INTELLECTUAL PROPERTY RIGHTS IN WTO AND DEVELOPING COUNTRIES

INTELLECTUAL PROPERTY RIGHTS IN WTO AND DEVELOPING COUNTRIES

Talwar Sabanna

SERIALS PUBLICATIONS
NEW DELHI (INDIA)

First Published - 2010

ISBN: 978-81-8387-260-7

Published by

SERIALS PUBLICATIONS
4830/24, Prahlad Street, Ansari Road
Darya Ganj, New Delhi-110002 (India)
Phone: 23245225 Fax: 91-11-23272135
E-mail: serials@satyam.net.in

CONTENTS

PREFACE

THE most avowed goal of the WTO, as set out in the promoting documents, is to create a fair and equitable, rule-based multilateral trade system. The most appealing aspect is that the new multilateral trade regime would be transparent and non - discriminatory. For the world trading community as a whole, every initiative on trade liberalization should ensure rewards in the form of large and expanding markets and greater trade flows for all participating members. Let us now look at some of the agreements and impact of these agreements on developing countries.

The subject of trade related intellectual rights (TRIPS) has always been very controversial. Intellectual Property (IP) refers to a creation of human mind that is a value to the society, while Intellectual Property Rights (IPRS) are rights granted by the state to persons over creation of their mind. In other words, patent owners exclusive property rights allowing them to prevent others from using the inventions covered manufactures wishing to use patented inventions must obtain licenses or authorizations from the patent owners who normally will require them to pay royalties. The areas of intellectual property that the TRIPs agreement covers are; plant and seed variety; micro organism; copyright and neighboring rights; trademarks, including services matters; industrial designs; geographical indications; integrated circuits; and trade secrets.

For each of these, certain norms of protection are prescribed. These norms do not necessarily have to be attained overnight. There is a transition period allowed legislations in most of these items are at various stages of formulation and implementation. In this book, an attempt is made to present the role of IPRs in WTO and developing countries.

CONTRIBUTORS LIST

Karishma Sarkar, Research Scholar, Department of Commerce, Gauhati University.

Nayan Barua, Professor, Department of Commerce, Gauhati University.

Anil Bhuimali, Professor in Economics, The University of North Bengal, Dist. Darjeeling, West Bengal.

Bhaskar Chaudhuri, Lecturer in Geography, Saheed Kshudiram College, Kamakhyaguri, Dist. Jalpaiguri.

Muzamil Jan, Lecturer, Extension and Communication, Institute of Home Science, University of Kashmir, Srinagar.

Dinesha P.T., Junior Research Fellow Department of Economics, Mangalore University, Mangalagangothri.

Jayasheela, Reader in Economics, and Coordinator, Chair in Rural Banking and Management, Mangalore University, Mangalagangothri.

V. Basil Hans, HOD of Economics, St Aloysius Evening College, Mangalore, Karnataka.

Sanjya Kumar Jha, Faculty-Member, Department of Economics, T.N.B. College, Bhagalpur, T.M. Bhagalpur University, Bhagalpur (Bihar).

Kamlesh Tayal, Sr., Lecturer, Department of Political Science, B.R. Government (P.G.) Girls College, Sriganganagar, (Rajasthan).

M. Tariq, Lecturer N.M. Law (P.G.) College, Hanumangarh Town, (Rajasthan).

J. P. Bhosale, Incharge-Faculty of Commerce, Coordinoter-P.G. Section, Arts, Commerce & Science College, Narayangaon Pune (MS).

D. M. Gujrathi, Chairman-BOS in Costing University Pune, Sangamner College Pune, Sangamner (MS).

H.D. Thorat, Pricnipal-Arts, Commerce & Science College Chakan, Dist-Pune (MS).

R. B. Dhande, Reader, Dept. of Commerce, S. P. H. Mahila College, Malegaon Camp, Nashik.

G. D. Kharat, Lecturer, Dept. of Economics, Arts & Commerce College, Yeola, Nashik.

B. R. Honparkhe, Professor, Vartak College, Vasai Road (W), Dist. Thane.

S. N. Yogish, Reader, Department of Economics, Kuvempu University, Jnana Sahyadri Shankaghatta.

A. Vinayagamoorthy, Reader, Department of Commerce Periyar University, Salem.

Benson Kunjukunju, Reader and PG & Research Department of Commerce, St. Thomas College, Kozhencherry, Kerala.

Mohan P. Philip, Lecturer Selection Grade, PG & Research Department of Commerce, St. Thomas College, Kozhencherry, Kerala.

M. Madhumathy, Lecturer, Department of Commerce and International Business, Dr. G. R. Damodaran College of Science, Coimbatore.

David Soundarajn, Lecturer, Department of Commerce and International Business, Dr. G. R. Damodaran College of Science, Coimbatore.

T.C. Brindha, Lecturer, Department of Commerce and International Business, Dr. G. R. Damodaran College of Science, Coimbatore.

R. Nithya, Lecturer, Department of Commerce and International Business, Dr. G. R. Damodaran College of Science, Coimbatore.

S. David Soundarajn, Senior Lecturer, Department of Commerce and International Business, Dr. G. R. Damodaran College of Science, Coimbatore.

J. P. Bhosale, Incharge-Faculty of Commerce, Coordinoter-P.G. Section, Arts, Commerce & Science College, Narayangaon Pune (MS).

Vinodh K. Natarajan, Ph.D. Research Scholar, Post-Graduate and Research Centre, Department of Economics, Scott Christian College (Autonomous), Nagercoil

J. Cyril Kanmony, Reader in Economics, Post-Graduate and Research Centre, Department of Economics, Scott Christian College (Autonomous), Nagercoil.

Jawahar Lal, Lecturer, Department of Commerce, B. D. Evening College, Patna, Magadh University.

Ranjana Sharma, Lecturer, Department of Commerce, B. D. Evening College, Patna, Magadh University.

Pramod Kumar Sinha, Lecturer, Department of Commerce, P. R. College, Sonepur, J. P. University, Chapra.

R. Kasilingam, Research Scholar, Alagappa Institute of Management, Alagappa University, Karaikudi.

G. Jayabal, Reader, Alagappa Institute of Management, Alagappa University, Karaikudi.

N. Radhakrishnan, Reader in Economics, Muthurangam, Govt. Arts College, Vellore, Tamil Nadu.

K. G. Selvaraj, Associate Professor, Department of Biostatistics, Christian Medical College, Vellore, Tamil Nadu.

N. Namasivayam, Professor and Head, Department of Commerce, D.D.E., M.K. University, Madurai.

C. Raja, Research Scholar Department of Commerce, D.D.E., M.K. University, Madurai.

K. A. Rasure, Professor and Head, Department of Economics, Nrupatunga Arts & Commerce College, SEDAM, Dist. Gulbarga-Karnataka.

M.C. Patel, Principal, N.S.Patel Arts College, Anand, Sardar Patel University.

S. M. Pillai, Lecturer, C.P.Patel & F.H.Shah Commerce College, Anand, Sardar Patel University.

R. Srinivasan, Senior Lecturer, Post Graduate Department of Corporate Secretary Ship, Bharathidasan Government College for Women (Autonomous), Puducherry.

B. B. Mansuri, Reader in Commerce, Women College, A.M.U. Aligarh.

M. K. Radhakrishnan, Reader and Head, Department of Commerce, Sri Vasavi College, Erode.

V. S. Ganesamurthy, Reader and Head, Department of Economics, Sri Vasavi College, Erode.

A. Sengottaiyan, Ph.D. Research Scholar, Sri Vasavi College, Erode.

Rama Shankar Singh, Asst. Professor, Department of Agronomy, TCA, RAU, Dholi, Muzaffarpur, Bihar.

Amalendu Kumar, Asst. Professor, Department of Agril. Economics, TCA, RAU, Dholi, Muzaffarpur, Bihar.

Mohammad Monirul Azam, is an Assistant Professor at the Department of Law, University of Chittagong, Chittagong, Bangladesh.

Abdul Hamid Chowdhury, is an Assistant Professor at the Department of Business Administration, International Islamic University Chittagong (IIUC), Bangladesh.

Kameshwar Pandit, Lecturer, Department of Personnel Management & Industrial Relations, Patna University,Patna.

R. Ezhil Jasmine, Lecturer in Commerce, Sarah Tucker College, Tirunelveli , Tamilnadu (India).

M. V. S. Srinivasa Rao, Associate Professor, Department of Management Studies, Maharajah's Post Graduate College, Phool Baugh, Vizianagaram.

Chapter-1

A STUDY ON INTELLECTUAL PROPERTY RIGHTS (IPR) IN WTO AND DEVELOPING COUNTRIES

Karishma Sarkar & Nayan Barua

INTRODUCTION

Intellectual property rights are a bundle of exclusive legal rights over creations of the mind, both artistic and commercial. It is covered by copyright laws, which protect creative works in the industrial, scientific, literary and artistic fields.

These rights give statutory expression to the moral and economic rights of creators in their creations. Intellectual property rights safeguard creators and other producers of intellectual goods and services by granting them certain time-limited rights to control the use made of those productions. These rights also promote creativity and the dissemination and application of its results and encourage fair-trading, which contributes to economic and social development. Thus, Intellectual property refers to the creations of the human mind and human intellect.

The idea or the thought itself could not be protected since it was completely intangible or invisible. However, the end product of the human thought, the outcome which is tangible could have been protected, thus the legal concept is created where a capital gets converted into a property. A property concept gives the owner a clear right over his asset and this is recognized by law. Thus, an intellectual capital gets converted to an intellectual property when it gets legal acceptance.

INTELLECTUAL PROPERTY IS DIVIDED INTO TWO CATEGORIES

Industrial Property-which includes patents for inventions, trademarks, industrial designs and geographical indications and

Copyright and Related Rights-which cover literary and artistic expressions (e.g. books, films, music, architecture, art), plus the rights of performing artists in their performances, producers of phonograms in their recordings, and broadcasters in their radio and television broadcasts which are also referred to as neighboring rights.

Most of the intellectual capital is protect able by the various forms of intellectual and industrial property rights created over the last 200 years and governed by international treaties and regional and national laws. Patents and utility models protect technical innovations. Trademarks protect brands. Design patents or registrations protect industrial designs. Copyright protects literary and artistic works as well as software. Circuit design registration protects integrated circuit architecture, and so on.

IMPACT OF INTELLECTUAL PROPERTY RIGHTS IN DEVELOPING COUNTRIES

Independent commission finds intellectual property rights impose costs on most developing countries and do not help to reduce poverty. In presenting its final report to the British government, the Commission on Intellectual Property Rights declared the internationally-mandated expansion of intellectual property (IP) rights unlikely to generate significant benefits for most developing countries and likely to impose costs, such as higher priced medicines or seeds. This makes poverty reduction more difficult. The report entitled 'Integrating Intellectual Property Rights and Development Policy' makes some 50 recommendations aimed at aligning IP protection with the goal of reducing poverty in developing nations. Topics include IP and health; agriculture; traditional knowledge; copyrights, software and the Internet; and the role of WTO and WIPO in advancing developing country interests. The Commission on Intellectual Property Rights called on developed nations, the World Trade Organization (WTO) and the World Intellectual Property Organization (WIPO) to take the circumstances of poor countries and their development needs properly into account when seeking to develop international IP systems.

INTELLECTUAL PROPERTY RIGHTS (IPR) AND THE CASE OF DEVELOPING COUNTRIES

(i) It has been a common practice among the developed countries to proceed on the assumption that what is good for them is likely to be good for developing countries as well. This trend of practice should strictly be curtailed.

(ii) Developing countries should not be encouraged or coerced into adopting stronger IP rights without regard to the impact this has on their development and poor people. They should be allowed to adopt appropriate rights regimes, not necessarily the most protective ones.

(iii) The intellectual property rights system, as a whole is less advantageous for developing than for developed countries in many areas of importance to development, such as health, agriculture, education and information technologies. The system increases the costs of access to many products and technologies that developing countries need.

(iv) The extension of IP rights globally will diminish the degree of competition worldwide for many products and services. For example, the degree of competition in developing country markets for patented pharmaceutical products will diminish when major suppliers of generic versions of such medicines will have to apply patent protection under TRIPS (WTO's Agreement on Trade-Related Aspects of Intellectual Property Rights). This is particularly important for those countries where competition is already weak.

(v) Developing countries are now being urged to adopt a complex set of rules more suited to advanced economies. When their economies were at comparable stages of maturity, most developed countries did not follow the stringent intellectual property standards they now advocate for developing countries.

(vi) The developed nations should take the economic needs of developing countries fully into account when seeking to craft international intellectual property rights systems.

(vii) Developed countries should pay more attention to reconciling their commercial self interest with the need to reduce poverty in developing countries, which is in everyone's interest.

(viii) Higher IP standards should not be pressed on developing countries without a serious and objective assessment of their impact. The impact of IP rights on poor people will vary according to socio-economic circumstances. IP systems should be tailored to a country's state of development and its particular circumstances.

INTELLECTUAL PROPERTY RIGHTS AND WTO

Today the WTO has 132 members with another 31 in the process of accession. Of the 132 members, 98 are developing countries, including 27 nations categorized as the least developed countries (LDCs).One of the commonly used yardsticks to measure the success of the WTO is the volume of world trade. The results seem excellent in this respect, with world trade up 25% in the last four years. But the benefits of increased trade are not widely shared. For example, the LDCs represent 20% of the world's population, but they generate a mere 0.03% of the trade flows. Although purportedly a democratic institution, the WTO is dominated by the leading industrialized countries and by the corporations of these countries. The logic of commercial trade pervades the WTO. The development goals articulated when GATT was first formed have been put aside—or are wrongly assumed to be the natural consequence of increased trade.

DEVELOPING COUNTRIES HAVE LITTLE POWER WITHIN THE WTO FRAMEWORK FOR THE FOLLOWING REASONS

1. Although developing countries make up three-fourths of WTO membership and by their vote can in theory influence the agenda and outcome of trade

negotiations, they have never used this to their advantage. Most developing country economies are in one way or another dependent on the U.S., the EU, or Japan in terms of imports, exports, aid, security, etc. Any obstruction of a consensus at the WTO might threaten the overall well-being and security of dissenting developing nations.

2. Trade negotiations are based on the principle of reciprocity or "trade-offs." That is, one country gives a concession in an area, such as the lowering of tariffs for a certain product, in return for another country acceding to a certain agreement. This type of bartering benefits the large and diversified economies, because they can get more by giving more. For the most part, negotiations and trade-offs take place among the developed countries and some of the richer or larger developing countries.
3. Developing countries have fewer human and technical resources. Many cannot cope with the 40-50 meetings held in Geneva each week. Hence they often enter negotiations less prepared than their developed country counterparts.
4. Developing countries have discovered that seeking recourse in the dispute settlement system is costly and requires a level of legal expertise that they may not have. Furthermore, the basis on which the system is run—whether a country is violating free trade rules—is not the most appropriate for their development needs.

The international institutions principally responsible for the development of global IP policy, WTO and WIPO, should take into account the needs and interests of those adversely affected by IP rights, not just the interests of potential beneficiaries of those rights.

POINTS TO BE CONSIDERED IN FAVOUR OF DEVELOPING NATIONS

(i) The voice of developing countries and, in particular, consumers needs to be better heard and the decisions taken better informed by evidence of the impact of IP rights in those countries.

(ii) WIPO must give explicit recognition to both the benefits and the costs of IP protection for developing nations.

(iii) It has been observed that IP system hardly plays any role in stimulating research on diseases particularly prevalent in developing countries unless there is also a substantial market in the developed world.

(iv) As IP rights are strengthened globally, the overall cost of medicines in developing countries is likely to increase unless steps are taken to counteract this trend.

(v) Differential pricing would allow prices for drugs to be lower in developing countries, while higher prices are maintained in developed countries. If this is to work, then it is necessary to stop low priced drugs leaking back to developed countries.

(vi) Developing countries should also aim to facilitate in their legal systems the ability to import patented medicines if they can get them cheaper elsewhere in the world. They should also make provisions in their law that will facilitate entry of generic competitors as soon as the patent has expired on a particular drug.

CONCLUSION

Developing countries need to shape their IP laws to promote development generally and keep in mind some of the negative impacts of overly generous IP protection. IP rights are only one factor among many in the development process. Their importance should be recognised, but not overstated. Even the complete absence of IP rights would not solve the lack of sufficient resources for adequate health facilities, health workers and medicines for all in developing nations. In particular, countries need other measures to stimulate development in the interests of poorer people, including increased public funding for health and agricultural research. The IP system is not well suited to encouraging this. Neither is the international IP system particularly effective at promoting the transfer of technology or foreign investment, despite this being an objective of TRIPS. To accomplish these goals, countries need a combination of increased international funding; specific initiatives to support research into areas that lack a lucrative market (for instance, many drug companies hesitate to develop malaria drugs or vaccines because most countries that need them cannot afford them); and support for increased education and training within developing countries. The governments which dominate the WTO, especially the United States, the European Union, Japan and Canada, and the transnational corporations which have benefited from the WTO system have refused to recognize and address these problems. They are still intent on further liberalization, including through the expansion of the WTO, promoting free trade as a goal in itself. Nelson Mandela rightly commented on the Uruguay Round that the developing countries were not able to ensure that the rules accommodated their realities... it was mainly the preoccupations and problems of the advanced industrial economies that shaped the agreement. He added that rules applied uniformly are not necessarily fair because of the different circumstances of members.

The time has come to acknowledge the crisis of the international trading system and its main administering institution, the WTO. Need is there to replace this old, unfair and oppressive trade system with a new, socially just and sustainable trading framework for the 21st Century.

REFERENCES

Intellectual Property Rights in the WTO and Developing Countries. Jayashree Watal. Boston: Kluwer Academic Publishers, 2001.

Intellectual Property Rights, the WTO and Developing Countries: the TRIPS Agreement and Policy Options. London, New York: Zen Books, Ltd., Penang, Malaysia: Third World Network, 2000.

Annual report (2006) of the Council for TRIPS, Geneva, WTO 2006', 4 p. Doc.no.

Annual report (2007) of the Council for TRIPS, Geneva, WTO 2007', 4 p. Doc.no.

Guide to the WTO and Developing Countries, Peter Gallagher. WTO Guide Series, Vol. 2. The Hague; Boston, Mass.: Kluwer Law International, 2000

The WTO, IPR and the Knowledge Economy, Cheltenham (etc,); Elgan; 2004, XX, 628, p.

Cultural Survival Quarterly. Summer (1991), *Intellectual Property Rights: The Politics of Ownership.* Cultural Survival Inc: Cambridge.

Greaves, Tom (ed.) (1994), *Intellectual Property Rights for Indigenous Peoples, A Sourcebook.* The Society for Applied Anthropology: Oklahoma City, OK.

Nair, M.D. (1993), 'Intellectual Property Rights and the Indian Pharmaceutical Industry.' *Journal of Scientific Affairs.* 1993 April, V52 N4: 278-283.

Park W.G., Ginarte, J.C. (1996), 'Intellectual Property Rights in a North-South Economic Context.' *Science Communication.* Mar, Vol. 17, No. 3: 379-387.

Posey D., Dutfield, G. Plenderleith, K. (1995), 'Collaborative Research and Intellectual Property Rights.' Nov., Vol. 4 , No. 8, 892-902.

Blakeney, Michael (1996), "The Impact of the TRIPs Agreement in the Asia Pacific Region." *European Intellectual Property Review*, Vol. 18-10 October, 544-554.

Bronckers, Marco C.E.J. (1994), "The Impact of TRIPs: Intellectual Property Protection in Developing Countries." *Common Market Law Review*, Vol. 31:6, December , 1245-1281.

Chapter-2

ENERGY SECURITY AND LESSON FOR INDIA

Anil Bhuimali & Bhaskar Chaudhuri

DEFINING ENERGY SECURITY

U.N. Economic Commission for Europe (UNECE) Energy Security Forum of water resources and deforestation defines energy security as the accessibility to exploitable energy supplies, at the point of final use, in adequate amount and timeliness in order that, given due regard for energy efficiency, the economic and social progress of the country is not materially inhibited. Energy security, as Daojiong (2005)[1] viewed is not be perplexed with self-reliance or energy independence, may be termed as 'a sound balance between energy supply and demand serving the purpose of facilitating sustainable economic and social development.' By 'balance' he did not just denoted the connection between the general amount of supply and demand, but the fit between a diversity of energy supplies and a multifaceted set of needs.

As India is reliant on overseas supply for approximate 74 per cent of its oil requirements, India's import oil bill has also rushed notwithstanding the 12.5 per cent rise in the value of the Indian rupee in respect of the dollar in large part of 2007. The precariousness in global crude market continued to threaten India's energy security and corroded the bottomlines of many oil companies in 2007, even as quite a few fresh hydrocarbon discoveries were made and oil possessions acquired abroad to protect India's fuel requirements. For overcoming the crisis, the government also initiated another round of auctions for oil and gas possessions in the hope to draw $3-3.5 billion in investments, besides $8 billion attracted in exploration in the earlier six rounds. The Indian energy sector would call for investments of $120-150 billion over the next five years as demand is predicted to more than double. And as indicated by the 11th Five Year Plan also, India's crude oil requirements would jump from the 127 million tonnes in 2006-07 to 145 million tonnes in 2011-12, even as home production has to increase to 40 million tonnes from 34 million. The government efforts followed 49 discoveries by private and joint endeavour in 15 blocks, inviting an investment in the range of $8 billion. However, while the government maintains that the Indian sedimentary basins are still poorly explored in terms of well density; suggesting more likelihood to access oil and gas in the country, it seems improbable to for oil and gas only to meet India's massive demand in the 21st century. As India's reliance on imports for crude oil continued to grow up during 2007, India appeared as net exporter of fuels similar to petrol and kerosene. Regarding cross-border pipelines, importing gas from Iran via Pakistan faces stumbling block not only due to pricing and access charges, but the looming threats of terrorism posing clear and imminent danger to continued supply of oil.

ENERGY CRISIS

The 20th century has been "the century of war". The 21st century has witnessed the invasion of oil-rich Iraq by the United States, without global endorsement or legal explanation. Rightful stability and supply matters are also distressing. For a case in point, places like Nigeria, Iran etc. all produce oil even though problems, as apprehensions range from steady supply, to stable government. Others, such as Venezuela threaten to use oil and its related profits to build up their own region even more. The US has massive military spending in part to defend global oil areas for their benefit. Several other large countries are getting more concerned in the global showground because of energy related worries, including China and Russia fuelling a fear of geopolitical war in near future. With rapid pace of industrialisation the developing countries will naturally need more energy to satiate the growth thirst. Thus China and India will be more involved in international affairs, especially in some untapped resourceful regions like Africa.

The present global oil crisis has been aggravated by a plethora of factors that need to be discussed in brief. First, the devaluation of dollar translates into higher purchasing power for the developing countries. Second, high demand for oil definitely leads to dearer petroleum. Apart from the industrialised countries like the United States and the European nations, the growing economies such as India and China now hugely consume oil. The third factor is OPEC–massively controlling the production and selling price of oil. The reserve of oil is steadily diminishing in the major oil producing nations. The crisis is compounded by the absence of any major discovery of oil field. Nonetheless, the intention of OPEC is guided by their astute future preparation to coin money as soon as possible before the great rush for oil ends within a few decades. The OPEC countries have a massive stake in the western business enterprises as well as the growing economies of India and China. The excess money they make now shall ensure a safe and secure future for these heavily oil dependent countries. Finally, terrorist attacks on pipelines pose a major threat to Nigeria, causing production-slump. The US-Iran imbroglio adds to uncertainty, while the supply from Iraq is still below hope. There exists a massive regional disparity in demand for oil. Reuters/OPEC estimates suggest that the demand for petroleum (million barrel/per day) in America in 2005 was 25.5, compared to south Asia's 3.1 and China's 6.5. The demand is poised to rise to 26.1 in America in 2010, whereas in South Asia the corresponding figure is 3.9 and in China it is going to be 8.7 million barrel/per day demand for petroleum. A United Nations (2007) report holds bad weather in the Gulf of Mexico, apart from high global demand for oil as one of the main reasons for the recent surge in oil prices.

The global petroleum-energy supply revolves around OPEC countries. Certainly, non-OPEC supply had a feeble show in 2007, particularly in view of preliminary prospects projecting a strong rebound for that year. But, regardless of some increase in the first half of 2007, non-OPEC supply increase was well below prospect, and the year ended with cumulative growth of only 800,000 b/d (see Graph 1). Furthermore, non-OPEC supply showed weakness when prices began to rise. For 2007, non-OPEC supply growth averaged a meagre 0.6 mb/d, even less than half the early prediction of 1.3 mb/d (see Graph 2).

GRAPH 1: Cumulative Growth: Oil Supply vs. ORB

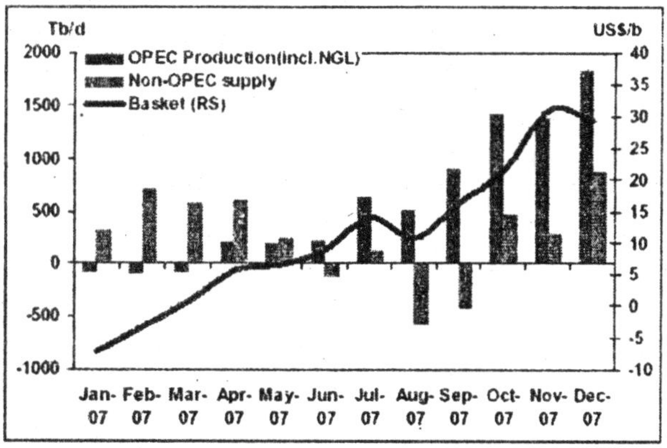

GRAPH 2: Range of Uncertainty for non-OPEC supply growth (mb/d)

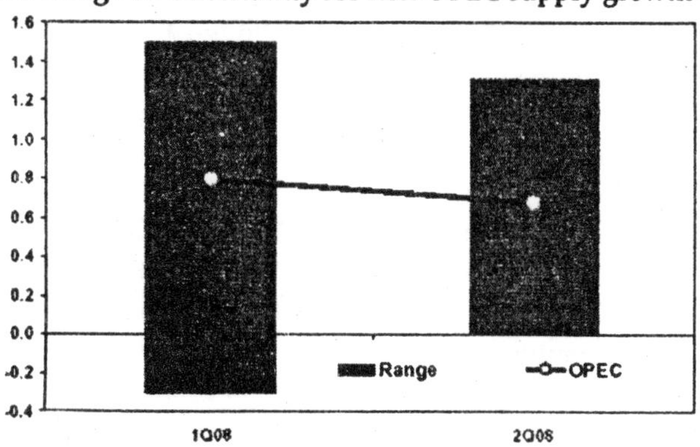

Source: OPEC Monthly Oil Market Report, January (2008).

OPEC suggests that in April 2008, crude-prices increased on geopolitical issues in the Middle East and supply interruptions in West Africa and Europe. The waning US dollar and financial ambiguity added to market instability, along with quick descending revisions to demand forecasts that were counterbalanced by symbols of strong demand in China. The buoyant impetus continued in May 2008 on geopolitical drift and strike-related distractions. The estimated demand for OPEC crude in 2007, according to The Monthly Oil Market Report, May (2008) was average 32.0 mb/d resulting in a boost of 280 tb/d over 2007. In 2008, the requirement for OPEC crude is anticipated to average 31.8 mb/d, causing 120 tb/d lower demands than 2007. The explanation put forward by OPEC hardly seems plausible; obvious from the recent exit of Indonesia from OPEC on the ground of crude-price issue. OPEC nations – it becomes obvious, are not increasing production despite high demand and available storage of oil in their lands. Even if Russia tops the crude production in the Q-1 of 2008, surpassing even Saudi Arabia, there has been negligible impact on the global crude price in 2008.

The global economic growth ought to lose in the process of rising crude value and inflation. The global economic growth is demonstrated below in Table 1.

Table 1
Economic Growth at 008, %

Years	*World**	*OECD*	*USA*	*Japan*	*Euro-zone*	*China*	*India*
2007	4.9	2.7	2.2	2.0	2.6	11.9	8.6
2008	3.9	1.7	1.1	1.4	1.6	9.7	8.0

**World aggregate growth rate now based on country weights calculated from updated 2005 purchasing power parity exchange rates.*

Source: OPEC Monthly Oil Market Report, May (2008).

In China and India a keen consciousness of the geopolitical connotation of energy supply and demand has rendered energy questions an escalating importance both in their domestic and foreign policies. Possibility of 'resource wars' need to be overlooked but emphasis is to be put on economic competition, and on seeking to maximise each country's position on the international energy marketplace. Fears are expressed by experts regarding growing resource rivalry contributing to augmenting clashes in regions where national jurisdiction has been fluid such as East China Sea and South China Sea, in addition to some of the energy exporting realms. Before June 2008 the International Energy Agency Meet, China and India were evasive to IEA regulations as they are not member nations. Nevertheless, during this Meet China and India's willing involvement in the Emergency Response Exercises with the IEA for intensive measures in the event of supply disruption signals the oil crisis the major oil consuming countries are experiencing. It is assumed that as fallout, the veteran nations will assist China and India to create oil stockpile structure and bring in

modus operandi on how to utilize the stockpiled assets in case of oil crisis. Visibly, these methods are short-term in nature and may be termed as panic reaction.

Menotti (2006) views that prosperous countries are trying to exploit the *World Trade Organization* (WTO) to form a newest global policy structure for "energy security" that essentially redefines, under the reason of "free trade in services," who can access energy assets, which ones are utilized and how, and who will profit mainly from their use. Finalizing such an arrangement could institute the WTO as an authoritative global tool to put into effect a new energy planning, shifting power over the international economy's most tactical resource—oil—to transnational corporations like *Halliburton*. Developing countries are under enormous strain in present WTO discussions to make liberal offers to unfasten their domestic markets to a variety of services and goods in return for first world's opening their bazaars to more agriculture imports. As the thrust of rich countries' demands aspires to take apart state-owned oil companies in the chief energy-exporting nations and big budding economies, extended WTO systems could also hold back energy policymaking in the wealthy countries themselves, particularly existing priorities akin to plummeting dependence on imported energy and/or changing to sustainable resources. If left uncontested, existing WTO talks could lessen governments' authority to control at a moment when democratic management over energy strategy has become a worldwide imperative for dealing with incomparable security, financial, social, and environmental threats. Energy specialists consider the globe as entering an era of momentous changeover, where energy security has become the novel lens through which governments observe global relations. Europe is alarmed over Russia's limitations on gas exports. Brazil feels defenceless after Bolivia's choice to nationalize its energy business, China's chase for energy possessions has worried many, whereas the US continues to muster even more ambassadorial and armed strength to protect supplies. In view of the energy anxiety," India should uphold full elasticity to decide their own energy prospect and not to be subsidiary to arduous fresh disciplines under the WTO.

In any case two aspects are powerful energy services liberalisation in the WTO. Firstly, seventy per cent of the global one trillion barrels of crude assets are controlled by state-owned oil companies, as per the *International Energy Agency*. The chief obstacle to better energy security and steady oil prices are the present policies in energy-exporting countries that hinder access by overseas financiers and foreign oil services corporations. Elimination of the obstacles that foreign companies abhor most, for example restrictions on foreign investment, necessities to associate with domestic companies, employ neighbouring labour, or relocate novel know-how. Second, globalisation has had key brunt on oil companies like Exxon-Mobil, Shell, and Chevron-Texaco who no longer make use of permanent employees to explore, remove, and sell abroad energy resources. Nowadays, the oil heavyweights function as mostly executive offices managing manifold contracts with oil services suppliers, reminiscent of Halliburton, who again sub-contract human resources and rent out paraphernalia as required carrying the principle of the "just in time" approach to management. As oil reserve declines, increasing partnership or contract with the state-owned companies holding the seventy per cent of residual coffers will be in vogue. By locking in these industry developments enforceable through the WTO due to which corporations like Halliburton have earned extremely, the state-owned oil companies would be obliged to outsource more service agreements to foreign business establishments. Subjecting energy to WTO regulations might even result in the disintegration of public sector companies. Diversifying economic activities seem to be a viable option for ensuring energy security. It is perilous for a country to be over-dependent on solitary segment, and without diversifying the own economic pedestal further than a lone sector is reasonably dicey. Consequently submitting one's nationalised energy segment to run by foreign parties through new WTO system would jeopardize sinking a nation's capacity to branch out its economy into added sectors.

SUBSTITUTING OIL

Experts view that it would make tactical and ecological sense to dispense more funds into the R&D of substitutes to fossil fuels[2]. The galloping price rise of oil in recent months forces customers to mull over more about energy preservation and substitutes. Nuclear power as one option has ruffled many political feathers in India. Environmentalists however, apprehend the penalty and costs of catastrophe and radioactive waste of nuclear energy. Economic Survey 2007-08 cites that there will be a few factors causing slower growth in the imminent as the much-debated US recession, the upward rupee negatively impacting export-oriented as well as employee-intensive areas, inflation, and finally, the static agricultural production. Since oil prices as well impact our financial system, significant policy programmes are essential to put up and shield the long-standing energy security of the country. The emphasis on privatisation of old unprofitable oil fields to recover output through application of technology is laudable, as higher production would decrease India's import reliance. To meet up the go-getting growth objectives, India requires energy on a sustained basis and at reasonable price.

Our energy security policy rests on two planks—the enhancement of domestic supply and the management of demand. Its success hinges on the continued availability of technocrats. India's energy sector has little scarcity of skilled experts but in near future India may face bottlenecks. This is because of the 'graying' of energy professionals worldwide. It is projected that 50 per cent of the technocrats in the oil/gas industry will retire by 2015 and 80 per cent by 2020. So, it is necessary that technical manpower be developed in hydel power and other renewable resources in order to meet future demand. Another explanation relates to the exploitation of technology.

Gregory (2007) emphasises upon the availability of technical expertise and technology is a sufficient condition for efficient utilisation of technology – hence energy security. He emphasises on the following aspects of energy security policy. First, it is insufficient to access futuristic technology. We have to also inaugurate systems and procedures in addition to the equipment to efficiently make use of this technology. Second, we should evaluate the organisational and management configuration of our foremost energy corporations. The purpose must be to guarantee the most creative utilisation of our technocrats, money and know-how. And third, we ought to prevent an 'energy brain drain' through a deep-seated renovation of the accessible financial and career scenario of the energy experts. The elements of supply improvement and demand management are labour force and know-how. Our energy security policy need not undervalue the significance of the line between the two.

Biodiesel

Since 2001, ethanol production has grown from 1.6 billion gallons (2000) to about 6.4 billion gallons in 2007, with the huge majority belonging to corn. The United States was the world's leading ethanol producer in 2005, and in 2007, the U.S. produced almost half of global ethanol production. The US administration is also investing in next generation biofuels for instance in cellulosic ethanol made from wood chips, switch grass, and other agriculture yield. By 2050 the US will be self-sufficient in bio fuel production. Over the last five years, the U.S. has spent approximately $1.2 billion in eco-friendly hydrogen R&D to help bring hydrogen fuel cell vehicles to market. By 2050, the U.S. will be self-dependent on solar energy. The approach to produce sustainable energy in the form of biofuels draws brickbats from the environmentalists. The looming question is whether biofuel crops like corn and soyabeans in the United States, sugarcane in Brazil or palm oil in South East Asia will in the long run compete for land with food crops. The six billion plus population in this planet is already facing worst food security problem; for which the diversion of land meant for food crops to biofuel crops in the US may be held partly responsible. In fact, achieving energy security seems difficult in the absence of uniform global energy policies for the betterment of mankind. The US government subsidises corn cultivation though levying lofty tariffs on much more energy- efficient sugar ethanol from Brazil. So, energy security can hardly be achieved at the cost of food security. Investing in right feed stock is *de rigueur* along with steadily erecting political and industrial espousal for the progressive expansion of biofuel production from non-food crops as well as in R&D of viable energy sources like photovoltaic cells, solar energy, and development of hybrid cars run by hydrogen fuel etc. can prove to be doable choice in future.

For India proper utilisation of grain stalks, shavings and waste biomass for biofuels ought to be a good preference, but the energy security achieved in this method will be at the cost of further green house gas emission and consequent global warming. Human civilisation cannot withstand further damage to our environment. In recent period India has been busy in stretching its arms of cooperation with the oil-rich African and South American countries. India at the Indo-Africa summit 2008 was positive towards ensuring huge reserve of energy in Africa untapped so far. Nevertheless, India's high economic growth necessitates energy supply from infinite sources which Africa can not deliver. Besides, the recent Chinese interest in Africa apart from the western powers is not a welcome news for Indian authority vis-à-vis future supply of energy. It is imperative to look beyond finite resources and explore countries like Scotland where many companies have gained expertise in the efficient utilisation of wind as well as wave energy. The cost-effective renewable energy exploitation technology is something India ought to aspire for.

Nearly all biofuels are produced and guzzled in home markets, and only a diminutive amount of trade takes place in biofuels these days. So far, only Brazil has an exportable excess in ethanol, and intra-EU trade of biodiesel is still very limited[3]. As there are a number of drivers pushing for larger biofuel production currently, some of them are evidently keen on domestic production and utilisation. Greater energy security may be achieved by becoming less reliant on petroleum imports from geopolitically unstable regions and by generating more energy domestically. Countries have also gripped biofuels since they provide market for their peasants' farming possessions and hold the prospective for promoting rural progress. Many countries, chiefly the signatories to the Kyoto Protocol, are looking for more eco-friendly transportation energy. Governments are also aiming to decrease their spending on oil. The aspiration for cost-efficient or more ecologically sustainable biofuels is not inevitably attached to domestic production. Countries using biofuels may seek for suppliers ahead of their borders.

There is accordingly a possibility for trade in biofuels, mainly because the nations where biofuels can be generated without difficulty and inexpensively plus the countries with the maximum latent demand for biofuels are not alike. The developing countries located in tropical and sub-tropical region may have a relative lead in generating biofuels owing to longer growing seasons, huge quarters of accessible cultivable land, and lesser labor costs, the export of biofuels to temperate zone developed countries is a potential opportunity. Some developing nations sense that there are considerable export openings in this sector. Malaysia, for example is planting large acreages of plantation for palm oil as India is also to produce considerable amount of biodiesel from jatropha plant grown in wastelands. Thailand will also produce ethanol in bulk for the Japanese market. Most developing countries can not provide government support resembling the developed countries. So, developing countries depend profoundly on private capital to promote the business of biofuels. A transparent and international trading system can draw steady financing and investment capital. Arguments are also in favour of the production of ethanol from sugarcane as being less energy consuming and more ecologically sustainable than with corn as the feedstock and that rapeseed, which is high yielding annual broadcrops for oil manufacturing. Some high efficiency strains of rapeseed can produce as much as 140-145 U.S. gallons per acre annually, vis-à-vis soy which at present yields nearly 40 U.S. gallons an acre of oil (IFATPC, 2006). However, application of foodstuff for biodiesel has its flipside also. Rising demand for bioethanol and biodiesel–as our experience shows will inevitably cause depletion of the area of rainforest, as it is happening in Malaysia; or the use of maize in ethanol in the United States seriously causes a shift from food crop to maize for higher profitability. It is noteworthy that experimentation with biodiesel is exceedingly risky at a decisive juncture when food crisis is intimidating the survival of human civilisation. Even the FAO (2007) educated guess suggests that regardless of abundant harvest in 2007, the poorest countries will have to pay more for cereal import bill causing an increase by one quarter in the existing season alone owing to the biofuels demand[4]. On the contrary some are of the opinion that while the developing countries like India are at the receiving end, they can reap maximum dividend out of the rising demand for biofuels also. Karmakar (2007) views that given the growing demand for biofuels there is enormous potential of agricultural export from developing countries such as India. But in that case, how motivated should the WTO negotiating strategy of India be? The likelihood is that developed countries may be converted into net agricultural importers in specific food crops and oilseeds, or start importing bigger quantities of biofuel from developing countries like Brazil, South Africa, Columbia, Malaysia, Indonesia, and potentially India because of favourable weather settings for biofuel feedstocks. Karmakar's opinion seems to be on the verge of absurdity, because the developed world possesses enough might to invest in R&D for other renewable energy like fuel cell and solar power as long-term developmental objective.

Bearing the gravity of situation in mind there has been a fresh attempt by some consumers in America to convert their gas guzzling automobiles into electric one. A recent European study of IISD (2008) shows that while biofuels do dislodge some fossil fuels, thus reducing GHG emissions, the study finds that the price tag for getting a unit of CO_2-equivalent reduction in the course of biofuel subsidies is too high. The cost of subsidy per tonne of CO_2-equivalent removed is projected to be from € 575 to € 800 for ethanol prepared from sugar beet, about € 215 for biodiesel finished from old cooking oil, and more than € 600 for biodiesel prepared from rapeseed.

The present crisis involving food security and energy security are inextricably linked, as is reflected in the 2008 Rome food summit. The three-day "High-Level Conference on Food Security", an urgent world food summit, convened by the Food and Agriculture Organisation of the United Nations, held in Rome on June 5, 2008 sadly ignored the basic problem. The summit decided to react immediately to requests for support from the concerned countries and to provide instantaneous support for farm production and trade in the hope, that abolition of trade limitations by food-exporting countries

(Vietnam, Cambodia and India made some assurances to export rice) would drastically decrease global cereal prices. The summit planned a set of medium and long-term actions like greater investment in agriculture (including in R&D), managing the challenge of climate change, liberalisation of worldwide agricultural trade, and dealing with the "challenges and opportunities posed by bio-fuels". Unfortunately a deal with regard to global trade in agriculture under the Doha round of the WTO is nowhere imminent[5].

Obviously, India needs to develop biodiesel without endangering food availability or environment. India deems bio-diesel as a probable fuel, which can be a successful option to encourage rural development, generate jobs in rural areas and facilitate energy security. The Desert Development Programme (DDP) of India allocated Rs 50 crore in 2007 to endorse the farming of Jatropha in rural areas. The accessibility to quality planting stuff, appropriateness of waste lands, precipitation, fitting agronomic practices for farming of non-edible oil seed making plants, are significant features for the cultivators. About 84 per cent of rural families in the country have fuel wood, farming residues and dung cakes as prime source of cooking energy. In such energy situation there are main challenges in providing uncontaminated and affordable energy to every one[6]. Still the official approach towards reduced greenhouse gas emission of biodiesel and ethanol seems to be largely unfounded and ill-conceived.

SOLVING THE RIDDLE

Nevertheless, the application of renewable energy has its pitfalls. Solving the riddle of ensuring energy security is no mean business. Renewable energy expertise brings in novel conflicts. The supply of renewable energy is controlled by availability of land. Now over 99 per cent of the global food supply originates from land. With about 75 per cent of the whole US land area exploited for cultivation and forestry, comparatively small land is obtainable for other purposes like biomass production with solar technologies. Population growth further exacerbates the crisis of land. As a result, future land conflicts could be severe, if other cost-effective sustainable sources are not invented (Pimentel, *et al.* 1994). By 2050, the United States will be self-reliant on solar energy. Presently, a strong deterrent has been the prohibitive cost of raw material for solar technology, i.e. silicon for solar panels. In near future, cheap silane gas holds the potential of replacing solar panels; thus making solar power more customer-friendly. The US and Australia are making vigorous efforts to set up solar panels in deserts and other regions receiving high solar insolation. Rajasthan boasts of a solar plant being constructed with foreign collaboration, capable to produce up to five MW. Other renewable energy technologies that have the potential to provide future energy supplies include: biomass systems, hydroelectric systems, hydrogen fuel, wind power, photovoltaic, and passive and active heating and cooling systems. India needs to explore every available option, like producing biodiesel from local plants such as jatropha grown on wastelands; constructing energy-conserving buildings also deserve enough attention. Chikkatur *et al.* (2008) finds that development of ground-breaking energy infrastructure need dealing with many key challenges concurrently. The challenges are: (a) increasing energy security together with rising general resource checks; (b) funding large energy infrastructure with ample capital expenditure (c) increasing development in the interrelated support infrastructure; (d) plummeting social and environmental impacts of a growing energy infrastructure; in addition the final factor is also significant, i.e. (e) concentrating on climate change outcomes, modification and mitigation. Fruitfully dealing with these energy-challenges will demand transformations in India's socio-economic strategies and institutional structures.

GOI report (2005) suggests India to lower energy intensity. Lessening energy intensity through efficiency is like making a fundamental source of unused domestic energy. A unit of energy saved by a consumer is bigger than a unit produced, because it saves on production losses, in addition to transport, broadcast and distribution losses. Therefore a "Negawatt", created by plummeting energy requirements save over a Megawatt generated. The Committee views that upto 25 per cent decrease in India's energy intensity is probable over existing levels. The report also finds that efficiency can be amplified by energy pull out, energy alteration, energy transportation, plus energy consumption. India's energy security needs something to do with the unremitting accessibility of main marketable energy as a low-priced commodity. Other most vital procedures to increase energy security include reducing energy demand and increasing energy use efficiency. Yet, it is still essential to categorize that India's growing assurance about energy import that enhances ambiguity concerning ease of use of energy at reasonable prices. There are some policy anomalies regarding policy implementation in India[7]. Diesel is the single major petroleum produce consumed in India since the emphasis was on the movement of freight by road and not by rail, although rail movement is merely one-seventh as energy intensive as road transportation. The sustained stress on widening and boosting the four-lane highway network has encouraged freight traffic more in that direction. However, the growing use for generating power derives from diesel, particularly for industries demanding quality electricity- as the power production and management programmes are still poor. Petrol occupies a minute percentage of total petroleum use, but this is also growing fast due to the government backing since 1991 given to the private automotive industry with its taxing policy.

The risk to energy security occurs from the vagueness of availability and cost of imported energy, and also from the probable interruption or deficit in home production. In absence of little disruption of supply there may be the market risk of an unexpected jump in crude price. Alternating imported energy by domestic fuels; by expanding fuel options like gas, ethanol, tar sands etc have been suggested as successful actions to embark upon the journey to tide over the crisis. Threats can also be addressed by widening the ability to endure supply shocks; capacity to import energy and experience market risks etc. as ways to address technical risks. The industrial market economies embarked on their voyage to energy-efficiency in 1973 with a series of public inventiveness, legislations and guidelines that built on the rising shift in prices and forced their customers towards more competent use of oil. Quite the reverse, India has done little by either legislating or promoting through other means a less oil-intensive mode of growth.

Some progress has been made in renewable energy sector in recent times. India possesses a grid power capacity in excess of 11,000 MW from renewables, that is almost 8 per cent of the total established facility in India. Access to power in over 4,000 villages and hamlets through renewable sources has become possible through indigenous resources and people's participation, while producing jobs. Still India has miles to go. So, India's governmental effort to begin compulsory labelling for a variety of electrical and electronic merchandise is a stride towards effective energy conservation. However, all such efforts are in vain if energy conservation does not become part and parcel of public policy. Energy audit ought to be essential in all government offices. Governmental apathy towards using energy-efficient transport just because the taxpayers pay the money for oil bill in due course is a self-destroying approach with a constricted vision. If we take a cue from other countries like France, for example, there are active instances of policy interventions like a new mandate necessitating at least 20 per cent of new cars in public fleets to be electrically driven vehicles (EVs). In Italy about 30 per cent rebate is allowed in the case of EVs. Japan has allocated $ 20 billion for the R&D for efficient battery. While the Delhi and Chandigarh territory governments can offer rebates in the range of 29 per cent, other governments may emulate the example. Initiating programmes for developing lightweight, high-power batteries like lithium-ion for EVs, can successfully replace lead-acid batteries, whose basic design is vintage type. In order to make EVs competitive alongside petrol automobiles, vigorous governmental support is needed for building charging points in city centres as well as major car parks[8]. Interestingly, Honda has launched a hybrid car in India. But the present import duty of 104 per cent on completely built units results into staggeringly high retail price of the commodity. On the contrary, the United States also imports the eco-friendly and oil saving hybrid cars, but subsidy factor positively boosts the widespread use of hybrid cars in the US. In India, there are virtually no enticements to auto-manufacturers for offering their next-generation green technology like hydrogen car to the country. As a result, the auto-giants such as Honda face the obstacle to mass-produce hydrogen cars in India.

Even the public and private buildings requires urgent overhaul in terms of energy-efficiency. Of late, some innovations promise us a silver lining in the dark cloud. The Australian scientists' effort to send water through a deep rig inside the earth crust and obtain the superheated water to produce electricity could be an endless source of energy for us. Another invention, which needs mention, is reproducing fuel from carbon dioxide emitting no green house gases (GHGs). The very recent British experiment to produce electricity for thousands of bulbs in the shopping malls by foot tapping by the unaware customers is a laudable one. The future source of renewable energy should be not only green but also less capital-intensive also.

India in its drastic attempt is trying to catch a straw in the volatile whirlpool of oil crisis, by seeking the central Asian oil reserve. By this, the politically unstable gulf region (the present Iran-Israel political imbroglio is also held responsible for the rising market graph of oil) as a source area may be avoided. But the geographical proximity of China to central Asia may negate the favourable factor for India in near future. The finite stock of oil can be denied at our own peril. Thus, central Asia as a long-term source area hardly offers a promising future.

NOTES

1. Cf. Zha Daojiong (2005), "China's Energy Security and Its International Relations." (Beijing:unpublished paper), August 2005.: *The China and Eurasia Forum Quarterly,* Volume 3, No. 3, November. *Website: http:/ www.silkroadstudies.org/new/docs/CEF/Zha_Daojiong.pdf* (accessed on 25.05.2008). This paper is a slightly updated version of a paper, under the same title, presented to the Third IISS Global Strategic Review, Geneva, 16-18 September.
2. Chairman, Shell Group in India was interviewed in the Indian Express, New Delhi edition on March 04, 2008.
3. Reuters, September 4, 2006. Available at: *http://today.reuters.com/news/ ArticleNews.aspx?type=reutersEdge&storyID=2006-09-04T130344Z_ 01_HKG352919_RTRUKOC_0_US-ENERGY-CHINA, (accessed on 03.06.2008).*
4. FAO (May 2007), *Crop Prospects and Food Situation,* Vol. No.3, Rome. Also the FAO Food Outlook (June 2007, No. 1) calculates approximately that worldwide expenses on imported food look set to exceed USD 400 billion in 2007, roughly 5 per cent above 2006. The volume of the increase can be levelled against increasing prices of imported coarse grains as well as vegetable oils-the commodity groups featuring a great deal in bio-fuel production.
5. See editorial *Right to Food versus right to Profit,* of *Economic & Political Weekly,* June 14, 2008.
6. Addressing a National Convention on Climate Change and Bio-Diesel 2008 at FICCI auditorium, the Union Minister for Rural Development Dr Raghuvansh Prasad Singh highlighted that bio-diesel can assist reducing green house gas emissions.
7. See editorial *Blinkers on oil Consumption,* of *Economic & Political Weekly,* June 14, 2008.
8. Read article 'Neither Fie No Smoke' in *The Times of India,* by Praful Bidwai on 20th June, 2008.

REFERENCES

Chikkatur, Ananth and Shoibal Chakravarty (2008), Modelling Institution in India, *Economic & Political Weekly*, May 24.

Clark, Gregory (2007), *A Farewell to Alms: A Brief Economic History of the World* (Princeton Economic History of the Western World), Princeton University Press, July 24.

IFATPC (2006), *WTO Disciplines and Biofuels: Opportunities and Constraints in the Creation of a Global Marketplace*, IPC Discussion Paper, October 2006, International Food & Agricultural Trade Policy Council.

International Institute for Sustainable Development [IISD] (2008), *Biofuels: At What Cost? Government Support for Ethanol and Biodiesel in the European Union*, (for the Global Subsidies Initiative), October, Geneva, Switzerland.

Karmakar, Suparna (2007), *Subsidies on Biofuel Crops: Farm Support or Industrial Subsidy*, ICRIER-SRTT Quarterly WTO Newsletter, WTO News and Views, April-June, Vol. 3, No.2.

Menotti, Victor (2006), *The Other Oil War: Halliburton's Agenda at the WTO*, A Policy Brief on the Energy Services negotiations in the World Trade Organization (WTO) June, International Forum on Globalization.

OPEC (2008), Monthly Oil Market Report, May.

OPEC (2008), Monthly Oil Market Report, January.

Pimentel, David, G. Rodrigues, T. Wane, R. Abrams, K. Goldberg, H. Staecker, E. Ma, L. Brueckner, L. Trovato, C. Chow, U. Govindarajulu and S. Boerke (1994), Renewable Energy: Economic and Environmental Issues, *BioScience*, Vol. 44, No. 8, September.

United Nations (2007), *Key Economic Developments and Prospects In The Asia-Pacific*, ESCAP, New York, pp. 9-10.

CHAPTER-3

EMANCIPATION OF WORLD ECONOMY THROUGH COOPERATIVE SECTOR

MUZAMIL JAN

INTRODUCTION

THE last decade of twentieth century has witnessed an era of liberalization. Globalization of world trade has become an accepted phenomenon (Balaksishan, 2000). In the world as a completely cooperative movement emerged as a response to the industrial revolution, which for the first time brought into existence the factory system and the two economic classes antagonistic to each other viz. the capitalists and the workers. The latter were exploited and hence came together to form cooperatives to save themselves from economic exploitation. Cooperative business enterprises are known to operate in almost every area of economic and social activity. They are known to be of major significance in almost every sector and sub-sector in at least some country. Their internal and external components are very significant, and functionally essential, component of advanced market economies (Figure 1). This economic status, when combined with the social and environmental conscience which characterises cooperative business enterprises and the international cooperative movement, is of major significance for women's advancement. Although to a less predominant extent than in the primary sector, cooperative enterprises are significant in manufacturing, not least because of the vertical expansion of agricultural supply cooperatives into the manufacture of inputs, and the converse expansion of marketing cooperatives into food processing. In many countries, very large numbers of persons are self-employed in worker-owned manufacturing cooperatives, ranging from small-scale and labour-intensive handicraft enterprises to highly capitalized large-scale heavy industry. In 1993 an estimated 10 crore persons were self-employed in such enterprises world-wide (International Cooperative Alliance, 1995). Today, Cooperatives are bustling hubs of commerce that operate in virtually every industry. More than 750,000 cooperatives serve some 760 million members in more than 100 countries. Cooperatives operate in every industry including agriculture, childcare, energy, financial services, food retailing, and distribution, health care, insurance, housing, purchasing and shared services, telecommunications, and others. Cooperatives range in size from large enterprises, including U.S. Fortune 500 companies, to small local storefronts (Gupta, 1993).

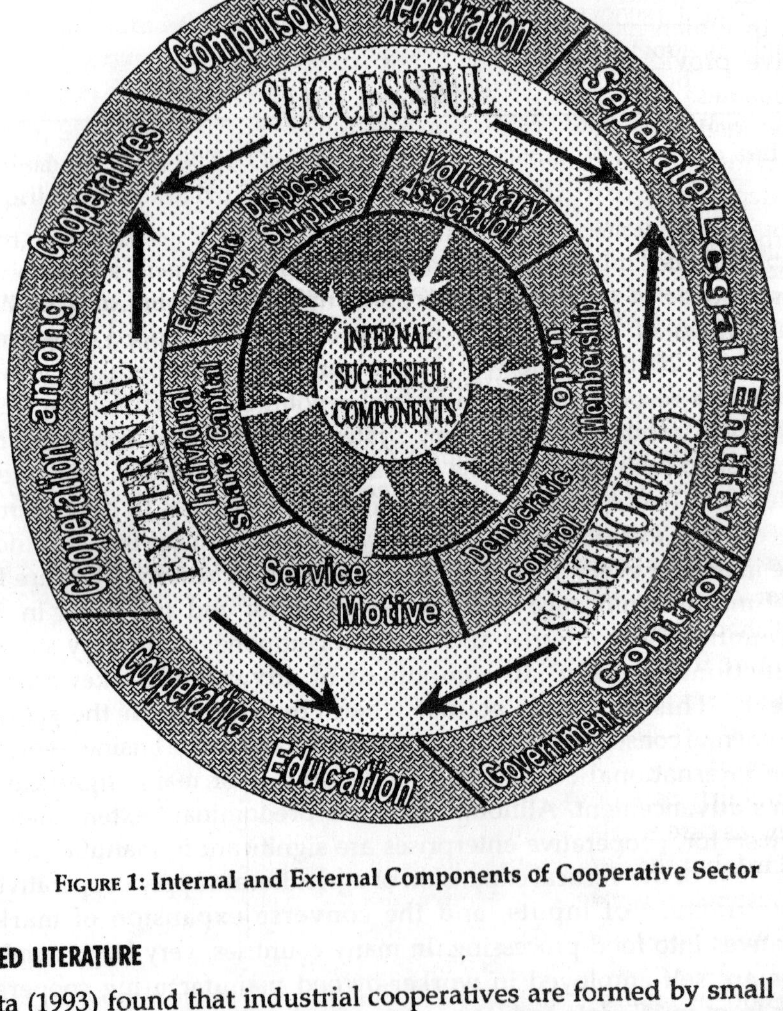

FIGURE 1: Internal and External Components of Cooperative Sector

RELATED LITERATURE

Gupta (1993) found that industrial cooperatives are formed by small artisans and craftsmen to secure the benefits of collective and large-scale production so that they may survive against the competition of organised large-scale producers. International Cooperative Alliance (2006) exemplified such cooperatives as: Land O' Lakes, Sun Kist, Sun Maid, Blue Diamond, and Ocean

Spray, (US), which is farmer owned cooperatives with strong brand recognition and market power; Gujarat Cooperative Milk Marketing Federation (India), which is a federation of 12 milk cooperatives with 2 million farmer-members that are now the country's largest food products marketing organization; and National Agricultural Cooperative Federation (Korea), which is a federation accounting for 45% of the local agricultural market, serving 5 million farmers.

Drake and Llewellyn (2001) analysed that membership-based businesses have been very successful. Financial services such as savings and loans, lending for house purchase, life and non-life insurance, and pensions provision are all concerned with directing flows of money and spreading risks. They do not really need injections of capital from a separate class of investors. The mutual form, in which members lend, borrow, and agree to insure each other, is effective, provided they do not take too many risks or invest too far from their core business. In the last decade there has been a wave of demutualization of mutual insurance (UK, South Africa, and Australia), building societies (UK), and savings and loans (USA). The reasons given are usually that more capital is needed, or that they need to escape regulatory restrictions, or that they will be more efficient after conversion. There is also a large amount of self-interest among managers who want to enrich themselves with higher salaries and share options, sometimes helped by members who will receive large 'windfall' payments on conversion (Nilsson, 2001).

Nilsson (2001) assessed that Canada has one of the highest concentrations of credit cooperatives. In the French-speaking Quebec region, there are 1300 *caisses populaires*, with five million members and more outlets than the banks. They have more than a third of the region's savings on deposit, and make a third of all consumer loans. In English-speaking Canada, they have not such a large market share, but in Saskatchewan 57 per cent of the population belong to one. In the USA, some very large cooperative banks account for about a quarter of the credit needs of US agriculture. Credit unions are also well established; there are over 12,000 of them, serving 70 million members and with more than $300 billions in assets. They have 13 per cent of the consumer credit market and eight per cent of consumer savings.

Taylor, et. al (2002) found that in developed countries, there is a growing problem of how to care for elderly people. The burden of care of the elderly rests unfairly on women, both those who care for relatives and those who make a living as care workers. These workers may not be poor by the United Nations standard, but they are among the lowest paid workers in developed countries. For these reasons, care cooperatives are being developed in several countries. There are around forty care cooperatives in the UK, and the sector is expanding rapidly, with local authorities seeing them as alternatives to public sector provision In Japan, over 30,000 care helpers have been trained, and thirty agricultural cooperatives have signed partnership agreements with local authority social care departments. In Canada, Sweden and the United States cooperatives providing day care for children are important. However, it is in

Italy that we find the most established cooperative care sector. Around 2,000 health and social care cooperatives attract about thirteen per cent of the total budget for social welfare. They employ around 40,000 people, and mainly take the worker cooperative form, but increasingly care cooperatives around the world are experimenting with multi-stake holding, having workers, carers and those being cared for as members (Birchall, 2004). Most of the cooperative credit sector as per Smith (2003) has stood firm against this trend. In the UK, the building society sector has shrunk to around 30 per cent of its previous size, but the remaining societies are outperforming the investor-owned banks and gaining new business. They are also considered by customers to be much more trustworthy than their competitors.

Birchall (2004) studied that agricultural cooperatives are really the best known example of a broader type, the primary producer cooperative. Others include fishing and forestry cooperatives. Statistics are hard to find, but the market share of the Korean Federation of Fishing Cooperatives is 71 per cent and this is not untypical of the picture in many other countries. In Norway, cooperatives produce 76 per cent of forestry products, in Canada 73 per cent Birchall (2004) also enumerated that about 17 per cent of housing cooperatives are in Sweden, and 14 per cent in Norway, are now cooperative. In Britain, the USA, Germany and Canada cooperatives are a much smaller minority tenure, but in their common ownership form they provide an alternative to public sector housing (often being developed to take over failing public estates), and in their market value form a way for elderly people securely to house themselves. *Brazil* has the largest system of provider-owned health cooperatives in the world

International Cooperative Alliance (2006) observed that consumer cooperatives operate worldwide in areas of retailing, energy, financial services, health care, housing, and others. Examples of most popular Consumer Cooperatives areas as per ICA (2006) are: Kooperativa Forbundet (Sweden), which is a network of consumer-owned cooperative retailers that enjoy 25 per cent of the national retail market; Deutsche Genossenschafts-und Raiffeisenverband (Germany), which is a federated system of credit unions and other consumer cooperatives throughout Germany; Oxford, Swindon & Gloucester Cooperative Society (UK), that is the largest retailer in a five county area with over 150,000 member and 3,000 workers; Co-op Atlantic (Canada), which is the second largest regional cooperative wholesaler in Canada with a membership of 136 cooperative enterprises and stores that serve over 200,000 member families; and Crédit Mutuel (France), which is the fourth largest bank in France providing financial services to 9.6 million members and clients. ICA (2006) further bring forth the most successful workers cooperatives in world which are: Burley Design Cooperative. (US), which is a bicycle products manufacturer owned and governed by its 88 workers, with $8 million in annual sales; and Mondragon (Spain), which is a major global producer of food and industrial products owned and governed by some 50,000 worker owners. It is the eighth largest corporation in Spain.

OBJECTIVES FOR STUDY

The present study was carried out with following objectives in view:

1. To study the evolution of cooperatives across the world.
2. To analysis the present status of world cooperatives.
3. To assess millennium development goals *vis-à-vis* cooperative development.

METHODOLOGY

The study is based on secondary data. Such data was collected from International Cooperative Alliance, Macro Data, Gender Disaggregate Statistics-Cooperative Members, from ICA Databank and Supplemented with reports from ICA Global Women's Committee, National Resource Centre, New Delhi and various websites and other literature. Content analysis using quantitative as well as qualitative approach was done to understand the research study. Data are scrutinized and analyzed, keeping the objectives in order to determine inherent facts and meanings. Appropriate statistical tables were presented in order to understand the problem under consideration and attempt was made to draw right inferences out of it.

RESULTS AND DISCUSSION

The evolution of cooperatives in the world can be traced from time immemorial; beginning from the day individual first joined hands for the advancement of common movement is generally dated from the foundation of Rochdale Equitable Pioneers at the end of 1844. In December 1844, the first cooperative society was established in United Kingdoms. This was named as "The Rochdale Equitable Pioneers Society" and it was registered under "English Friendly Societies Act, 1846" (Hajela, 1982). Rochdales are called as pioneers of cooperative movement on earth because they were first who organized and run the first industrial society of the world successfully with the working capital of 28 pounds only. The structure and the rules of the Rochdale Cooperative Society of Weavers formed the model for countless successors not only in England but also in other countries and continents. Germany is the birthplace of cooperative credit movement. The two pioneers Raiffeisan and Schulze organized credit cooperative society in 1850. Raiffeisan started the cooperative credit movement for rural areas and Schulze for urban areas (Britt and Boyd, 1968). However, the first Dairy Cooperative was setup in Hjedding with the initiate of a young dairy man 'Stilling Anderson' in 1882 in Denmark (Sehgal, 1990).

United Kingdoms: Britain is the homeland of cooperative movement. It was the outcome of radical changes that took place in the latter half of the 18th century, in the economic and social systems of Britain, under the impact of the Industrial Revolution. On 21.12.1844, the Rochdale Pioneers established a society with a working capital of £ 28. The Rochdale Society had a record of brilliant successes. In the beginning, however, the progress was very slow. At the end of first year the membership was 74, the sales amounted to £ 22. In 1847, the society suffered a setback owing to general depression in trade. In 1850, the membership increased to 600 and the capital to £ 2300. The savings rose to £ 13,180 and profit to £ 9,910. This enabled the society to undertake more and more services like drapery, tailoring, butchery, and footwear. A new room and library were also added. The same year the pioneers entered into production and started a cooperative corn mill. After surmounting the initial difficulties the mill, in 1852, made a profit and by end of 1853, its assets exceeded its liabilities. Subsequently, the pioneers establish a number of producers' societies, viz., the Rochdale Cooperative Manufacturing Society, The Rochdale Equitable Provident Sick and Burial Society, The Rochdale Cooperative Card Manufacturing Society, The Cooperative Building Society, and the Cooperative Insurance Society. It played a leading role in establishing the Cooperative Wholesale Society in 1863.

In the initial stages of the development of cooperative movement in Britain, the educational; activities of the cooperative societies were confined to organizing classes in scientific, technological, art, commerce and general subjects. This was a good effort in its own place but it resulted in the neglect of cooperative education. Much of this educational activity was taken over by the local authorities, leaving the movement's funds and energy for producing co-operators. Fortunately, the cooperative union had from the beginning being actively concerned with education in cooperation. The leaders of the movement in various conferences emphasized the importance of cooperative education. In 1854, Christian Socialists started workers' college where the noted economists, philosophers and co-operators delivered lectures to the workers in the night classes. The chief contribution of Christian Socialists lies in their efforts for getting the Industrial Provident Societies' Act passed for the cooperatives, in 1852. Prior to this Act, the Cooperative Societies were registered under the Friendly Societies Act, 1846. In August 1863, 'The North of England Cooperative wholesale Agency and Depot' was registered. It started business on 14 March 1864. In 1867, its name changed to 'Cooperative Wholesale Society' (CWS). Several branches, depots, and salesrooms were opened and by the end of the century, there was a network of branches to serve the retail society. Since the wholesale society was established for enjoying the economies of large-scale trade, buying depots outside England were also set-up. The CWS also started undertaking production. In 1889, it started cooperative dairy, in 1900 bacon factories and in 1913 purchased tea estates in Ceylon. In 1976, it had total sales of $2167 million. In 1957, a subsidiary society named Cooperative Retail Services Limited was started. Its main function was to establish retail stores at those places where such stores were not in existence.

In May 1868, the Scottish Cooperative Wholesale Society was registered. It commenced business on September 8, 1868. This society also went on developing, more or less, on similar lines as those of CWS i.e. the same pattern of development from groceries to dry goods, increase in departments, opining of branches and depots, entering into cooperative production like, furniture, footwear, brushes, tobacco, tin ware, soap, food stuffs, paints, leather goods, mulberries, jute, farming, clothing, printing, building and engineering.

Although agricultural societies were formed in England as early as 1829, the organization of agricultural cooperatives on systematic lines could be possible only towards the beginning of the present century. In 1925, a separate department for agriculture was established in the cooperative union in collaboration with the CWS. This, however, did not suit the CWS, which withdrew itself in 1927. In 1930, the National Cooperative Authority was set-up to deal with the activities and policies of the cooperative movement. The Cooperative Housing Council, a central, organization was constituted in 1965.

The Cooperative Credit Movement in Britain has not made appreciable progress, chiefly because Britain is a highly industrialized country and agriculture is not in a backward state. The experiences show that credit movement has flourished only in those countries, which are predominantly agricultural and where the peasants are hard-pressed In Britain the farmers are quite well off and do not depend on the moneylenders. The property owners are always ready to help the peasants. Consequently, the atmosphere has not been favourable for the development of credit movement. Another reason for the slow growth of the movement is that in Britain, no concerted effort has been made to organise the movement. However, cooperative societies have been established, are more or less inactive. Hence, there is hardly much to record about the credit movement (Hajela, 1982). Vague complaints in the Cooperatives press and a decline in consumer movement rates suggest that wheel-like changes may have occurred in the British Cooperative Movement (Britt and Boyd, 1968).

United States of America: Although cooperation—working together—has been a way of life in the US since colonial days, cooperative business enterprise, even in its most elementary form, did not emerge, even in its most elementary form, did not emerge until the early 1800s. Four Connecticut dairy farmers organized the first marketing cooperative in US recorded in 1810. In the 1840s, with the support and encouragement of labour unions, a number of cooperative stores were tried, but failed within a few years. The Union Cooperative Association in Philadelphia, the first US consumer cooperative established on the Rochdale Plan, opened its store in 1864; a hasty and unwise expansion forced the store to close two years later. It was not until the 1860s that grain-marketing cooperatives emerged -in the East. These early cooperatives, for the most part, were dependent on their members' savings or on the monies, which the members could borrow. Most of the members were poor; the money they borrowed was at high interest rates. In hard times, many early cooperatives failed because they lacked the capital and strength of membership to survive.

It was not until the National Grange promoted cooperatives in the nation's agricultural areas in the 1870s that cooperatives began to emerge as a vital force in the US economy. Following the decline of the Grange, the Farmers Alliance, then the Farmers Education, Cooperative Union, and the American Farm Bureau Federation boosted the cooperative cause.Credit unions and housing cooperatives also trace their origins to the early 1900s. In 1909, a dime opened the first credit union account in the US Alphonse des Jardins, who started this first credit union in a New Hamshireparish church, assisted in Massachusetts' passage of the first general state credit union law that same year. Early cooperative housing efforts were traced to Finnish artisans who, in 1918, organized the Finnish Home Building Association in Brooklyn, New York. However, it was not until the mid 1920s when organized labour became interested in cooperative housing, that this type of cooperative, advertised by the Amalgamated Clothing Workers of America as 'offering members a housing choice based on economy and good living' really took hold. During this period the first two national cooperative trade organizations were formed—the Cooperative League of the USA (CLUSA) and the National Milk Producers Federation—both in 1916. By 1920, in addition to local cooperatives, large scale federated and centralized cooperatives were actively marketing the produce of American farmers.

Supply cooperatives were born in the 1920s—largely to purchase fuel in bulk quantities and make deliveries to the farmers directly—a service that oil companies refused to provide. World War II greatly stimulated cooperative growth. Regional farm supply cooperative started to explore for crude oil and to refine petroleum—so that farmers could be guaranteed adequate fuel during the War. Soya-bean oil mills, first established in the early 40s, helped meet critical shortages of protein feed that followed World War II. The War boosted cooperative processing of dried milk and dehydrated and canned fruits and vegetables. In California, cooperative wineries began to assume real importance. The Cooperative League became involved in international activities in June 1944 when it launched the Freedom Fund as part of a celebration of the 100th anniversary of cooperatives. The Fund was used to rehabilitate European cooperatives. One of the most dramatic investments was a $ 30,000 advance to help launch CARE, which subsequently changed its name to Cooperatives for American Relief Everywhere. One of the largest programme activities was an additional solicitation of contributions for the establishment of an Italian lending agency for cooperatives, IFCAI.

In 1955 the Fund was made perpetual and its chief purpose then became technical assistance to cooperatives in the developing nations. In 1957 the Freedom Fund was renamed the Fund for International Cooperative Development (FICD). In 1962, FICD launched a Worldwide Cooperative Partners Campaign as a special solicitation of individuals and cooperatives. The same year FICD contracted with AID for the organization of a cooperative fiancé institution in Latin America. FICD helped to finance long-term CLUSA technical assistance to rural agricultural and consumer cooperatives in northeast Brazil from 1962 to 1967. In addition, it provided major resources for the CLUSA work in India, which had begun in 1954. In the period ending December 1975, the proportions of farm supplies handled through cooperatives totalled 35 per cent for petroleum, 30 per cent for fertilizer and lime, 29 per cent for farm chemicals, 18 per cent for feed and 16 per cent for seeds. This accounted for nearly 75 per cent of the total business volumes for supply cooperatives.

Related service cooperatives provide those services that affect the form and quality of location of the farm products or supplies handled by cooperatives. These include trucking, storage, grinding, drying, application of fertilizer and pesticides. General Service cooperatives provide unique and distinct services such as electricity, telephone, artificial breeding and mutual irrigation. Membership in related service cooperatives (which numbered 155 in 1975) declined 75 per cent until 1980—mainly because the majority of both farm supply and marketing cooperatives provided specialized services such as cotton ginning, livestock trucking, storage, grinding, and drying. In 1980s, there were more than 50 million people -one out of three US families -belonged to some type of cooperative. These ranged from 1,000 consumer goods cooperatives to the 8,000 businesses owned by farm families to purchase supplies, insurance or marketing services. Social and economic benefits of US cooperatives spread beyond the confines of the individual cooperatives and their members. Fairly and openly posted prices, access to credit, improved consumer information service—these are just a few ways US cooperatives have improved the quality of life for all Americans. Currently, CLUSA has active cooperative assistance programmes in India, Thailand, Indonesia, Panama, Switzerland, Rwanda and Zambia (Felder, 1980).

Germany: Germany is the birthplace of co-op. credit movement. Famine, poverty, exploitation, indebt-ness etc. were very common in the middle of 19th century. Moneylenders exploited the poor farmers and labourers heavily under debt. Mostly trade were in the hands of the Jews. Even the agricultural produce used to be sold to them. In every household, the farmland was encumbered with debt. All these necessitated the introduction of new ideas of cooperation in Germany in the middle of 19th century. Moved by the miserable condition of farmers and labourers, two pioneers—Herr F. W. Raiffeisan mayor of Weyerbusch and Herr Franz Schulze the judge and mayor of Delitzeh made experiments of various methods of relief. Raiffeisan took grains as loan from government and started bakery to supply bread at cheaper rate. When transferred to Flammrsfeild commune, they organised the 'Union in Aid of Impoverished Farmers' in 1849. The needy farmers joined it. The union was grand success and farmers were saved from the clutches of usury. Schulze started a charitable bakery to distribute bread to the poor with contributions from friends. Soon he realised the superiority of self-help and mutual help over charity. He found his first 'Friendly Society of Shoe-makers' in 1849 with the objectives making purchases of raw materials in bulk and to supply to members. In 1850, he found the credit society. Thus, Raiffeisan started the Cooperative Credit Movement for rural areas and Schulze for urban areas.

Raiffeisan stressed on the concept of self-help mutual help, social equality, non-profit motive and joint liability. The primary societies were federated into 12 regional federations for audit purposes. These regional federations were further federated in Raiffeisan Federation. The Prussian Cooperative Act 1867 made applicable for whole of Germany in 1889.

After German defeat in 1945, the country was divided into German Democratic Republic (GDR) and Federal/Republic of Germany (FRG). In GDR Russian pattern of collective farms had been organised whereas in FRG, rural societies, urban societies, housing societies and consumer cooperatives were organised (Sehgal, 1990). The position of the various societies in 1976 in the two Germanys was quit different. The German Democratic Republic had 198 consumer cooperatives, with 4,275,141 members and $ 12,246,329 thousand retail turnover. Whereas, Federal Republic of Germany had 76 consumer cooperatives with 160,00 members, 3242 credit cooperatives comprising 2600000 members, 9275 agricultural cooperatives with 3300000 members and 1263 housing cooperatives with 1,577,975 members. The retail turnover of consumer cooperatives during the period was $3,991,525 thousand at retail level and $ 1,440,678 thousand at wholesale level. Similarly, agricultural societies had retail turnover of $ 23,250,082 thousand. Thus, Federal Republic of Germany overtook the cooperative movement. In Germany the cooperative movement and the workers' movement have been helping each other and fostering the interest of the entire nation (Hajela, 1982).

Denmark: The first Cooperative Dairy was set up in Hjedding with the initiative of a young dairyman Mr. Stilling Anderson in 1882. Since then the continuous efforts have been made to develop the Cooperative Dairy Movement. The country is called the 'Cooperative Denmark'. The dairy cooperatives play an important role in the country's socio-economic development. Up to 1995, there were 750 primary dairy cooperatives at primary level. These primary cooperative dairy societies consisted of number of milk producers associated with process and disposal of milk and milk products as a joint enterprise. At present, there are more than 24 Regional Dairy Associations in Denmark. The primary dairy cooperatives are associated with the regional dairy associations. Even private dairies at the primary level are associated with the regional associations. The policy behind associating the private dairies is to preserve them to maintain the spirit of healthy competition between the two sectors. These associations are managed democratically. The main function of the associations is to look after the dairy industry besides helping the member institutions.

The cooperative movement in Denmark grew spontaneously and naturally, credit of success goes mainly to the efforts of members and their self-generating energy. Finances are available not from the government but from the National Cooperative Bank having branches throughout the country and from the private commercial banks. Cooperatives in Denmark are of single purpose rather than multipurpose. The belief in specialised and decentralised activity of each branch has developed its own regional and national federations. About 70 per cent of the dairy products including butter, cheese, cream and milk powder is exported and 30 per cent is sold in the home market. Prices of milk are paid to producers based on fat contents, weight and hygiene quality of milk (Sehgal, 1990).

Sweden: The Swedish movement was started with a modest beginning more than a century ago and during this period; it passed through many vicissitudes. The most important land-mark in the history of Swedish movement was the emergence of the Central Organisation of the Cooperative Union and the Wholesale Societies known as "KF" – KOOPERATIVE FORBUNDET" – founded (Kamat, 1978) in 1899 at Stockholm to advise and guide the primary cooperatives and for making publicity. Subsequently, in 1904 it started supplying goods to primaries. It took agencies from a number of private companies. The subsidiary organisations of KF were organised as the Samarbet Fire Insurance Society in 1908, the Folket Life Insurance Society in 1914 and the Marine and Transport Society in 1949 (Sehgal, 1990). In 1949 KF also evolved an arrangement for distribution of goods to retail societies with the help of a regional warehouse system. A separate Domus Department Stores Association was set up in 1956, to assist the societies wishing to establish new Department Stores. Since 1966, the societies themselves were responsible for the Department Stores, although there was a close collaboration with the retail division of the KF. The local consumer societies in Sweden worked in close collaboration with KF. The size of the societies varied greatly both with regard to membership and geographical area. The process of amalgamation made the number of societies from 668 in 1958 to 258 in 1968 (Kamat, 1978). In 1985, KF's share in consumer retailing was 18 per cent, food trade 20.5 per cent and non-food trade 14 per cent (Ganesan, 1982a). Up to 1995, KF established more than 50 factories for producing most of the consumer goods. Important among these were bakery, oil, flour footwear, polish, baking powder, staple fibre, clothing, rubber, electric lamps, sewing machine, electric bulbs, vacuum cleaners, washing powder, ceramics, furniture, insulated materials, super-phosphate, paper, oil extraction, etc. It also established its own canning mill and fruit and vegetable preservers. It also maintained fruit farm in the decade on 90s (Sehgal, 1990).

Today, however, cooperative movement has come to occupy a commanding position in the economy of Sweden. The structure has been so evolved there that in terms of organisational and financial strength, meticulous planning, effective member participation, efficient management and economic success, the Swedish movement has come to be regarded as the successful cooperative endeavour in the world. Approximately 50 per cent of the total number of households and 20 per cent of the total retail trade have been covered by the Swedish Consumer' Cooperatives. KF has grown from strength to strength. It is one of the largest purchasing organisations in entire Europe. The KF has a number of factories doing extensive commercial business and is a part owner of a number of concerns. It ha also entered into several international joint cooperative ventures. He KF provides leadership through a special body to secure coordination in activities of local societies and in turn with central societies. There is a coordination division consisting of departments of planning, location, establishment of units, an office of architects and engineers and an audit service. A whole range of consultancy services is made available to the retail units (Kamat, 1978). Agricultural cooperatives in Sweden have been organised on a single purpose basis. Swedish lending cooperatives have achieved self-sufficiency in funds. Deposits raised by the primaries are remitted to the regional cooperative banks. These banks lay down policies for local societies in respect of deposits and loans, system of loaning, security to be taken by way of mortgages, auditing and inspection. Primary societies can borrow up to 85 5 of their deposits with the regional banks for lending to their members. To rationalise the marketing systems as a whole grading, standardisation and quality control is practised for various agricultural products. Improved and scientific methods of packing as well as sales promotion are used to popularise the products of cooperatives (Ganesan, 1982).

Thailand: As in other developing countries, the cooperative sector in Thailand was established and promoted by the government as a means to improve income and livelihood opportunities for small farmers. The country's first cooperative, in the form of a small village credit cooperative called the *Wat Chan Cooperative Unlimited Liability,* was established by the government on 26 February 1916 in Phitsanuloke province (AWCF, 1999 and AWCF and CULT, 2000). This first cooperative society was established among the small paddy farmers. It was known as a village credit cooperative with unlimited liability, based on the Raiffeisan model. The primary intention of the then government was to relieve farmers from severe indebtedness and maintain their land ownership. At the initial stages, the government directly provided the cooperatives with funds to be loaned to their members against land mortgages and guarantors. The success of the first group of village credit cooperatives led to a moderate expansion of the cooperatives of this type later on. But all these cooperatives were registered called "The Civil Association (Amendment) Act, B.C 2459 (1916)" [CLT, 2001]. The cooperative societies' act B.E.2471 (1928) was promulgated in 1928 paving the way for further development of cooperatives of various types. But it was not until 1932 that other types of cooperatives were organised, such as, land hire purchase, land settlement, marketing and processing, consumers', land improvement, cottage industry, fisheries and thrift and credit cooperatives. In 1943, the bank for cooperatives was organised to serve as a financing centre of the agricultural cooperatives and to take the places of the government's direct lending (Sharma, 1992).

With the success of the Wat Chan cooperative, the government expanded its support to a large number of small village credit cooperatives all over the country. The Bank for Cooperatives was set up in 1947 (CPD, 2002). Two provincial cooperatives were established in Chiang Mai and Uttaradit provinces in 1952 and 1953 (FAO, 1998a). Multi-purpose cooperatives were set up in 1959 to meet additional demands of farmers. During this period, the government policy of cooperative amalgamation encouraged small credit cooperatives to merge with other types of cooperatives to form bigger bodies able to conduct a bigger volume of business for their members (FAO, 1998b and 1998c; ILO, 2000; and Kane and Tototo, 1992). Two provincial cooperative banks were organised with equity from the government and the credit cooperatives in 1952 and 1963. These banks were subsequently reorganised into federations because of enactment of commercial banks law in 1952. In 1966, a state enterprise called Bank for Agriculture and Agricultural Cooperatives (BAAC) came into being. For the first time a cooperative society act was enacted, which paved way for establishment of cooperative league of Thailand. This apex level organisation brought about systematic growth of cooperatives in Thailand (Krishna, 1997). The Bank for Agriculture and Agricultural Cooperatives (BAAC) as a state-run financial centre for agricultural cooperatives lend directly to individual farmers as well. Two years later, the Cooperative Society Act B.E 2511 was enacted to strengthen the cooperative movement (Kindervatter and Range, 1991). Also, in 1968, the Cooperative Act was amended to permit the establishment of the Cooperative League of Thailand (CLT) to function as the apex cooperative promotion organization (Patrawart and Stiftung, 1995). In 1968, the cooperative societies act; B.E. 2511 (1968) was promulgated, repealing the cooperative societies act B.E. 2471, in order to facilitate the expansion and improvement of the cooperatives. This legislation embodied two new features, i.e. the amalgamation of the cooperative league of Thailand (Sharma, 1992). The federation of savings and credit cooperatives of Thailand Ltd.(FSCT) came into existence in 1972 (Krishna,1997).

By 1990 BAAC had a network of 71 branches, 47 sub-branches or district branches and 604 field offices, covering the entire country. The total staff of the bank was 7,330, of which 6,181 were working in branch offices or field offices. About 1.9 million farmers were registered as direct clients of the bank. Direct clients borrowed 28,013 million Baht (US$1.120 million). Of this total, 16 per cent of the value of all loans was long-term investment loans. About 812 agricultural cooperatives were also BAAC clients. Agricultural cooperatives were legal entities organised at the district level and administered by the cooperatives promotion department (CPD) of the Ministry of Agriculture and Cooperatives (MOAC). The cooperatives borrow from the BAAC at interest rates three percentage points below the rates for direct clients and on-lend to their 833,711 farmer members at the same rate paid by direct clients, currently 12.5 per cent for most loans. Total BAAC disbursements to cooperatives amounted to 5,794 million Baht (US$232 million) in 1990. In 1992, Thailand comprised 3,163 different types of cooperatives ; out of which 1,464 were agricultural cooperatives with 1,007,637 members; 26 fishery cooperatives with 6,236 members; 94 settlement cooperatives with 95,604 members; 858 thrift and credit cooperatives with 1,399,449 members; and 302 service cooperatives with 86,913 members (Sharma, 1992). In 1997, FSCT raised funds through issue of promissory notes. The federation had an outstanding of Rs. 7000 million. These funds were used for providing loans to the member cooperatives. The outstanding loans to the cooperatives by the FSCT was around Rs. 5400 million (Krishna, 1997).

The most recent amendment to the Cooperative Act in 1999 stipulated that all cooperatives would be affiliated to the CLT. Alongside, the government set up the National Cooperative Development Board to advise it on policy and guidelines for the promotion and development of cooperatives. The Act also provided for setting up of a Cooperative Development Fund in the Ministry of Agriculture and Cooperatives for providing financial assistance to cooperatives (UNDP and UNIFEM, 2000 and APCO, 2001). The existing cooperative system in Thailand is weak and there is a need for a new attempt to establish a new kind of organisation, which genuinely belong to the farmers and have a strong commercial orientation. The BAAC has considerable experience working with both individual farmers and farmer institutions, learning many lessons along the way (Sharma, 1992). Steps are being taken to upgrade and strengthen the management capabilities of the agricultural cooperatives in poor financial conditions. An increase is observed in foreign aid in assisting and fostering the growth of cooperatives, particularly in the field of agricultural cooperatives (Ganesan, 1982b).

Japan: In Japan, Cooperatives emerged in the second half of the 19th century when Japan entered the modern world. These Cooperatives were strongly oriented towards Western Models. But it was not until 1900 that the large number of already existing Cooperatives could be based on National Cooperative Legislation by adopting the 'Industrial Cooperative Act' which was drawn up in the line with the German Cooperative Act (Burkner, 1998). The Japanese Consumer's Cooperative Union (JCCU) started the Tokyo Consumer's Cooperative society in 1969 (Nakabayashi,1976). The Central Union of Agricultural Cooperatives of Japan (CUAC) convened the first national conference for the stabilisation of fruit shipment in May 1981, and fixed 1981 production target of 'Unshu Mikan' (looking like Mandarin Organe) at three million tons on the basis of n estimated domestic demand. At the second national conference for the stabilisation of fruit shipment held on September 10th 1981 centred on the transformation of 'mikan' plantations into other farms. It was reported at the conference that 'mikan' plantations in 1980 was 9,693 hectares, far surprising the target of 7,000 hectares. In 1981, it was reported, the total transformed area had, far exceeded the target of 7,000 hectares by one per cent (Ganesan, 1982c). The membership in all types of cooperatives raised to 4.6 million in 1982, with turnover of 4.6 billion US Dollars (Ganesan, 1982b).

The primary agricultural cooperative societies in Japan are mainly of multipurpose type and provide a variety of services to their members such as credit, supply of inputs including farm machinery, marketing of members produce, mutual insurance, farm and better living guidance. There are also single purpose primary societies for certain crops and live stocks. Due to amalgamation of small societies into larger and more viable cooperative societies, the primary level societies in Japan are strong and viable. They enjoy the loyalty of their membership. The apex cooperative organisations of Japan are strong and play a key role in agricultural cooperative development. The organisational structure of the cooperative movement is well defined and there is smooth coordination and cooperation among the primaries, prefecture level and apex level organisations avoiding duplication of activities. Provision of integrated services at the primary level and specialised services at the prefecture and national levels enables the membership to get comprehensive services from the movement (Ganesan, 1982a).

Hungry: The development rate of Hungarian Cooperative movement has been dynamic. From 1976-81, the agricultural growth rate was higher than seven per cent. This result was partly due to advancement of mechanization. In 1946, only 5 per cent of Hungarian agriculture was mechanised while in 1981, this rate was 95-99 per cent and 33 per cent in animal breeding. In 1961, the property of Hungarian cooperatives reached 55000 million forint, which rose to 110,000 million forint in 1981. In the decade of 90s, 50 per cent of cooperative land was in the possession of the members, 48 per cent was owned by the cooperative and 2 per cent was state owned. About 1350 cooperatives were established during the period and provided employment to nearly 650,000 people and 800 agricultural specialists. The employment of cooperative members became more even during the period. Because of state measures, members and employees working in the positions especially in working time, pay, retirement age, social welfare benefit and generally in working and living conditions. About 400 farms under best cooperatives were able to adjust very well to the higher demands of economic policy. However, at a slower rate, the majority of farms with medium quality were also able to continue their development. But nearly one third of the cooperatives fell short of the requirement although they did make some advances. This was primarily due to the lack of initiatives and means and to adverse natural conditions. The agriculture cooperatives achieved significant results in a historically short period. This attracts attention also abroad and today increasing number of foreign specialists study the Hungarian cooperative movement (Dev, 1981).

Russia: Over its 100 years, the cooperative system in Russia has become economically highest. The Moscow Regional Union for Consumer System (MRUCS) spreads to thousands of villages, small towns and district centres. It's purchasing turnover increased by 80 per cent since 1986. It was accidental that the share of the cooperative's own resources in total sales of foodstuffs rose to 32 per cent, whereas the average for the system was only 23.8 per cent. The new approaches to the development of foreign trade were incorporated in the social and economic development plan of the Moscow Regional Consumer Society adopted in December 1989. The society enhanced its role in supplying the region with foodstuffs and manufactured goods with due regard for the market economy. This was done by increasing its own output and extending its export and import operations. The region's consumer market was satisfied by all-round restructuring of the economic mechanism and by contractual relations. In 1991, MRUCS had about 5,000 retailing outlets and over 1,500 catering enterprises. In order to improve the supply and to relieve the social tension the co-operators are doing their best to build up the output and to extend foreign trade operations. At present, the cooperative system in Russia is constantly developing. The closest economic ties are maintained with the Sofia and Varna cooperative unions of Bulgaria. The collaboration is also being made with Yugoslav cooperatives and Canadian cooperatives (Marinichev, 1991).

Malaysia: The Malaysian cooperative movement is governed by the cooperative act 1993 and the cooperative regulations 1995, which were enacted after consolidating different legislations governing cooperatives in the country. A government authority to promote and regulate cooperatives in Malaysia was established as far back as 1922 in the form of department of cooperative development of Malaysia. The Malaysian Cooperative Insurance Service (MCIS) was established in 1954 and gradually raise in its popularity over the period of time. As the cooperative movement grew particularly in the period after attainment of independence by Malaysia in 1957, two separate authorities, one called the Farmers Organisation Authority and the other Fisheries Development Authority were set up to monitor these two sectors of the cooperatives. However, all other cooperatives were left under the control of Department of Cooperative Development, which functions under the Ministry of Land and Cooperative Development of Malaysia (Krishna, 1997). In the fourth Malaysian Plan beginning 1981-1985, about 30,000 housing units were constructed by various cooperative housing societies Ganesan, 1982b). In 1997, there were 465 credit societies/banks with total assets of over Rs. 100 billion. Of these 465 societies, three societies functioned as full-fledged banks offering all the banking services. Finance/banking, housing, transport services, industrial plantation and consumerism are the sectors in which cooperatives has very good presence. The insurance sector has only one cooperative society (MCIS), built it is the largest organisation in the insurance sector in Malaysia. MCIS has achieved tremendous success to the grassroots level contracts, introduction of schemes suited to the lower middle class and middle class and excellent personalised service (Krishna, 1997). New ventures in Malaysian cooperatives include cooperative printing, rubber and palm oil processing, establishment of mini estates of palm oil and rubber, and the consolidation of the batik manufacturers (Ganesan, 1982b).

Turkey: The first cooperative in Turkey was organised in Pirot town by Mithat Pasha (General Mithat) in 1867. After the organisation of the Republic of Turkey, various laws related to cooperatives were passed through parliament, including Agricultural Unions Law No.498 in 1924; Agricultural Credit Cooperatives Law No. 1470 in 1929; Agricultural Credit Cooperatives

Law No. 2836 in 1935; Agricultural Marketing Cooperatives Law No. 2834 in 1935; Rural Development Cooperatives Law No. 1165 in 1969; and Agricultural Credit Cooperatives Law No. 1581 in 1972. Initially only agricultural credit cooperatives were established in the country. Gradually rural cooperatives spread in almost every region and in every part of the country. In the beginning of 1990s, the cooperative movement in Turkey boosted and the number of cooperatives reached 19501. Formerly, the cooperative movement was supported through the Ministry of Commerce. However, since 1990 government transferred the activity to the Ministry of Village Affairs with a view that it would reach the small farmers particularly. The number o agricultural marketing cooperatives increased from 635 in 1972 to 653 in 1994. These cooperatives were organised in the region of the country where agricultural commodities were mainly produced for commercial purposes. The village development cooperatives were 4,514 with more than 30,000 in 1993. They were organised to develop rural environment and rural living. The main objectives of their work covered not only agricultural activities but also the development of rural industry. Since the Turkish Government believes that, the cooperative movement is god for the rural people and that it will improve their economic position and strengthen the economy of Turkey the cooperatives are supported by the government in many ways. These incentives can be mentioned in two groups: guidance and technical assistance and financial aids. Incentives of financial aids are of three types that the government uses to support village development cooperatives to carry out projects successfully. These are credits, subventions, and labour quotas for the European countries. At one point, the cooperative movement in Turkey is considered to be at the beginning. So far, they have been very limited in number. Now, the Turkish government is preparing to help the cooperatives with new understanding and to meet all their needs until they can stand on their own and start playing an important role on the economy of the country (Yardimci, 1995).

Sri Lanka: In the history of Cooperative movement in Sri Lanka, 1911 to 1930 is regarded as the period of Cooperative Credit Societies development. The other types of Cooperatives developed during 1931 to 1941 (Prakesh, 1992). The government of Sri Lanka, in 1980, accepted the Devanayagam Report (on the reorganisation of the cooperative movement) – one of the recommendations of which was the settling up of an Advisory Council to advise the government and the ministry on cooperative policy. This advisory committee was appointed in 1981. National Institute for Cooperative Management has been set up in Sri Lanka along with a coordinating committee to formulate policy on cooperative education and training. At present credit cooperatives are being revived in the country (Ganesan, 1982c).

China: The present strong representation of cooperatives in Chinese economy is a product of both cooperative history in China and deliberate policies of the government, particularly after the foundation of the People's Republic in 1949. As early as around 1900, cooperative credit societies were organised in Northern china (now Inner Mongolia). Later agricultural marketing cooperatives were widely organised in cotton-growing regions. Based on indigenous forms of mutual aid and with their roots deeply imbedded in Chinese soil, small-scale farmers back, in history, further used to pool their scarce resources in some kind of cooperatives to compensate for shortage of draft animals, implements and work force, particularly during sowing and harvesting periods. All these type of cooperatives gradually convulsed the rural areas into multi-purpose cooperative providing a multitude of services to their members. In urban areas, workers and students formed consumer cooperatives in 1920. The first cooperative law in china was promulgated in 1935, after a national cooperative conference. During 1930 to 1940, when the country was under the pressure of invading foreign troops and civil war, industrial cooperatives provided for the war efforts and the farmers with arms, tools and consumer goods. This network of industrial cooperatives also provided a lot cooperative education and training, as cooperatives were expected to play an important role in the rebuilding of post-war china.

The most striking feature of immediate post-1949 development was the clear consensus that cooperatives should be the major instrument for achieving the transition to a socialistic economy. A second major characteristic feature of the post-war government policies was to focus on enlisting the peasants in rebuilding the nation. This was different from, for example, the Russian concentration on urban industrial workers, but easily understandable, as in China the peasants constituted and still constitute the major part (about 80 per cent) of the population. The need for a cooperative approach in agriculture was further emphasised by the passage in the mid-1950s of the land reform act, which redistributed to landless farmers more than two-fifths of the total cultivated land in china. In the mid 1950s, 'elementary cooperatives' were set up, comprising 25-40 households in each cooperative. The individual peasant retained, however, private ownership of their land and means of production. By 1955, more than two thirds of China's farmers had joined such cooperatives. Main stages in the cooperative element of the revolution were expected to be Mutual Aid Teams (MATs), Advanced Agricultural Producer Cooperatives (APCs), and Communes. The earlier MATs were merged into large agricultural producer cooperatives; at first made up of 25-40 families, often the usual population of a village. Later it was expanded to enrol 125 families and finally even up to 400 households. The purpose was to stimulate the rural productivity, by creating larger and more effective planning units, by promoting rationalization of land use and use of mass labour for large-scale capital constructions.

Despite the warning signs indicating a serious imbalance in the agriculture, the freed collectivisation was accelerated in mid-1957. This was partly a consequence of experienced grain shortage, need for more investment funds for the industry development and a remaining belief in large collection as such, without considering the actual situation and real factors of importance. The former about 750,000 advanced agricultural producers' cooperatives were further forcibly merged into some large-sized 26,000 communes. The purpose was the same—mass labour mobilisation and intensive infrastructure investments. Prior to 1958, the township government was the lowest level of local government in rural areas. Several townships formed a country, which with other countries formed a province. Under each township government was a number of agricultural producers cooperatives, compiling up to a few hundred households, performing the economic function in the area. In 1958, however, the formation of the huge communes usually at country level, embracing several villages or townships put both political and economic function under the institution. As of 1985, some 90 per cent of all oils and about 50 per cent of sheep and goats were raised by households under the contract with cooperatives.

Today, the cooperative sector plays an important role in the Chinese economy, as one of the three main sectors; the other two are the government sector and the private sector. In some areas, cooperatives dominate, for example, in marketing of farm produce and supply of farm needs, covering about 70-80 per cent of the markets. In some areas, the cooperative sector is even given formal monopoly rights, for example, in buying cotton from farmers and providing fertilizers to farmers (Sharma, 1992).

Vietnam: The first National Congress of Vietnam Cooperatives, held in October 1993 resolved to the change the organisational task as well as the activities of cooperative economic sector. The cooperatives in localities are being transformed to the model of share-holding cooperatives and instructed to revalue total assets, funds and clearly affirm members' ownership etc. Such units are being set up on voluntary and democratic basis and according to principles of cooperation and members' requirement. In the year 1994, more than 120 cooperative groups were established without official registration on legal status. The Central Council of Vietnam Cooperative Unions has affirmed that the role of training and skill improvement of cooperative managers was important at that stage. Two training centres were established in 1993, so that every activity in training could be consolidated and gradually completed in respect of lectures/trainers; training programme for the improvement of new managers for cooperative economic sector, and materials and equipment for learning and teaching.

After the seventh Resolution of the Communist Party of Vietnam and the government's new policies, the cooperative economic sector has found the development direction in the fields of production of small and handicraft industry, transportation, construction, trade and services. However, many difficulties are still faced in the context of the market economy. Since turning to the market economy, cooperative economic sector has been declining substantially, including the reduction of number of cooperatives, its labour force, production and business value as well as its position in the economic structure of each corresponding branch. At present, there are in total 6,000 cooperatives and cooperative groups such fields as small and handicraft industry, transportation, construction, trading and service, out of which only about 40 per cent have adapted themselves to the new structure; only these could hope to work effectively and be able to exist and develop. The rest are in a weak and difficult condition in many aspects like capital, technology, knowledge of management. These days, efforts are being made to deep influence on the cooperative movement throughout country and create a new thinking and correct understanding about its role and the contribution for developing state economy and cooperative economic sector (Trong, 1995).

France: France has been the torchbearer for other countries of the world in the field of 'producers' cooperatives'. The French cooperative movement has been essentially a workers' movement. In no other country of the world, workers' societies have attained those heights of success, which have been attained in France. The seed of the cooperative movement was sown as early as the beginning of the 19th century by Charles Fourier, a great Utopian socialist, the world has ever known. The cooperative movement in its present form could only be started after the revolution of 1948 and it gained momentum after the passage of act of 1863. Although the cooperative movement has diversified its activities, like its counterparts in other countries, the workers' cooperatives still occupy a dominant position.

An Agricultural Syndicate French Cooperative Institution was set up under the Act of 1884. The first rural credit bank was established in 1885. This bank was set up at a time when the state-supported association was very popular. The law of 1894 provided facilities for the organisation of credit societies as union of the syndicate. These societies were allowed to give loans only to members of the syndicate. With the passage of the law of 1899 the bank of France was compelled to grant an interest-free loan of 40 million francs to agricultural banks and a grant of 2 million francs every year in addition to it. The Cooperative Bank of French Workers' Productive Societies was established in 1893. The National Bank was set up in 1920. More than 50 per cent of its members were government nominees and the rest were elected by the regional banks. It also accepted deposits from the regional banks. Workers' Cooperative Organisations were organised for the first time in 1945. In 1955, 708 workers' societies were its members. The bank provided normal banking facilities to the societies and the regional federations. It generated short-term loans to societies for executing their contracts. It also granted credit for three to five years for the purchase of equipment. Its affairs were managed by the committee consisted of nine members. In 1955, the total reserves of the bank stood £ 2 ½ millions. Up to 1971, cooperative credit societies on the pattern of Luzzatian People's Bank were set up. In 1978, the housing movement had 300 cooperatives organised in 40 departments, grouping approximately 16000 families. Its importance not only in economic field but also in social life as far as consumers were concerned was unquestionable. Up to 1982, there were 13 fish trade cooperatives, which played a very delicate role. School cooperatives were 40,000 in number and they represented two million pupils i.e. one-fifth of the total school population of that time.

A unique feature of the French cooperative movement is that the entire movement is not governed by any one ministry and different cooperatives fall within the jurisdiction of different ministries. The agricultural cooperatives, thus, fall within the jurisdiction of the Ministry of Agriculture. Again, not all the cooperatives are governed by one act or statute. Agricultural societies are of two types: credit and non-credit. Credit societies have been providing short-term credit to the farmers. In fact, cooperative agricultural credit societies have made great contribution in the moral and material advancement of the people and hence such societies are more important than producers' cooperatives. The cooperative agricultural credit societies are of two types: (i) those, which get government assistance, and (ii) those, which do not get any assistance from the government. Of these the former type of societies are the most important. The structure of the cooperative credit movement is the same as in other countries, pyramid in form, i.e. the village banks or rural credit societies at the base, the regional banks at the centre and the national agricultural credit bank at the top (Hajela, 1982).

Italy: Cooperative dairy is the oldest form of cooperation in Italy. These dairies are run on modern lines and are equipped with modern equipment for processing. Their functions are to process the milk of the members, help them in the sale of their products and give them advices for improving the quality of their products and their cattle. Their membership is limited to all cow-owners residing in the area of operation of the society. The members are bound to supply all the milk in excess of their family requirements. Delinquent members are expelled from the society and their share capital is forfeited. The administration of these societies is similar to that of other cooperative organisations. Cooperative societies in winemaking, tobacco growing and raw silk production have made good progress. The agricultural societies have federated into national federations. The National Union includes all cooperative organisations except the credit societies whose national organisations are grouped with private banks. The National Federation of Cooperative Labour Cultivation Societies, the National Federation of Cooperative Purchase and Marketing Societies and the National Federation of Processing and Marketing Societies have their offices in Rome. The objectives of these federations are: to act as legal representatives of the member societies, to intervene in the collective labour contracts and to act as consolidators in controversies; to promote coordination work; to look to their technical and economic development; and to promote the organisation of new societies. Some cooperative societies in Italy have also opened up testing stations and have started experimental farms. They have also taken up drive against insects and pests. The surplus is distributed in proportion to the purchases after deducting expenses and taking out for the reserves (Hajela, 1982).

Kenya: Cooperatives are important economically in Kenya, including 700,000 rural households, and about two million wage earners who belong to savings and credit societies. The Cooperative Bank is Kenya's third largest bank. Cooperation in Kenya has extensive government involvement, which the study claims has diminished incentives for active member control. Cooperatives have generally operated in markets that are controlled through government-approved monopolies and non-market pricing arrangements. Cooperation has been viewed as a means of advancing the interests of small producers as new markets have been opened to them since the late 1950s, just before independence, and as new farming technologies have been introduced and taken up. Coffee societies collect coffee from their members and process it into parchment for further processing by the Kenya Planters Cooperative Union. Smallholder growers produce about 65 per cent of coffee exports and are required by law to belong to primary coffee societies, of which there were 243 in 1993. Coffee processing factories, called pulperies, may be operated only by cooperative coffee societies or by farms of more than 10 acres. Coffee society membership varies widely, from 5,000 to 20,000, and many own more than one factory. The Ministry of Cooperatives directs that the expenses of each coffee society should not consume more than 20 per cent of the value of the crop and that members should receive at least 80 per cent of the value of their harvest. The payment system is complex and not always efficient.

Milk production in Kenya is virtually entirely a smallholder activity. About half of total output is consumed on the farm and half is marketed. Producers' cooperatives handle about 79 per cent of marketed milk, which is sold locally as raw milk or delivered to Kenya Cooperative Creameries (KCC) for processing. Recent liberalization of the market has increased producer prices as well as competition, putting pressure on primary societies. Private processors now compete with KCC. There are more than 200 registered dairy societies. Some multipurpose societies have milk collection as their principal activity, and an estimated 192 primary societies are "dairy" societies, with total membership exceeding 200,000. Dairy societies have from 100 to 3,000 members. Their main investment is in vehicles used to collect and market raw milk. Cooperation in Kenya remains heavily regulated and micro-managed. Ministry regulations require that 80 per cent of the value of milk collected be paid to members, limiting society expenses. This rule, regulated prices and KCC inefficiencies have contributed to pushing half of the milk societies into dormancy and liquidation. Clearly, this rule works against capital formation. Cooperative law in Kenya requires written government approval for any bonus or dividend; that 25 per cent of net surplus be transferred to a statutory reserve; that the dividend rate cannot exceed 10 per cent per annum; that all surpluses due to members be allocated, although a society can postpone cash payment by issuing bonus certificates redeemable from a revolving fund; and that a 35 per cent tax be paid on a base consisting of total income less qualifying expenses and distributions. Taxation has led to increases in payouts for produce. Municipalities also tax produce handled by each local society (Von, 1995).

India: The overriding reason for the establishment of cooperatives in India was the dire need for improvement in the conditions and quality of life of the rural masses, most of whom were abjectly poor. The first sustained growth in cooperatives occurred around the turn of the century in respect of credit cooperatives, primarily because the village moneylenders greatly exploited the poor when providing credit. Although some efforts at establishing cooperatives had been made earlier, they were not very successful. In 1895, the government of Madras deputed Sir Frederick Nicholson to look into the possibility of introducing land and agricultural banks in the province. However, the first cooperative society was started in the Punjab in 1891 for controlling the common land of the village. This functioned until 1922. The concept of cooperatives was concretized only in 1904 with the passing of the first Cooperative Credit Societies Act under which cooperatives were established in the field of credit, with limited liability (IGNOU, 1997a). The object of the Act as defined in the preamble was to encourage thrift, self-help among agriculturists, artisans and persons of limited means. The Act empowered the local government to appoint Registrar whose duties were to registrar societies. The Registrars were required to train the rural population in the management of the societies and carry out propaganda for spreading the principals of cooperation. They were also made responsible for the annual audit of the societies. The Act provided for the starting of credit societies only. It made a distinction between rural and urban societies. A society was classed as rural, if 4/5th of its members were agriculturists, and urban if 4/5th of its members were non-agriculturists. Rural societies were to have unlimited liability and to carry over the profit to Reserve Fund. The Act was passed with a view to evolve simplicity and elasticity. It merely laid down the general outline and the provinces were left free to fill in details accordingly to local conditions. To encourage the movement, the government gave some concessions such as exemption from income tax, stamp duty, registration fees, etc.

The years that followed 1904, revealed, certain omissions and defects in the Act of 1904. The Act did not provide for the registration of central societies. In some provinces like Punjab and Madras, rural societies had raised a substantial amount of share capital and the total prohibition o profit in rural societies caused hardship to members. The classification of societies into rural and urban was unscientific and inconvenient. For these reasons, the government came forward with a new Act in 1912. It gave recognition to non-credit societies. It recognized Central Societies as distinct from other societies. The old classification into rural and urban was given up and societies were scientifically classified as unlimited or limited liability societies. All central societies were limited liability societies and all societies of which the majority was agriculturists were to be of unlimited liability societies. Societies with unlimited liability were also permitted to declare dividends.

After 1912, there was a rapid increase in the number of societies and membership (Dev, 1992). There were 8,177 cooperative societies in 1912 compared to just 843 in 1906 (IGNOU, 1997a). Central Banks began to develop rapidly. Non- credit cooperatives were also being gradually developed. In 1914, government appointed a committee under Sir Edward Maclegan to express whether the movement, especially in the higher stages, and its financial aspects, was progressing on sound lines and to suggest measures for improvement, which seemed to be required. Its report published in 1915 is one of the authoritative reports on the working of cooperatives societies in the country. They observed that societies were then so rapid over all parts of India and advantages, which their members were obtaining, were potent, that it was impossible to doubt the movement (Dev, 1992). However, the Government of India in 1919 made cooperation a provincial subject. Cooperative societies made substantial progress in terms of growth in numbers throughout the twenties but subsequently slowed down. In 1927, the Central and Provincial Banking Enquiry Committee made suggestions for its improvement. In 1935, the Reserve Bank of India (RBI) was established and its Agricultural Credit Department was given the task of studying the problems faced by the cooperative movement. In 1937, the RBI recommended the establishment of multipurpose cooperative societies (IGNOU, 1997b). The review of cooperative movement in India in 1939 by RBI highlighted the decaying conditions of cooperatives due to mounting over-dues, inefficient administration etc. The cooperative Planning committee (1946) made certain suggestions to revitalise the cooperatives of India. At the end of June 1947, there were 1.39 lakh societies having a membership of 91 lakhs; with a total working capital of Rs. 156 crores. The progress of cooperatives during pre-independence period was limited, mainly due to lack of professional managers, opposition from stakes, financial delinquency, limited area and scope of operation, overemphasis on honorary services etc. (Suresh and Joseph, 1990).

Today cooperative movement in India is one of the largest movements in the world (Table 1). Initially it was started with a limited spectrum of activities or dispensation of rural credit has now entered in all fields of economic activity with social content. The movement has covered 100 per cent villages and 75 per cent rural households. It has been playing a significant role in disbursing agricultural credit, distribution of agricultural inputs, providing market support, processing, etc. Over the last more than hundred years (1904-2007), cooperatives have made substantial contribution to the country, particularly to the rural poor. Notwithstanding their achievements and phenomenon growth, cooperatives are beset with several issues and confront with challenges in the era of economic reforms. The cooperative sector in India has more than 5.49 lakh societies of various types with membership of more than 22.95 million and working capital of about Rs. 3,827,496,000 thousand as on 31st March 2003 (Department of Agriculture and Cooperation, 2006). The membership in cooperatives has risen from 142.1 million in 1984-85 to 229.4 million in 2002-

2003. The employment generated through cooperatives is 15 per cent at national level, in addition to 14.79 million self employed persons via cooperatives (National Resource Centre, 2004).

Table 1
Indian Cooperative Movement at Central Level (2001-2002)

(Rs. in Lakhs)

Name of Cooperative	*No. of Societies*	*Total Membership*	*Working Capital*	*Total Borrowings*
Credit Cooperatives				
Central Cooperative Bank	370	1857715	10233098.43	1835203.30
Credit Total	370	1857715	10233098.43	1835203.30
Non- Credit Cooperatives				
Marketing Cooperatives	388	3290672	148942.81	21948.10
Consumer Cooperatives	712	2637910	53939.73	12963.36
Weavers Cooperatives	36	4268	3068.25	1102.90
Industrial Cooperatives	119	26026	3144.34	749.01
Dairy Cooperatives	396	108964	205520.04	125585.03
Fisheries Cooperatives	108	20803	1971.74	849.73
Labour Contract Cooperatives	92	2618	397.21	2.60
Forest Labour Cooperatives	26	NA	NA	NA
Cooperative Unions	264	83156	NA	NA
Ghee Unions	379	9323	82.30	7.12
Non-Credit Total	2520	61837490	417066.42	6737.93
Credit Total	370	1857715	10233098.43	6699992.08
Grand Total	2890	8041455	10650164.85	6706730.01

Source: National Resource Centre, 2004.

Cooperative Movement in Other Countries": The major milestone in the cooperative movement of the ***Philippines*** are the establishment of National Food Authority (NFA) and Kilusang Kabuhayan Sa Kaunlaran (KKK)—the national livelihood movement in 1981. Cooperative marketing system is being developed through cooperative marketing projects for the integration of credit expansion, production and marketing of farm produce. Unification is seen in the cooperative movement in Philippines. There is transfer of responsibility of the government's cooperative development programme from the Ministry of Local Government and Community Development to Ministry of Agriculture. In 1980, Cooperative Academy for Western ***Indonesia*** in Bandung was established with the capital sum of Rupiah 250 million. With the commencement of the Third Five Year Development Plan, Secondary cooperatives were gradually involved in guidance and development activities, like channelling of fertilisers, pesticides marketing of agricultural products, channelling of consumer goods. Government assistance and guidance seem to lead to government's control or interference, but through decentralisation of cooperative organisations and management, government involvement gradually reduced to guidance on infrastructures only. State interference is mostly to break across sectorial barriers. There is a tendency for greater involvement participatory activities of members in cooperative movement of the country. Profitable economic activities are being carried out through cooperatives -rice processing and marketing channelling of agricultural inputs, marketing of other agricultural products like copra, rubber pepper, cloves marketing, rural electricity supply and supply of consumer goods. Cooperatives have also commenced handling sugarcane.

On 15th August 1981, ***Korea*** celebrated 20th anniversary of the founding of multipurpose agricultural cooperatives in the country. In the same year, amendment as made in Agricultural Cooperative Law and reorganised the agricultural cooperatives into two-tiered system of Primary Cooperatives and National Academy of Cooperative Federation (NACF) [Ganesan, 1982a]. In South Korea, the number of agricultural cooperatives have decreased from 21,500 in 1961 to 1,463 in 1986 (Dev, 1992). The country formulates Five Year Primary Cooperative Development Plan to develop primary cooperatives into member farmers. There is also an indirect election system for the appointment of presidents of Primary Cooperatives and Special Cooperatives. In South Korea, the number of agricultural cooperatives have decreased from 21,500 in 1961 to 1,463 in 1986 (Ganesan, 1982a).

An ineffective cooperative structure is a prominent inherent problem in ***Pakistan.*** Of the total agricultural credit requirements of Pakistan, only about 15 per cent is channelled through the institutional sources like cooperatives and government Taccavi loans. The credit provided by the cooperatives has not only been inadequate but highly ineffective. The cooperatives too like other agencies have not been able to meet the large demand for credit. Cooperatives are subservient to political rather than economic motives and there is lack of proper marketing cooperative societies. The primary cooperatives in Pakistan also have weak financial base. The problems relating to agricultural credit, cooperatives and agricultural marketing are interlinked and are eating into the vitals of country's economy. Without their total elimination or to the desirable extent, the agricultural sector cannot develop satisfactorily upon which the edifice of the Pakistan's prosperity can be built (Yardimci, 1995).

In ***Bangladesh,*** village-based Cooperative Societies were organized in 1960 at South Rampur and Monsasan and in 1963; the Bangladesh Cooperative College was located on the Academy Kotbari Campus (Raper, 1970). Cooperatives in ***Singapore*** have had to make constant adjustments in view of the spectacular growth of the country's economy in the last 10-15 years. Singapore no longer has any poor or lower middle classes who are generally the sections served traditionally by the cooperatives, so, the cooperatives are adjusting themselves to be more useful to the members and the society they are operating. Therefore, many of the employees' cooperative societies and vocation specific societies like leaders' cooperatives, etc. are diversifying to become multipurpose societies (Krishna, 1997). ***African*** Cooperatives were started from the marketing end. Though there are Craft men's Cooperatives, the movement is dominated by marketing only. It is quite natural that in a number of mono-crop economics of Africa, Cooperative history is replete with battle between the movement and crop authorities, especially on the returns to farmers. This is true in case of ***Uganda, Nigeria, Zambia, Ghana, Kenya*** and ***Tanzania***, where the movement have been 'hard done by' Governments (Ramanujan, 1997). The Nationals where the Cooperative Movement has shown much strength are the United States of America, Britain, Germany, New Zealand, France and Japan and with that there have been found signs of new efforts to spread the movement in a number of other countries (Sarojini, et. al., 1997).

PRESENT STATUS OF WORLD COOPERATIVES

In many countries membership in all cooperatives is equivalent to a high proportion of the adult population. Although censuses do not yet record the numbers of persons who are members of at least one cooperative enterprise, it is possible, by comparing the known numbers of members of cooperatives (some of whom are likely to be members of two or more such enterprises) with the total population of economically active age, to arrive at an index of the dimension of cooperative membership within national populations. This index, limited to individual membership in those cooperative enterprises themselves members of the International Cooperative Alliance, was in 1994 as high as between 70 and 79 per cent in Austria, Canada, Cyprus, Finland, Israel and Uruguay. In France it was 61 per cent, in Belgium and Norway between 50 and 59 per cent. It was between 40 and 49 per cent in Denmark, India, Japan, Malaysia, Portugal, Sri Lanka and the United States of America.

A total of 740,000,000 women and men have been members of cooperative business enterprises in 1995, which have associated together in national federations and unions, which are members of the International Cooperative Alliance. Not all cooperatives, and not all national federations, are yet members of the Alliance, and it is estimated that the total number of co-operators - that is, members, and hence owners, of cooperative enterprises - is about 800,000,000 world-wide. To this total maybe added the numbers of persons employed by cooperative enterprises but not members of them: an estimated further 100,000,000. Membership of, or employment in, a cooperative enterprise has economic and social significance also for the immediate families of members and employees. If the average size of families or households affected to some significant extent by association with a cooperative-whether as a producer or as a consumer, client or user-is taken to be four persons, then the global total reaches 3,600,000,000-more than half or the world's population.

In no country does the system of national accounts yet distinguish between cooperatively organized and other types of private business enterprise: hence it is not easy to calculate the contribution of cooperative enterprises to GNP. However, in Sweden it was calculated that this share in 1993 reached 8 per cent (with an annual turnover of 20 billion European currency units - ECU). In the Basque region of Spain in 1989 it was estimated that cooperatives accounted for 15 per cent of regional GNP. On the basis of what is known of cooperative shares in certain sectors it may be presumed that in most developed market economies the cooperative share of GNP is between 5 and 20 per cent. In those developing market economies where production and export of agricultural commodities is of major significance, the cooperative contribution to GNP is likely to be between 10 and 20 per cent, given that cooperatives are responsible for most activity in these sectors. In the Costa Ivoire, the share has been calculated as 15 per cent. In almost all market economies cooperatives owned by independent agricultural, forestry and fisheries enterprises account for major shares of the purchasing and supply of inputs and the marketing of outputs, and are an essential organizational component or rural economies. For example, in 1993, in the countries of the European Union, together with Austria, Finland and Sweden, 14 million agricultural enterprises were member-owners of cooperatives which supplied 55 per cent of their inputs and marketed 60 per cent of their outputs: these cooperatives employed 800,000 persons and had an annual turnover of 205 ECU. In Sweden 99 per cent of dairy production is marketed by cooperatives owned by independent farmers. In Norway 75 per cent of forest products are processed and marketed by cooperatives. In Italy 60 per cent of wine is produced by marketing cooperative, these cooperative enterprises handle 95 per cent of rice and 90 per cent of fisheries output. In the United States of America in 1992 agricultural supply and marketing cooperatives served four million members who were independent farm enterprises. Fourteen of these cooperatives were included in the "Fortune 500" list of the largest corporations. In 1991 they supplied 45 per cent of American farmers' input of fertilizers, 43 per cent of their input of petroleum and 28 per cent of their input of chemicals. Their percentage share of marketed outputs was 81 per cent for milk, 38 per cent for cotton and cotton seed, and also for grains and oilseeds, and 18 per cent for fruits and vegetables. In Canada in 1992, 8 of the top 10 agricultural firms were cooperative enterprises. Those in the Prairie Provinces marketed 75 per cent of western Canadian grain and oilseed.

In many developing market economies rural supply and marketing cooperatives pay an equally significant role. This is so in respect to production for the internal market, as well as for export. For example, in India the AMUL dairying cooperative system, composed of 6 million independent farm producers–most of whom are women-organized in 57,000 cooperatives and in State level and national level federations, supplies the greater part of milk consumed nationally. In Tunisia 60 per cent of milk production was marketed by cooperatives in 1993, and in Bolivia 60 per cent of chickens and 30 per cent of eggs. The proportions of exported agricultural commodities handled by marketing cooperatives owned by independent producers reached in Kenya 100 per cent for cotton, 87 per cent for pyrethrum and 52 per cent for coffee; in

Brazil these proportions were 50 per cent for wheat and 40 per cent for cotton.

In many countries significant proportions of services are provided by cooperative enterprises which are owned by the individuals, households or enterprises which are the users or customers. For example, in the United States rural electricity cooperatives supply 25 million persons: in Costa Rica about 10 per cent of electricity consumed is supplied by cooperatives. Housing cooperatives provide significant shares of shelter in many countries.High proportions of the population, particularly in advanced market economies, are members of retail consumer cooperatives: in December 1991 in the European Community, the Nordic countries, Switzerland and the then Czechoslovakia, such cooperatives had 21,6 million household members, 393,000 employees, and a turnover during 1991 of 45,639,000,000 ECU. They accounted for over half of retail food sales in Switzerland, 34 per cent in Denmark and 30 per cent in Finland.

Savings and credit cooperatives (often known as "credit unions") are significant in the financial sectors of many advanced and developing market economies. The proportions of the working age population who were members at the end of 1993 was between 30 and 49 per cent in five countries (including 44 per cent in Ireland and 36 per cent in the United States), and between 10 and 29 per cent in another 16 countries. At the end of 1993 members of credit unions which were associated in national or regional federations which were themselves members of the World Council of Credit Unions (WOCCU) totalled 93,216,000. Their 55,186 credit unions had savings amounting to US$ 383 billion, loans of 248 billion, reserves of 17 billion and assets of 425 billion. This type of cooperative had the most dynamic growth of any: between 1972, when global statistics were first collected by WOCCU, and 1993, both savings and loans had grown by an annual rate of 15 per cent, and assets by 16 per cent.

These were not the only types of cooperative in the financial sector, but in many countries cooperative banks were dominant in the economy: for example the largest European Bank, the French Credit Agriculture cole, Rabo bank, the third largest bank in the Netherlands, and the Raiffeisen movement in Germany, Austria and Switzerland, are all cooperatives: that is they are owned by their members, who are account holders. Cooperative insurance enterprises are of major significance in many advanced market economies. For example, in Sweden about one half of the adult population has at least one policy with the Folksam group. In Japan the farmers' insurance cooperative is the largest agricultural insurance enterprise in the world (International Cooperative Alliance, 1995).

In the United States, the first child-care cooperative was established in 1916. Today, more than 50,000 families send their children to cooperative day care centres (National Cooperative Business Association, 1995). In Sweden more than two-thirds of private day care centres are either parental or worker cooperatives day care services (Pestoff, 1994). Day care cooperatives are functioning in a number of countries including Canada, Hungary, Italy,

Norway, Spain, Portugal and the United Kingdom to list just a few (International Cooperative Alliance, 1994).

The latest surveys conducted by International Cooperative Alliance (ICA) across the world for assessing the percentage of women in membership of cooperatives, show that Russia and Romania is leading in women membership in their cooperatives by 78 per cent and 70 per cent respectively. Among the countries, where cooperatives are also headed by half or more than half percentage of women membership comprise Chile, Colombia, Egypt, Hungry, Japan, Lithuania, Philippines, Sri Lanka, Sweden, U.K, and USA. In the cooperative movement of Turkey, not even a single percentage of women is involved in cooperatives. Bulgaria has also shown least percentage of women membership in cooperatives. In case of India, it ranks third from the bottom, just above Bulgaria, comprising least percentage of 3.5 per cent only. Thus a wide difference can be seen in the women membership in cooperatives ranging as high as 78 per cent in Russia to as low as 3.5 per cent in India (International Global Women's Committee, 2005) (Table 2).

Table 2
Percentage of Women in Membership of Cooperatives across the World

Country	*Latest Survey*	*Percentage*	*Country*	*Latest Survey*	*Percentage*
Brazil	1999	43.3	Nepal	1996	7.0
Bulgaria	2003	3.0	Norway	2003	13.0
Chile	2000	50.3	Peru	1999	8.3
Colombia	2001	63.4	Philippines	2001	62.0
Denmark	2001	23.0	Poland	2003	48.1
Egypt	2001	54.6	Romania	2003	70.7
Hungry	2003	59.3	Russia	2003	78.4
India	2003	3.50	Singapore	2001	47.4
Italy	2003	31.0	Spain	2003	42.0
Japan	2003	63.0	Sri Lanka	2000	58.1
Korea	2001	17.3	Sweden	2001	62.5
Lithuania	2003	63.4	Turkey	2003	0.55
Malaysia	2001	35.6	Uganda	1996	42.0
Malta	2003	5.7	U.K	2003	51.5
Mexico	1999	40.1	*USA	2000	59.0

Source: *http://www.ica.coop/gender/stats.htm*
*WORLD, World Council of Credit Union Magazine, Vol. 2, Issue 2, June 2000.
Macro Data, Gender Disaggregate Statistics- Cooperative Members, from ICA Databank and Supplemented with reports from ICA Global Women's Committee.

COOPERATIVES AND THE MILLENNIUM DEVELOPMENT GOALS

The Millennium Development Goals (MDGs) are based on a set of fundamental values: freedom, equality, solidarity, tolerance, respect for nature, and shared responsibility. MDGs goals are linked to the economic, social and cultural rights set out in the UN's Universal Declaration of Human Rights. This means they

Table 3
Cooperatives and the Millennium Development Goals

Title	*Country*	*Sector*	*Relevant MDGs*
Dairy Cooperatives	Bangladesh	Agricultural cooperatives	Goal 1, targets 1 & 2; Goal 3
Tribal People's Cooperatives	Orissa, India	Community cooperatives	Goal 1, targets 1 & 2; Goal 3 & 7 target 9
SAGUAPAC Water Cooperative	Santa Cruz, Bolivia	Utility cooperative	Goal 7 targets 10 & 11; Goal 4, target 5
Uganda Shoe shiners Cooperative	Uganda	Shared service cooperative	Goal 1, target 1; Goal 4, target 11
Indigenous People's Organisations	Philippines	Community cooperatives	Goal 1, targets 1 & 2; Goal 7 target 9
The ACOPAM Programme	Sahel, Sub-Saharan Africa	Agricultural; women's; credit; resource management cooperatives	Goal 1,Target 2;Goal 3;Goal 7 target 9
Cooperatives in the Informal Economy	South Africa	Worker cooperatives, shared service cooperatives	Goal 1, targets 1 & 2; Goal 3
Rural Electric Cooperatives	Bangladesh	Consumer cooperatives	Goal 1,targets 1 & 2; Goal 2; Goal 3 indicator 11; Goal 4 target 5; Goal 6 target 6
Popular Housing Initiatives	Latin America	Housing cooperatives	Goal 7, target 11
Credit Union Remittances	Latin America andthe Caribbean	Credit unions	Goal 1,target 1 Goal 3

Source: Birchall, 2004

are not just pious hopes but 'claimable rights', and action to achieve them is not just charity but an obligation for which we are all–as citizens– accountable (Birchall, 2004). The track record of global goals is not good. Previous goals that the international community signed up to in the decades leading up to the Millennium included providing health care for all, access to safe water, and universal primary education by the year 2000. Obviously, these goals were not met, though there were modest achievements, and other goals that relied on simple interventions such as mass immunization against infectious diseases succeeded very well (United Nations, 2003). The potential contribution of cooperatives to the MDGs can be enumerated as (Table 3).

Goal 1: Eradicate Extreme Poverty and Hunger

Goal 2: Achieve Universal Primary Education

Goal 3: Promote Gender Equality and Empower Women

Goal 4: Reduce Child Mortality

Goal 5: Improve Maternal Health

Goal 6: Combat HIV/AIDS, Malaria and Other Diseases

Goal 7: Ensure Environmental Sustainability

Goal 8: Develop a Global Partnership for Development

SUMMARY AND CONCLUSION

Cooperatives are bustling hubs of commerce that operate in virtually every industry. More than 750,000 cooperatives serve some 760 million members in more than 100 countries. Cooperatives operate in every industry including agriculture, childcare, energy, financial services, food retailing, and distribution, health care, insurance, housing, purchasing and shared services, telecommunications, and others. Cooperatives range in size from large enterprises, including U.S. Fortune 500 companies, to small local storefronts (ICA, 2006). In the new millennium, a serious challenge, which is being faced by cooperatives, relates to WTO Agreement on Agriculture. Cooperatives are closely attached with agricultural and agro-based activities in the rural areas. Members of cooperative fraternity are expressing concern that the implementation of various provisions of Agreement on Agriculture will seriously affect the farming community in terms of their income levels, levels of living and quality of life. This aspect is particularly important as 70 per cent of our population is dependent on agriculture and agro-based activities: whereas, only 4 per cent of population is dependent on agriculture and allied activities in case of developed countries. Further, it has to be ensured that food security in terms of providing minimum food for various sections of Indian population does not get adversely affected by the WTO Agreement on Agriculture and hence there is the need for providing a separate "Food Security ox" under WTO provisions with emphasis on encouraging on food production and per hectare productivity of various crops. Various segments of cooperative movement should be encouraged for improving their operational challenges of competitive culture.

REFERENCES

APCO (2001), *Cooperative Newsletter-September*. Bangkok, Angthong Provincial Cooperative Office.

AWCF and CULT (2000), *A Training Manual on Gender and Cooperatives in Thailand.* Manila, Asian Women in Cooperative Development Forum and Credit Union League of Thailand.

AWCF (1999), *A Development Link: A Look at Women Cooperatives and the Community.* Manila, Asian Women in Cooperative Development Forum.

Balakishan, S. (2000), Globalization of Cooperatives, The Co-operator's Bulletin, XXXXIII (5-6), June, Jammu, Jammu and Kashmir Cooperative Union.

Birchall, J. (2004), Cooperatives and the Millennium Development Goals, Cooperative Branch and Policy Integration Department International Labour Office, Geneva Committee for the Promotion and Advancement of Cooperatives.

Britt, S. H., and Boyd, H. W. (1968), *Marketing Management and Administrative Action,* New Delhi, McGraw-Hill Company.

Burkner, A. (1998), *The Japanese Cooperatives,* IRU Courier, Raiffeisan, 1, April, Adenauralle, International Raiffeisan Union.

CLT (2001), *The Cooperative Movement in Thailand and the Cooperative League of Thailand.* Bangkok, Cooperative League of Thailand.

CPD (2002), *Cooperative Promotion in Thailand.* Cooperative Promotion Department, Bangkok, Ministry of Agriculture and Cooperatives.

Department of Agriculture and Cooperation (2006), Cooperation, New Delhi, National Cooperative Union of India.

Dev, J. (1981), Agricultural Cooperatives in Hungary, Co-operator's Bulletin, XXIV(7), Jammu. Jammu and Kashmir Cooperative Union.

Dev, J. S. (1992), *Cooperatives and Development,* Co-operator's Bulletin, XXXV (9), Septt. , Jammu, Jammu and Kashmir Cooperative Union Limited.

Drake, L. and Llewellyn, D. (2001), The Economics of Mutuality: A Perspective on UK Building Societies, in Birchall, J, (ed.) *The New Mutualism in Public Policy,* London: Routledge

FAO (1998a), *Report of NEDAC Regional Workshop on Financial Viability of Agricultural Cooperatives.* Bangkok, FAO Regional Office for Asia and the Pacific.

FAO (1998b), *A Study of Cooperative Legislation in Selected Asian and Pacific Countries.* Bangkok, FAO Regional Office for Asia and the Pacific.

FAO (1998c), *The Role of Fishery Cooperatives in Promoting Sustainable Coastal Fisheries in Thailand.* Bangkok, FAO Regional Office for Asia and the Pacific.

Felder, A. C. (1980), *The United States Cooperative Movement Today,* Cooperative News Digest, XXXI (10), Oct., Bombay, Reserve Bank of India.

Ganesan, A. H. (1982a), *Agricultural Cooperation,* ICA Regional Bulletin, 22(1), Jan., New Delhi, International Cooperative Alliance.

Ganesan, A.H. (1982b), *Cooperative Development in South-East Asia during 1981,* ICA Regional Bulletin, 22(1), Jan., New Delhi, International Cooperative Alliance.

Ganesan, A.H. (1982c), *Regional News Round Up: Japan,* ICA Regional Bulletin, 22(1), Jan., New Delhi, International Cooperative Alliance.

Gupta, C. B. (1993), *Business Organisation and Management,* 2nd Edition, New Delhi, Sultan Chand and Sons.

Hajela, T. N. (1982), *Principles, Problems and Practice of Cooperation,* Delhi, Shiva Lal Agarwala Company.

ICA (2006), What are Cooperatives? One Member, One Vote, One Domain, COOP, Available at: http://*www.coop.org/ica/info/*

IGNOU (1997a), *Cooperatives in Rural Development: Rural Development Administration,* 3, RD.D.I, *'Rural Development: Indian Context',* New Delhi, Indira Gandhi National Open University.

IGNOU (1997b), *Development of Rural Women: Rural Social Development,* RD.D.4, I, New Delhi, Indira Gandhi National Open University.

ILO (2000), *Rural Women in Micro-enterprise Development: A Training Manual and Programme for Extension Workers.* Geneva, International Labour Organization.

International Cooperative Alliance (1995), Dimension of the International Co-op Movement, Fourth World Conference on Women: Action for Equality, Development and Peace, Beijing, China, 4-15 September, the contribution of cooperative business enterprise and the international cooperative movement to achievement of the strategic objectives of the draft platform of action, New York, Prepared Jointly, Pursuant To General Assembly Resolution 49/155, by the international cooperative alliance and The united nations department for policy coordination and sustainable development.

International Global Women's Committee (2005), Gender Disaggregate Statistics: Percentage of Women in Membership of Cooperatives, ICA, Geneva.

Kamat, G. S. (1978), *New Dimensions of Cooperative Management,* 1st Edition, Bombay, Himalaya Publishing House.

Kane, K. and Tototo Home Industries (1992), *Business Training for Women's Groups.* Boston, USA FAIDIKA.

Kindervatter, S. and Range, M. (1991), *Appropriate Business Skills for Third World Women, Marketing Strategy: Training Activities for Entrepreneurship.* USA, Overseas Education Fund.

Krishna, D. (1997), *Cooperatives in Thailand, Malaysia and Singapore – A Report,* Urban Credit, *A Journal of NAFCUB,* XIX (2), June, New Delhi, National Federation of Urban Cooperative Banks and Credit Societies.

Marinichev, Y. (1991), Saturating The Consumer Market, The Co-operator's, XXIX(3), August, New Delhi, National Cooperative Union of India.

Nakabayashi, S. (1976), *New Trends in the International Cooperative Movement: Economic Growth and Cooperative Principles,* Anthology of Cooperative Thought, II, New Delhi, National Cooperative Union of India.

Nation Resource Centre (2004), Indian Cooperative Movement – A Profile, Centenary Celebrations, New Delhi, National Cooperative Union of India.

National Cooperative Business Association (1995), A Day in the Life of Cooperative America, p. 26.

Nilsson, J. (2001), 'Farmer Cooperatives: Organisational Models and their Business Environment in Birchall, J, (ed.) The *New Mutualism in Public Policy,* London: Routledge.

Patrawart, J. and Stiftung F. E. (1995), *A Research Report* on Guidance *for Production and Marketing Development of the Cooperative Women's Group Enterprises in Thailand.* Bangkok, Friedrich Ebert Stiftung.

Pestoff, Victor A. (1994), Beyond Exit and Voice, in Delivering Welfare; Repositioning Non-profit and Cooperative Action in West European Welfare States. CIES, Barcelona (Spain).

Prakesh, D. (1992), *Rural Women Leaders of Agricultural Cooperatives in Asia: A Report,* New Delhi, International Cooperative Alliance.

Ramanujan, K.N. (1997), *Women Cooperatives and Economic Development,* Co-operator's Bulletin, XXXX (1), Jan., Jammu, Jammu and Kashmir Cooperative Union Limited.

Raper, A. F. (1970), *Rural Development in Action: The Comprehensive Experiment at Comilla – East Pakistan,* London, Cornell University Press.

Sarojini, T. B., Vijayalakshmi, B. and Himachalam, D. (1997), *The Growth of Consumer Movement,* Indian Consumer Co-operator, 24 (4), Oct-Dec., New Delhi, National Cooperative Consumer's Federation Limited. International Technical Meeting, Capital Formation in Agricultural Cooperatives Rome, 8-10 November, copac Committee for the Promotion and Advancement of Cooperatives.

Sehgal, M. N. (1990), *A Text Book of Cooperative History,* Jammu, Jammu and Kashmir Cooperative Union Limited.

Sharma, B. D. (1992), *Agricultural Cooperatives in Thailand: Social Background of Cooperative Movement in Thailand,* The Co-operator, XXIX(13), March, New Delhi, National Cooperative Union of India.

Sharma, B. D. (1992), *The Cooperative Sector in Chinese Economy,* The Co-operator, XXIX(12), February, New Delhi, National Cooperative Union of India.

Smith, S. (2003), Network Externalities and Cooperative Networks: Stylized Facts and Theory, Laixiang Sun (Ed) *Ownership and Governance of Enterprises,* Basingstoke: Palgrave/Macmillan.

Suresh, K. A., and Joseph, M. (1990), *Cooperatives and Rural Development in India,* New Delhi, Ashish Publishing House.

Taylor, M., Hameenaho, S., Pinion, D. (2002), *Options for Cooperative Care*: Promoting and Supporting Cooperative Solutions to Social Care Delivery, Manchester: Cooperative Union.

Trong, N. V. (1995), *Cooperative Training System in Vietnam*, COOPNET, Human Resource Development for Cooperative Management and Networking, Update for Asia and Pacific, 2 (1), March, Pune, International Labour Organisation.

UNDP and UNIFEM (2000), *Gender and Development. Facts and Figures in Thailand.* Bangkok, United Nations Development Programme and United Nations Development Fund for Women.

United Nations (2003), *World Development Report.*

Von Pischke J. D. (1995), Capital Formation in Agricultural Cooperatives in Developing Countries: Research Issues, Findings and Policy Implications for Cooperatives and Donors, Synthesis Paper, Report of the COPAC.

Yardimci, B. (1995), *Problems with Credit, Marketing and Cooperatives,* in Verma, R.K., (ed.), *Rural Development and Anti-Poverty Programme,* 5, Jaipur, Rupa Books Pvt., Ltd.

CHAPTER-4

HEALTH INFRASTRUCTURE IN INDIA: PRESENT CHALLENGES AND FUTURE PROSPECTS

DINESHA P.T., JAYASHEELA & V. BASIL HANS

INTRODUCTION

HEALTH is one of the vital indicators reflecting the quality of human life. It is a basic need along with food, shelter and education and is a precondition for productivity and growth. That there is a positive correlation between the health status of people and the economic development of the country is a well-established fact. It is also one of the key variables that determine "growth with a human face" even as health economics has emerged as an important area of research (Hans, 1997). There are three principal ways by which health programmes can affect the pace of economic development in the developing countries: *One*, increasing the number of man-hours of work available, *two* Increasing the quality of productivity of the existing work force, and *three*, changing the attitudes towards innovations and entrepreneurship. Though health has been considered a fundamental human right since the Alma Alta Declaration (1978), yet expenditure on health in India is often lower than expected and the condition of health infrastructure in the country is not good enough.

Keeping the above facts in view this paper has the following objectives; (i) to understand the status of health indicators in India, (ii) to understand the problems faced by health infrastructure and (iii) to consider policy alternatives.

STATUS OF HEALTH IN INDIA

As per the United Nations Development Programmme's (UNDP) Global Human Development Report (HDR) 2007, India ranks at 128 among the countries with medium human development out of 177 countries of the world. In terms of Gender Development Index (GDI), India ranks 113 out of 157 countries. India's HDI rank reflects low relative achievement in the level of human development and it also indicative that the country has done better in terms of per capita income than in other components of human development. The condition of India's neighbours like China and even Sri Lanka with respect to health indicators including HDI values is far better than India (GOI, 2008).

The status of health indicators in India is in deplorable condition. As the Table 1 reveals that crude birth rate in India is 23.5, total fertility rate is 2.5, life expectancy at birth in India is 63, infant mortality rate is 57 and maternal mortality rate is 301. From these figures we can understand the unhealthy condition of health status of our country. Again the serious matter of concern is that, even the improvement in health indicators since Independence is slow.

Table 1
Selected Indicators of Health in India

Details	*1951*	*1981*	*1991*	*Current level*
Crude birth rate (Per 1000 population)	40.8	33.9	29.5	23.5 (2006)
Crude death rate (Per 1000 population)	25.1	12.5	9.8	7.5 (2006)
Total fertility rate (Per 1000 woman)	6.0	4.5	3.6	2.5 (2005)
Maternal mortality rate (Per 100,000 live births)	NA	NA	437 (1992-93)	301 (2001-03)
Infant mortality rate (Per 1000 live births)	146 (1951-61)	110	80	57 (2006)
Child (0-4) mortality rate (Per 1000 children)	57.3 (1972)	41.2	26.5	17.3 (2005)
Couple protection rate (per cent)*	10.4 (1971)	22.8	44.1	48.2 (1998-99)
Life Expectancy at Birth				
Male	55.4 (1981-85)		59.0 (1989-93)	62.3 (2001-05)
Female	55.7 (1981-85)		59.7 (1989-93)	63.9 (2001-05)

Note: Dates in brackets indicates year for which latest information is available,* National Family Health Survey, N A: Not Available.

Source: GOI, *Economic Survey of India* 2007-08, pp 252 and *Office of the Registrar General of India.*

Though there has been a steady increase in health care infrastructure available over the plan period (Table 2), progress is not satisfactory, as, there is a shortage health centers and infrastructure to the existing population norm. Further, almost 50 per cent of the existing health infrastructure is in rented buildings, Poor upkeep and maintenance and high absenteeism of manpower in rural areas have also eroded the credibility of the health delivery system in the public sector (GOI, 2008).

Table 2
Trends in Health Care

	1951	*1991*	*2005/06*
SC/PHC/CHC*	725	57,353	171567 (March 2006**)
Dispensaries and Hospitals (all)	9,209	23,555	32156(1-4-2006***)
Beds (Private and Public)	1,17,198	5,68,495	9,14,543 (Jan 1 2002-CBHI****)
Nursing Personnel	18,054	1,43,667	1481270 (2005***)
Doctors (Modern System)	61,800	2,68,700	660801 (2005***)

*SC/PHC/CHC: Sub centre, Primary Health Centre and Community Health Centre.
** RHS: Rural Health Statistics, *** National Health Profile 2006.
****CBHI: Central Bureau of Health Statistics,

Source: GOI, Economic Survey of India 2007-08, pp. 254.

Another serious matter of concern of health sector is the disparity in the condition of health indicators between the states. The table 3 shows that condition of Kerala is with respect to Life Expectancy at birth, Infant Mortality Rate, Birth Rate as well as Death Rate are far better than other states. Condition of states like Assam Uttar Pradesh, Rajastan is worse than other states in some indicators.

Table 3
Selected Indicators of Human Development for Major States

	Life expectancy at birth (1998-2002)			*Infant Mortality Rate*			*Birth rate (per 1000)*	*Death rate (per 1000)*
State	*Male*	*Female*	*Total*	*Male*	*Female*	*Total*	*2003**	*2003**
Andhra Pradesh	62.0	64.6	63.5	59	59	59	20.4	8.0
Assam	57.7	58.1	57.9	69	65	67	26.3	9.1
Bihar	61.4	59.5	60.8	59	62	60	30.7	7.9
Gujarat	62.4	64.4	63.4	54	61	57	24.6	7.6
Haryana	64.7	65.4	65.2	54	65	59	26.3	7.1
Karnataka	62.8	66.2	64.5	51	52	52	21.8	7.2
Kerala	70.8	75.9	73.5	11	12	11	16.7	6.3
Madhya Pradesh	57.0	56.7	56.9	77	86	82	30.2	9.8
Maharashtra	65.0	67.4	66.2	32	54	42	19.9	7.2
Orissa	58.4	58.5	58.5	82	83	83	23.0	9.7
Punjab	67.4	69.5	68.5	46	52	49	20.6	7.0
Rajasthan	60.5	61.6	61.1	70	81	75	30.3	7.6
Tamil Nadu	64.2	66.3	65.2	44	41	43	18.3	7.6
Uttar Pradesh	59.4	58.5	59.1	69	84	76	31.3	9.5
West Bengal	63.3	64.8	63.9	45	46	46	20.3	6.6
India	61.6	63.3	62.5	57	64	60	24.8	8.0

Source: Office of the Registrar General of India, Ministry of Home Affairs, *Provisional.

PROBLEMS IN THE HEALTH INFRASTRUCTURE

Following are the some of the reasons for the poor growth of health infrastructure in India.

Inadequate Financial Resource

The paucity of financial resources because of poor allocations has often proved to be a major obstacle in the execution of health programmes. Public health investment on health infrastructure in the country over the years has been comparatively low. India spends about 5.1% of its GDP on health, but 82% of total health care expenditure is spent by the private sector and almost all of this represents private out of pocket expenditure (Acharya and Ranson, 2005). Moreover, with shrinking budgetary support and fiscal shortage most state governments are finding it difficult to expand their public facilities to cater to the growing health care needs of their population. Thus, the state health sector only partially serves the needs of rural and urban poor in the informal sector. So lack of adequate finance has become the strong reason for the under development of the infrastructural facilities.

Inadequate Buildings

Health sector also faces the problem of shortage of buildings for health centres. Many health centres are functioning in buildings whether government or rented which have limited available space. In rural areas about 49.7 per cent of the sub-centres, 78.0 per cent of the PHCs and 91.5 per cent of CHCs are located in the government buildings. The rest are located either in rented buildings or rent free Panchayat/Voluntary Society buildings. As on September 2005, overall 60,762 buildings are required to be constructed to house sub-centres. Similarly, for PHCs 2948 and for CHCs 205 additional buildings are still required (Laveesh Bhandari and Siddhartha Dutta, 2007). Besides these there is no sufficient availability of residential accommodation in remote rural areas, which are acting as a great deterrent in motivating medical officers to work in such areas.

Inadequate Physical Infrastructures

Health facilities in India face many operational difficulties. These include inadequate funding for drugs supplies, diagnostic facilities, laboratory equipment, urinals, latrines, bathrooms, ambulances, phone, fax etc and these are in extremely hopeless condition which a very sad reflection on the functioning of health centres and a general deterioration of physical infrastructure. Lack of adequate hospitals and clinical persons is another problem. According to HDR 2002, in India there is only one hospital for every 68,881 population and one hospital bed for every 1498 population and 51.8 doctors for every one lakh population. This clearly reveals the poor condition of health infrastructure in India (Karne, 2007).According to a survey by the Jan Swasthya Abhiyan, only 38% of all PHCs have all the critical staff. A survey by the International Institute of Population Sciences found that only 20% of PHCs have a telephone. So not only is the infrastructure inadequate, we don't even have the staff to use the existing infrastructure (Srinivasan, Sandhya, 2005).

Absence of Effective Personnel and Materials Planning

In most of the hospitals there is no personnel planning resulting in the under utilisation of resources. The hospital authorities must ensure that the existing staff in the various departments has been deployed consistent with the workload and are according to the prescribed norms. Periodic studies of the functioning of hospitals are needed to enable the administrators to mange them effectively.

Absence of Good Transport Facilities

Another problem of health infrastructure is the lack of good transport facilities between the villages and hospitals. The data reveals that only 73.9% of villages are well connected with the roads to health centres (Laveesh Bhandari and Siddhartha Dutta, 2007). According to the NCAER, nearly 20% of cases rural households travelled more than 10 km for treatment. In Meghalaya, in 54.56% and in Orissa 33.47% of rural illness cases, patients travelled more than 10 km. Studies shows that in Andhra Pradesh nearly 75% of PHC's are located at agency area where the villagers are scattered widely. It has become very ardous for the tribal and the down trodden people to reach the PHC's as there are no link roads in most of the villages (Himanshu Sekhar Rout, Prashant Kumr Panda, 2007).

Imbalance between the Rural and Urban Areas

There has been an imbalance in the availability of medical facilities and health manpower in rural area and urban areas. The National Health Policy (NHP) 1983 envisaged a three-tier structure of primary, secondary and tertiary healthcare facilities to bring the services within the reach of the rural population. In spite of the three-tier system of rural health infrastructure the condition of rural health infrastructure has been deplorable. A Review of Rural Health Care Infrastructure Development by the Central Council of Health and Family Welfare in April 1999 revealed not only in the establishment but also in the amount of man power required.

Table 4
Rural Health Care Infrastructure 2000-01

Service (per population)	*Existing*	*Required*
Primary Heath Centres 1 per 20,000-30,000	22,842	24,717
Sub Centres 1 Per 3,000-5,000	137,311	148,303
Community Health Centres 1 Per 100,000	3,043	7,415

Source: Srinivasan, Sandhya (2005).

Table 4 clearly shows the mismatch between the existing and required health infrastructure. For instance, if we should have one CHC for every 100,000 rural populations, we need at least 7,415 CHCs, but we have less than half of what we should have. In the 3,043 CHCs that we do have, only 440 have a paediatrician, only 704 have a physician only 780 have a gynaecologist and 781 a surgeon.We need 76,622 midwife nurses (one per PHC and seven per CHC). We have planned only for 44,143 and only 27,336 are in place.

In the case of other rural healthcare personnel too there are similar and dramatic differences between what we *need*, what is *allocated*, and what is *actually in place* : we have cnly 71,053 male multipurpose workers compared to the 13,73,311 planned and the 148,303 needed; 137,407 auxiliary nurse midwives compared to the 160,153 planned and 173,020 needed; 19,927 male health assistants compared to the 22,842 planned and the 24,717 needed; 19,855 lady health visitors compared to the 22,842 planned and the 24,717 needed; 21,118 pharmacists compared to the 25,885 planned and the 32,132 needed; and 13,262 lab technicians compared to the 25,885 planned and the 32,132 needed (Srinivasan, Sandhya, 2005).

Studies reveal that one of the reasons for the reluctance of doctors to serve in SCs, PHCs and CHCs is lack of adequate drug suppliers and paramedical support services, which place them in an embracing position vis-à-vis the patients. Lack of communications and other facilities in rural areas is also a reason for doctors to flee or keep away from the country side.

SUGGESTIONS TO IMPROVE THE CONDITION OF HEALTH INFRASTRUCTURE

India does have a systematic health policy. What need to be done are its effective implementation, monitoring and evaluation for promoting holistic health and economic welfare of the people. The following suggestions are made to improve the health of the health infrastructure.

Creating New Infrastructure and Strengthening Existing Infrastructure

The availability and accessibility of good quality health-care services need to be extended to larger population. In the long run, new infrastructure (hospitals and essential equipments in the hospital) need to be created to make quality services available to a larger population and wider area. It is possible to restructure and rationalise the existing health care institutions to improve their service delivery and enhance outreach in the short run. Besides creating new infrastructure existing health infrastructure should be strengthened with appropriate infrastructures like beds, laboratories, ambulances, telephones, medicines etc.

Refocus on Government Expenditure

A major chunk of the resources needs to be deployed for development of health infrastructure and amenities. Government expenditure should cover both healthcares for the poor and health promotion and disease prevention for all. There should be a shift from the current emphasis on curative, advanced and urban services to increase funding for preventive services and better services in the rural areas. Government expenditure on healthcare services should be increased and spread across regions based on the principle of 'equity'.

Filling up the Vacant Posts

Vacant posts should be filled up with the appropriate staff. If a state finds it difficult to fill up vacant specialist positions in hospitals simple medical graduates should be recruited so that the people get at least minimum services. Convenient and standard residential accommodation needs to be provided for at least the key staff as a motivation for them to stay on so, as to ensure the availability of services to the people. The mismatch between manpower and infrastructure facilities should be done away with so as to enhance efficiency as a whole.

Use of Technology

Technological innovations make it possible for delivery of health care facilities at cheaper cost. A detailed plan for use of information technology in health care delivery, referral, training and administration should be formulated and implemented. There should be emphasis on continuous training for both medical and paramedical professionals (Thomas, 2007).

Supporting Involvement of VO/NGO's

Committed and reputed NGO's may be involved in the development of primary health care system by handing over certain proportion of infrastructural facilities namely SC or PHC along with building , funds and staff with relatively more management freedom to VO/NGO's depending upon their capability of funds, staff etc, after ascertaining their credibility. Initiatives in health care by private sector and NGOs can be encouraged through appropriate tax breaks and other healthy incentives.

Constructing of Buildings in Ideal Location for Hospitals and Staff

There is an urgent need to provide adequate buildings for hospitals to provide good service. Besides the construction building for hospitals, houses for the staff should be constructed to increase the morale and efficiency of the personnel working there. While opening a new health centre care may be taken in selecting such a site which should be easily accessible to largest number of people in the block.

Proper Supply of Drugs and Other Health Equipments

Steps may be taken to ensure adequate and timely supply of medicines and equipment to health centres. They should maintain adequate stock of drugs. For efficient discharge of curative functions the health centres should be provided sufficient equipments like x-ray and laboratory facilities, oxygen cylinders, operation tables, indoor beds and surgical instruments etc.

CONCLUSION

The past sixty years have witnessed the development of a vast health care infrastructure and manpower aimed at providing health care to the population.

Several programmes for health care are evolved and implemented both at national and state level. Even after these efforts, lower and middle strata of the society are being exploited by the private dominated health care industry. So, Health policy and strategies of its implementation in the New Millennium should be geared towards strengthening the state-run health infrastructure by increased allocation of funds and community involvement to ensure an efficient and effective referral system. There is a need to provide greater resources for the rural health services. More attention should paid to improve the health status of the population by providing additional resources to the provision of safe drinking water, education, nutrition better housing and sanitation etc. Since health is an important determinant of productivity countries like India, which depend on "human capital" for their rapid economic progress must accord higher value to having a healthier work force to hasten the progress of economic development. Further, addressing the health inequalities along with general health would not only bring about growth but also development with a human face.

REFERENCES

Acharya, Akash and M. Kent Ranson (2005), "Health Care Financing for the Poor. Community Based Health Insurance schemes in Gujarat", *Economic and Political Weekly*, September, Vol. XL, No 38, pp.17-23.

"INDIA 2006", Research, Reference and Training Division, Publication Division, Ministry of Information and Broadcasting.

GOI (2008), *Economic Survey of India* 2007-08.

GOI (2006), *Economic Survey of India*, 2005-06.

Hans, V. B. (1997), *"Nature and Scope of Health Economics–A Survey of Literature"*, Unpublished M.Phil Dissertation, Mangalore University, Mangalagangothri.

Himanshu Sekhar Rout, Prashant Kumr Panda(2007), *"Health Economics in India"*, New Delhi, New Century Publications.

Karne, Manisha (2007), Public Health Care in India Issues and Problems, *Health Action*, December, pp. 8-11.

Laveesh Bhandari and Siddhartha Dutta (2007), "Health Infrastructure in Rural India", *India Infrastructure Report 2007*

Reddy, Byre V. J. and Manjunath S. J. (2006), "Health Inequalities in India", *Southern Economist*, Vol. 45, No. 1, May 1, pp. 61-63.

Srinivasan, Sandhya (2005), *'Public Health Infrastructure: What we need and what we have'*, Info Change India News & Features, June. *http://www.infochangeindia.org/HealthIbp.jsp*

Summary of the Report on Workforce Management Options & infrastructure Rationalization of PHC, Planning Commission, available at *http://planningcommission.nic.in/reports/peoreport/peoevalu/peo_NCAER.doc*

Thomas, George (2007), "Striking a Balance", *The Hindu*, Open Page, Sunday, March 11, pp. 15.

CHAPTER-5

MICROFINANCE: AN EFFECTIVE TOOL FOR FINANCIAL INCLUSION

DINESHA P.T. & JAYASHEELA

INTRODUCTION

THE banking industry has shown tremendous growth in volume and complexity during the last few decades. Despite making significant improvements in all the areas relating to financial viability, profitability and competitiveness, there are concerns that banks have not been able to include vast segment of the population, especially the underprivileged sections of the society, into the fold of basic banking services. Thus, important challenge facing the banking sector is to extend financial services to all sections of society. At this juncture the introduction of "financial inclusion" comes from the recognition that this can serve the interests of both society and the banking system. As a complementary to this, micro-finance[1] can work as a powerful tool to fight poverty became the effective approach of financial inclusion.

Keeping the above facts in view this paper has the following objectives

- To highlight the nature and extent of exclusion
- To study the role and importance of microfinance as a strategy of financial inclusion.
- To suggest some policy prescriptions

NATURE AND EXTENT OF EXCLUSION

Credit is one of the critical inputs for economic development and its timely availability in the right quantity at an affordable cost goes a long way in contributing to the well-being of the people especially in the lower rungs of society. Further, access to finance will empower the vulnerable groups by giving them an opportunity to have a bank account, to save and invest, to insure their homes or to partake of credit, thereby facilitating them to break the chain of poverty. But India is lagging behind in this respect so it has become a serious matter of concern.

The Situation Assessment Survey (NSSO, 2003) indicated that out of the total 89.3 million farmer households in the country, 51.4 per cent of households were non-indebted. Further, out of the total 43.4 million indebted households, 20.3 million (46.8 per cent) households had availed financial services from informal sources. The report also shows that 45.9 million farmer households out of the total 89.3 million households do not access credit either from institutional and non-institutional sources. Further, only 27 per cent of the total farm households are indebted to formal sources; in other words 70 per cent of the farmhouses do not have access to formal credit sources. Exclusion is most acute in Central, Eastern and North-Eastern regions–having a concentration of 64% of all financially excluded farmer households in the country.Only 36% of ST farmer households are indebted (SCs and Other Backward Classes-OBC-51%) mostly to informal sources.(GOI , 2008)

There are over 397 million workers in India, out of which 123 million are women workers. Only a small proportion, 18 million, is in the urban areas while 106 million are in rural areas. Not only do a higher percentage of women than men work in the informal economy, women are concentrated in the lower-income segments, working in survival activities or as casual wageworkers or home workers. About 30% of the total workers are poor in India (using the 1999–2000 poverty line at Rs.336 per capita per month in rural areas and Rs.451 in urban areas). In general a large proportion was poor.

Analysis of the data provided by RBI thru' its Basic Statistical Returns reveal that critical exclusion (in terms of credit) is manifest in 256 districts, spread across 17 States and 1 UT, with a credit gap of 95% and above (GOI, 2008). In these districts, only 10 per cent or less out of 100 persons have access to credit from the fact that the exclusion is large, there is also a wide variation across regions, social groups and asset holdings. The poorer the group, the greater is the exclusion (Rangarajan, 2007).

The inference of these findings is that in spite of a large network of the institutional credit system, it has not been able to adequately penetrate the informal rural financial markets and the non-institutional sources continue to play a dominant role in purveying the credit needs of the people residing in rural areas.

One common measure of financial inclusion is the percentage of adult population having bank accounts. Going by the available data of 2005 on the number of savings bank accounts and assuming that one person has only one account, (which assumption may not be correct as many persons could have more than one bank account) we find that on an all India basis 59 per cent of adult population in the country have bank accounts–in other words 41 per cent of the population is un-banked. In rural areas the coverage is 39 per cent against 61 per cent in urban areas. The un-banked population is higher in the North Eastern and Eastern regions (Thorat, 2007b).

The following table shows that in Northern Region out of 100 persons only 43 persons hold an account in a bank. While coming to the North Eastern Region it is quite low that is just 19. Thus table reveals that access to bank services is low, as well as there exists a large variation across the regions in credit accessibility. Another thing is while compared to the developed world; the coverage of our financial services is quite low. For instance, as per a recent survey commissioned by British Bankers' Association, 92 to 94 per cent of the population of UK has either current or savings bank account (Leeladhar, 2005).

Table 1
Coverage of Banking Services in India

Region	*Current Accounts*	*Savings Accounts*	*Total Population*	*Total No. of accounts*	*No. of acc. Per 100 of population*
North	4215701	52416125	132676462	56631826	43
North East	476603	6891081	38495089	7367684	19
East	1814219	47876140	227613073	49690359	22
Central	2202217	64254189	255713495	66456406	26
West	3178102	49525101	149071747	52703203	35
South	4666014	83386898	223445381	88052912	39
All India	16552856	304349534	1027015247	320902390	31

Source: Situation Assessment Survey 59th Round, National Sample Survey Organisation 2003.

The figures ultimately reveal that there is lack of outreach of banking services to the population, at this juncture micro finance services doing well as a tool of financial inclusion in bringing excluded population to the main stream of formal banking system.

MICRO FINANCE AS AN EFFECTIVE STRATEGY OF FINANCIAL INCLUSION

Financial inclusion is delivery of banking services at an affordable cost to the vast sections of disadvantaged and low-income groups. Although credit is the most important component, financial inclusión covers various financial services such as savings insurance, payments and remittance facilities by the formal financial system to those who tend to be excluded (Mahendra S, 2006).The broad objective of Financial Inclusion is to extend the scope of activities of the organized financial system to include within its ambit people with low incomes. Through graduated credit, the attempts must be to lift the poor from one level to another so that they come out of poverty.

Microfinance through Self Help Groupsv(SHG) has been highly successful in furthering financial inclusion. The cooperation between the formal banking system and micro-finance organisations has also been encouraging. SHGs are groups of usually women who get together and pool their savings and give loans to members. Members of the group are mostly come under below poverty line so; generally they are excluded from the formal banking habits. Usually there is a Non-Governmental Organisation (NGO) that promotes and nurture these groups. National Bank for Agriculture and Rural Development has played a very significant role in supporting group formation, linking them with banks as also promoting best practices. The SHG is given loan against guarantee of group members. The recovery experience has been very good. Banks provide credit to such groups at reasonable rates of interest. However the size of loans is quite small and used mostly for consumption smoothening or very small businesses. In some SHGs, credit is provided for agricultural activities and other livelihoods and could be several times the deposits made by the SHG.

Microfinance has drawn attention to an entire sector of borrowers who had been previously poorly served by the formal financial sector - and MF has demonstrated how to make lending to this sector a viable proposition. The financial inclusion attained through SHGs is sustainable and scalable on account of its various positive features. One of the distinctive features of the SHG-Bank Linkage Programme (BLP) has been the high recovery rate. However the spread of SHGs is very uneven and is more concentrated in southern states. This regional imbalance needs to be corrected and special efforts in this regard may have to be made by NABARD. SHGs also needed to graduate from mere providers of credit for non-productive purposes to promoting micro enterprises. However, there is no need to provide interest rate subsidy to the SHGs. Banks do provide them credit at reasonable rate of interest.

Micro Finance Institutions (MFIs) have been playing an important role in substituting moneylenders and reducing the burden on the formal financial institutions. With the objective of ensuring greater financial inclusion and increasing the outreach of the banking sector, banks have been allowed to use the services of NGO's, SHGs, MFIs and other civil society organizations as intermediaries in providing financial and banking services through the use of business facilitator and correspondent models. Provision for this kind of financial intermediation has opened new and diverse avenues to address the issue of financial inclusion by banks (Mahendra S, op. cit.).

The SHG-Bank Linkage Programme launched by NABARD in 1992 continues to be the predominant Micro-Finance (MF) model in the country. It is a proven method of financial inclusion, providing un-banked rural clientele with access to formal financial services from the existing banking infrastructure. During the year 2006-07 6, 86,408 new SHGs were credit linked with banks as against 6, 20,109 during 2005-06, taking the cumulative number of credit linked SHGs to 29, 24,973. The phenomenal outreach of the programme has enabled an estimated 409.5 lakh poor households to gain access to MF from the formal banking system as on March 2007, registering a growth of 24.2 per cent over the previous year (NABARD, 2007). So, large section of financially excluded population mostly including women came under the formal banking system and microfinance successfully inculcated banking habits among the people.

From the above description it could be stated here that, formation of SHGs in rural areas has kindled new hope of change and development in the status and role of women folk, who are otherwise powerless and marginalized members of the society. Now they are able to grow economically and socially as members have also accepted the changed role of their women folk and most of the time they are supportive to them. In addition they are able to get financial assistance from women folk, which were not possible earlier (Patil, 2006).

POLICY PRESCRIPTIONS

Following are the some of the suggestions for strengthening movement of financial inclusion through microfinance.

- For addressing financial inclusion effectively banking system has to develop a holistic approach in creating awareness about financial products, education, and advice on money management, debt counselling, savings and affordable credit.
- Technology can be a very valuable tool in providing access to banking products in remote areas. According to Prof. M.S. Swaminanthan, the noted agricultural scientist, "SHGs, will however, become sustainable only if they have backward linkages with technology and credit and forward linkages with processing and marketing organisations" (Swaminanthan, 2006). So, technology should be upgraded to bring down the transaction cost, while extending loan, etc...
- The banks need to redesign their business strategies to incorporate specific plans to promote financial inclusion of low income group treating it both a business opportunity as well as a corporate social responsibility.
- In dealing with the needs of rural enterprises and of small and medium enterprises in urban areas, banks have to look for new delivery mechanisms. These must economize on transaction costs and provide better access to the currently under-served. To serve new rural credit needs, innovative channels for credit delivery will have to be found.
- Till now, micro financing has been a grey area in the finance sector as the current laws allow only the entities registered with RBI to raise deposits and lending activities. In view of the rising micro-financing activities in the country, a need has been felt to regulate the unregulated business in this sector and also provide legal framework to facilitate the credit flow in rural areas (Tiwari, 2006).
- Micro-insurance is a key element in the financial services package for people at the bottom of the pyramid. The poor face more risks than the well off. It is becoming increasingly clear that micro-insurance needs a further push and guidance from the Regulator as well as the Government (The Hindu Business Line 2007).
- Government should initiate the SHG programme through state programmes in identified regions where spread of SHG movement is less. There should be machinery in each State to monitor the spread of SHGs.

- The MFIs should be strengthened with the tools of managerial expertise, user-friendly technology and with the principles of good governance and social responsibility.

CONCLUSIONS

Microfinance in India has emerged as a powerful tool for financial inclusion. The 'SHG – Bank Linkage' programme plays a predominant role in the financial inclusion of poor. But there is a need to strengthen the SHG-Bank Linkage Programme to fully mainstream it with the commercial banking system. The variations in performance across the regions, both in terms of reach and quality needs immediate attention.

NOTES

1. Microfinance: Micro finance is a financial service ot small quantity provided by financial institutions to the poor. These financial services may include savings, credit insurance, leasing, money transfer, equity transactions etc. that is any type of financial service provided to customers to meet their normal financial needs life cycle, economic opportunity and emergency.
2. Micro Finance Institution (MFI): A MFI is an organization that acts as an interface between the formal credit delivery institutions and credit seekers, with an aim to assist for the socio economic development of poor and marginalized people. The geographical distribution of MFIs is very much concentrated in the Southern India where the rural branch network of formal bank is excellent.
3. Self Help Group (SHG): A Self-Help Group (SHG) is a registered or unregistered group of people having homogenous social and economic background voluntarily, coming together to save small amounts regularly, to mutually agree to contribute to a common fund and to meet their emergency needs on mutual help basis. Each group consists of 10-20 members. A group could be exclusively male or female, or even mixed. However majority of SHG's are female groups.

REFERENCES

Fisher, Thomas and M. S. Sriram (2002), *Beyond Microcredit': Putting Development Back into Micro-finance*, Vistaar Publications, New Delhi.

GOI (2008), *Report on the Committee on the Financial Inclusion*, January.

Karmakar, K.G. (2002), Micro-finance revisited, *Financing Agriculture*, Vol. 34, No.2, April-June , pp 18-22.

Leeladhar (2005), *Taking Banking Services to the Common Man–Financial Inclusion*, at FedBank Hormis Memorial foundation, at Ernakulam on December 02.

Mahendra Dev S. (2006), Financial Inclusion: Issues and Challenges, *Economic and Political Weekly*, Vol. 41, No. 41, October 14-October 20.

NABARD Annual Report 2007.

Patil, Shobhadevi R. (2006), Role of Self Help Groups in Sustainable Development: an NGO experience, *Participative Development*, Vol. 5, No 1, Jan-Mar, pp 55-64.

Patnaik, Priti (2006), Nabard to Oversee Micro-lenders, *The Economic Times*, Friday, 27, p. 3.

Rangarajan C. (2007), *Financial Inclusion: Some Key Issues*, Lecture delivered at Mangalore University, Mangalore, and August 10.

Satish P. (2005), Mainstreaming Indian Micro Finance, *Economic and Political Weekly*, Vol. 40 No. 17 April 23 - April 29, 2005, pp. 1731-1739.

The Hindu Business Line (2007a), Micro-finance Bill tabled, March 20. Available at *http://www.thehindubusinessline.com/2007/03/21/stories/2007032105170600.htm* (accessed January 30, 2008).

Thorat, Usha (2007a), *Taking Banking Services to the Common Man–Financial Inclusion*, Deputy Governor, Reserve Bank of India at the HMT-DFID Financial Inclusion Conference 2007, Whitehall Place, London, UK, June 19.

Thorat, Usha (2007b), *Financial Inclusion–The Indian Experience* Text of speech by Deputy Governor, Reserve Bank of India at the HMT-DFID Financial Inclusion Conference 2007, Whitehall Place, London, UK, June 19.

Tiwari, Ravish (2006), Micro-finance Bill referred to GOM after objections, *The Indian Express*, Dec 16. Available at *http://www.indianexpress.com/story/18680.html (accessed on January 30, 2008).*

CHAPTER-6

WOMEN EMPOWERMENT IN WTO REGIME: A CASE STUDY OF ARARIA DISTRICT OF BIHAR

SANJAY KUMAR JHA

INTRODUCTION

WOMEN constitute nearly half of total population of India and yet the participation rate of women in employment is not up to the mark. Women are half of the world's population, work 2/3 of the world's income and own less than 1/10 of the world's property. But, rapid influx of women into empowerment world wide over the past three decades has become a key factor in the growing independence of women, economically, socially and legally. On an average, women the world over receive 30 to 40 per cent less than men for work of comparable value-whether in cash or kind, in benefits or food. In cash terms alone, women's earnings continue to fall short of men's. In the United Kingdom, women earn on average 70 per cent of men's wages; In Kenya 74 per cent; In Brazil 51 per cent; In the Republic of Korea 15 per cent; In Japan 43 per cent women also represent a disproportionate share of the unemployed in every age group and in every region (Women Labour in India, V.V. Giri National Labour Institute).

Empowerment is the process of challenging existing power relation and of gaining greater control over the sources of power. The goal of women empowerment is to challenge patriarchal ideology, to transform the structures and reinforce and perpetrate gender discrimination and social inequality and to enable poor women to gain access to and control over both material and informational resources. Empowerment is not internally bestowed upon people but instead, the women need to be the agents of their own empowerment, outsiders and outside generation can only help create the conditions favourable to women empowerment and can support the process that work in these directions.

NEED FOR WOMEN ENTREPRENEURSHIP DEVELOPMENT

Women entrepreneurs are the women or a group of women who initiate, organise and operate a business enterprise. It is said that "educating a woman in as good as opening a school" and "enterprising a woman is as good as opening an industry in rural areas".

The women in Bihar have been neglected and they have not been actively involved in the mainstream of development even though they represent of bulk of the population and labour force. Primarily, women are the means of survival of their families, but are generally unrecognised and undervalued, being placed at the bottom of the pile. Ideologically as well as in practice, women are considered inferior to males. Thus, the inequalities in here in our traditional social structure, based on caste, community and class, have a significant influence on the low status of women in different spheres. Thus, the main issue, which is still being debated, is the kind of strategy to be evolved for raising their status and participation in the process of development. Hence, the emergence of women as entrepreneurs in Bihar should be viewed as a resurgence of the rightfully respectable socio-economic status of women.

In Bihar, women are not given required scope for education. The pattern of existing education system is not geared towards instilling of entrepreneurial instincts in young minds in general and women in particular. The higher levels of education too, especially commerce and management education are not directed towards generating entrepreneurial skills.

The present study encompasses the following objectives:

(i) To analyse the various factors influencing the rural women entrepreneurs.

(ii) To identify the problems encountered by the women entrepreneurs.

(iii) To suggest measures to promote large scale rural women entrepreneurship.

METHODOLOGY

Araria district was purposively selected as this district has the potential to probe into the entrepreneurial behaviour of rural women. Besides, it is noted for cottage industries. Four blocks Araria, Forbesganj, Narpatganj and Raniganj were selected. Twenty respondents from each block were selected randomly comprising the total of eighty (80) samples.

RESULTS AND DISCUSSION

The factors which influence the entrepreneurship among rural women were classified as technological, personal, economic, physical and market factors. The respondents were asked to indicate which factors under each influenced their entrepreneurship and the percentage analysis is used.

From the above table, it is clear that availability of SHGs for consultancy as the technology factor influencing their entrepreneurship expressed by 75% of the respondents followed by NGO which is expressed by 65% of the respondents. Among the personal factors, self confidence was expressed y 95% of the respondents. About 90% of the respondents had expressed the personal factor-own interest as a factor influencing their entrepreneurship. Among the

Table 1
Factors Influencing Entrepreneurship

Factors	*Percentage*
Technological Factors	
• Guidance from private agencies	40
• Guidance from extension personnel	08
• Guidance from SHG	75
• Guidance from NGO	65
Personal Factors	
• Own Interest	90
• Self-Confidence	95
• Eagerness to evaluate enterprise	43
• Risk taking ability	20
• Achievement motivation	18
• Anticipation of future possibilities	18
• Experience	60
• Educational Qualification	20
Economic Factors	
• Initial Involvement	55
• Possession of ancestral property	05
• Demand for the products	80
• Resource recycling	05
Physical Factors	
• Availability of inputs	63
• Good transport facilities	93
• Own Vehicle	03
• Good roads	05
Market Factors	
• Good market potential	80
• Response prices	83
• Nearness to the market	03

economic factors, demand for the product was expressed by 80% of the respondents. Higher demand results in higher economic gain from the enterprise. The next important economic factor as expressed by 55 per cent of the respondents was initial investment. Initial investment must be strong to set up or to maintain or to expand. The enterprise. High investment makes the enterprise viable and therefore the returns are high. Physical factors which influenced the entrepreneurship were good transport facilities and availability of inputs. Regarding market factors, responsive prices 83% and good market potential 80% were major factors influencing entrepreneurship. Potential market and responsive prices will influence one to set up the enterprise and expand.

PROBLEMS AND WOMEN ENTREPRENEURS

The major problems faced by women entrepreneurs are as follows:

(i) Financial constraint was expressed by most of the respondents (nearly 95%). This was due to poor family background.

(ii) Marketing of products was one of the major problems faced by the women in the district.

(iii) Lack of technical know-how was another problem faced by the women entrepreneurs in the district.

(iv) Non-availability of space to keep the manufactured produced was expressed by more than 65% respondents.

(v) Low female literacy rate is the major problems faced by rural women entrepreneurs. Due to this, they became unaware of technological development, marketing trends etc. Even among educated, the bookish knowledge gathered by them is not sufficient to face the challenges in the business field.

(vi) In the present set up, a woman's duty is to look after her children and family members. Her family involvement restricts her economic involvement.

(vii) Inferiority complex: They are easily disheartened by failure.

(viii) Corruption, unnecessary delay, humiliation etc. at the government level (i.e. in government offices, banks etc.) make entrepreneurial life miserable for women. The cases of dropping out the business idea due to such difficulties are not uncommon in Bihar.

CONCLUSION AND SUGGESTIONS

Following measures should be taken to promote entrepreneurial skill among women:

(i) Re-orientation of educational system for women with due emphasis on career guidance, entrepreneurship awareness should be started with school curriculum itself.

(ii) Group entrepreneurship should be promoted to bring out the hidden talents of the individual entrepreneur.

(iii) To make wide publicity of various schemes of government and other agencies through electronic and print media is must, to promote entrepreneurship in remote rural areas.

(iv) Follow-up support in marketing the products of women entrepreneurs should be properly executed.

(v) The skill of existing women entrepreneurs should be upgraded.

(vi) At the national level and state level, there is a need to set up Women Industrial Development Bank.

(vii) 'Women Entrepreneurs Guidance Cell' in every district should be established to promote and guide the women entrepreneurs.

(viii) More and more research work is to be conducted to identify the problems, faced by rural women.

(ix) Efforts should be made to get the active involvement of Mahila Samaj or Women's organisations by launching village adoption schemes.

In the globalisation era, there is an urgent need to nurture and create an enabling entrepreneurial climate in the country. Enterprising rural women will enrich themselves and will induce stability to their family activities, will build up social capital and will reduce urbanisation. So, it is the need of the hour that if we have to develop Bihar, entrepreneurship among rural women should be developed.

REFERENCES

Ashley, C. and D. Carney (1999), Sustainable Livelihoods: Lessons from Early Experience DFID, London.

Reynolds, P. D., W. D. Bygrave, E. Autio, L. W. Cox and M. Hay (2002), Global Entrepreneurship Monitor (GEM) 2002 Executive Report. London Business School, U.K.

Roling, N. (1988), Extension Science: Information Systems in Agricultural Development. Cambridge University Press, Cambridge, Great Britain.

V. G. Patel (1997), "Entrepreneurship Development Obstacle-causes and Remedies", Bodh Publication, Kanpur.

Wayne, B.G. (1978), The Village Entrepreneur, Harvard University Press, London.

Prasad, H. and Verma, B. L. (2006), Women Entrepreneurship in India. *The Indian Journal of Commerce*, Vol. 59, No. 2, April-June.

C. B. Gupta and S. S. Khanka (1996), Entrepreneurship and Small Business Managment, S. Chand & Sons, Delhi, p. 10.

Anand Neeta (2003), Working Women: Issues and Problems, *Yojana*, March, pp. 11-14.

Human Development Report (2003), Millennium Development Goals: A Compact among Nations to End Human Poverty. United Nations Development Programme (UNDP). Oxford University Press, New Delhi.

Grover Indu and Deepak Grover (2002), Empowerment of Women (Ed.) Udaipur, Agrotech, p. 384.

CHAPTER-7

ANTI-DUMPING MEASURES UNDER WORLD TRADE ORGANIZATION (WTO)

KAMLESH TAYAL & M. TARIQ

INTRODUCTION

ANTI dumping is, perhaps, one of the most controversial issues in the realm of international trade policy. Some leading trade theorists have described the use of anti-dumping measures as being akin to disguised transfer payment from consumers to local high-cost producers. Not withstanding the controversies around it, anti-dumping measures today play an important role in modulating trade flows deriving legal sanctions under the WTO Agreements.

Anti-dumping measures are taken against the practice of 'Dumping'. Simply, 'Dumping'; is the difference between 'Normal value' and Export price. Dumping takes place when an exporter sells the goods in the territory of another country at cheaper prices than his domestic market price of below costs.

Dumping is defined in the Oxford Dictionary as sale of goods in foreign market at low price.[1] 'Dumping' has been referred to by economists as 'price discrimination between national markets.[2] But legally, to determine dumping, a comparison is to be made between the export price' of the product and the 'normal value' of the like product in the exporting country. If the 'export price' is less than the 'normal value', then the product is considered to be dumped. The difference between the two is the dumping margin. It is impossible to determine whether a good is being dumped just by knowing its export price. A product may be cheap but not 'dumped. just by knowing its export price. A product may be cheap but not; dumped', or may be expensive and yet; dumped.

Dumping is condemned only if it causes or threatens to cause material injury to domestic industry in the importing country of materially retards the establishment of a domestic industry. The "degree" of dumping is reflected by the margin of dumping judged by the quantum element of dumping, that is, whether it is voluminous so as to cause 'injury' to the domestic industry or is 'de minims'. The "effect" of dumping has reference to the impact of dumping on the domestic industry in the context of injury caused by the volume of dumping of the product under investigation. But determining, whether or not to impose anti-dumping measures, is never so simple and more often that not involves a series of complex analytical steps.

Under the GATT rules[3] a product was considered to be dumped if its export price was lower than its normal value. This definition is restricted to the concept of price discrimination between national markets in relation to goods. It does not cover all forms of international price discriminations. Some of the practices that have been excluded from its domain are: Service dumping, Freight dumping, and these are Service dumping, Freight dumping, Exchange dumping, Bounty dumps and Social dumping.

CAUSES OF DUMPING

Economists have enumerated various causes of dumping. Supporters of anti-dumping policies argue that anti-dumping is a justifiable attempt by importing country governments to offset the market access restriction existing in an exporting firm's home country market, that underlie the ability of such firms to dump. Such restrictions may consist of import barriers preventing arbitrage, but may also reflect the non-existence or non enforcement of competition law by the exporting country. Thus, the United States had claimed that lax Japanese antitrust enforcement permits Japanese firms to collude, raise prices, and use part of the resulting rents to cross subsidies (dump) products sold on foreign markets.

Viner developed the first original theoretical rationale for anti-dumping law. He argued that anti dumping duties may be needed to protect domestic consumers from predatory dumping. Most economists however contend that predatory dumping is an exception rather that a rule. Viner distinguished three forms of dumping: sporadic, short run, and long run. Only the second form justified a reaction in his view, as only this form of dumping can be construed as anti-competitive. In the first case injury to firms is transitory; whole the gains to consumers outweigh the losses to domestic producers in the last case.[4]

'Dumping' could occur on account of variety of reasons, such as:

- Exporting surplus production while continuing to produce at full capacity in order to achieve/maintain the economy of scale.
- The motive could be to maximize short-term gains by exporting at a price, which is slightly more than the marginal cost of the product though lower than its average cost.
- An exporter might dump in order to gain foothold into a market, or to maintain his position there, or his aim might be to achieve other corporate objectives, such as maintenance of full employment/ avoiding retrenchment of labour.
- Another motive could be predation, aiming to eliminate the competitors in the importing country or induce them to share the market there on his terms.

- In order to maintain domestic prices in the country of origin/export by disposing 01 the surplus stocks.
- An exporter may be simply following the price trends of his competitors who may be exporting at a lower price on account of geographical proximity or preferential tariffs. This occurs because- importers expect all supplies to be made at the cheapest of such prices, which may compel the other exporters (who may not have the advantage, for instance, of geographical proximity or preferential access to the market) to follow the trend in prices.

Dumping may also be caused by what is known as transitional dumping. It occurs when an exporter needs to price below marginal cost in order to maximize sales and expand market share. In this case below cost pricing is a kind of investment in the marketing of the product. deemed to be worthwhile if profits can be earned in the long run. Because this may require fixing price below marginal cost, it may be treated as predatory pricing, yet clearly it is not. The main argument advanced for taking measure against it is that it ensures that national producers get beater experience than the foreign firms. It is frequently argued that such industries bring special advantages to a country either because they enable domestic factors of production to earn higher returns than in other sectors of the economy or because they generate externalities or spillover benefits for the rest of the economy. Even if these arguments are accepted it must still be demonstrated that anti-dumping policy is the best instrument for achieving these objectives. Economists contend that it is not. Theory shows that a superior instrument would be production subsidy granted to domestic producers sufficient to correct for the market distortion.

ANTI DUMPING UNDER LEGAL FRAME WORK

The Anti-dumping Agreement provides a legal framework; providing redressal not only against the dumped imports but also against an unjustifiable anti-dumping action. It has 18 Articles and two Annexes attached to it. One of the major contributions of the WTO to the world trading system has been the predictability of trade policy through clear commitments that is tariff bindings.

However, this certainty of the law, in the Anti-dumping Agreement has been lacking. The Agreement has asymmetries and gaps in its text, which are on account of a consensus because of the existence of divergent national interests. This resultant lack of clarity has also enabled the Members to include subtle variations in their national anti-dumping legislations and has led to different interpretations, understanding and applications by the WTO Members.

The Agreement is vague and ambiguous on quite a few issues, which enable the administering authorities to interpret it in an unduly protectionist manner. This is also because like any other International Agreement, the Anti-dumping Agreement is also the result of a negotiated compromise emerging out of varying negotiating positions of the Members during the Uruguay Round and was put place at the eleventh hour and therefore has many technical deficiencies.

This lack of coherence and vagueness is manifest in the Agreement, fur instance, we find that action against dumping can only be taken by the authorities if such dumping is causing injury to the domestic industry, but this requirement is not of much consequence as the definition of injury itself is unclear, especially what could be termed as 'material' in this regard.

The result of the uncertainty of some provisions of the present Agreement is that an exporter/producer is not really able to determine in advance, the quantum of anti-dumping duty when an investigation starts. At times, it is even difficult to determine whether or not he is dumping, as the dumping calculator practices of the different administering authorities vary.

Many Members have tabled suggestions for improving the application of anti-dumping measures. It is apprehended that unless the negotiators plug file gaps in the existing Agreement, it may lead to increased use of anti-dumping measures, especially by the developing Members, as their domestic industry is likely to clamor for protection against imports resulting from lowering of Customs tariffs and dismantling of the Quota systems.

The indiscriminate use of this instrument is causing a concern amongst tie Members. This sentiment has been the guiding principle of current negotiations on the subject, which are underway as per the mandate of Doha Ministerial Conference of the WTO (2001). The Doha mandate, *inter-alia,* provides fur negotiations aimed at clarifying and improving disciplines under the Anti-dumping Agreement, while preserving the basic concepts, principles and effectiveness of the Agreement. The relevant excerpts of the Ministerial Decision at Doha read thus:

> *"In the light of experience and of the increasing application of these instruments by Members, we agree to negotiations aimed at clarifying and improving disciplines under the Agreements on implementation of Article VI of the GA? I 1994..., while preserving the basic concepts, principles and effectiveness of this Agreements and their instruments and objectives, and taking into account the needs of developing and least-developed participants. in the initial phase of the negotiations, participants will indicate the provisions, including disciplines on trade distorting practices, that they seek to clarify and improve in the subsequent phase.*[5]

It needs to be appreciated that the rules governing anti-dumping measures have been refined over the years and additional rules developed; however, the essence of these rules is that they all restrict the freedom of the importing country to take recourse to this protective measure.

DISPUTE RESOLUTION SYSTEM

Article 13 of the Anti-dumping Agreement requires that each Member whose national legislation contains provisions on anti-dumping measures shall maintain judicial, arbitral or administrative tribunals or procedures for the prompt review of administrative action relating to final determinations and review of determinations within the meaning of Article 11. Such tribunals or procedures shall be independent of the authorities responsible for the determination or review in question?[6]

Besides recourse to "Judicial Review" under the domestic law of the Member imposing anti-dumping measures, the agreement on anti-dumping provides for Consultation and Dispute Settlement through WTO with respect to any matter affecting the operation of the Agreement.

Dispute Settlement System under GATT, 1947

The rules for dispute settlement under GATT 1947 system were contained in Articles XXII and XXIII. Both these articles have been carried over without any change into the WTO system under GATT 1994. Article XXII of GATT, 1994 deals with consultations between WTO members. Article XXIII on the other hand is concerned with the concept of "nullification and impairment". This refers to the loss of benefit that would have been received had a particular action not been tal: by a WTO member. If the consultations failed, GATT members were to examine the matter, issue rulings or recommendations and authorize possible retaliation. The system did not yield much result due to blockage action by the erring member country. Articles XXII and XXIII are now supported by a detailed understanding on Dispute Settlement Procedure. The Uruguay Round Understanding on Rules and Procedures Governing the Settlement of Disputes has transformed GATT rules, which themselves evolved over forty years. The whole accent is on speedy resolution of disputes and prevention of deliberate blocking of action by the erring member country.

The dispute settlement system in the WTO is a major change from the previous GATT system.[7] For the first time, an independent judicial system to enforce the WTO law is in place. The Dispute Settlement Panels have powers equivalent to those of judicial benches. The power to enforce an international law is major breakthrough in international affairs. WTO is perhaps the only international institution which has the legal power enforce rules. The International Court of Justice in Hague too has similar powers but they come into play only when both sides to the dispute agree to move to the court.

The dispute settlement system is designed to provide security and predictability to the multilateral trading system. It serves to preserve as well as to clarify rights and obligations under the agreements.

Regarding the Anti-dumping measures WTO oversees their application by Members at various levels:

(a) It reviews the Anti-dumping legislations of Members and the application of Anti-dumping measures by Members.

(b) If a Member wants, the Agreement provides mechanism for consultation with another Member affecting the operation of the Anti-dumping Agreement.

(c) It provides mechanism for dispute settlement.

(d) It provides for Arbitration for implementation of the rulings of the Panel and the Appellate Body.

Before taking recourse to the dispute settlement procedure there has been a provision for consultations under the 1979 Code as well as the present Agreement.

Para 1 of Article 15 of the 1979 Code provided, "Each Party shall afford sympathetic consideration to, a shall afford adequate opportunity for consultation regarding representations made by another Party with respect to any matter affecting the operation of this Agreement." Further, Para 2 provided, "If any Party considers that any benefit accruing to it directly or indirectly under this Agreement is being nullified or impaired, or that the achievement of any objective of the Agreement is being impeded, by another Party or Parties, it may, with a view to reaching a mutually satisfactory resolution of the matter, request in writing consultations with the Party or Parties in question. Each Party shall afford sympathetic consideration to any request from another Party for consultation. The Parties concerned shall initiate consultation promptly". Para 3 obligated the Committee on Anti-dumping Practices, "In cases where matters are referred to the Committee for conciliation, the Committee shall meet within thirty days to review the matter, and through its good offices, shall encourage the Parties involved to develop a mutually acceptable solution. Para 4 obligated the Parties that they "shall make their best efforts to reach a mutually satisfactory solution throughout the period of conciliation".

DISPUTE SETTLEMENT SYSTEM

In case of failure of consultation there has been provision for dispute settlement in the 1979 Anti-dumping Code as well as the present Anti-dumping Agreement[8]. Article 15(5) of the 1979 Code provided, "Ii no mutually agreed solution has been reached after detailed examination by the Committee under Para 3 within three months, the Committee shall, at the request of any party to the dispute, establish a Panel to examine the matter.

Similarly, Article 17.4 of the present Agreement on Anti-dumping provides that if the Member that requested consultations has failed to achieve a mutually agreed solution, and if final action has been taken by the administering authorities of the importing Member to levy definitive Anti dumping duties or to accept price undertakings, it may refer the matter to the Dispute Settlement Body (DSB). When a provisional measure has a significant impact and the Member who requested consultations considers that the measure was taken contrary to the provisions of para 1 of Article 7 of the Agreement that Member may also refer such matter to the DSB.

The only difference between the two provisions is that while previously it was the Committee on Anti-dumping Practices that established the Panel, now it is the responsibility of the Dispute Settlement Body.

Similarly, both the 1979 Code and the present Agreement provide that the Panel shall examine the matter based upon:

(a) a written statement of the party making the request indicating how a benefit accruing to it directly or indirectly under this Agreement has been nullified or impaired, or that the achieving of the objective of the Agreement is being impeded, and

(b) "the facts made available in conformity with appropriate domestic procedures to the authorities of the importing country."

Thus, both the 1979 Code and the present Agreement are similar in that they provide that the establishment of the Panel will be to examine if there has been nullification or impairment of any benefit to the party or the achievement of the objective of the Agreement has been impeded.

However, the present Anti-dumping Agreement further clarifies the role of the Panel. Article 17.6 of the Agreement provides:

(i) in its assessment of the facts of the matter, the panel shall determine whether the authorities' establishment of the facts was proper and whether their evaluation of those facts was proper and whether their evaluation of those facts was unbiased and objective. If the establishment of the facts was proper and the evaluation was unbiased and objective, even though the Panel might have reached a different conclusion, the evaluation shall not be overturned;

(ii) the Panel shall interpret the relevant provisions of the Agreement in accordance with customary rules of interpretation of public international law. Where the Panel finds that a relevant provision of the Agreement admits of more than one permissible interpretation, the Panel shall find the authorities, measure to be in conformity with the Agreement if it rests upon one of those permissible interpretations.

Article 17.6(i) was clarified in the case of United States. Antidumping Measures on Stainless Steel Plate in Coils and Stainless Steel Sheet and Strip from Korea.[9] In that case the Panel held that Article 17.6(i) 'speaks not only to the establishment of the facts, but also to their evaluation. Therefore, the Panel must check not merely whether the national authorities have properly established the relevant facts but also the value or weight attached to those facts[10] and whether this was done in an unbiased and objective manner. This concerns the according of a certain weight to the facts in their relation to each other; it is not a legal evaluation".[11]

CONCLUDING REMARKS

The study of anti-dumping is the study of regulation of unfair trade practice. The purpose of WTO is to maximize liberalization of trade between countries within the sphere of internationally agreed rules. It's Endeavour for liberalization of trade includes removal of tariff as well as non-tariff barriers such as anti-dumping measures; its realm of rules condemn unfair trade practices such as dumping.

As for the existing provisions, the Panel and Appellate Body have most of the time given decision based on legalistic interpretation of the provisions and have tried to balance the rights and obligations of the parties, keeping in view the purpose of the provision.

Without getting into the normative aspects of dumping and alternative dispute measures, it is very much clear to say that the last twelve years of its operations by WTO member countries have led to a vast array of legal jurisprudence with regard to the application of alternative dispute measures. During this period, more than three thousands anti-dumping investigations were initiated and almost two thousand anti dumping measures were taken; a minefield for any person willing to dig his heels to analyze the various facets of anti-dumping and how the instrument has been used by member countries around to globe.

NOTES AND REFERENCES

1. The Concise Oxford Dictionary, Dictionary, (10th Edn.).
2. See, Boulding, Economic Analysis, (revised edition, New Your. 1948), p. 557.
3. Article VI, para, I. GATT.
4. J. Viner (1966), Dumping: A Problem in International Trade, 262.
5. Paragraph 28 of 4th Ministerial WTO Conference in Dhoa.
6. There was no corresponding provision in the 1967 Code or the 1979.
7. Arun Goyal and Noor Mohammad (Ed.) (2001), WTO in the New Millennium, 585 (5th Edn.).
8. The 1967 Anti-dumping Code did not contain any separate provision for dispute settlement. The provision under GATT Articles XXII and XXIII were the only provisions applicable.
9. WT/DS 179/R, adopted on 22 December, 2000.
10. In the Case of Thailand-Anti-dumping Duties on Angles, Shapes and Sections of Iron or Non-Alloy Steel and H-beams From Poland WT/DS 122/R adopted on 28th September, 2000, It was clarified that Articles 17.5 and 17.6(i) required a Panel to examine the facts made available to the investigating authority of the importing Member. These provisions do not prevent a Panel from examining facts that were not disclosed to, or discernible by, the interested parties at the time of the final determination.
11. Panel Report, United States-Anti-dumping Measures on Stainless Steel Plate in Coils and Stainless Steel Sheet and Strip from Korea, WT/DS 179/R, adopted on 22 December, 2000. para 6.18.

Chapter-8

WTO BRAND EXTENSION– AN EMERGING STRATEGY OF MARKETING

J. P. Bhosale, D. M. Gujrathi & H. D.Thorat

INTRODUCTION

The level of interest in the subject of branding and in brand related topics has increased dramatically in the last two decades Brands are considered as some of the best important assets of an organization

A brand mean a name, term sing symbol or design or a combination of than services of one seller or a group of sellers and to differentiate them those of competitors.

In the last decade, Indian market has been witnessing the dazzling entry of numerous multinational brands across various product categories.. We have to be faithful to the process of LPG (Liberalization, Privatization and Globalization). By this the Consumer's in India got some opportunity to choose. Though the trend is very much appealing to the Indian Consumers, Multi - National Corporations (MNCs) find it a thorny affair. The ways and strategies, which have been going their way in other markets is proved to be wrong when, applied in the Indian Market.

OBJECTIVES OF THE STUDY

1. To know & study the concept of brand &brand Extension.
2. To know & study the types Brand.
3. To Study the Tips for Successful Brand Extension

CORPORATE BRANDS

Brands have been defined by the American Marketing Association as names, terms, signs, symbols or designs that identify the products and services of individual sellers and differentiate them from those of competition. Companies use several types of brands in practice In recent years, there has been an increased focus on corporate brands. A company is said to be engaged in corporate branding when it markets itself as a brand. Thus, the corporate brand can be seen as a brand that spans the entire company and conveys expectations about what the company will deliver in terms of products and services. In simple terms, a corporate brand represents who the company says it is, or wants to be The construct of corporate branding has evolved from two different streams. Firstly, from the side of a marketing perspective with a consumer focus, via brand image, brand positioning, brand identity and corporate associations. On the second side, it has evolved from a multi-disciplinary perspective with an organization focus via corporate image, corporate personality, corporate identity and corporate reputation.

Corporate brands have been considered to be powerful symbols. Brands like IBM, GE, McDonalds and Coca Cola are well known throughout the world. Corporate brands have been considered to be especially influential in emerging countries where they are supposed to have an impact in diverse areas ranging from product and service choice to attracting high potential employees. The corporate brand can serve as a master brand that endorses and provides credibility for other brands in the company's brand portfolio. Corporate brands are believed to provide several benefits in terms of reduction of communication costs; providing community to customers; providing a seal of approval and providing common ground for other brands.

BRAND AWARENESS

Brand awareness is an important concept in both branding theory and practice. It has been defined as the ability of a consumer to bring the brand to mind in a choice situation or decision task. It also refers to the consumers' ability to recognize and recall the brand and identify it under different conditions. Brand recognition relates to the consumers' ability to confirm when the brand is present and it has been encountered earlier. Brand recall relates to the ability of a consumer in the absence of the brand, to retrieve the brand from memory in response to a product category mention, category need, usage situation.

Brand awareness is an important component along with brand image in consumer brand knowledge. Brand awareness has been described as essential to the communication process to occur as it precedes all other stages in the process.

Brand awareness is also an important concept in memory theory where it is indicated as a first step in melding a bundle of associations which are anchored to the brand in memory.

MANAGING GROWTH THROUGH BRAND EXTENSIONS

The ever-changing marketplace dynamics, increased competition of the global economy and the evolving customer needs and preferences have amplified the role of brands to an unmatched level. Companies frequently launch new products to meet the above challenges. Launching new products is an attractive and proven growth strategy, but not without risk.

An increasingly popular approach that companies follow to reduce risk during new product launches, has been to leverage on the equity of the existing brand. The two most common approaches to leveraging the equity of the established brands are line extensions and brand extensions. Line extension is the use of an established brand name for a new product in dies same product category. The new product is different from the original product in relatively minor ways like composition, price, size, etc. On the other hand, brand extension refers to stretching the brand name into different product categories. According to Keller, a brand extension is defined as a branding strategy "when a firm uses an established name to introduce a new product." Companies can capitalize on the recognition and goodwill of the existing brand, thereby increasing the chances of product success.

These benefits are mostly due to the transfer of parent brand's awareness, reputation and association to the new product. There are various case studies relating to successful brand extensions. Dettol, which was predominantly in the antiseptics' segment, extended its brand by launching products like shaving creams, soaps and Other Men grooming products. Meera soaps recently launched Meera shampoos and Meera hair wash herbal. The Taj Group of Hotels ha successfully ventured into adventure tourism, an luxury residencies. Similarly, Nyle brand ha extended its brand to include cold cream am moisturizing lotion Reliance too successfully extended in to telecom, petrochemicals and retail. Successful brand extensions have a positive spillover effect on the parent brand reputation and image. I also increases the parent brand awareness am recall, and in some cases, it even revitalizes am renews the attitude of the consumers toward: the parent brand.

TYPES OF BRAND EXTENSIONS

Brand extensions are of two type:

(i) Extension into related categories;

(ii) extension into unrelated categories.

An example of the first is *Cinthol* soap launching a lime fresh/cologne fresh version or becoming a talcum powder. An example of the second category is the name *Tata* being used for both steel and tea. There is noth-ing common to steel and tea. Yet *Tata* as a brand name established itself successfully in both the categories and hence called an unrelated extension.

Related Extensions could Further take Two Routes

(i) extension into the same product category

(ii) extension into a category that is different but similar in benefits, association and appeal to the parent brand. An example of the first is *Cinthol* soap launching its lime fresh/cologne fresh/spicy fresh versions. Here the product has not been changed but stretched to ac-commodate variety. Both *Cinthol* (Old) and *Cinthol Lime Fresh* are soaps. This could be called *category-related extension.*

In the second case, however, *Cinthol* from a toilet soap becomes & talcum powder. Though products are different, they are linked by the appeal they hold for customers. Both are cosmetics. This has been labelled as *image-related extension.*

Classification of Brand Extension

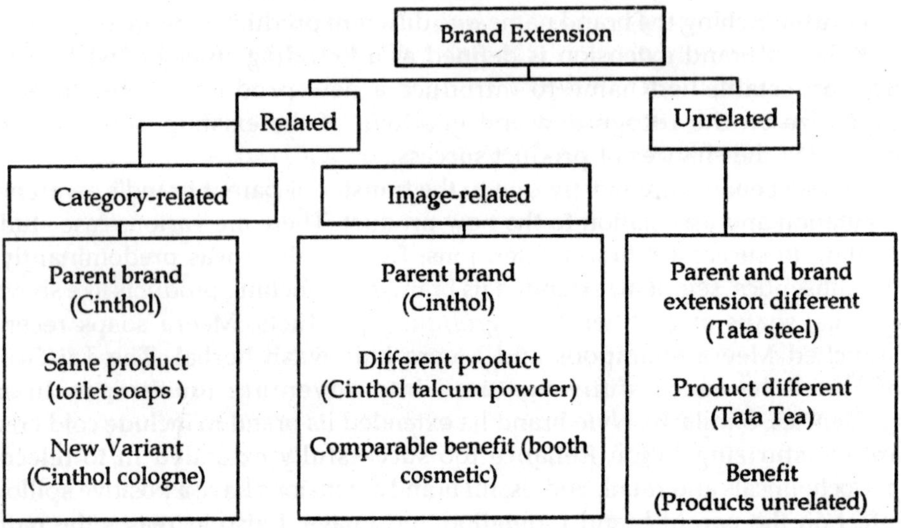

TIPS FOR SUCCESSFUL BRAND EXTENSIONS

1. Extend those brands which are well-known and have high awareness and reputation.
2. Brand extensions should have a ht or similarity with the parent brand.
3. Brand extensions must leverage on parent brand and corporate brand.
4. Brand extensions that create confusions or dilution of the parent brand image should not be undertaken.
5. Brand extensions should create meaningful value to the consumers.
6. Brands should not be over-stretched or stretched across many categories.
7. Brand extensions that do not create synergy tor the parent brand should not be undertaken.
8. Every' brand extension should create a new category for the firm.
9. Think sub-brands.

The strategic use of brand extensions for growth involves five steps. In the first step, the future desired market position tor the parent brand is determined. The second step involves identifying the conditions tor extension or the product categories where the extension is most likely to succeed. This is where fit and relevance come into picture. The third step involves planning and implementing marketing strategies to facilitate the success of the extension. The fourth step involves management of the associations between the parent brand and the brand extension using one of the fortification processes.

CONCLUSION

Brand Extension should Create Meaningful Value to the Consumers

Many companies have started using the brand extension strategy to get a foot or two into a new product category. However, the process of transferring the values and attributes of the parent brand to its extensions is often a daunting task. Brand extension is more an art than a science. The failure of an extension not only dilutes the parent brand but also the corporate image; therefore, companies should do everything to ensure success when extending the brand. The key to successful brand extension is "ability to bring meaningful value to the customer."

In Short Brand Extension is an Emerging Strategy of Modern Marketing.

REFERENCES

J. Venkatesh , Dr. V. Balachandran (2006), Recent Issues in Changing of Global Brands to Domestic Brands. *Indian Journal of Marketing,* Feb.

M. S. Balaji (2006), Brand Extension, *The ICFAI Journal of Marketing Management,* Nov.

Avinash Mulky, Rajendra Nargunkar (2005), *The ICFAI Journal Marketing Management, Aug.*

www.brandxpress.net

Aaker, D. A. (2004), "Leaverging the Corporate Brand". *California Management Review.*

Aakler, D. A. and Joachimsthaler, A. (2000), Brand Leadership, New York: Free Press.

Keller, K. L. (2003), Strategic Brand Management, New Delhi, Prentice Hall of India Pvt. Ltd.

Globalbrands.org

Bambooweb.com

Y. L . R. Moorthi, Brand Management, Vikas Publishing House, New Delhi.

Chapter-9

IMPACT OF WTO ON AGRICULTURAL MARKETING

R. B. Dhande & G. D. Kharat

INTRODUCTION

The world agricultural trading system has been experienced a tremendous change during the second half of the 20th century. The tread on agriculture was signed at the ministerial meet on 15th April 1994 by 125 nations and the agreements of agriculture (AOA) become effective from 1st Jan 1995 with the establishment of WTO.

The WTO agreements are a milestone in the development of International trade in agricultural commodities; agriculture has been brought under international discipline. It is very difficult to foresee that exact outcome of WTO.

Agriculture marketing was tilled recently, not fully accepted as an essential element in agricultural development in the countries of Asia Agricultural marketing occupies as fairly low place in agricultural development policies of developing countries. Agricultural development means not only enough to produce a crop but also we must see it to be satisfactorily marketed. The present paper has been described the need for better agricultural marketing. Foreign customers demand quality products. The challenges left before the agriculturists providing them an opportunity for making some heroic efforts to capture the world market. Traditionally, plantation & fiber crops occupied primary position in agricultural exports of our nation.

OBJECTIVES OF THE STUDY

The present study is an attempt to–

1. Examining an impact of AOA on Indian Economy.
2. Identifying the need for better agricultural marketing.

HYPOTHESIS

The marketing (both domestic and export) of agriculture is a decisive issue & hence requires an intensive strategy with structural & infrastructural facilities for the development of well built marketing system.

METHODOLOGY

The methodology is designed with an intention to make a critical appraisal of the present day agriculture & identify the challenges. The study is based on secondary source of data.

Agreement of Agriculture (AOA)

Agreement of agriculture (AOA) is related to reforms in agricultural trade over time. Accordingly member countries have to formulate market oriented policies. The commodities under AOA are to be fulfilled through–

(a) Providing market access

(b) Reducing domestic support

(c) Containing export subsidies

The member countries have to provide market for agricultural products to the extent of 3% of domestic consumption by end of implementation period i.e. 2000 & 5% latter on. In order to move towards free trade, member countries have to reduce tariffs. Developed countries have to reduce import tariffs by 36% for all products (at least 15% per product) whereas developing countries 24% of all products (at least 10% per product) from present level. Under WTO these have been replaced by tariffs that provide equivalent levels of protection. If the domestic prices were 25% higher than the prices prevailing in International Market, now import tariff called tariffication could be 25%

As a part of AOA, subsidies & other form of support to agriculture including minimum support prices & procurement prices have to be used less intensively by the member countries, to promote agriculture sector in their respective economies.

WTO categorized the domestic support in terms of trade distorting called as 'amber box', 'green box' & 'blue box'.

'Amber box' includes the domestic support policy induce farmers to produce more than the domestic requirement. The presence of over production forces the Govt. to provide subsidies to clear it out. The trade distorting domestic support is measured in terms of Aggregate Measure of Support (AMS). It means the difference between minimum support price & external price quoted in the International Market.

'Green box' includes minimal trade distorting domestic support toward scientific research, disease control, development of infrastructure & to ensure food security (to maintain PDS). It also includes the direct payment made by Govt. to sustain incomes of farmers on the one hand & other to discourage farmers to cultivate certain crops & to limit the production through declaring crop holiday.

The domestic support in the form of direct income payments to farmers is called as *'Blue box'*. The members can continue other domestic support on small scale, called as *'Special & differential box'*.

The other major issue related to agriculture is containing export subsidies. The member countries have to contain the quantity of subsidized export as well as the amount earmarked towards exported subsidy. The developed and developing countries agreed to cut the subsidized quantity & amount of money they spend on export subsidies.

IMPACT OF AOA ON INDIAN ECONOMY

Agreement of Agriculture is biased in-favor of developed nations. Provision of marked access clause adversely affects the developing nations particularly India. It is fact that, there is huge market for agricultural products in developing nations and at the same time, there is surplus food production in developed nations. In the guise of AOA & its market access clause, the developed nations will dump their surplus food grains in developing countries.

MARKET ACCESS CLAUSE

India has reached to stage of self sufficiency in food grains. We do not need impact of food grains. But under this clause, we have to provide market access for agricultural products to the extent of 3% by spending precious foreign exchange. AOA has been structured in such away to deny increased market access to developing nations. India could not derive any advantage from market access clause. Being a member of WTO & a party of AOA, India has to fulfill its commitments by allowing impacts of agricultural products in the presence of adequate domestic supply of agricultural products. The import of agricultural products even in the presence of glut of output has adverse impact on Indian economy in terms of fall in prices of agricultural products & income levels of farm community.

DOMESTIC SUPPORT

The second major issue under AOA is related to containing domestic support especially subsidies to agriculture sector. AOA stipulated that total subsidies to agriculture should not exceed 10% of the value of GDP of agriculture sector.

The developed nations providing subsidies to agriculture well beyond stipulated limits. USA spends more than 1/3rd of GDP from agriculture, Japan 1/4th of the GDP from agriculture, Canada & European Union around 10% of GDP from agriculture towards green box subsidies.

In India, the amount of subsidies extended to agriculture sector constitutes less than 10% (near about 6%) of GDP from agriculture. In our economy the adverse impact of weather, defective seeds & rise in fertilizers prices on overall crop yields. Under these conditions, the government has to provide subsidies to protect farm sector & to ensure food security. If the Indian Government under AOA in near future, agricultural output may fall due to lack of incentives to farmers & focus our millions of people to look at developed countries to satisfy their hunger. This is the final outcome that the developed nations aim to achieve under AOA. Though we are a party of AOA, we should not fall in the trap of developed nations.

EXPORT SUBSIDIES

Regulation of export subsidy is a major factor that adversely affects the performance of agriculture sector. Under AOA, the government has to regulate export subsidy in terms of duty drawbacks, cash compensatory support, etc. The aim of developed nations, under the guise of AOA, is to make the exports of agricultural products from developing nations less competitive in the international market through regulation of export support. The provision of market access, containing domestic support & regulation of export subsidies clearly indicates that, developed nations have to clever vision in terms of expecting a huge market for their agricultural products in developing economies. According to the clause of "technical barriers to trade "also prepared in favor of developed nations. Under this clause, developed nations can effectively prevent imports of agriculture & allied product from India, on health grounds, environmental issues & citing violation of human rights in the form of employing child labor.

NEED FOR BETTER AGRICULTURAL MARKETING

Agricultural marketing plays an important role not only in stimulating production & consumption but in accelerating pace of economic development. Marketing of agricultural produce is complex phenomenon. It requires special treatment at all levels with government & institutional support.

Indian farmers are poor and illiterate; consequently do not acknowledge the new technology in pre harvest operations. All sort of pre- harvest operations are not market oriented & sustainable. Quality of production also annoyed due to natural calamities & climatic conditions. Crop protections measures are becoming costly. Cost of input also remains high. There is no guarantee of prices to be paid for farmers produce. The producer's share in consumer rupee is tremendously less in India. All the lacunars deserve to have Institutional and infrastructural facilities to be made available to the farmers by government authorities. The government has taken various steps to improve the conditions of the agricultural marketing, but these steps are not meeting the required demands. In the wake of globalization, the farmers have to face lot of challenges ahead to market his product. Some of the initiatives needed for tomorrow's better marketing are as follows:

Expansion of Co-operative Marketing and Processing

Expansion of co-operative marketing facilities for all commodities assures reasonable prices so as to remove all exploitation of the farmers by the middlemen. A network co-operative at the national level, state level and primary level needed to help farm producers to get best markets and best prices for their product. These markets have their own storage and warehousing facilities which results in better control over the flow of supplies and influence the prices.

Electronic Trading

It may facilitate the direct interaction between buyers & sellers. Agricultural market committee can also set up the special information kiosks for this purpose. The issue in the concept calls for the dual role of farmers as producers & seller. With the present infrastructural facilities can we justify it?

Information Network System

The ministry of agriculture has recently implemented an IT based central sector scheme to link 710 important regulated markets spread all over the country including the state Agricultural Marketing Board & Directories. Under this scheme, an agricultural information system network is being set up to computerize 27 major commodities with online data of daily market arrivals, prices, storages, dispatches with destination cost, sold & unsold stocks, infrastructural facilities, etc with this advances the world has become a small place and a larger market at one can go.

Forward & Future Markets

In the wake of WTO, the government has withdrawn its intervention from commodity sector to ensure that the demand & supply forces will determine the market prices in the new economic environment. The Forward Markets Commission (FMC) performs the functions of advisory, monitoring, supervise & regulating in future and forward trading. In the century, currently future controls are traded for nine commodities in twenty commodity exchange. The linkage between spot & future markets seem to be poor due to domination of speculators. The government therefore has to continue its efforts to strengthen traders. Efforts have also to be made to extend the role of exchange in other traders and other services like warehousing, financing, investments and market intelligence which could improve the existence of the future markets.

Creation of Cold Storage Facility

In India, presently, the total warehousing in both urban & rural areas which accounts to 35 million tones (2000-2001) capacity. Now, the need of the hour ahead is creation of cold storage facilities to growing demands of fruits & vegetables, where we have to convert our comparative advantage in the production & process of fruits & vegetables, to competitive advantage which is still untapped potential. Very merger efforts have been made in a form location specific Agri-Export Zone [AEZ] in this area which could not sufficient. It may be noted that plantation crops like tea, coffee, spices, coconut, cashew, dairy products require storage facilities. Efforts will have to create crop-specific storage capacity during the 11th five year plan.

Linkage of Roads

As compared to railway, the road transport system has definite advantages. Road development in India was neglected in past years for various reasons. In the first place, central & state governments did not appreciate the importance of developing the road system. During the next three plans, the planning commission provided for a total outlay of Rs.8600 corers on road programs & for road transport. One of the most ambitious projects launched in independent India is the National Highway Development Project (NHDP), which is expected to go a long way in promoting economic development of the country & integrating remote regions with the main stream economic activity and ensuring connectively of the rural roads.

Private Investment

The decline in the share of Investment in Agriculture as percentage of GDP has been an area of continued concern. This decline was attributed mainly to near stagnation or fail of public investment in agriculture. For the development of agricultural marketing, private sector must invest their share in agriculture in the coming years.

Price Support Policy

Food grain marketing has been a subject of considerable debate in the recent past. The government intervention in food grain market in case of rice & wheat in a farm price support, buffer stocking & PDS helped a lot in reaching the rural poor. Today food security is one of the prime importances of the nation. There are only 24 agricultural commodities which are covered under minimum price support policy & have regulated markets throughout the country. There are several other commodities which of high economic significance that need urgent coverage through comprehensive price stabilization as well as establishment of regulated markets in the respective agro climatic regions. There is a need for policy which should have high market intervention and it should increase the operational efficiency of purchasing agencies in the context of cost efficient purchases vis-à-vis competitive sales as to avoid or reduce loss. There is a need for bringing uniformity in the state level tax structured for better efficiency.

The infrastructure under government ownership & management has, however, proved thoroughly inefficient and corrupt. The demand for infrastructure facilities & services has always out paced supply, besides the quality of the existing supply is extremely poor. The widening gap between demand and supply of infrastructure & the extremely poor quality of the existing supply raises important questions concerning the sustainability of economic growth of the country in the coming years.

After considering the above issues, it is sure that we are able to develop well built marketing system.

REFERENCES

Acharya, S. S. and Agrawal, N. L. (2004), "Agricultural Marketing in India". Oxford and IBH Publishing Co. Pvt. Ltd

Arunachalam, R. (2002), "An Analysis of India's Steucture and Direction of Foreign Trade". *'Agricultural Growth & Economic Reforms'*, p. 215-225.

Mercia Selva Malar, S. (2005), 'WTO in Support of Agriculture Trade', Kisan World, p. 63.

Prasad (2005), "*Encyclopedia of Agricultural Marketing*", Vol. XI.

FAO (2005), The State of Food and Agriculture, Rome, Italy.

Josling, T. and S. Tangermann (1999), Implementation of the WTO Agreement on Agriculture and Developments for Next Round of Negotiations. *European Review of Agricultural Economics*, 26(3):371-388.

Dr. A. Nakula Reddy (2006), Multilateral Trade Agreement on Agriculture–Impact on Indian Economy, *Osmania Journal of International Business Studies*, July-December, p. 51-56.

Chapter-10

WTO: INDUSTRIALIZATION AND GLOBAL ENVIRONMENTAL DEGRADATION

B. R. Honparkhe

INTRODUCTION

Industrialization has two sides, positive and negative, positive side is useful and essential for society's welfare or to lift the standard of living. Industrialization is necessary for utilization of natural resources for production activities to provide different types of goods and services for society. Due to industrialization generation of employment opportunities to skilled, semiskilled and unskilled people in their respective areas such as production, purchase, marketing, finance, personnel department and other areas. For economic development and quality human life industrialization is a must.

But the negative side of the industrialization is harmful to human health and life because of rapid unplanned industrial progress creates many more different types of pollution problems such as air, water, noise and soil. Maintaining clean environment and ecology balance is essential for survival of human life. This is the social or moral responsibility of business towards society.

MEANING/NATURE OF ENVIRONMENT AND ECOLOGY

1. *Environment*: The sum of all external conditions affecting the life, development and survival of an organization.
2. *Ecology*: The relationship of living things to one another and their environment, or the study of such relationship.

DEFINITION OF ENVIRONMENTAL POLLUTION

Environmental pollution can, therefore, be defined as any undesirable change in the physical, chemical or biological characteristics of any component of the environment (air, water, soil), which can cause harmful effects on various forms of life or property.

OBJECTIVES

The present paper has been prepared with the following objectives

1. To know the different types and causes of environmental pollution.
2. To know the nature and indicators of environmental degradation.
3. To know the ways to prevent industrial pollution.
4. To study the current issue of global warming.

TYPES OF ENVIRONMENTAL POLLUTION

The different types of environmental pollution are given below:

Air Pollution: Air pollution is a broad term applied to any chemical, physical (e.g. particulate matter), or biological agent that modifies the natural characteristics of the atmosphere. The atmosphere is a complex, dynamic natural system that is essential to support life on planet earth. Stratospheric ozone depletion due to air pollution has long been recognized as a threat to human health as well as to the earth's ecosystems.

Water Pollution: Water pollution has a large set of adverse effects upon water bodies (lakes, rivers, oceans, ground water) caused by human activities. Although natural phenomena such as volcanoes, storms, earthquakes etc also cause major changes in water chemistry and the ecological status of water, these are not deemed to be pollution. Water pollution has many causes and characteristics. Humans and other farmed organisms produce bodily wastes which enter rivers, lakes, oceans and other surface waters. These wastes increase the solids suspended in the water (turbidity), they can increase the concentration of bacteria and viruses leading to potential health impacts.

Thermal Pollution: Thermal pollution is a temperature change in natural water bodies caused by human influence. The main cause of thermal pollution is the use of water as a coolant, specially in power plants, water uses as a coolant is returned to the natural environment at a higher temperature. Increases in water temperature can alter aquatic organisms by (a) decreasing oxygen supply, (b) killing fish juveniles which are vulnerable to small increases temperature and (c) affecting ecosystem composition.

Noise Pollution: Noise pollution is unwanted human-created sound that disrupts the environment. The dominant form of noise pollution is from transportation sources, principally motor vehicles, aircraft noise and rail transport noise. Other diverse sources are factories, amplified music, air conditioners, and construction work.

Soil Pollution: Soil sustains innumerable microbes and a large number of plants and animals along with plenty of mineral reserves for purposeful exploitation. Soil has different meaning to different people. Chemists consider the soil like an object endowed significantly with high buffering capacity while to a geologist, soil is a means for ascertaining the age of the earth from a large number of isotopes present in it.

REASONS FOR ENVIRONMENTAL POLLUTION

Natural Pollution: Nature causes air pollution enormously. Dust storms, dirt and debris into the air, natural forest fires cast a pall of smoke over mountain valleys, and lightening creates certain chemical compounds. The pollution from volcanoes is phenomenal. The Director of the United States Geological Survey states that only three eruptions in the last 150 years. Krakotoa in Java in 1883, Mt. Katmai in Alaska in 1912 and Hekla in Iceland in 1947 have produced more air pollution than mankind in all of history.

Population Explosion: Population explosion, characteristically called, the population bomb, is probably the biggest source of pollution. It is estimated that world population is doubling every thirty-five years. If existing rates continue, population of over three billion will be over six billion by the year 2000.

Standard of Living: Industrialization has raised the standard of living enormously. Increased standard of living act as a source of pollution. As people consume more, their consumption tends to create more wastes. The more elegant their tastes for food become, the more garbage and other refuge they produce. The more they buy, the more paper and packaging are required, most of which become refuge.

Deforestation: Forests are an essential part of the environment. They check soil erosion, counter floods and landslides, shelter vast variety of flora and fauna and cause rainfalls. The Chipko slogan best sums up the importance of forests. The slogan reads thus:

"What do the forests bear
soil water and pure air.
Soil, water and pure air
are the bases of life".

Vehicular Traffic: Damage to the environment caused by vehicular traffic is equally significant. Moving vehicles cause both air and noise pollution. Pollution of the air is the severest and there are agencies to monitor the magnitude of the problem.

Heavy Irrigation: Heavy irrigation schemes like canals and dams are pollutants. Water logging and increased salinity and alkalinity of soil are the manifestations of this type of pollution.

Agriculture: Agriculture also cause pollution. Dust from fallow field increased turbidity of run-off water, nitrate pollution of surface and ground water, pesticide pollution and water-logging are some of the forms of pollution arising out of agriculture.

Industry the Scapegoat: Unfortunately, the industry is held the scapegoat for disrupting ecology, though other agencies as explained earlier causes equal if not more damage to the environment.

NATURE OF ENVIRONMENTAL DEGRADATION

In many parts of the world, environmental degradation deterioration of the natural environment, including the atmosphere, bodies of water, soil, and forests is an important cause of poverty. Environmental problems have led to shortages of food, clean water, materials for shelter, and other essential resources. As forests, land, air, and water are degraded; people who live directly off these natural resources suffer most from the effects. People in developed countries, on the other hand, have technologies and conveniences such as air and water filters, refined fuels, and industrially produced and stored foods to buffer themselves from the effects of environmental degradation. Global environmental degradation may result from a variety of factors including overpopulation and the resulting overuse of land and other resources. Intensive farming, for instance, depletes soil fertility, thus decreasing crop yields. Environmental degradation also result from pollution. Polluting industries include mining, power generation, and chemical production. Other major sources of pollution include automobiles and agricultural fertilizers.

In developing countries, deforestation has had particularly devastating environmental effects. Many rural people, particularly in tropical regions, depend on forests as a source of food and other resources and deforestation damages or eliminate these supplies. Forests also absorb many pollutants and water from extended rains; without forests, pollution increases and massive flooding further decreases the usability of the deforested areas. Some indicators of environmental degradation in major agro ecological zones and urban areas (Jodha, 1991).

- Tropical dry lands sheet erosion, wind erosion (deflations) lowered water tables, ground water Stalinization growing prevalence of inferior annuals and thorny and woody shrubs (i.e. reduced availability of useful biomass), declining crop productivity, declining availability of common property resources.
- Mountain areas increased landslips, gully erosion, terrace abandonment, decline in species diversity in pastures and forests, substitution of cattle by sheep and goats, substitution of deep-rooted crops by shallow-rooted ones, persistent decline in agricultural productivity. Increased distance and time involved in gathering fodder and fuel wood increased seasonal migration reduced fallowing, intercropping and crop diversification.
- Tropical moist forests declining, species diversity decline, in forest area reduction in length and deterioration of vegetation composition of fallows, decline in useful species present in bush and fallow, gully erosion.
- Tropical wetlands decline in useful macrophytes through eutrophication, chemical pollution and presence of metals, soils drying and hardening of irrigated lands, water-logging, Stalinization, mining of productive soil components (organic matter, available macro and micro-nutrients).
- Rain fed cropland sheet and gully erosion, declining crop productivity, increased yield variability/increasing rainfall variability, increasing

crop disease and pest damage reduced fallowing, intercropping and crop diversification.

- In urban areas increased presence in human environment of pollutants and micro-organisms damaging health, specially excreata, increased presence of toxic wastes in air and water, declining availability of clean drinking water, decreased quality and increased overcrowding of housing.

WAYS OF PREVENTING INDUSTRIAL POLLUTION

There are basically three ways of preventing pollution.

Self Realization: As a part of the social responsibility of business, a businessman is expected to realize the need for maintaining a clean environment. Without being enforced, he should take all possible steps to prevent pollution. Examples are not lacking.

A 56 kms long effluent disposal channel is jointly set up in Baroda by the Indian Petrochemicals Corporation Ltd, Gujarat Refinery, Gujarat State Fertilizers Company, Nandesari Industrial Estate and small industrialists.

The Rs. 13 crore massive channel designed to carry 145 m litres of liquid waste and on the way, the effluents are treated before letting into the Arabian Sea. Earlier, they were dropped into the mini river polluting the water. The channels have been built voluntarily.

The Electroporcelains Division (EPD) of BHEL, Bangalore essentially deals with clay and therefore, generates lot of dust. Calcination and crushing of raw material generated dense smoke and heavy dust posing health hazards to the employees and people living around. Realizing their social responsibility, management sub contracted calcination and crushing to outsiders, hiked the materials cost by 10 per cent.

In the same plant, water with lot of slurry was let into open space earlier. Now the discharged water is treated before letting it into sewers. Foundry of the EPD also generates lot of dust. To prevent the dust from settling on neighbouring residential houses, management undertook a massive tree plantation programme around the foundry. In one year, about 1200 eucalyptus saplings were planted.

Environmental Movement: Environmental movement is a voluntary association formed to protect the environment from pollution. The movement took its birth in our country in 1968 and the genesis was settling the river Ganga ablaze by the effluents discharged into it by the Barauni Oil Refinery. Since then, the movement has grown in strength and as of today there are 54 voluntary organizations located in different parts of the country. The Chipko movement and save silent valley are the two major successes of the voluntary bodies. The other projects opposed are the controversial Tehri Dam in river Al Kananda, The Koel Karo and Suvernekha in Bihar, the Pollovaram in Andhra Pradesh, the Upper Indravati Project in Orissa and the Inchampalli and Bhopalpatnam dams on the borders of Maharashtra and Andhra Pradesh. The most important agitation against any development project seems to be the Sardar Sarovar Project across Narmada river.

Government Interference: The Govt. of India came out with a series of statutory provisions and fiscal incentives in order to protect the environment from industrial pollution.

Statutory Provisions

- The central government enacted the water (Prevention and Control of Pollution) Act, 1994. Under the Act, the Center and States (majority) have constituted centre and state boards for the prevention and control of water pollution. Land pollution is also covered by the Act.
- In 1997 the water (Prevention and Control of Pollution) Cess Act was enacted with a view to enable the pollution control boards to levy cess on the consumption of water by specific industries and local bodies at the rates specified in the schedule to the Act. The amount thus collected will be used by the boards to discharge their functions effectively.
- The Government of India enacted the Air (Prevention and Control of Pollution) Act in 1981 in order to control air pollution. Latest in the series is the comprehensive legislation called the Environment (Protection) Act, 1986. The main objective of the Act is to protect and improve the environment and the prevention of hazards to human beings, other living creatures, plant and property.
- Then there is the Dept. of Environment in Delhi, set up in 1980, where clearance is now made compulsory of any new industrial enterprise to be set up.
- Fiscal and financial incentives: With a view to encourage industrial units to undertake pollution control measures and to foster a clean environment, the Govt. of India has offered several fiscal incentives. Accordingly, fiscal sops in the form of tax exemption, depreciation allowances at increased rates, reduction in water cess etc. have been offered to industrial units which introduce pollution control devices.

GLOBAL POLLUTION AND THE WTO

As Jagadish Bhagwati explains very clearly, much of the analysis so far has been addressing what I called domestic pollution problems. But something must be said about global problems such as global warming, ozone layer depletion, acid rain, another cases where there are externalities for other countries—effects on them from what one country does within its own jurisdiction or in the global commons where no country has jurisdiction. Remember, however, that while these are global problems, they are not necessarily a consequence of globalization.

Thus the ozone layer gets depleted partly because people use aerosol cans, and global warming is intensified by the carbon-emitting belching of Indian cows and by the clearing of carbon absorbing forests, the latter often reflecting in part the traditional practice of slash and burn agriculture.

By now, many of the global environmental problems hav been addressed through negotiated treaties and conventions, typically described as multilateral environmental agreements (MEAs). They often have fewer parties than the WTO, the membership of which has steadily grown to over 145 today, with several others, including Russia, standing with hat in hand at the door. Several of these MEAs allows the use of trade restrictions against members, whom they describe as "Free riders". A good example of the former concerns the use of CFCs in refrigerators. This is a forbidden by the Montreal Protocol on substances that contribute to the depletion of the ozone layer. But if non members still use them, the signatories then want to be able to use trade sanctions against such non-members, the free riders.

GLOBAL WARMING

Troposphere, the lowermost layer of the atmosphere, traps heat by a natural process due to the presence of certain gases. This effect is called green house effect as it is similar to the warming effect observed in the horticultural green house made of glass. The amount of heat trapped in the atmosphere depends mostly in the concentrations of "heat trapping" or "green house" gases and the length of time they stay in the atmosphere, the major green house gases are carbon dioxide, ozone, methane, nitrous oxide, chlorofluoro carbons(CFC) and water vapours.

The average global temperature is 15°C. in the absence of green house gases this temperature would have been -18° C. Therefore, greenhouse effect contributes a temperature rise to the tune of 33° C. heat trapped by green house gases in the atmosphere keeps the planet warm enough to allow us and other species to exist.

The two predominant green house gases are water vapours, which are controlled by hydrological cycle, and carbon dioxide, which is controlled mostly by the global carbon cycle. While the levels of water vapour in the troposphere have relatively remained constant, the levels of carbon dioxide have increased. Other gases whose levels have increased due to human activities are methane, nitrous oxide and chlorofluoro carbons. Deforestation has further resulted in elevated levels of carbon dioxide due to non-removal of carbon dioxide by plants through photosynthesis.

Warming or cooling by more than 2°C over the past few decades may prove to be disastrous for various ecosystems on the earth including humans, as it would alter the conditions faster than some species could adapt or migrate. Some areas will become inhabitable because of drought or floods following a rise in average sea level.

CONCLUDING REMARKS

For the welfare of mankind in every respect, a proper lively and pollution free atmosphere should be available. This is possible only in the case when people are getting better surroundings for living with all the amenities available with a proper planning of water, drainage, electricity and gas and of course free space available for gardening and plantation and thereby taking the indirect benefit of pollution free climate.

Government should take up the public awareness programme by educating people for all sorts of age groups right from child to an elder generation for better living environment. In addition to that, either government should seek help from the private sector or all the private sector sources should come forward for creating better environment for better living by helping in every way.

A thought of public transport by railway running on electricity should be enhanced fully. Instead of transport facility increase by means of road, the fuel required for road transport comprises petrol and diesel which consequently develop pollution by means of smoke hot scattering in the atmosphere.

Today, ethanol is a best option as a bio-fuel to reduce vehicular pollution. According to Pramod Chaudhri, Chairman of Praj Industries Ltd and Chairman of the CII, National Bio-Fuels Committee in his own words, "Ethanol is the most widely used bio-fuel in the world. Thanks to technological advances, the cost of producing and processing it has come down. Brazil has replaced petrol-only engines with engines that use pure ethanol or a 78:22 petrol-ethanol blend. The shift has benefited Brazil environmentally and economically. Ethanol, one of the best tools to fight vehicular pollution, contains 35 per centoxygen that helps complete combustion of fuels, thus reducing tailpipe emissions".

Concluding the subject of industrialization and its positive and negative effects on society and atmosphere would be something like this to meet the evergrowing demand of the people because of continuous increase in population, sufficient steps should be taken on industrial grounds which should be properly planned taking into consideration of safety, pollution free atmosphere so that the climate/atmosphere shall be without pollution which is the basic need of mankind.

Dignitaries engaged in the various fields, scientists and world leaders are worried about the global warming which is increasing with a superfast speed because of the negligence of industrialist for taking proper action and to the great extent of government machineries which are not emphasizing the law connected to environmental technology.

REFERENCES

Madhu Raj, Dictionary of Environmental Economics, Published by Ivy Publishing House, Delhi-110095, p. 115.

Madhu Raj, Dictionary of Environmental Economics, Published by Ivy Publishing House, Delhi-110095, p. 104.

Prof. Anubha Kaushik and Prof C.P. Kaushik, Perspectives in Environmental Studies (2nd edition), New Age International Pvt. Ltd., Publishers (formerly WILEY

Eastern Ltd.) New Delhi, Bangalore, Chennai, Cochin, Guwahati, Hyderabad, Jallandhar, Calcutta, Lucknow, Mumbai, Ranchi, p. 123.

S. P. Mishra, Environmental Pollution, Avishkar Publishers & Distributors, Jaipur-302003 (Raj), India,p. 27, 28, 32, 33, 39, 41.

P. R. Trivedi, Encyclopedia of Environment, Pollution, Planning and Conservation (A set of 6 volumes) (Environmental Education Volume 5), p. 154.

K. Aswathappa, Essentials of Business Environment, Himalaya Publishing House, Mumbai, Delhi, Nagpur, Bangalore, Hyderabad (8th edition), p. 618-623.

K. Aswathappa, Essentials of Business Environment, p. 627-629.

Abhijit Dutta, Sunita Dutta and P.N. Pandey, Environmental Economics, Published by Kulbhushan Nangia, APH Publishing Corporation, 5, Ansari Road, Dharyaganj, New Delhi-110002, p. 144-95.

Jagdish Bhagwati, In Defence of Globalization, Published by Manzar Khan, Oxford University Press, YMCA Library Building, Jaysingh Road, New Delhi-110001, p. 158-59.

Prof. Anubha Kaushik and Prof C. P. Kaushik, Perspectives in Environmental Studies, p. 179-180.

Pramod Chaudhari (2008), An Article on 'The Bio-fuel Option', *Business India*, April 20, p. 122.

CHAPTER-11

WTO AND LABOUR STANDARDS

S. N. YOGISH

THROUGHOUT the 1990s, both International Labour Organization (ILO) decision making bodies and World Trade Organization (WTO) agenda -setting meetings extensively debated whether and how trade policy should address issues of labour standards. In the WTO labour standards were debated in Ministerial Conferences in Punta del Este in 1986 and in Marrakesh in 1994. The debate became especially heated in the last two ministerial meetings in Singapore and Seattle in 1996 and 1999 respectively. Since 1994 a working party in the ILO Governing Body on the social dimension of the Liberalization of International Trade has debated how the ILO, in an international economy increasingly subject to market forces that frequently denigrated labour rights, should protect and promote core labour standards—i.e., the rights to freedom of association and collective bargaining, the prevention of child and forced labour, and the outlawing of discrimination.

The debate has sharply divided WTO member governments between developed and developing countries. The latter claim that any policy or institutional linkages between trade and labour standards would be a slippery scope to protectionism. The U.S has been the most vocal developed country to argue that linkages exist and to propose that they need to be recognized and dealt with the WTO.

Developed country support for the U.S. position on a working party in the WTO has varied. Belgium, France, and Norway have consistently proposed similar WTO agendas. Germany under the Christian Democrats has been unhelpful, and the United Kingdom was not enthusiastic about any EU proposal at the Seattle ministerial conference regarding WTO involvement in labour standards.

Developing country opposition to U.S proposals is more unified and is reinforced by strong legal arguments to the effect that the WTO does not have the competence to deal with labour standards. Developing countries contend that:

1. The WTO is a commercial contract based on rules and disciplines governing commercial activity and free and fair trade; it is not based on judgments about other aspects of member states domestic policies, including worker rights and other non trade issues. Its rules aim to discipline the use of trade measures and reduce barriers to trade. Member states are free to conduct their domestic policies in whatever way they see fit.
2. To introduce judgments about member countries domestic policy choices into the WTO would fundamentally change the legal nature of the agreements. In this regard, Article xx refers to the protection of conditions in the importing country. Introducing labour standards would undermine existing, most notably negotiated rights to market access, without introducing reciprocal obligations.

Developing countries have also thus far succeeded in staunching the establishment of a working group on labour standards by claiming that it is motivated by protectionist demands in the United States. Developing countries, especially the least developed, who see their low labour costs as essential to their export competitiveness, give considerable credibility to this charge. Beyond their legal arguments, they contend that U.S and EU use of antidumping measures—permitted in the WTO when intended to prevent the sale of imports at prices lower than the costs of production—are abused and become essentially protectionist measures. These charges were aggravated by president Clinton's statement of demonstrators in Seattle that ultimately sanctions could be used, in dire circumstances, to enforce core labour standards.

CORE LABOUR STANDARDS AND THE WORLD TRADE ORGANIZATION

A sharp divide between developed and developing countries on the relationship between core labour standards and the international trade rules played an important role in the failure of the 1999 Seattle ministerial conference of the World trade Organization (WTO). In the post-Seattle debate on the future of the international trading system, labour standards, environment and human rights have become known as the 'trade and agenda' Developed countries face domestic pressures from labour unions, environmentalists, social action groups, and churches among others to expand the use of trade rules to meet broad public policy goals. Developing countries reject this agenda as a blatant attempt to impose the values and norms of developed countries as a condition of participating in international trade. The result is a debate with no center. Until a consensus emerges on the effective treatment of the trade and agenda, especially on labour issues, either within world trade rules or through the strengthening of the rules and institutions on global governance more generally, the prospects of launching a new round of multilateral trade negotiations will remain weak.

The debate over the incorporation of labour obligations in to the WTO has fed long-standing anxieties in developed countries about the impact of international trade on employment and incomes. During the public debate on the Canada- US free trade Agreement in the 1980s, unions and their supporters argued vociferously that Canadian workers could not compete against the allegedly low-cost, non-union jurisdictions of the united states, especially in the south.

Advocates of incorporating an obligation to respect core labour standards into the WTO find powerful ammunition in the inclusion of an Intellectual Property chapter in the WTO. Indeed, there is a plausible argument that prior to the WTO, Intellectual property rules and institutions, notably the WIPO and the Paris and Berne conventions, bore a strong resemblance to the weakness, especially of enforcement mechanisms, of the international rules and institutions on labour rights.

THE ROLE OF THE ILO

The ILO was the first international organization to be created after world war one, predating the League of Nations. It has four main functions: it passes resolutions or international economic and social policies, it provides technical assistance to member governments, employers, and workers' organizations; it writes conventions setting out minimum labour standards; and it reviews compliance with ILO conventions through an adjudication process. The ILO has a unique tripartite governance structure consisting of representatives of governments, employers and worker representatives. Its principal bodies are the annual legislative conference, a governing council of 56 members, and a secretariat in Geneva.

The ILO is best known for the adoption of conventions on labour standards, which now number 183. The conventions are binding, of course only on those countries, which ratify them. In many countries, including Canada, the basic intent of a convention will be reflected in law and practice but the convention may not be ratified because of inconsistency with constitutional or legal Practices or the failure to provide exceptions to reflect local preferences. This has proven to be a serious problem in federal countries, which assign some or all labour issues to sub-national levels of Government, which are under no constitutional or political obligation to conform to the treaties signed by the national government. Although some progress has been made in recent years in increasing the number of countries ratifying the conventions, as of June 2000, only just one-third of the ILO member countries have ratified all the conventions.

In 1998, the ILO adopted a Declaration of Fundamental Principals and Rights at work. The Declaration stated that all members of the ILO, even if they not ratified the conventions in question, have an obligation arising from membership to respect promote, and realize the principle of those conventions. These are: freedom of association and the effective recognition of the right to collective bargaining; the elimination of all forms of forced or compulsory labour, he effective abolition of child labour, and the elimination of discrimination is respect of employment and occupation . The follow-up procedures require all member countries, which have not ratified one or more of the eight conventions associated with these rights to report annually on their efforts to promote the principles of the Declaration.

The ILO has a variety ot measures to monitor application of its conventions, including performance by its members. Regular supervision is based on ratification of conventions and their associated obligation to provide regular, periodic reports on measures taken. Special systems provide for examination of complaints by employers or workers organizations concerning alleged failure by a country to apply a convention it has ratified. An ILO committee (the committee of experts on the application of conventions and Recommendations) reviews both reports each year and reports to the Annual conference. The conference examines individual complains and may invite governments to explain how it is complying with its obligation under the relevant conventions. There is also a process to review performance by members under ungratified conventions. For all this elaborate procedure, the ILO tools are limited to 'sunshine and carrots', the former being exposure of labour practices country of ILO conventions and the latter the provision of technical assistance to help countries with compliance.

The pressure to build a labour standards obligation into international trade rules derives from the perceived failure of the ILO tools to secure practical enforcement of its conventions. In the early years of the ILO, there was some support for the use of economic sanctions in enforcement actions. Under its original procedures a commission of enquiry was empowered to propose economic measures against a government, which defaulted on its obligations. No such recommendations were ever made. Over the years, the ILO has been hesitant in promoting the incorporation of a social clause in trade agreements, In part, this reticence stems from the tripartite governance structure, making consensus difficult to achieve, and in part due to the emphasis upon cooperation and conciliation. Most developing country governments and many of the workers representatives from these countries have been strongly opposed to any such linkage and employers groups from almost all countries have resisted such linking as well.

The discussion of a social clause was taken up in the 1990s in the face of pressure on the ILO to contribute to the debate. In 1994, the Governing Body engaged in open discussion of the issue for the first tomes. The Director-General stated that the ILO should not advocated restrictions on trade nor the harmonization of social costs since both would be contrary to the premises of the ILO, that free trade contributes to economic development and that the ILO traditions is to rely on cooperation, not coercion. Subsequently, he suggested that acceptance of the ILO conventions on freedom of association and collective bargaining, which are the most widely ratified ILO conventions, could be made a condition for membership in the new WTO. Following the 1994 conference, the Governing Body established a working party to discuss all relevant aspects of the social dimensions of international trade. The report prepared by the Secretariat, ' the social Dimensions of International Trade', rejected the concept of the equalization of social costs and pointed out that while trade liberalization presupposes a level of harmonization, equalization of wages and social protection should not be an end in itself. The working paper then proceeded to a wide-ranging discussion of possible means for including a social dimension in the GATT/WTO. He working paper suggested that the ILO complaints procedures could be used to determine violations of the obligations of the standards. If under these procedures, a violation were found, it would be for the WTO member to take appropriate action.

Other than launching a series of studies on the implications of globalization and trade liberalization for the achievement of the ILO's social objectives, no action was taken on the report. In the 1998 Declaration, the members reiterated their long standing view that 'labour standards should not be used for protectionist trade purposes and that the comparative advantage of any country should in no way be called into question by the declaration. Any move by the ILO to search for a role in applying trade sanctions thus seems unlikely for the foreseeable future.

TRADE AND LABOUR STANDARDS

Currently, labour standards are not subject to WTO rules and disciplines. But some WTO member governments in Europe and North America believe that the issue must be taken up by the WTO and the global trading systems are to be strengthened. These member governments argue that the rights such as, the freedom to bargain collectively, freedom of association, elimination of discrimination is the work place and the elimination workplace abuse, are matters for consideration in the WTO. Several member governments have suggested that the issue be brought into the WTO through the formulation of a working group to study the issue of trade and core labour standards. Bringing the matter to the WTO. These member governments believe, will incentives for WTO member governments to improve conditions for workers around the world.

Most developing countries and many developed nations believe the issue of core labour standards does not belong in the WTO. These member governments see the issue of trade and labour standards as a guise for protectionism in developed-country markets. Developing-country officials have that efforts to bring labour standards into the WTO represent a smokescreen for undermining the comparative advantage of lower-wage developing countries.

Many officials in developing countries argue that better working conditions and improved labour rights arise through economic growth. They say that if the issue of core labour standards became enforceable under WTO rules, only sanctions imposed against countries with lower labour standards would merely perpetuate poverty and delay improvements in workplace standards.

The issue of trade and labour standards has been with the WTO since its birth. At the Ministerial conference of he General Agreement on Tariffs and Trade held in Marrakesh in April 1994 to sign the treaty than formed the WTO, merely all ministers expressed a point of view on the issue. the chairman of that conference concluded there was no consensus among member governments at the time, and thus no basis for government on the issue.

ILO member Governments argued to respect and promote this core convention even if they have not ratified all of them. As a follow-up the ILO will issue annual reports in which ILO officials obtain information from governments, which have not ratified also f the conventions on any changes that may have taken place in national laws or regulations and which may impact these fundamental labour rights.

In 1999, ILO member governments agreed to prohibit and eliminate the worst forms of child labour, member governments defined the worst forms of child labour as all forms of slavery, child prostitution and pornography, the use of children to traffic in drags and work which is likely to harm the health, safety or morals of children.

ILO member governments said they recognized that child labour is largely a function of poverty and that the long- term solution to elimination of exploitative and harmful child labour is through sustained economic growth.

A recent World Bank study estimated that less than 5% of child workers in the developing world are involved in export related activities.

CONCLUSION

Much of the current discussion about incorporating labour rules into the WTO proceeds on the basis of functional rather than substantive analysis and thus misses the central issue. It is, of course, possible to graft labour rules onto the WTO and make them enforceable through the dispute settlement mechanism. There is no serious procedural obstacle to expanding the interpretations of existing trade rules to justify the application of trade actions to violators of over loading the WTO with new tasks but such risks were faced and overcome in the expansion of the WTO into new areas such as services, intellectual property, and investment.

International discussion should terms to ways and means of strengthening the ILO. Charnowintz (1995) discusses a variety of approaches including the establishment of standing ILO bodies is forced labour and child labour, the pronunciation of social labeling programmes, and the development of codes of conduct. These and other like approaches warrant close examinations before the WTO is embarked upon a fruitless and damaging quest for a role in the enforcement of labour standards.

REFERENCES

Chairman of the Trade Negotiations countries of the multinational Trade Negotiations of the Uruguay Round at Marrakesh, GATT Doc. MTN. TNC/ MIN (94) 16 (April 15. 1994).

E. A. Londay (1996), 'The effectiveness of International Supervision: Thirty Years of ILO experience (lobour: Stevens and Sons, 178.

Gary Hufbaner and Jeffery J. Schote (1993), NAFTA; An Assesment (Washingtons: Institute for International Economics.

J. T. Shotwell, (ed.) (1934), The origins of the International Labour Organizations (New York: Colembia University Prek, Vol. II Documents 37 and 47.

Kimberly Ann Elliote (2000), 'The ILO and Enforcement of Core Labour Standards', International Economic Policy Briefs, Institute of International Economics, July.

Martin Khor (1997), "The WTO and the Battle over Labour Standards", Third World Network Features, Jannuary 13, pp. 1-4.

W. A. Dymand, (Springs 2001), Canadian Foreign Policy ISSN 1192-6422, Vol. 8, No. 3, pp. 99-114.

Chapter-12

WTO AND INTELLECTUAL PROPERTY RIGHTS

S. N. Yogish

The subject of Intellectual Property Rights (IPRs) has assumed significance in global trade. The term " Intellectual Property" as a subject is growing in importance in a developing country like ours.

Intellectual Property enjoys Protection within a country under specific rights given by the national laws of the purpose. Thus intellectual property Rights (IPRs) are subject to territorial limitations. The IPRs available within a country are not automatically extendable within a country are not automatically extendable to another country if no agreement exists between the two countries in that respect. If laws for IPRs were substantially different from one country to another, the flow of technology and intellectual resources/property would be severely impeded, which in time would gravely undermine the economic growth and development. The owners and creators of intellectual wealth would be reluctant to send their wares to a country, which would be lax in safeguarding their interests.

OBJECTIVES

The important objectives are,

- Discuss the initiative taken at the Paris convention.
- Explain the Provisions of the Patent cooperation Treaty.
- Understand the role of WIPO.
- Discuss the agreement on the Trade Related Aspects of Intellectual Property Rights (TRIPs of WTO).

PARIS CONVENTION

The Paris convention constitutes a union of member countries for the protection of industrial property (patents, utility modes, industrial designs, trademarks, and service marks, trade names, indications of source or appellations of origin and the repressions of unfair competition). A utility model is an invention that is new and useful but fails to quality for patent protection. In several countries, including France, Italy, Germany, Japan, Korea, Taiwan and Brazil, such small inventions of demonstrable practicability can be protected, without the rigorous examination required for the subject matter of a patent, for a period, generally the years or less. A trade name is the name of an enterprise. The Paris convention stands for three basic principles:

1. ***National Treatment*:** Nationals of any country of the Union shall enjoy, in another country of the union, the same treatment as that other country extends to its own nationals in respects of the protection of industrial property.
2. ***Independence of Patents*:** Patent applied for by a national of a member country of the union, in other countries of the union, is independent of patent obtained fort the same invention in any other country. It does not matter whether the country where the patent has been granted is a member of the union or not.
3. ***Right to Priority*:** If a national of a member country of the union has applied for patent in a union country, he can claim the same priority date for application in any other country or countries of the union for the same invention as for the first application, provided the subsequent applications are made within a period of twelve months from the filling of the first application.

The last revision of the Paris Convention in 1967 also led to the establishment of an international organization for administering and fostering intellectual property, called as the World Intellectual Property Organization (WIPO).

THE WORLD INTELLECTUAL PROPERTY ORGANIZATION

The world Intellectual Property Organization (WIPO) is one of the specialized agencies of the United Nations (UN) system of Organizations. The convention establishing the World Intellectual Property Organization was signed at Stockholm in 1967and entered into force in 1970. However, the origins of WIPO go back to 1883 and 1886, with the adoption of the Paris convention and the Berne convention respectively. Both of these conventions Provided for the establishment of international secretariats, and both were placed under the supervision of the Swiss Federal Government. The few officials who were needed to carry out the administration of the two conventions were located in Berne, Switzerland.

Long before the United Nations was established, BIRPI was the responsible intergovernmental organization in the field of intellectual property. WIPO, the successor to BIRPI, became a specialized agency of the United Nations when an agreement was signed to that effect between the United Nations and WIPO, which came into effect on December 17, 1974.

MISSION AND ACTIVITIES

The mission of WIPO is to promote through international cooperation the creation, dissemination, use and protection of works of the human mind for the economic, cultural and social progress of all mankind. Its effect is to contribute to a balance between the stimulation of creativity world wide, by sufficiently protecting the moral and material interests of creators, on the one hand and the provision of access to the socio-economic and cultural benefits of such creativity world wide, on the other hand.

ADMINISTRATION

The convention establishing WIPO provides for four different organs: The General Assembly, the Conference, the Coordination Committee, the International Bureau of WIPO or Secretariat.

The General Assembly consists of all the states, which are members of WIPO and also of any of the unions. The conference consists of all the states, which are members of the WIPO. The General Assembly is the supreme organ of WIPO. Among its other powers and functions, the General Assembly appoints the Director General upon nomination by the Coordination Committee, it reviews and approves the reports and activities of the Coordination Committee as well as the reports of the Director General concerning WIPO; it adopt the financial regulations of WIPO and the biennial budget of expenses common to the unions; it approves the measures proposed by the Director General concerning the administration of the international agreements designed to promote the protection of intellectual property; it determines the working languages of the Secretariat taking into consideration the practice of the United Nations, and it also determines which states not members of WIPO and which intergovernmental and international non-Governmental organizations shall be admitted to its meetings as observes. The fourth organ of WIPO is the Secretariat. The Director General heads it.

MEMBERSHIP

The convention establishing WIPO declares that membership shall be open to any state which is a member of any of the unions, and to any state which is not a member of the any unions, provided that it is a member of the United Nations, of any of the specialized agencies of the United Nations, or of the International Atomic Energy agency, or is a party to the statute of the international court of justice or is invited by the General Assembly of WIPO to become a member. Thus, only states can be members of WIPO or, indeed, of any other specialized agency of the United Nations.

THE IPRs AND INDIA

It is a well-known fact that the role of Intellectual Property (IP) protection has expanded at an unprecedented pace during the last two decades. In the process IPRs have been modified or new provisions have been created in order to cover new areas of Science and Technology, such as Information Technology, Biotechnology, and now service sector. It may be observed that World Trade Organization (WTO) agreement on Trade-Related Aspects of Intellectual Property Rights (TRIPs) has extended minimum standards for IP Protection globally. There are continuing discussions in World Intellectual Property Organization (WIPO) aimed at further harmonization of the patent system. Moreover, agreements between Developed and Developing countries also include mutual commitments to implement IP regimes that go beyond TRIPs minimum standards. Hence, India is under pressure to increase the levels of IP protection in our own regime, based on standards in developed countries.

In one dimension it is observed that IPRs help stimulate economic growth and reduce poverty in developed countries, but the same concept may not do the same in developing countries. However, IP rights can do little to stimulate inventions in countries like India. The ownership of intellectual property is a crucial issue that impacts market position and profitability of industries. India is realizing this fact and this is evident from India's number 3 position in Patent Cooperation Treaty (PCT) filings and its highest growth rate of 50% in the segment of developing countries. The changes in the IPR regime have necessitated technological self-reliance, as borrowing of technology from developed countries will no longer be economically viable.

Our country is rich in genetic resources and traditional knowledge, which are of great value to us and to the world at large but we lack desired efforts to protect and exploit them. Historically, developed countries used IP protection as a flexible instrument to help promote their industrialization. Strong evidence suggests that certain types of companies in developed countries, particularly the pharmaceutical industry, consider IPR as essential in promoting innovation.

INTELLECTUAL PROPERTY (IP)

IP as a general term refers to subject matter of the laws that give rise to proprietary interests in creations of the mind. That is, it refers to intangibles that arise and derive their intrinsic value out of innovative or creative activities. The various tools of IPR that are used to protect innovations are copyrights, industrial Designs, Data protection, Geographical indications, patent and Trademark.

COPYRIGHT

It is concerned with protection of creative works that are musical, literary, artistic, lectures, plays, art reproductions, models, photographs, computer software, etc. It is valid for the lifetime of the author and minimum 50 years after the death of the author. The 1999 amendments have made the Copyright Act fully compatible with Trade- Related Aspects of Intellectual Property Rights (TRIPs) Agreement. With these amendments the Indian copyright law has become one of the most modern copyright laws in the world.

PATENT

It pertains to pragmatic innovations and aims to protect inventions that are novel, non- obvious and useful. Patents are given only for inventions. Inventions are solutions to specific problems in the field of technology. An Invention may relate to a product or a process. Patents have a term of 20 years from the date of filling a complete specification.

TRADEMARK

It is related to commercial symbols and concern to protect distinctive mark, such as words/signs including personal names, letters, numerals, figurative elements (logos); devices, visually perceptible two or three dimensional signs/ shapes or their combinations audible signs.

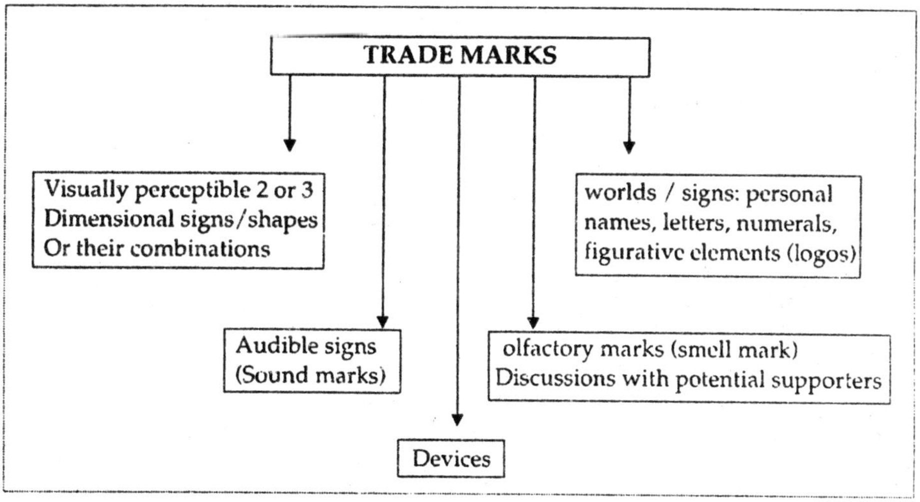

FIGURE 1: Components of Trademark

Some countries have also registered sounds and distinctive smells as trademarks. It can be perpetually renewed from time to time.

The latest amendments also include the concept of 'service marks'. Service marks are trademarks used in the services sector like hotels, education, airlines and IT enabled services.

Industrial Designs

It protects novel non-functional features of shape, configuration, pattern, ornamentation or composition of lines or colours, applied to any article either two or three dimensional or in both forms by any industrial process or means whether manual, mechanical or chemical, separate or combined which in the finished article appeal to and are judged solely by the eye. This registration has a specific term (initially 10 years renewable for another term of 10years).

Geographical Indications (GI): Geographical Indications of goods are defined as that aspect of industrial property, which refers to the country or to a place of origin of that product. The term is renewed perpetually. Before the TRIPs GI was not protected in India.

DATA PROTECTION

Concerning pharmaceutical and agricultural lest data, it is related to protection of undisclosed information such as strategies and trade secrets.

Discussion on various components/tools of IPR that are used to protect innovations won't be complete without a discussion on the way the ideas have converted into intellectual property and the way they can be efficiently managed–the process flow of mined to market.

Seven phases in the process of converting innovations/creative activities to intellectual property, thereby effectively converting them to intellectual assets that have a potential and realizable value, are shown in Figure 2.

Conversion of Concepts and Ideas to Intellectual Property

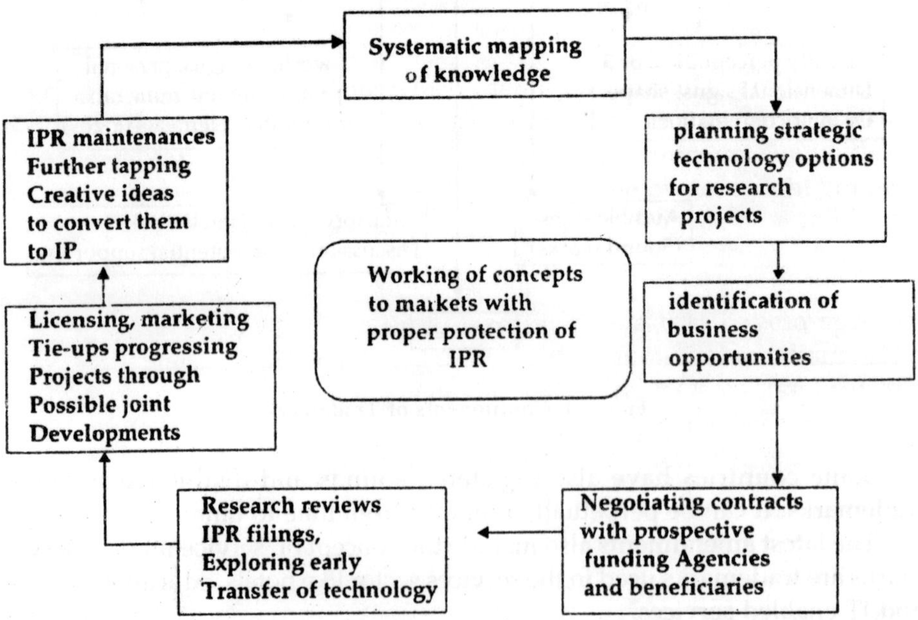

FIGURE 2: Representation of the Process of Flow of Mind to Market, with Proper Protection of IPR.

PATENTING IN TEXTILES

The present study mainly pertains to machinery and devices used in textile manufacture. Patent applications filed and as published in the Gazette of India part III.

FILINGS BY INDIANS AND INDIAN COMPANIES

The major players in this area are foreign companies of the total 470 applications filed in the area of textile machinery only 74 were filed by the Indian individuals and Indian companies, which constitute just 16% of the total applications filed. Major Indian players, who have filed patent applications, are listed in the Table 1.

Table 1

Indian Company	*No. of Applications*
Indian jute Industries Research Association	6
Lakshmi machine works Ltd.	5
Ahmedabad Textile Industry's Research Association (ATIRA)	4
Star spin and Twist Machines Ltd.	4
Central silk Technological Research Institute	3
Indian council of Agricultural Research (ICAR)	2
Indian card clothing co Ltd.	2
South Indian Textile Research Association (SITRA)	2

The central coir Research institute, Indian precision Bearing manufacturing Ltd. Indian Institute of Science, North Indian Textile Research Association (NITRA) and Electronic Research Development Corporation (ERDC) all have filed a single application each during this period

FILINGS BY FOREIGNERS AND FOREIGN COMPANIES

Foreigners and foreign companies filed 396 applications, which constitute 84% of the total filings. The companies filing more than ten applications are listed in Table 2.

Table 2

Company	*No. of Applications*
Machinen fabrik Rieter AG	54
Wschlafhorst AG & Co.	22
Zellweger Luwa AG	16
Barnag AG	15
Kinberly clark corp	14
Trutzschler GMBH and co KG	11
Roeter Ingolstade	13

Areas in which most patent applications have been filed are given in Table 3 along with the number of applications filed.

Table 3

Subject	*Patent applications*
Spinning (machine, devices, rings, frames, wet spinning, dry spinning)	128
Yarn manufacture	49
Guiding units (yarn winding, feeding, take-up devices)	48
Quality control devices	39
Fibre (treatment, identification improvement)	35
Knitting machines	23
Webs	22
Thermal treatment of fibre/yarn cooling device	12
Weaving looms (including circular looms)	7
Carding machine	6
Screen printing machine	5
Cabler machine	4
Others	84

The patent applications included in the others category include a variety of sub areas in the field of textile manufacturing.

IMPORTANCE OF INTELLECTUAL PROPERTY

Intellectual property protection is the key factor for economic growth and advancement in the high technology sector. They are good for business benefit the public at large and act as catalysts for technical progress. Whether IPRs are a good or bad thing; the developed world has come to an accommodation with them over a long period. Even if their disadvantages sometimes outweigh their advantages, by and large the developed world has the national economic strength and established legal mechanisms to overcome the problems so caused. Insofar as their benefits outweigh their disadvantages, the developed world has the wealth and infrastructure to take advantage of the opportunities provided. It is likely that neither of these holds true for developing the least developed countries. (Extracts from Report on Commission on IPR London September 2002).

IPR MAINTENANCE AND FURTHER DEVELOPMENT

IPR has to be renewed from time to time to ensure the protection of the rights from any infringement. Companies should expand their programmes of IP-related technical assistance and raise the additional finances if required. Also, the system for monitoring and evaluation of IP-related development should be made stronger.

MULTI–PRONGED–FRAME WORK FOR EFFECTIVE CREATION AND MANAGEMENT OF IPRS

Co-ordination of the R & D activities of all units of a company is very important particularly in a manufacturing company. Proper co-ordination of process is required in the case of service sector. This objective can be achieved to a greater extent by effectively managing intellectual property rights information system (IPR-IS), because a large part of IP related work is document intensive and involves laborious tasks. Hence, significant amounts of IP work likePatent drafting; search, analysis, prosecution and litigation support can be made easy by proper documentation and maintenance of such documents.

Creation and management of IP require a customized internal system plan based on the following framework.

Planning /Requirement analysis
• Planning for intellectual property • Planning or up gradation of IP Infrastructure • Defining internal polices • Through knowledge of National IP policy. and IP Legislation. • Patent search, and analysis • Developing strategic framework for IP creation &
Management
• Cost-benefit Analysis • Identifying potential Donors and other sources. • Schedule of above activities • Strategy
Organizing
• IP committees for Research, Project Management and Audit. • Organizing of Information systems such as Decision support system, expert system, and artificial intelligence. • Technology options, Strategic options • Technical assistance team or Tie-ups with expert group. • Alert checks
Execution and coordination of activities related to
• Research • Formulation • Testing and pre-implementations • Implementation • Audit trail
Controlling IP
• Maintenance of IP • Protection of IP • Development of IP • Audit trail

FIGURE 4: Representation of the Phases in Creation and Management of IP.

EFFECTIVE UTILIZATION OF IPR INFORMATION

Effective utilization of IPR information is an organization is very important. As represented in Figure 5, database is created based the facts and events happening in the process of creation and management of IPR, such created database when further processed, becomes information. Regular updating of IPR-IS (Intellectual Property Rights Information System) will ensure not only accurate, up-to-date, and valid information but also helps in taking accurate and prompt decisions.

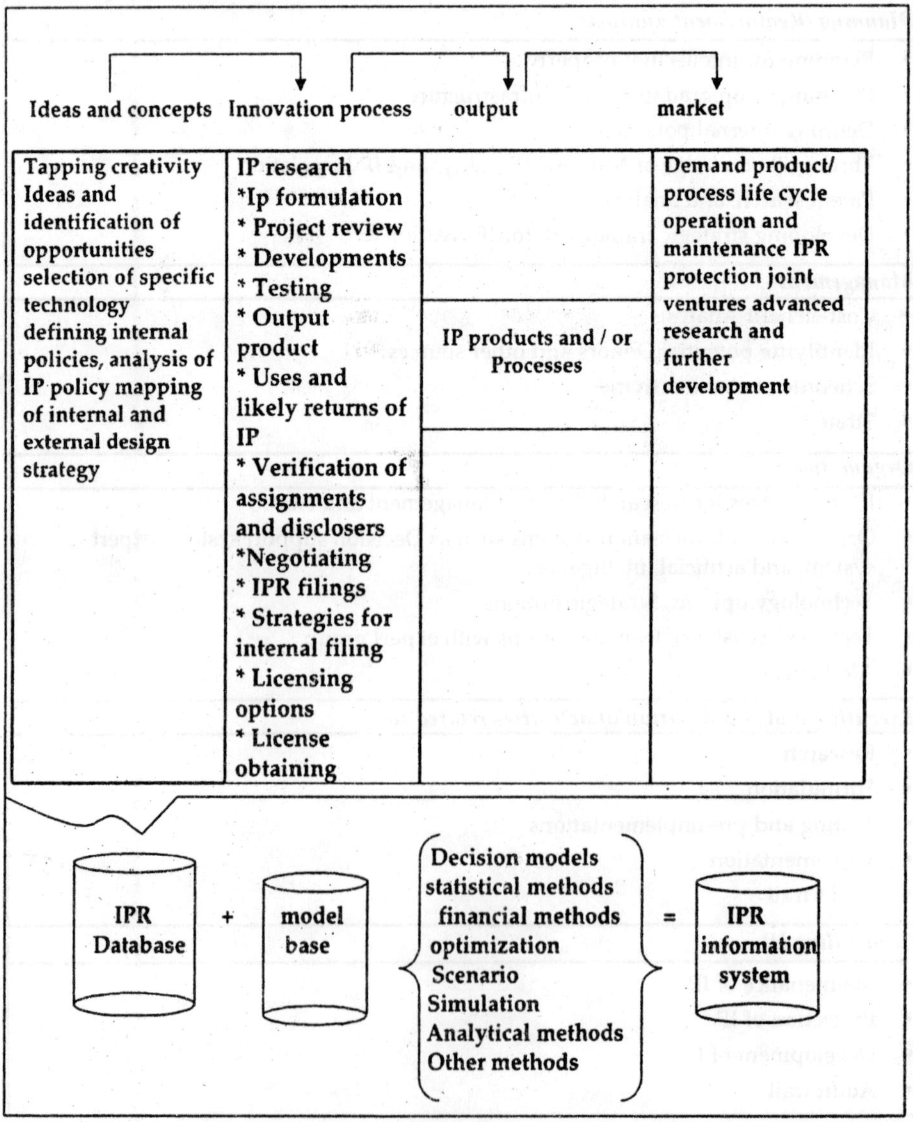

FIGURE 5: Intellectual Property Rights Management

THE FUTURE OF WTO

WTO members are on schedule as far as meeting deadlines set by the TRIPs agreement developed countries met their 1996 deadline, and almost all the developing nations completed implementation by their deadline, January 1, 2000. As part of implementation, WTO members have established laws protecting various forms of intellectual property, including copyrights, geographical indications, integrated circuit layouts and patents. They also have established formal judicial channels to enforce IPRs and legislated penalties to deter potential violations. WTO members have also created national intellectual property regimes that are controversial in that they involve substantial administrative changes and costs. Least-developed countries, have been granted an extended deadline; they must implement the agreement by 2005, but are exempt from applying patent protection to some pharmaceuticals until 2016.

CONCLUSION

There is a distinct set of issues that arises in management, maintenance and protection of IPR. Here, it is a challenge to design and operate institutional innovation processes that would preserve intellectual excellence and at the same time amicably fit into a disciplined formal IPR management system.

- Indian industries and R & D institutes have not really excelled in the area of innovation due to various factors. But new IP-regime sounds really encouraging.
- Form the intuitional point of view, the major challenge is to develop and train techno legal manpower to mange critical issues in management of IPR.
- Government must think of setting-up required number of advisory body/council in order to render services regarding IPR information, protection, and further development.
- With growing pharmaceutical, software and entertainment industries, India has much to gain from implementing a more robust IPR regime. Increased intellectual property protection would boost bilateral trade and investment with the United States. Hi-tech trade and collaborative research and development are growing, but there is a need to do it faster.

REFERENCES

Mrs. A. Santhosh Kumari and Dr. Raghunatha Reddy, JNT University, Hyderabad, p. 725-732.

WTO Web Pages Dedicated to TRIPs News, License Announcements, and Relevant Texts.

"A Gift Bound in Red Tape", Statement by NGO's about TRIPS Agreement, September 10,2003.

WTO Voted to by Pass Patents on Medicines; Cheap Generics go to Poor nations", Washington Post, August 31, 2003.

"Drugs, Patents, and the WTO: Symptomatic Relief," Economist, September 4, 2003.

Vandana Vaidya, "Intellectual Property Rights", A Boon to Indian Companies", pp. 1-3.

CHAPTER-13

SOLID WASTE MANAGEMENT

A. VINAYAGAMOORTHY

INTRODUCTION

SOLID waste management is a planned system of effective control of the production, storage. Collection, transportation, processing and disposal or utilization of solid wastes in a sanitary, aesthetically acceptable and economical manner and includes all administrative, financial, legal and planning function as well as the physical aspects of solid waste handling. Thus, solid waste management involves management of activities associated with generation, storage, collection, transfer and transport, processing and disposal of solid waste which is environmentally compatible, adopting principles of economy, aesthetics, energy and conservation.

GENERATION

Wastes differ in the rate of generation, quantity and quality depending upon the area of generation. The quantity and quality depend upon the source like residential areas (which may into vary widely), commercial areas or industrial areas and also may vary at different times of the year, which will have a marked effect on the selection of method for its collection, processing and disposal.

STORAGE

The generated waste is stored within the premises in commercial and industrial areas, whereas in residential areas, occupants take it out and transfer to community storage bins. Plastic cans with lid are preferred for temporary storage in houses though they are subjected to damage by rats.

COLLECTION

Citizens deposit the wastes by the roadside from where the conservancy staff-transfer it to the community bins using wheelbarrow or other equipment. The location of the refuse containers should be easily accessible to both the residents and the municipal staff.

TRANSPORTATION

The material collected in community dust-bins is transferred to transport vehicles for transport to the processing or disposal site. The fleet of transport vehicles should have sufficient capacity for average and peak loads and should be utilized at optimum levels. Regular disposal of refuse is essential to maintain proper sanitation.

PROCESSING AND RECOVERY

A large quantity of waste has to be processed before suitable disposal, to reduce its potential nuisance value. Occasionally recovery of useful constituents is also carried out as an independent process. Garbage may be separated from ashes and rubbish for its use as hog feed.

DISPOSAL

The waste may come for disposal either directly after its transportation or after processing. Disposal could be on land or water logged areas for reclamation. The different functions are interdependent and interrelated which could be better managed by a system approach.

EDUCATION

Man is the main animal responsible for pollution and has no desire for cleanliness. He strongly believes in his 'out of sight is out of mind concept' and is addicted to live in unhygienic environments. The people should be educated to keep their surroundings clean. Yet, many people do not know the ill-effects o the dirty surroundings.

CHARACTERISTICS OF REFUSE

The main components of a refuge and their characteristics are:

1. *Garbage:* It consists of putrescible wastes resulting from the growing, handling, preparation, cooking and consumption of food. During summer, the amount of garbage is more, when vegetable wastes are more abundant. The increased use of processed and packaged foods has reduced garbage but increased the combustible rubbish. It requires careful handling and frequent removal as otherwise it attracts and breeds flies and other insects, supplies food for rats and generates unpleasant odors due to rapid fermentation. It may be utilized as hog feed and yields a valuable fertilizer or soil conditioner after composting.
2. *Rubbish:* It includes all non-putrescible wastes except ashes. It consists of both combustibe and noncombustible substances such as cans,

paper, brushes, glass, cardboard, wood, scrap metals, bedding, crocker, and yard clippings. Rubbish becomes a nuisance only if it is scattered by wind or careless handling.

3. ***Ashes:*** Ashes result from the combustion of fuels like coal, wood or dung, used in houses or industries. Use of natural gas and oils and fuels has greatly reduced the quantity of ashes.
4. ***Dead Animals:*** Dead animals such as cows, horses, donkeys, pigs and dogs must be removed as early as possible and finally disposed of by incineration or deep burial in specified locations.
5. ***Street Sweepings:*** They consist of materials worn from street surfaces, leaves, sweepings from sidewalks, dirt and bits of waste paper.
6. ***Industrial Wastes:*** As far as possible industries are insisted to have their own solid waste handling and treatment systems as otherwise they produce obnoxious odors and cause severe problems to public health authorities.

The refuse may also be classified as:

(a) ***House Refuse:*** Ashes, cinder, rubbish, debris from cleaning and demolition of structures, vegetable and animal waste matters.

(b) ***Street Refuse:*** Street sweepings, dirty materials dropped from vehicles, tree leaves, empty match and cigarette boxes, fruit peels and empty packets.

(c) ***Trade Refuse:*** Solid wastes from factories, business centers, slaughter houses, etc.

(d) ***Mixed Refuse:*** The weight of the mixed refuse varies from 300 to 600 kg per m^3. The weight of garbage varies from 450 to 900 kg/m^3. It should be handled carefully, because flies, insects, rats, etc. breed in it. Density of rubbish is between 50 to 400 kg/m^3. The density of ashes is between 700 to 850 kg/m^3. The average composition of refuse by weight is about 25% cinder, 27% fine dust, 15% ashes, 4% empty tin cans, 14% putrescible matter, 2% glass and crockery, 2% rag, 1% bone and 10% miscellaneous matter.

DISPOSAL OF REFUSE BY DUMPING

The disposal of refuse can be done by various methods viz.,

(i) by dumping into sea

(ii) by sanitary land filling

(iii) by incineration

(iv) by composting

(v) by ploughing in fields

(vi) by hog feeding

(vii) by grinding and discharging to sewer

(viii) by salvaging and

(ix) by fermentation or biological digestion.

Dumping into Oceans: The disposal of refuse by dumping into sea is possible only in case of coastal cities. While dumping the refuse, care is taken to take the refuse in barges, sufficient distance away, 2 to 3 km from the beach and dumped there. The refuse may be washed ashore under tidal conditions. This method is very costly and is not used in India.

Open Dumping: Some components of refuse are suitable for open dumping. These include street sweepings, ashes and incombustible rubbish. However, serious nuisances and hazards will result if garbage or mixed refuse it disposed of in this manner. They include odors, dust, wind-borne paper, fires flies, rats and mosquitoes that will breed in rain-water held in cans. Low lying areas, which may be brought up to grade by filling are generally chosen for the dump. Ashes and street sweepings, though dusty, permit the construction of a fairly stable landfill.

HOG FEEDING

The feeding of garbage to hogs has been practiced for many years. It is estimated, private individuals feed that about 25 per cent of the total quantity of garbage produced to hogs. Garbage feeding is profitable and many hotels and restaurants dispose of their garbage to farmers who are willing to collect it themselves. Usually they collect daily and furnish clean cans. While garbage is the most potentially valuable element of refuse, it is most difficult to handle in a sanitary manner and is responsible for the majority of the nuisances and health hazards associated with the refuse program.

Hog farms are frequently the cause of complaints of odors, flies, rats and other nuisances and sanitation hazards. The presence of extraneous matter and dangerous materials, such as razor blades and glass, in residential and institutional garbage makes it the least desirable garbage for hog feeding. Garbage from hotels and restaurants is much higher in nutritive value. Each hog can eart about 10 kg of garbage per day and may gain about 0.5 kg in weight per day.

INCINERATION

Incineration is a method of treating refuses to reduce the volume and weight and to leave an innocuous residue. The conventional incineration involves the burning of solid wastes at a high temperature. This is a widely used method of refuse disposal with the following merits and demerits.

1. A modern incineration plant is usually constructed where landfill disposal sites are distant from the center of generation of refuse, making transfer and transportation of refuse a costly proposition.

2. Less land is required than for landfills.
3. A central location is possible. A well-designed building, careful operation and landscaped grounds are acceptable in many neighborhoods, especially in industrial areas. This may allow short hauls for the collection service.
4. Ash and other residue produced are practically free of organic matter, nuisance-free and acceptable as fill material.
5. Many kinds of refuse can be burned. Even the noncombustible materials will be reduced in bulk.
6. Climate or unusual weather does not affect it.
7. Flexibility is possible. Incinerators may be operated for 8, 16 or 24 hr/day.
8. It is possible to get some income through the sale of waste heat for steam or power. Some cities charge industries and businesses for incinerator service.
9. Incinerators are high in first cost.
10. Operating costs are relatively high and skilled employees are required for operation and maintenance. The High and skilled employees are required for operation and maintenance. The high temperatures, dust and type of materials handled have a bad effect upon machinery and furnace interior and hence expensive repairs are frequently needed.
11. There may be difficulty in getting a site. Many property owners will object to refuse disposal in any form near their property. Many will also object that truck traffic to and from the plan is a hazard and a nuisance.
12. Land pollution is converted to air pollution by incineration. The main air pollutants released from a incinerator are dusts (SPM), fly-ash, SO_x, NO_x, HC1, HF and other metallic fumes and acidic mists.

The Principal Features of an Incinerator are

Charging Apparatus: Dumping the collection trucks on the charging floor charges an incinerator. The refuse is then pushed into charging doors by hand or bulldozer. Larger incinerators usually have storage bins into which the refuse is dumped by the trucks. A crane and bucket is then used to move the refuse to the charging doors.

Furnaces: This includes the grates on which the material is deposited for burning. Grates allow fine ash to fall through to the ash pit below. Moving grates also are used sometimes.

Combustion Chamber: This is located between the furnace and the stack and its purpose is to permit mixing of the hot gases and allow time for combustion to take place. Some plants provide for the burning of dead animals in this chamber. It also allows completion of burning of fly ash, which otherwise would emitted from the chimney to present a fire hazard. A temperature of at least 650°C is necessary for complete burning of combusitble gases and 800°C is desirable to ensure against escape of odorous gases. Temperature in the furnace or combustion chamber should not exceed 1100°C or the refractory brick lining may damaged and require replacement. Successive heating and cooling is undesirable as it encourages 'spalling'. Continuous operation of incinerators reduces this effect.

Chimney or Stack: The incinerator stack serves to discharge the gases into the atmosphere and is also a means for providing air movement or "stack draft" through the incinerator system. The chimney height should be designed to enable adequate dilution of gases with air and to minimize fly-ash problems. A minimum stack height of 30m is recommended.

Miscellaneous Features: Provision must be made for temporary storage and removal of ashes. Most plants utilize a system of ash-pits, which receive the noncombustible wastes and are equipped with a water spray system of other quenching device. Air supply by forced draft is generally used, which requires a fan or blower and the necessary ducts to force air below the grates and up through the bed of burning material, but no father. The theoretical total requirement is 5 kg of air per kg of combustible refuse, but this is usually doubted in designing air requirements. Preheating of the air supply is also an operational practice that is considered economical in plants of more than 75 tons capacity. The air discharged below the grates is preheated by passing it through ducts where it may absorb heat from the chimney gases.

Control apparatus should include thermometers for checking temperatures of the burning chambers, the preheated air and the stack gases. Scales for weighing the refuse and ashes are desirable. Special flyash removal apparatus may be necessary or the incinerator may violate the local air pollution control requirements. Filters, baffle devices, centrifugal or cyclonic separators. Water-spray chambers and electrostatic precipitators may be used for this purpose.,

On-site Incineration: This term applies to incineration of refuse at the homes, apartments, commercial buildings, hospitals or industrial sites. Backyard burning by open fires or in simple outdoor incinerators is banned by many cities because of fire hazard and air pollution by particulates and hydrocarbons. Refuse collection and disposal can be reduced by satisfactory on-site incineration.

SANITARY LAND FILLING

Sanitary landfill differs from ordinary dumping in that the material is placed in a trench or other prepared area, adequately compacted and finally concerned with earth at the end of the working day. The term 'modified sanitary landfill' has been applied to those operations where compaction and covering are accomplished once or twice a week. Where compacted refuse is placed in the fill to a depth of 6 ft., it is estimated that 1 acre of land per year will be required per 10,000 population. It is one of the most common forms of disposal of refuse. 70 to 90% of world's refuse is being disposed of by the landfill method only. The method is al called 'controlled tipping' or 'Land fill method'. In either case, the refuse is adequately covered and compacted to allow traffic over the fill.

Prospective landfill sites should be evaluated with respect to type of soil available, drainage, prevailing winds and availability of access roads, possible contamination of ground and surface water etc. Sandy loam is considered the most suitable landfill soil, although other soils also can be utilized. Poor surface drainage may hinder the operation, and care should be exercised to prevent interception of an underground water stratum in constructing the fill. The type of sites being used for disposal are:

(i) Mineral excavations

(ii) Low lying land

(iii) Valleys

(iv) Areas involving the reclamation of land from water

(v) Flat land to build up a feature

The three broad classifications of operational methods are: the trench method, the area-ramp method and the area-fill method. In either case, the working face should be maintained at about a 30° slope, compacted and covered as a part of the daily operational routine. Six inches of earth is placed over the compacted refuse on the slope, and at least 2 ft. of compacted earth should be placed on top of that portion of lthe fill that is completed each day. Earth cover must be compacted to prevent fly emergence (6 in. will be sufficient). Where level terrain is available, the trench method is usually chosen. Trenches are usually 6 to 10 ft. (1.8 to 3 m) in depth and depending on local conditions, 10 to 40 ft. (3 to 12m) in width. The area-ramp method is well suited for moderately sloping terrain. Actually, this method can be utilized to bring a sloping area to grade t secure cover materials and side ramps.

Characteristics of the Fill: Chemical, bacteriological and physical changes occur in the buried refuse. In about 4 days after placement and at about 3 ft. below the surface, temperatures rise rapidly to 55-65° C. They remain at this point for about 60 days and then fall gradually for about 10 months to near air temperatures. The composition of landfill materials, which include only about 15 per cent garbage, is responsible for the slow decomposition of wastes. Most of the settlement occurs within the first 12 months, and by the end of 2 years most fills settle completely.

Use of Filled Land: Such filled areas can be used for parks, golf courses and other recreational areas, airports, parking lots etc. Construction should be limited to single-story buildings, although heavier buildings may be constructed if foundations are carried through the fill to undisturbed earth or if reinforced-concrete mat foundations are utilized. Water pipes and sewers passing through the fill require special precautions against corrosion, contamination and settlement as methane gas is produced in the decomposition process.

Advantages and Disadvantages of Sanitary Fill: Sanitary fill has the advantages of minimizing odour and fire nuisances and of eliminating such health hazards as insect and rodent breeding; cheapness and simplicity, since no separation of refuse is required; the only manpower requirement at many landfills is a machine operator; landfill operations are usually enough to take care of usual quantities of refuse caused by expanding populations and marginal land can often be reclaimed for profitable resale. The principal disadvantage is that in the absence of careful and continuous supervision, the fill may deteriorate into an ordinary dump. Also since land requirements for sanitary landfill operations are large, bigger cities experience difficulty in obtaining suitable sites at reasonable prices.

COMPOSTING

The Process where bulk organic matter is converted into fertilizing manure by biological action is called Composting. Here, about 5 cm thick layers of animal dung are placed over a 30 cm thick refuse layer. Trenches of size 10m x 3m are filed with alternate layers of refuse and dung and finally the top is covered width 5 to 10 cm thick earth layer to prevent insects, loss of moisture and public nuisance. In 3 to 4 months, manure is ready for use. If composting is practiced with the help of earthworms, it is called 'Vermin Composting'. In a good composting process C: N ratio of about 30:1 to 40:1 and a moisture content of 30 to 40% is maintained.

Thus, composting is a biological process in which the organic material of refuse is converted to a usable stable material by the action of microorganisms present in the refuse and soil. Composted refuse is an excellent organic additive for agricultural soils. However, because of the cheap availability of inorganic fertilizers, demand for compost has not yet materialized. Composting includes the following:

Removal of Non-Compostables: Several components of mixed municipal refuse are of no value in the compost process. Some of these, such as cans and other metals and glass can sometimes be recovered for sale. While magnetic devices will remove the ferrous metals, some provision must be made for hand picking the wastes.

Grinding/Shredding: To speed up bacterial action, the raw refuse is shredded to about 5 cm in size prior to placement in piles, digesters or bins for decomposition.

Blending or Proportioning: The optimum carbon-nitrogen ratio in the refuse for speedy bacteria action is 30-35:1. A ratio above 35:1 requires a considerable increase in composting time. Blending is not necessary when the carbon-nitrogen ratio is 25-30:1. This may be done at the plant if loads containing much paper, straw and sawdust, which are deficient in nitrogen, can be combined with other loads high in nitrogen, such as slaughter house wastes, fish scrap, blood, night soil, or sewage sludge. The optimum moisture content for aerobic composting is 40 to 60 per cent.

Placement: Open piles or windrows are placed on the ground, on a paved area in shallow pits, if aerobic conditions are to be maintained by frequent timing, windrows or piles are used. Windrows should be about 8 to 12 ft. (2.5 to 3.5 m) wide at the bottom and piles of about the same diameter. The windows or piles are turned at such intervals that aerobic conditions are maintained. This may be every 2 or 3 days if the moisture content is high or a total of three or four times in a 15 to 21 day composting period. The optimum temperature range is 50 to 70° C. Temperatures will be established naturally and will be highest in the middle of the pile or windrow. Excessively high temperatures, over 75° C are injurious to bacterial action. Turning has little effect upon temperature, but lowering the windrow height can control excessive temperature. In order to maintain optimum temperature in cold weather, the height may be increased. A drop in windrow temperature may mean that anaerobic conditions have developed.

Mechanical Methods: Here, the refuse is received on a conveyor and transported to a building where solvable material such as white glass, cardboard, non ferrous metal, rages and paper are removed and where paper sacks and containers re torn open. Thereafter a magnetic separator removes ferrous metals. The remainder is then ground and conveyed to a digester for a varying period during which moisture, temperature and aeration are closely controlled. Prior to digestion the material is screened to remove large undigested items and is passed through a separator to remove glass. It is then trucked to an adjacent area where, if digestion is incomplete, it is windrowed for further aerobic action.

Composted material is stable i.e., it undergoes a little or no further decomposition, and has only a slight musty or earthy odor. Its color will be grayish or brownish black. Its principal value when applied to the soil is as a conditioner. It lightens the soil, promotes aeration and helps to retain moisture by adding humus. It has some fertilizing value when applied to the soil as a conditioner. It lightens the soil, promotes aeration and helps to retain moisture by adding humus. It has fertilizing value. It contains about 1.5% N, 1% P_2O_5, 0.8% K_2O, 30% C and 40% ash. Compost itself presents no health hazards, as the heat developed during composting kills the pathogens and the eggs of parasites. The killing temperature extends only to within 10 to 20 cm of the surface of the pile. Turning, therefore, also lays a part in ensuring destruction of pathogens and parasites.

Fly production can be expected where composting is conducted in the open. Completely composted material is not attractive to flies. Composting may become more popular in the future if farmers recognize its considerable soil-conditioning value as an adjunct to its modest fertilizing value. This is a possibility for use for certain soils and for farms and market gardens near cities. The composting plant will be at a disadvantage because of its greater volume of residue, but if this can be disposed of free of charge to the city or by sale at some price, composting can compete with incineration.

DISCHARAGE TO SEWERS

Three methods for the disposal of garbage with sewage are in use- the installation of individual grinders in homes and commercial establishments; the installation of municipally operated centrally located grinding stations; and the installation of grinders at sewage treatment plants. If garbage of all the population contributing sewage is ground at a central grinding plant and then discharged into the sewers, the suspended solids will be increased by about 50 per cent and the biochemical oxygen demand will be increased by about 30 per cent. The waste consumed with the grinding will amount to about 5 lpcd. This method is a rarely practiced one.

SALVAGING

Paper, cardboard, glass, metals, rags, garbage and miscellaneous commercial wastes are the principal elements of refuse having marketable value. Clean paper can be reused in the manufacture of paperboard or cardboard. Glass has some value, if it can be hand sorted according to size and color. Broken glass is quite limited in value. Cans and other metals have value because of their tin coating and solder. Commercial areas are often the source of such solvable refuse as sloth and leather trimmings, some wood materials and cardboard cartons. Careful evaluation of potential local markets for solvable goods should precede municipal salvage activities. Refuse can also be tried for landscaping in parks etc. as in Chandigarh.

Separation of Salvage: The separation of refuse is most essential when it is disposed by incineration, because it contains dust and other materials of low calorific value. During the process of separation the salvage is discharged into the receiving hopper of separation plane and then raised to the primary screen by internal spiral. Now the refuse is carried forward to the screen by internal spiral. The dust is removed by primary screens, which are rotated at 15 rpm and have fine mesh of size 5-10 mm. The material passing through 5 cm mesh is transferred to secondary screen, through which the dust is further separated and the clean cinder is removed by means of garbage extractor. The materials from primary and secondary screens and garbage are passed on a 1.2 m wide picking belt moving at 10 m/min in case of hand picking. The ferrous metals are separated out by means of a magnetic separator or magnetic pulley. Other usable materials such as glass, paper, metals, rags etc., are separated at the picking belt. The remaining refuse is discharged by a moving tripping mechanism to a cross belt from where it is charged into an incinerator or other loading hopper of transport for composting.

Be Broad-minded

When a person is convinced that his basic relationship behind all other worldly, physical or work relationships is that of 'Spiritual brothers' because all are children of God, then one's angel of vision changes. It widens one's concern from what has made a man look towards a small family or a small circle of fiends to the whole family of mankind as 'Vasudhaeka kutumbam' or 'Global Village'. One's love is no longer directed towards a few but to all. This awakens in man the attitudes or qualities of sympathy, service and fellow-feeling and puts his behavior on a new and a higher pedestal. Let sky be your limit, star be your goal.

CONCLUSION

Solid waste analysis is necessary to know the proper methods of collection, treatment and disposal. Solid wastes are to be analyzed for Moisture content and Temperature, to know about putrescibility and bacterial activity; Bulk density, to study compressibility; Volatile solids and ash content, to know the economic viability of incineration; Carbon-Nitrogen ratio and the NPK Value to find its Fertility value; and Organic matter and Calorific value to know its value as a fuel.

REFERENCES

Viegas, Philip, Menon, Geetha (1989), The Impact of Environmental Degradation on people, Indian Social institute, New Delhi.

Nilsen, Richard, (Ed.) (1991), Helping Nature Heal-An Introduction to Environmental Restoration, Point Foundation, USA.

Balasubramanian, A. (1995), Ecology, Environment & Pollution, Indira Publishers, Mysore, India.

National Academy of Sciences (1991), One Earth One Future-Our Changing Global Environment, Affiliated East West Press Pvt. Ltd., New Delhi.

Beyond interdependence-The meshing of the World's Economy and Earth's Ecology (1991), Oxford University Press, New York.

Eldon D. Enger & Bradley F. Smith (2000), Environmental Science–A Study of Interrelationships, McGraw Hill, New Delhi.

Tyler Miller Jr. G. (1996), Living in the Environment, Wardsworth Publishing Company, London.

Gadgil, Madhav & Guha, Ramachandra (1995), Ecology and Equity–The Use and Abuse of Nature in Contemporary India.

Agarwal, K. C. (1996), Environmental Biology, Agro Botanical Publishers (India), New Delhi.

Ecology-Individuals, Population and Communities, (1990), Blackwell Scientific Publications, Australia.

Trivedi, P. R. and Gurdeep Roy (1992), Management of Environmental Education and Research, Akashdeep Publishing House, New Delhi.

Ministry of Environment and Forests, Government of India (June 1992), National Conservation Strategy and Policy Statement of Environment and Development.

Agarwal, V.P. (1990), Forests in India-Environmental and Production Frontiers, Oxford & IBH Publishing House, New Delhi.

State of Environment, India, 2001.

World Resouraces Institute, Sustainable Agriculture, Agenda 21, Chapter 14, *www.wri.org*

Care2-alerts@australia.care2.com

Environmental Concerns of India-An Introduction, C.P.R. Environmental Education Centre, 1, Eldams Road, Chennai, (2003)

Pollution and Helath, C.P.R. Environmental Education Centre, Chennai. *www.unep.org.*

Chapter-14

LOCAL AREA BANKS–PROBLEMS AND PROSPECTS

Benson Kunjukunju & Mohan P. Philip

INTRODUCTION

It has been the endeavor of the Reserve Bank and the Government of India to improve the credit delivery system by freeing it from procedural hassles and thereby make available the basic banking services to a large section of society. Despite widespread expansion of the banking sector during the last four decades, a substantial number of households, especially in rural areas, are at present outside the coverage of the formal banking system.

The guiding principle of the Government of India is to release the farmers, rural artisans and the downtrodden from the stranglehold of moneylenders. In consonance with the above policy, the Reserve Bank of India has undertaken a number of measures for attracting the financially excluded population into the mainstream of the financial system particularly in the rural areas.

The Reserve Bank's broad approach to "financial inclusion" aims at 'connecting people' with the formal banking system. Financial inclusion refers to delivery of banking services at an affordable cost to the vast sections of disadvantaged and low-income groups who tend to be excluded from the formal banking channel. Efforts towards "no frill accounts" and 'financial inclusion' include sensitizing the banks about the banking and financial needs of the common person and there by ensure access to basic banking facilities. In accordance with the above approach, the Reserve Bank has initiated a number of measures of late for attracting and absorbing the financially excluded population into the formal financial system.

Regardless of the periodic policy for improving the rural credit delivery system, for the last fifteen years, it is seen that on an average one rural branch of a scheduled commercial bank gets closed every working day. In the same period, bank branches in urban and metros doubled, opening at a rate of more than one every day.

The Reserve Bank of India's Hand Book of Statistics on the Indian Economy (2006-07) shows there were 30,639 rural branches of SCBs in 2007. That is 4,750 less than there were in 1993. In other words, an average of 26 bank branches shut down each month, or one every working day.

The share of rural credit as a percentage of total credit disbursed by all scheduled commercial banks including Regional Rural Banks stood at just around 7.93 per cent in March 2007. The corresponding figure for the previous year was 8.39 per cent. Much less than the 10 per cent, it stood at in 2001. Of the total rural credit disbursed the percentage share of farmers account for only a part of it.

ORIGIN OF LOCAL AREA BANKS

Man Mohan Singh the then Finance Minister, in his budget speech in the Parliament in 1996, highlighted the need for a separate financial institution in the rural areas, capable of meeting the credit needs of the local people. The primary objective of these institutions should be to bridge the gap in the credit availability in rural areas. These institutions considered as alternative source of rural credit, which the commercial banks and co-operatives fail to provide. Thus, in the multi- agency approach, Local Area Banks have to play an important role in the rural credit structure, along with co-operatives and commercial banks.

In 1996 with great expectations, the Union Government took initiative to establish the Local Area Banks and there by strengthen the institutional credit framework in the rural and semi-urban areas. In this connection in August 1996, the RBI issued the necessary guidelines for the establishment of the Local Area Banks (LABs) in the private sector.

STATUES APPLICABLE TO LABS

Local Area Banks (LABs) are unique form of banking institutions governed by the provisions of the Reserve Bank of India Act of 1934, the Banking Regulation Act of 1949, and Regional Rural Banks Act of 1976 and of the Indian Companies Act of 1956. A Local Area Banks can also be established as a public limited company in the private sector under the Companies Act of 1956. These banks will be licensed under the Banking Regulations Act of 1949 and will be eligible for inclusion in the second schedule of the Reserve Bank of India Act of 1934 subject to the fulfillment of the eligibility criteria prescribed in the respective section of the RBI Act.

MEANING OF LOCAL AREA BANKS

Local Area Banks (LABs) are local private commercial banks established in the rural and semi-urban areas with jurisdiction over two or three adjacent districts. As per the Reserve Bank of India guidelines, the area of operation of a Local Area Banks was restricted to a maximum of three geographically neighboring districts. The Local Area Banks were allowed to open only one branch in an urban area in a district, other branches were allowed to be opened in the rural, and semi urban areas subjected to the regulations and guidelines of the Reserve Bank of India.

The primary objective of setting this type of rural financial institution was to experience and get familiarized with local needs, and also to remain a professionally managed alternative channel for credit dispensation to small and marginal farmers. Agricultural labourers, socially and economically weaker sections etc. of the population were its target group and their purpose was to develop agriculture, trade, commerce, small scale and cottage industry in their area of operation.

Local Area Banks were expected to mobilize resources from rural areas and make it available for investments in viable economic enterprises in their area of operation and thus strengthening the institutional credit framework in the rural and semi-urban areas.

LICENSING OF LOCAL AREA BANKS

Pursuant to the announcement of Local Area Banks (LABs) by the Finance Minister in his budget speech in 1996, the Reserve Bank of India announced a set of guidelines on 24th August, 1996, for the establishment of Local Area Banks in the private sector.

From the time of issuance of the notificatior in August 1996 to the end of June1999, the Reserve Bank of India received 215 applications from different states for the setting up of LABs. Till the end of March 2002, 227 applications were received by the RBI for the setting up of LABs.

Of the 227 applications received, 214 were rejected. Almost all applications were disposed off due to the lack of fulfillment of the terms and conditions, which were stated in the notification. 'In-principle' approvals for establishment of LABs were issued to 10 institutions and 3 applications are pending examination. Of the 10 applicants who were granted 'in-principle' approvals, four of them were withdrawn, due to the inability of the promoters to fulfill the conditions stipulated in the 'in-principle' approvals. One application remains pending for approval. The 'in- principle' approvals for setting up of LAB were granted to, one each in the states of Maharashtra, Punjab, Andhra Pradesh, Tamil Nadu, Rajasthan and Gujarat and two in Karnataka. Of these, licenses were issued only to five Local Area Banks under Section 22 of the Banking Regulation Act of 1949.

COMMENCEMENT OF BUSINESS BY LOCAL AREA BANKS

Following this Local Area Banks commenced their operations in their allotted districts;

(1) ***Coastal Local Area Bank Ltd., Vijayawada:*** The bank commenced its business on 27 December 1999, with its Head Office at Vijayawada. Its area of operations was limited to the districts of West Godavari, Krishna and Guntur in Andhra Pradesh,

(2) ***Capital Local Area Bank Ltd., Phagwara:*** The bank was established on 14th January 2000 with its Registered Office at Phagwara. Its area of operation was restricted to the districts of Kapurthala, Jalandhar and Hoshiarpur in the state of Punjab. Shri A.S. Samra and 25 individuals have promoted the bank.

(3) ***Krishna Bhima Samurdhi Local Area Bank Ltd., Mehboobnagar:*** The bank was established on 28th February 2001 with its Head Office at Mahabubnagar. The area of operation of the bank was restricted to three districts in two states. The bank will operate in the districts of Raichur and Gulbarga in Karnataka and Mehboobnagar in Andhra Pradesh.

(4) ***Vinayak Local Area Bank Ltd., Sikar:*** It was established on 21 October 2000 in the state of Rajasthan. The bank was permitted to operate in the districts of Jhunjhunu, Sikar and Churu.

(5) ***South Gujarat Local Area Bank Ltd., Navsari:*** Shri Kanaksinh M. Mangrola and nine others promoted the bank. The bank established was on 3rd October 2000 with its Head Office at Navsari. The bank established in the state of Gujarat was operating in three neighboring districts of Surat, Navsari and Bharuch.

6) ***The Subhadra Local Area Bank Ltd., Kolhapur:*** The Subhadra Local Area Bank Ltd., Kolhapur, was given the license on July 10, 2003. During the year 2002-03, RBI issued only one license for LAB. The bank commenced its business from September 30, 2003 in the districts of Kolhapur and Sangli in Maharashtra and Belgaum in Karnataka.

FAILURE AND MERGER OF LOCAL AREA BANKS

The year 2002 witnessed the cancellation of the license of the two year old "Vinayak Local Area Bank Ltd" and the year 2004 witnessed the merger of the four year old "The South Gujarat Local Area Bank Ltd." with a public sector bank.

(1) ***Vinayak Local Area Bank Ltd.:*** Of the Five LABs, which commenced their operations, the license in respect of one Local Area Bank viz., Vinayak Local Area Bank, Sikar established on 21st October 2000, was cancelled on 16th January 2002, because of major irregularities in their functioning.

(2) The South Gujarat Local Area Bank Ltd.: South Gujarat Local Area Bank Ltd., Navsari opened six branches (1 urban, 2 semi urban, 3 rural) in its area of operation, and it incurred net losses consecutively from its inception and got merged with the Bank of Baroda in 2004.

PERFORMANCE IN THE WORKING OF LABs

The Local Area Banks in India had a life span of only a very short period of only one decade. From this short span of ten years, it can be seen that the concept of Local Area Banks never got transformed into a vibrant institution of rural credit expansion. However, the commercial banking sector in India witnessed a robust growth during these periods. Local Area Banks could make only a little impact in their area of operation with regard to mobilization of deposits and lending of money. The short history of LABs reveals that they encountered a number of crises with the consequent failures and mergers. Of the total six Local Area Banks commenced, two banks failed and only four were functioning in the country at the end of March 2007. These banks were:

(1) Coastal Local Area Bank Ltd., Vijayawada;

(2) Capital Local Area Bank Ltd., Phagwara, Navsari,

(3) Krishna Bhima Samruddhi Local Area Bank Ltd., Mehboobnagar; and

(4) Subhadra Local Area Bank Ltd., Kolhapur.

The various indicators in the working of Local Area Banks viz. Deposits, Advances, Interest income, Interest expended, Operating profit, Net profit etc. from 2002-03 to 2006-07 are given in Table 1.

Table 1 reveals that the interest income of four LABs in total increased appreciably from Rs. 12.7 crore to Rs. 37.4 crore during 2003 to 2007. During 2006-07, the income of the LABs increased sharply mainly because of interest income.

Table 1
Financial Performances of Local Area Banks 2002-07 (Amount in Crore)

Particulars	*2002-03*	*2003-04*	*2004-05*	*2005-06*	*2006-07*
Interest Income (Rs.)	12.7	15.4 (21.2)	17.3 (12.3)	25.5 (47.3)	37.4 (46.6)
Interest Expenses (Rs.)	7.7	8.6 (11.7)	8.7 (1.2)	12.0 (38.0)	18.3 (52.5)
Operating Profit (Rs.)	2.7	2.9 (7.4)	3.4 (17.2)	5.4 (58.2)	10.2 (88.8)
Net Profit (Rs.)	0.2	0.1 (-50)	0.9 (800)	2.8 (211)	5.9 (110.7)
Deposits (Rs.)	113.4	157 (38.4)	200 (27.4)	290 (45)	343 (18.27)
Advances (Rs.)	76.8	103 (34.1)	130 (26.2)	197 (51.5)	230 (16.8)

Figures in bracket indicate percentage variation over the previous year.

The interest income in 2007 recorded (Table 1) an increase of 46.66 per cent over the previous year. Interest income recorded a three-fold increase over a five-year period. The interest expenditure of four LABS also went up from Rs. 7.7 to Rs. 18.3 crore during 2003 to 2007. The rate of growth in interest expenses during the year 2007 shows an increase of 52.5 per cent over the previous year.

Local Area Banks bank began showing profits since their inception. However, Subhadra Local Area Bank Ltd., Kolhapur, which commenced its operation in September 2003, suffered loss from the very first year of its operation. Table 1 shows that the operating profit of LABs increased significantly from Rs. 2.7 crore to Rs. 10.2 crore during the period 2002-03 to 2006-07 showing a 3.8 fold increase. The operating profit increased by 88.8 per cent in the year 2006-07 where as the corresponding percentage of increase for the year 2005-06 were only 58.2. The ratio of operating Profit to total assets represents 2.1 per cent in March 2007, which was higher than 1.5 per cent at March 2006.

The net profits of Four LABs also increased remarkably in the year 2006-07. It increased from a paltry amount of Rs. 0.2 crore in 2002-03 to Rs. 5.9 crore in 2006-07. Total net profits of LABs increased by 110.7 per cent in 2007 over the previous year. The ratio of net profit to total assets in March 2007 was higher at 1.2 per cent as compared with 0.8 per cent in the previous year.

During 2006-07, deposits and gross advances of all LABs increased significantly. The total Deposits of Local Area Banks aggregating to Rs. 343 crore at the end of March 2007 represented a spectacular increase over that of Rs. 290 crore as on March 2006. Deposits show a compound annual growth rate of 25.8 per cent over a five-year period. The total Advances of LABs in the country also increased substantially and steadily from Rs. 197 crore in March 2006 to Rs. 230 crore in March 2007, registering a compound growth rate of 25.5 per cent per annum. The compound growth rate in respect of deposits and advances over a period of five years are more or less same.

REVIEW ON WORKING OF THE LOCAL AREA BANKS

The Reserve Bank in consultation with the Government of India appointed a committee to give recommendations in order to ensure balanced growth of Local Area Banks (LABs) in the country. The Reserve Bank of India appointed a three member Review Group under the Chairmanship of Shri G.Ramachandran, Former Finance Secretary, Government of India, in July 2002, to carry out a review of the operations of Local Area Banks functioning in the country and to make recommendations for revitalizing them. The terms of reference of the Group were to examine whether the Local Area Banks have fulfilled their objectives and purposes for which they were formed. Review also included the question whether the Local Area Banks should be allowed to continue or not. The Review Group finalized and submitted its report in September 2002.

After wide discussions, the Group arrived at a conclusion that Local Area Banks, which were established with high expectations, have failed in achieving their desired objectives. However, in the preface of the report, the Group noted that Local Area Banks were in existence only for a short period and it would be difficult to draw a clear conclusion about their success or failure from this short period of their operation. They further observed that these banks would need a little more time to establish themselves firmly in the areas in which they were functioning and to win the confidence of both the investors and the borrowers.

The Group opined that Local Area Banks were tormented by a variety of problems such as poor mobilization of local resources, ineffective leadership, poor monitoring of end use of credit and mounting overdues. The Group further opined that Local Area Banks have not made any impact on the local communities amongst whom they are functioning in terms of any of the relevant indicators such as:

(1) Deposit mobilization
(2) Number of depositors
(3) Number of borrower accounts
(4) Amounts lent
(5) Number of rural branches and
(6) Number of poor people helped.

The Group also opined that a number of measures have to be initiated to strengthen them and new norms of capital and capital adequacy have to be laid down if the few banks, which have come into existence, are to survive and grow.

MAJOR ISSUES OF LOCAL AREA BANKS

Local Area Banks as a new comer in the field of banking industry was established for providing banking services to peoples in the rural areas especially to those on the lower rungs of the economic ladder. The policy developments concerning the operations of Local Area Banking system have direct and indirect implications on the performance of the LABs. Following are some of the major issues concurring Local Area Banks in India.

Competitive Environment

Nationalization of major commercial banks in 1969 and 1980 with the aim of social banking over an extensive geographical and functional area created competitive environment in the banking sector. Nationalization paved the way for extension of retail banking to the rural and semi-urban areas. The changed operating environment of the banking sector, underpinned by globalization, deregulation and advancement in information technology, has created intense competitive pressure on banks. The emergence of new private sector and foreign banks equipped with latest technology, further made competition stiffer among the banks.

An analysis of the progress in the working of Local Area Banks over a decade reveals that they are not in lead in respect of mobilization of deposits and lending of money in their area of operation. Local Area Banks having only a tenderfoot in the field of banking business is facing intense competition from the entrenched and well established commercial banks and cooperative banking institutions. The challenge before the Local Area Banks is to establish themselves firmly in their areas in which they are functioning and to win the confidence and trust of both the investors and the borrowers.

Lack of Up-to-Date Products and Services

The branches of Commercial banks both in urban and rural areas are operating in a highly sophisticated environment. They are offering up-to-date products and services with enhanced personnel efficiency attracting many new clients' especially big customers and high net worth individuals (HNI's). Commercial Banks are competing with one another to offer value added services to customers to expand and widen their customer base. Several Banks have been positioning themselves as "financial supermarkets" for all financial services with a comprehensive range of products, services with different delivery channels viz. deposits, loans, credit card, debit card, depository services, utility bill payments, investment advice, selling third products, ATM, electronic fund transfer facility etc. all under one roof. A good number of customers in rural areas are aware of these services and they are keen to deal with only those banks, which provide such services. Local Area Banks, which were in existence only for a short period, would need more time to provide such services. The prospects of Local Areas Banks depend up their ability to provide these modern services and products, which the nationalized commercial banks provide.

No Scope for Diversification in Business

LABs are mainly concentrating on traditional banking businesses viz. accepting deposits and lending money in the form of loans and advances. Under the present statutory and regulatory set up, there is only limited scope for immediate diversification and expansion of the businesses of Local Area Banks. Distribution of insurance products, mutual funds, providing financial advisory services etc. are the important prospective areas were the LABs could undertake to diversify their portfolios.

Too much Lending to Target Groups

Like commercial banks, as per the provisions of RBI act, LABs were also required to finance agriculture and allied activities, small-scale industries, agro-industrial activities, trading activities and in non-farm sector in their area of operation. Priority sector advances to these banks were fixed at a minimum of 40% of the net bank credit. Of the total priority sector advances, at least 25 per cent of the advances should be made to the weaker sections of the society i.e. small and marginal farmers, landless labourers, scheduled castes, and scheduled tribes and beneficiaries of government sponsored schemes. The advances to weaker sections should not fall below 10 per cent of the net bank credit.

Too much insistence on targeted lending at a lower rate of interest is not desirable to a newly started banking institution. The insistence of 40 per cent priority sector advances will adversely affect the profitability, liquidity, and solvency position of the bank.

Further, these institutions are not eligible for refinancing facility from NABARD and SIDBI. To strengthen and to improve their performance, LABs may be allowed to concentrate on non-target groups, deregulate their deposit and lending rates, and permitted to invest surplus funds in profitable ventures. For their lending to priority sectors, it would be advisable to extend refinancing facility from NABARD and SIDBI at reasonable rates of interest for the LABs.

Restrictions on Opening of New Branches

Even though Local Area Banks of not come under the category of scheduled commercial banks, they have to complete the entire procedural formalities akin to commercial banks when they open a new branch. They have to seek permission from the District Consultative Committee of the Lead Bank of the District. The licensing procedure is very slow and cumbersome. It will be better if these institutions are given autonomy in opening branches for a certain period and make the rules similar to co-operative banking institutions applicable to them.

Restrictions on Opening Branches in Urban Centres

At present Local Area Banks are permitted to open only one urban branch in a district. In order to expand and diversify the business and to attain viability, Local Area Banks should be given the autonomy to open more branches in urban centres in their area of operation. By opening, more branches in urban centres, LABs can attract more customers including business people and thereby to minimise their risk and to improve their profitability.

Too much Supervision and Regulation of LABs by RBI

The regulatory responsibility over the Local Area Banks is vested in the Rural Planning and Credit Department (RPCD) of the RBI. LABs would be subject to prudential norms, corporate governance, accounting polices and other policies stipulated by the RBI. From their inception these banks had to maintain capital adequacy at 8 per cent of risk weighted assets and comply with all the norms of income recognition, asset classification and provisioning with out any lapse. Two aspects of prudential regulation, which have assumed greater importance and relevance in the recent period relate to capital adequacy and provisioning. The Working Group recommended for enhancing the capital base of Local Area Banks to at least to Rs. 25 crore over a period of five years. The Group also advised the LABs to raise the capital adequacy from 8 per cent to a minimum of 15 per cent. The ability of the Local Area Banks to raise capital to meet CRAR norms is because of limited by certain peculiar features. The shares of LABs are quoted neither in the stock market nor are these banks allowed to raise capital in the market. To maintain the prudential and capital adequacy norms is the immediate challenge before the Local Area Banks.

Absence of Human Resource Management\Professional Management

HRM is one of the key factors defining the characteristics of a successful banking institution. Professional Management is essential for any banking system.

Employing and retaining skilled workers and specialists, training the existing workforce and promoting a culture of continuous learning are challenges for the LABs. There has to be a commitment and involvement of every employee in the functioning of the Bank.

Low Level of IT Implementation

The process of globalization requires banks to move towards global standards of customer service so as to effectively meet the growing demands of their customers. Electronic Banking services offered by many banking institutions can be a strategic weapon to attract good customers. Through electronic banking, banks are in a position to offer extensive range of products and services of varied content and sophistication. Improved customer service has become very important for banks to survive and to grow in the emerging deregulated financial market. LABs are deficient in technology-based products. Their institutional net works have not succeeded in providing banking services in a more user-friendly environment due to several reasons. LABs, lag in technology threatening their very existence.

Limited Income from Other Sources

With the introduction of the concept of Universal Banking, commercial banks have endeavored to improve their fee-based incomes. The percentage shares of non-interest income in total income of commercial banks have been increasing tremendously. Before the liberalization measures commercial banks concentrated on interest income and other incomes constituted only a small portion of their total income.

Interest on loans is the main source of income to the Local Area Banks and other income represent only a small portion of the total income. The difference between the accepting and lending rate represent the margin to the bank. A swing towards fixed deposits in the deposit -mix of the bank cannot be reckoned as a healthy sign because it leads not only to the erosion of profits but also affects the financial position of the bank. Therefore, special attention should be given by the Local Area Banks to mobilize low cost deposits such as current and savings bank. The financial position of some Local Area Banks are not showing significant improvement mainly due to its limited business flexibility with a narrow scope for expansion\diversification combined with smaller size of loans with higher exposure to risks.

Poor Credit Management

Local Area Banks lack Professional efficiency in financial deployment. It was found that a good number of LABs advance their funds to a small number of stockbrokers mainly for trading in securities. Trading in securities is an inherently risky business. The LABs located in rural areas with limited capital and meager financial resources trading heavily in securities are likely to become victims of the uncertainties of share market. It is also found that Local Area

Banks achieve their business target by utilizing the services of intermediaries such as agents and quasi agents. Depending too much on financial intermediaries is not advisable for a newly started financial institution. Poor credit management is likely to increase credit risk and consequent rise in non-performing assets.

High Transaction Cost

Majority of commercial banks are deriving the benefits of electronic banking, which provides an efficient and cost effective delivery mechanism for banking services. Cost of banking services offered through the electronic banking come to only, a fraction of costs incurred in conventional methods. Keeping transaction costs low, remains a challenge to the Local Area banks. This has to be achieved only through affordable infrastructure and the use of appropriate technology.

CONCLUSION

In spite of several efforts on the part of the Government and the Regulator (RBI), large sections of the population are still outside the coverage of formal banking system. There is immense scope and prospects for banking business in India in the rural and semi-urban areas. The Local Area Banks, a newcomer in the field of banking business can play a crucial role in freeing the farmers and the downtrodden from the control of moneylenders. In the long run LABs can be converted into vibrant and an effective Area Specific Business Units for the development of the rural economy.

Local Area Banks face severe competition from nationalized, private sector, and cooperative banks and poses a threat to its survival. Although LABs have shown some progress in attaining their objectives at the local level, there remains enormous practical and theoretical challenges that demand multidisciplinary approaches and strategies by those engaged in development. The problems faced by the LABs need to be addressed urgently not only to ensure future growth of these institutions, but also to secure orderly progress of the entire financial system.

REFERENCES

Benson Kunjukunju (2008), Commercial Banks in India- Growth, Challenges and Strategies New Century Publications, New Delhi.

Trends and progress in Banking, Reserve Bank of India, Bombay, Various Issues.

Annual Report, Reserve Bank of India, Bombay, Various Issues.

www. rbi. org.

Chapter-15

WTO IN PROTECTION OF INDIA'S IPR's

M. Madhumathy & David Soundarajan

The republic of India located in south Asia, is the seventh largest country in the world. India is a country with different cultures, languages, traditions, climate etc, It also has exports and import in every sector of industry and also has booming economy.

The current Indian economy has been characterized by optimistic growth strong GATT, is one of the main reasons for the smooth trade functions between countries. In the post WTO era, international trade has witnessed the dismantling or dilution of any trade barriers, especially the quantitative restrictions, that has encouraged freered flow of trade among the countries. Today globalization is a buzz word, while WTO works towards globalization and multilateralism in trade, the development taking place simultaneously is the emergence of regional trade agreements promoting intra regional trade.

WTO was established on 1st January 1995 as an outcome of Uruguay round negotiations(1986-1984), it is situated at Geneva, Switzerland having 151 member countries with 630 secretariat staff headed by Pascal Lamy(Director-General). WTO in general covers the rules of trade between countries at global or near global level. They hold the responsibilities of administration, providing technical support to the needy countries, analysis of trade policy and performance, settlement of trade dispute and providing advice to member countries government. WTO agreement is a broad one, which covers trade in service, trade in goods and in trade inventions, creations and designs (Intellectual property).

INTELLECTUAL PROPERTY

Creativity is an art, which is found in all fields like films, music's, Books, Software's, clothing, etc. New ideas and knowledge, part of trade helps to face the competition. Creators should be given the right to prevent others from using their inventions, designs etc., and to negotiate payment for using the right. The WTO's agreement on Trade-Related Aspect of Intellectual Property (TRIPS), introduced under intellectual rules in the multilateral trading system is a good step that was taken to safe guard these rights around the world by bringing them under common international rules. IPRs have been accepted and recognized as a mean of protecting intellectual creativity in a legal way. Generation, storage and protection of avenues of knowledge have become a top priority agenda for most of the nations. The ultimate objective of IPRs is not to provide exclusive benefit to private persons and corporate alone but to the public at large.

The Agreement Covers 5 Broad Issues

1. The basic principles of the trading system and how other international intellectual Property should be applied.
2. How countries should enforce those rights adequately in their own territories.
3. How to give adequate protection to intellectual property right.
4. How to settle disputes on intellectual property between members of the WTO.
5. Special transitional arrangement during the period when the new system is being introduced.

TYPES OF INTELLECTUAL PROPERTY

The following are the areas covered by TRIPS agreements.

- Copyright of related rights.
- Trade makers.
- Geographical indications.
- Industrial designs.
- Patents.
- Layout design.
- Undisclosed information.

Copyright

Just like the literary works, now computer programs are also protected by the TRIPS agreement. The agreement safeguards the authors of computer program by giving the owners rights to prevent unauthorized person from using it.

Trademarks

Trademark may be a sign, or a symbol which identifies the product separately from other products. TRIPS agreements enforce certain rights to the owners of trademark.

Geographical Indication

There are a large number of products which are identified by the place name. There is lot of scope for people to misuse the place name. So TRIPS agreements establishes various notification, registration of geographical indications.

Industrial Design

The industrial design, when protected under TRIPS agreement, will prevent other manufacturers from copying the design.

Patents

A products patent has to be protected. The TRIPS agreements describe the various rights to the patents owner, but if the patent owner misuses the rights in anyway, then the government interference will be present to safeguard the consumers internal.

Undisclosed Information

Any trade secrets or any information which has a value, towards business must be protected, in order to prevent unfair trade practices. These secrets of information can be protected by the TRIPS agreements.

INTELLECTUAL PROPERTY IN INDIA

TRIPS provides only general and standard guidelines that should be complied with by the member countries with respect to IP protection. It is solely helps the individual member nation to formulate legislation which suit their social and political set up, ensuring effective protection of creative property. This underlines the need to look into the social impact of legislation with respect to IP protection in a regionalized manner. Here we examine some of the implications of IPRs at the grassroots level of society, especially in the Indian context.

India is rapidly developing its information technology market and the number of internet subscribers is increasing every day .Along with this development, there is need to have better and more comprehensive laws to tackle the issues that may arise in the near future. Protection of intellectual property at an offshore location is one of the core subjects for the companies that are planning to execute some of their core projects offshore. All the companies should have a good understanding of IP rights in India, for protecting their own rights.

The rapid growth of technology and ever increasing access to the internet has made it possible to access information from anywhere in the world at a mere click and at the minimal cost .Thus, it has revolutionized the manner in which information is disseminated and internet users are able to access the information as well as distribute their work, instantaneously .However this easy access to information comes along with its drawbacks. In addition to various forma of violation of intellectual property in the real world, now the intellectual property owners risk their Intellectual Property Rights (IPR) being violated in the virtual world as well.

The Berne convention for the protection of literary and artistic works establishes minimum rights that all countries agree to. since 1996 the World Intellectual Property Organization (WIPO) and this signatories of the Berne convention including USA and India have been trying to develop a new international treaty, know as Berne Protocol, to protect copy right holders in the digital context .However, this proposed Berne Protocol does not deal with ISP liability in great deal but has left it to the national legislatures.

World intellectual property organization defines intellectual property as legal rights that result from intellectual activity. The concept of intellectual activity includes artistic works, scientific works, literary work and industrial. The Indian intellectual properties has 4 major section, they are copyright patent trademark and design protection.

INDIAN INTELLECTUAL PROPERTY RIGHTS—SOFTWARE INDUSTRIES

The Indian copyright act 1985 has the provision to protect the copyrights of computer software. The Indian copy rights law clearly explains:

- The rights of a copyrights holder.
- The rights to the user to make backup copier.

The Software field is a very sensitive field, where the scope for fraudulent practice is more. It is always very easy to manipulate the original software package, in such a way that it is too identical to the original one. So this paved the way for the need of copyright Act. The highlights of the law are:

- Copyrighted software should not be made or distributed without authorization from the concerned authorities.
- The person who violates the law will be punished under both civil and criminal law.
- Heavy punishment for the infringement of software copyright.
- The violators will be imprisoned from minimum 7 days extended up to 3 years.

The government of India and Indian enforcement agencies are actively participating ,to protect the intellectual property rights .they have framed some measures to strengthen the copyright law the measures are:

- To create awareness of copyrights laws in the society ,the government has published a Handbook and these handbook are circulated to state and central government officials and even in seminars, workshops which are connected to IPO's.
- The government of India is conducting several training program for the police and customs officers, it has also constituted Copyright Enforcement Advisory Council (CEAC) and created cells in 23 states.

- The number of cases registered has gone up mainly by the initiates taken up by the government by conducting workshops and seminars on copyright issues

Steps to Protect Offshore Intellectual Property

- A detailed knowledge of the laws undertaken by the offshore country.
- A team to monitor their intellectual property rights.
- Before entering into a vendor relationship ,review the history of the company with respect to intellectual property and define the IP violation clause.
- The history behind the off team members should be verified ,with reference to IP violations.
- Create a general awareness among the employees of the company and also off shore team to protect the IP.
- Perform periodic IP audit, examine the new works and get it copy righted.

THE NEW CONCEPT-COPY LEFT AN ALTERNATE TO COPYRIGHT

Computer software was not the golden goose that it is today in fact ,it was often thrown in gratis with the hard ware .but the scenario was to undergo a sea change with consecutive advancements in technology .As the US software industry burgeoned ,bonhomie came to be replaced by secrecy .What happened was this source codes (a set of instructions humanly readable and hitherto releases with the software for use as desired) came to be blocked by the software companies , a lucrative avenue, since user would have to knock on their door each time a new feature was desired or a bug was to be exterminated.

There is a little dispute to the fact that software is entitled to copyright protection as a literary work ,as per section 2(o) and 14 of Indian copyright Act,1957,section 102(b) of the US copyright Act ,1976,Article 10 of the TRIPS or any other like provision, albeit its very unique nature has at times proven to be a trifle difficulty to reconcile with establishment notions of the law of copyright, what with court in various decisions in this aspect making effort 'to fit the proverbial square peg in a round hole 'It is in context that the discussion has assumed significance. Although, the realm of copy left licenses is no longer confined to the domain of computer software, it cannot be gain said that the genesis of the movement lies here. The uniqueness of the whole concept may be noted from the fact that the system of copy left actually rests upon the institution of copyright, whilst attempting to rid itself of many of fetters otherwise imposed by the latter.

The copy left is an agreement allowing the software to be used, modified and redistributed freely on the conditions that a notice to this effect is included with it .In the realm of software too, the practice of blocking source code riled many, who protested that proprietary software was undermining the very values that were envisaged to be upheld by the idea of copyright. Arguments such as personality of the creator as well that of reward were frowned upon, and a separate norm was sought, which would foster 'the prosperity and freedom of the public in general, thus the birth of copy left.

A copy left license provide that any user must agree not to assert copyright t protect any improvement or changes to the license, and must distribute any changes and subject to the license, and must make publicly available the entire source code for those changes .this indeed, is the most intriguing part of the entire discussion, viz that the license covers not only soft ware in its original form, but all modifications and improvements that may be made upon it by subsequent users.

The various benefits that are claimed as the outcome of WTO trading system

- The system helps to promote peace among the member countries
- The dispute settlement procedure are vital and ensure the trade flows smoothly
- The WTO's principal rule book runs to some 30,000 pages ,rules makes life easier for all
- The freer trade between the member countries cuts down the cost of living of each member countries
- When countries are allowed to trade freely ,the quality of the goods are improved and there are wide choice of products to the people
- The revenue for the member countries have increased considerably by the WTO trading
- Trades stimulate economic growth.
- Governments are shielded form lobbying.

The opponents of the WTO pose some arguments against the functions

- Commercial interest take priority over development, environment health of safety
- Smaller countries are forced to join the WTO and are also powerless.
- WTO so the tool of powerful lobbies.
- WTO is undemocratic and dictates policy.
- It is for free trade at any cost.

CONCLUSION

Director General of WTO, Pascal Lamy in a lecture said that the global trading system during the past 60 years "has underpinned an unprecedented period of economic growth and development" the world trade is growing at a faster rate than the growth in world output, but still the world trade is dominated by developed countries, the share of developing countries is increasing but at a slow pace. The current provisions of the Indian Patent Act, 1970 has amended are not only in conformity with the international obligations but are also sufficient to provide protection to the emerging fields of technology. It has also been observed that patenting activities in the emerging field of technology are increasingly growing. However India has a long way to go to attain what has been achieved by indigenous investors in developed countries such as US, Japan, and even developing countries like China and South Korea. A sound knowledge of IPR would be a prerequisite for the companies. The recent interest started with curiosity and an element of apprehension in 1995, but has now graduated to a need based compulsion and a desire to understand the nuances of IPR so that, as a nation, Indian can position itself in the competitive world that has emerged after the formation of the WTO and the introduction of TRIPS agreement.

REFERENCES

Madhavan Mahesh (2003), Use of Copyright by Open Source Software Movement on Computer Software and its Implications, *Journal of Intellectual Property Rights*, 8(1), 37.

Vaidhyanathan Siva (2001), Copyrights and Copywrogs (New York University Press, New York), pp. 155-56.

Shah A. (2007), The Information Technology Act, 2000: A Legal Framework for E-governance, *http://www.sudhirlaw.com/cyberlaw-itact.htm (10 may 2007).*

Joseph B. G. and Wasylik D. P. (2003), Copyright issues on the Internet and the DMCA, Practicing Law Institute-Patents, Copyrights, Trademarks, and Literary Property Course Handbook Series, 451.

Unni V. K. (2007), Internet Service Providers Liability for Copyright Infriengement. How to Clear the Misty Indian Perspective, *Richmond Journal of Law and Technology*, 8(2001) 13. ISP Liability, *http://www.bitlaw.com/internet/isp.html(9 may* 2007).

Signitories of the Berene Convention, *http://www.copyrightaid.co.uk/copyright_information/berene_convention_signatories (14 may 2007).*

Kishore K. John (2008), Intellectual Propert Rights in the Indian Context, Facts for You May, p. 26 to 29

K. S. Kardam (2007), "*Journal of Intellectual Property Rights*", Jan.

Bhalla A. S. (1996), Facing the Technological Challenge (Macmillan Press Limited London), p. 9-12.

Rajan Sudesh Focus WTO–Vol. 9, Oct. 07.

CHAPTER-16

WTO AGREEMENT IN AGRICULTURE

T. C. BRINDHA, R. NITHYA & S. DAVID SOUNDARAJAN

SALIENT FEATURES

THE provisions of the WTO Agreement on Agriculture are contained in three broad areas of agriculture and trade policy: market access, domestic support and export subsidies.

Market Access

Tariffication, Tariff reduction and access opportunities are the concepts included. The Non- tariff barriers are grouped and termed as Tariffication which includes quotas, voluntary restraint agreement, etc. These non-tariff barriers need to be abolished and converted to its equivalent tariff. Ordinary tariffs, resulting form the inclusion of Tariffication are to be reduced by an average of 36 per cent with 15 per. Additional duties are allowed to be imposed as a special safeguard provision when the imports rise unexpectedly beyond a particular level.

Domestic Support

Domestic support policies, subject to reduction commitments are measured by the total Aggregate Measurement of Support (AMS). This should be reduced by 13.3 per cent in developing countries and 20 per cent in developed countries. Reduction commitments refer to total level of domestic support and not to individual commodities. Reduction commitments are excluded for policies which have no or have minimal trade distorting effect on production (Green Box–Annex. 2 of AOA). The policies which provide service or benefits to agriculture or rural community are included in the list of exempted green box policies.

The developing country members can avail the Special and Differential Treatment provision. It includes the sale from and purchase of food for security stocks at administered prices. For meeting the requirements of urban and rural poor, the developing countries are permitted untargeted subsidised food distribution. The investment subsidies are also excluded for developing countries.

Export Subsidies

The main provisions of the Agreement were the members' commitments to reduce export subsidies. The rate of export subsidy reduction was fixed as 36 per cent by value and21 per cent by volume in 6 years for developed countries. The percentage cuts for developing countries were 24 per cent and 14 per cent by value and volume respectively in 10 years, in equal annual instalments. Products not subject to export subsidy reduction would not be granted such subsidies in the future.

ISSUES FOR NEGOTIATION

Market Access

(i) A few WTO members impose high agricultural tariffs and tariff peak which act as a significant barrier to market access opportunities. A very careful articulation or it is required as India has to maintain a reasonable level of tariff protection on consideration of food security and rural employment concerns.

(ii) The fear of tariff escalation is another factor discouraging the developing countries from diversifying to processed value added agricultural products for export purpose.

(iii) The trade opportunities of new suppliers, particularly from developing countries, are limited by the operation of Tariff Rate Quotas (TRQ). Hence, it is essential to have guidelines to enhance market access opportunities.

(iv) Aspects of sanitary and phytosanitary measures and making the special safeguard provisions available to all developing countries also figured in the negotiations.

Domestic Support

(i) A number of member countries, particularly the developing countries, have experienced difficulty in the calculation of Aggregate Measurement of Support (AMS). Such issues related to implementation require clarification.

(ii) The policies listed in the " Green Box" are to be revised for further tightening of criteria.

(iii) The "Blue Box" policies, which make direct payments to farmers under production limiting programmes should either be totally dispensed or should be subject to reduction commitments.

(iv) Application of De minimis support and means of incorporating increased flexibility should be discussed.

Export Subsidies

(i) A complete outlawing of export subsidies would be highly demanded. India should have right to provide export subsidies upto an appropriate level as long as it is permitted by WTO's Subsidies and Countervailing Measures Agreement.

(ii) Rolling over export subsidies are observed in certain countries due to the ambiguity in the existing language of AOA. This is to be suitably addressed.

NON-TRADING CONCERNS

The Non-Trade Concerns (NTCs) alluded in Article 20 of AOA would be taken into account for negotiation. It not only includes food security but also includes the protection of environment and maintaining the economic viability of rural areas. This concept is called Mutifunctionalism, which has to be examined from the perspective of developing countries. The main NTCs which India would like to see addressed is the need to provide employment in pre-dominantly rural agrarian areas.

Biotechnology

The agricultural production and trade is highly affected by the Biotechnical inventions. There is increased productivity of genetically engineered varieties of crops that are more pest resistant.

Food Security

1. The main objective of the AOA was to bring about discipline in one of the most distorted sectors of trade. This could be obtained by regularising the unrestricted use of production and export subsidies and reducing tariff and non-tariff barriers.
2. The provisions of the Agreement and its consecutive implementation do not have any impact of the fine balance between trade and non- trade concerns. The agreement is based on the hypothesis that liberalisation is the universal remedy for all ill effects in the agricultural sector. A purely market oriented approach may not be appropriate for developing countries whose significant percentage of population is around poverty line. It is therefore important for the AOA to ensure a special consideration towards food security and other non-trade concerns.
3. Rapid liberalisation has enabled the procurement of food requirements internationally. This assumption would not be true to all developing countries whose foreign exchange reserves limit such procurement.
4. The rising level of urbanisation, simple barter system of marginal farmers for sustenance and rapid industrialisation has lowered the productivity level. The only possible way to sustain the agricultural growth is to increase the governmental support.

ISSUES OF INTEREST TO DEVELOPING COUNTRIES

Large number of developing countries, whose large percentage of population is dependent on agriculture, are predominantly agrarian countries. The concern of these people gradually grew from self sufficiency to market access which was emphasised in the Uruguay Round.

The focus areas, where special and differential treatment provisions have provided in the AOA, are:

(i) Commitment to domestic support
(ii) Food security
(iii) Market access
(iv) Commitment to export subsidy
(v) Notification requirement and technical assistance.

AGREEMENT ON AGRICULTURE IN DEVELOPING COUNTRIES

There are various issues concerned to the developing countries which are formally and informally discussed in the committee of agriculture. There are certain countries, specifically Nordic countries of EU, which prefer to continue their agricultural subsidies. Whereas there are certain countries (Cairns) totally opposing trade subsidies followed by EU and Japan. There is another dimension of group who neither belong to the opposing EU nor the Cairns group. The developing countries are on the decision process to form the fourth dimension.

The result of liberalisation had made EU strongly defend its "Blue Box policies". Incase of abolishing the Blue Box policies, the members will have to agree to the recent changes in the rules of Agreement on Agriculture.

Multifunctionalism is the concept followed by the Japanese. It includes agriculture, food security and the balance between rights and duties of the trading countries of farm products.

Food security issues related to developing countries can be resolved only with a certain degree of autonomy and flexibility. The articulation of these non-trade concerns is with the hope that forth coming negotiations would provide adequate opportunity for persuasion.

IMPACT OF GLOBALISATION ON INDIAN FARMERS

The pressure of rich economies have resulted in the ill effects of succumbing. The import of food grains into into India, along with the domestic source, has created the problem of 'over- stocking'. The Indian government has to invent methods to prevent its rotting and for its proper utilisation. Inspite of this over-stocking, almost all 40 per cent of our country people suffer from malnutrition.

The enormous production of food grains by the developed countries like USA and EU is mainly to establish a fair market trading system. Dr. Devinder Sharma, a well known food and trade policies analyst, has stated that the hidden focus of the misuse of provision is "war for food supremacy".

Proposals by India

The provisions of special and differential treatment in Agreement on Agriculture, made after the Uruguay Round, have benefited the developed countries, though it was made for the benefit of developing countries. The prevailing inequality and discrimination has disappointed the Indian government.

The proposals has deviated the stand of the Indian government. The diabolic attitude of the developed economies has been increasingly opposed in the Post-Marrakesh Era. The bullying attitude of the northern rich economies has been opposed by the recent Indian proposals. These countries misuse the WTO platform for conquering the developing and LDC by the weapon of food.

Domestic Support

The elimination of all farm subsidies within 10 years was agreed in the Uruguay Round. There was a great opposition from EU and OECD countries. The domestic support in developed countries was at peak during the base period at 1986 to 1988.

India in Critical Period

Indian government desired to follow the American model of economic development. The Russian model of development, followed under the leadership of late Pt. Jawaharlal Nehru, favoured India. The downfall of Russia has made to blindly follow the controversial model. India is thus exhibiting a slavish mentality forgetting the existence of some Bharatiya model which would guide India in the path of progress.

Table 1

	Percentage of subsidy in proportion to national production		
Name of the country	*1986-88*	*1992-94*	*1997*
Canada	42%	31%	20%
EU	48%	48%	42%
Iceland	82%	77%	68%
Japan	73%	74%	86%
Norway	74%	74%	71%
Switzerland	79%	80%	96%
OECR	32%	41%	34%

POLICY PERCEPTIONS

1. It is an individual farmer, who would make the Indian agriculture a high performing one. The global model of farming as in Western countries will not be possible in Indian.
2. The requirement of organic manure for soil has necessitated the reinstate of traditional organic farming with modern inputs as supplements.

3. Efforts to be made to increase the number and quality of cattle population since it are the fundamental input resource for farming. Immediate steps must be taken to prevent cattle slaughter.
4. The major reason behind the slow growth of Indian agriculture is the target which is 200kg per person per annum. It is the level of target to stave off famine deaths. Unless the production target is increased, our country cannot attain the status it should hold.
5. The main reason for the high cost of farming is chemical farming which is proved by the recent experiments and experiences.

   The government ahs to create large funds to subsidise the easy change-over of the farmers from the wrong agriculture method, on the wisdom of the government.
6. The state must vacate the areas where the community system is still working and must step into a substitute where it is unworkable.
7. Incentives and needed facilities must be provided to promote the rural living to make it legitimate and respectable. Emphasis on the environmental, social and financial issues are also considered essential.
8. The government must take up the responsibility of rural infrastructural development for the next decade. The local Panchayati Raj institutions must take up the operations and maintenance.
9. The rejuvenation of the traditional agricultural practices to be undertaken so as to protect our traditional intellectual property, which remains unresearched unrecorded.

CONCLUSION

It needs to be said finally that agricultural self reliance forms a vital underpinning for the growth of the GDP of agrarian developing economies since good agricultural production provides purchasing power to a large majority of a population, which in turn spurts industrial growth. Self-sufficiency in food production has therefore a specific developmental perspective as opposed to a purely commercial perspective. Hence, it is our view that developing countries need to be provided the requisite flexibility within the AOA to pursue their legitimate non- trade concerns. More specifically, developing countries need to be allowed to provide domestic support in the agricultural sector to meet the challenges of food security and to be able to preserve the viability of rural employment, as diffrent from the trade distortive support and subsidies presently permitted by the agreement. It is therefore important that a differentiation is made between such domestic support measures which are presently being used to carve out a niche in the international trade and between those measures which would allow developing countries to alleviate rural poverty.

REFERENCE

Focus WTO, November- December, 2007.

Foreign Trade Review, January–March, 2008.

Panel Report, India", Quantitative Restrictions on Imports of Agricultural, Textile and Industrial Products", Adopted 22nd September, 1999.

WTO Annual Report, 2007

WTO, Cancun 5th Ministerial, 2003, *http// www. Wto.org/ English/min03_12sept_e.htm (15, March 2007)*

WTO Agreement on Agriculture-A Back Ground Paper, *http//commin.nic.in, abhatia@ub.delhi.nic.in*

Impact of Globalisation on Indian Farmers, Baba Takwale, *http// www.wto.org/*

Trading in Food Security, Dr. Devinder Shrama, 2000.

Foreign Trade, Jeevanandam, Sultan Chand Publications, 2007.

Chapter-17

IMPACT OF GLOBALIZATION ON INDIAN SUGAR INDUSTRY

J. P. Bhosale

INTRODUCTION

We are all aware of the recently emerging information technology and its impact created on individual , organizational and social activities . The advancement in sophisticated information technology resulted in devising a number of electronic devices which have been rendering value added services and increase in socio-economic status to the people worldwide , These are the days of information revolution, new economic order information oriented society and the age of global communication, instantly accurately at faster rate over video, audio, graphics, across the boundaries of the world.

Explosion in information technology in recent years is to a great extent is attributed to a new vistas opened up from space observation platform and rapid advancement in remote sensing technologies which are based on the silicon chip, fiber optics, coaxial cable, laser, satellite etc. Information technology has been changing and reshaping the dreams of business organizations, individuals etc., and many of them are proffering modern technologies today corporation have been giving top priority and spending substantial amount on information technology.

India is second largest sugarcane sugar producer in the world, since 1991. During the year 1999 - 2000 it has produce over 18.20 million tonnes of sugar , contributed nearly 15 per cent of the world sugar production. The yearly turnover of the industry exceeds Rs. 20000 crores & play the annual wage bill more than Rs. 10000 crore. Over 45 million farmers are involved in sugarcane production and its, allied activities and the receive Rs. 5500 crores in the form of sugarcane prices. The area under sugarcane cultivation is nearly 40.76 lakh hectares. It is just 2.8 per cent of the total area of the cultivation land in the country. Though there are more than 700 registered sugar mill in the country but presently some 450 plus sugar mills are in operation in different part of the country.

If we concentrate on the qualitative progress of the industry, it is observed that the sugarcane yield per hectare has been increased from 32 m. tonnes per hectare in 1950-51 to 72.6 m. tonnes in 1999-2000 but the sugar recovery is hovering around 10 per cent only during the same period.

CURRENT SCENARIO

India is the leader in the world sugar production after Brazil. But its position in the world sugar market has become very vertical . At present it carries a huge stocks of 12 million tonnes which represents almost 38 % (per cent) of the world inventory . Globalization of the world sugar economy has been already started but the extent of it remains limited as compared to the manufactured goods . Historically sugar has been regarded as one of the most regulated agro industries in the world . Now the globalization has created obvious challenges for those whose cost of production is higher & benefiting to those cost of production is low. India stand third (increasing order) in the cost of sugar production . Thailand , Australia and Brail are the low cost sugar production in the world . On this background Indian sugar industry has to rearrange & strengthen its position very carefully so as to make it more competitive in the world market .

The world sugar market is now open under the regime of WTO . Millions of farmers are anxious to know the impact of WTO on Indian sugar industry in general and their income levels, levels of living and quality of life in particular.

FEATURE OF WORLD SUGAR TRADE

The main feature of the WTO Agreement on Agriculture is the opening up of world market for agriculture products. Under this competition is bound of increase. The enforced competition will have two fold effects on the sugar industry.

1. That will increase domestic competition between different sugar factories.
2. The commitment to improve will make them globally competitive in the world sugar trade scenario the major importers of raw refined sugar are developed countries like European Union, U.S.A., Japan & Russia. Izach of these countries has heavily protected their sugar market through (1) reduces consumption, (2) encourage domestic production & (3) restrict trade. It shows that these countries have shield their producer from world market prices through.
   (a) Import protection
   (b) Higher support prices to domestic producer &
   (c) Export—subsides particularly in Ruropean union.

Ultimately it leads to huge export subsides , large scale domestic support of producers, high tariff wall & selective little market access to developing countries.

Export of sugar from the E. U. have contributed 15% of the world exports over the past five years. Most of these exports are produced under price support management and are subsidized . The heavily subsidized export of E.U. sugar stimulated surplus production and contributed directly to lower the world sugar prices.

European union under common Agricultural policy , USA with its tariff rates & highly protected industry of Japan are mainly responsible for the distortion in the world sugar trade .Owing to this protective tariff policies the India could not export its sugar to the traditional markets. At the same time it has become a dumping ground fui uilnjio. If we ^ce the comparison between domestic & international prices, it is observed that not only for sugar but for major Agriculture products the extent of protection enjoyed by domestic producers in E.U. is quite substantial. For sugar this gap is highest. This can be seen with the help of following table .

Comparative Prices of Various Food Items in E.U. World during 1999-2000

Items	*E.U.*	*World*	*Average %*
Wheat	133	188	13
Maize	140	92	52
Rice	600	300	100
Sugar	650	250	160
Bananas	660	360	83
Tomato's	787	633	24
Butter	2954	1307	126

Source: EU's Everything but Arms proposal for LDCs Likely.

Impact for India's sugar Industry by chetan Bijesure. The above table indicates that the high cost producers of sugar (E.U.) are dominating the world sugar market at the cost of effective producers of sugar in the world . It is also observed that most of the developed countries, mainly offer two types of subsidies to their domestic producers namely.

1. Transparent subsidies &
2. Veiled Subsidies

To Protect the home sugar industry the developed countries like European Union, U.S.A., Japan & Russia charge duties 250 per cent & above on imported sugar, naturally it checks the import of sugar from developed countries, this is called as transparent or direct subsidies. While in the from of veiled subsides particularly Thailand, Australia & Brazil Government offer interest free loans of their sugar industries for modernization of sugar mills. They also give the exemption to their sugar mills from certain long tern loans. Ultimately it helps to bring down the cost of sugar production in these countries & indirectly help to their sugar industries to become more competitive in the world market.

IMPACT OF GLOBALIZATION ON INDIAN SUGAR INDUSTRY

The Indian sugar industry is required to concentrate on number of important areas so as to make it more cost effective as well as more competitive at the global level.

Need to Bring Down the Cost of Sugar Production

The world average production cost of sugar exceeds prices. Costs tend to exceed prices because many producers benefit from Government protection enable them to survive despite their costs exceed world price level .year after year the sugar price has shown a downward trend approximately 1.5%. This trend has clear posed a serious challenge before the sugar producer around the word.

A study of Dr. James Fray, managing Director of LMC reveals that in:

1. *Field Cost:* It is lowest in India followed by Australia, Thailand, world average & China increasing order.
2. *Factory Cost:* It is lowest in Thailand followed by Australia, India world average & China Increasing order.
3. *Total Cost of sugar Manufacturing:* Shows that it is lowest in Thailand, followed by Australia, India world average & China, It shows that though, India has an advantage of lowest field cost in the world but when the field + factory cost considered together, Indian sugar industry stand third (increasing order) It means the Indian sugar industries not able to exploit the benefits of lowest field cost in bringing down the final or total cost of sugar production. Thus Thailand & Australia sugar industries are more cost effective as compared to Indian sugar industry . In Thailand the average crushing capacity per day is 15000 M. Tonnes where as it is just 2500 + TCD in India . Naturally it items the industry ability to exploit economies of scale in capacity has been started in number of sugar mills in the country , so that it will help to bring down the final of sugar manufacturing .

Need to Rationalize the Sugarcane Prices

When we see the proportion of various cost components in the total cost of sugar manufacturing, it is observed that a single component i.e.. Cost of sugar cane alone contributes more than 75 per cent in the total cost of sugar production. Therefore to check the total cost of sugar production there is need to concentrate more on i.e. cost of sugarcane (Raw material) & its quality . At present the central government decides the minimum statutory prices per ton to each factory , below which no sugar mill can pay the sugarcane price to their sugarcane growers . Again state Govt. comes in & decides the prices for each sugar mill, which are always higher than the statutory minimum prices decided by the central Govt. really this is the central crux the problem. It is observed that during the last 7 tears in U.h*., the state Advised prices have been increased by 55 per cent practice of arbitrarily determining a state Advised price (SAP) invariably far higher than the M.S.P. fixed by the central Govt. In southern states, this proportion is comparatively lower than the northern state of India .ultimately this leads to increase the cost of sugar manufacturing.

Therefore to rationalize the sugarcane price is the most important task before the industry for bringing down the total cost of sugar production. Ultimately that will help to make it more competitive at the international level.

Need to Concentrate on High Sugar Contents and High Yielding Varieties of Sugarcane

India is second largest producer of cane sugar in the world after Brazil. It contributes over 15% of the world sugar production . But even after this if we take a review of sugarcane yield per hectare & the quality of sugarcane produced the picture is grim. In spite of introduction of early mid & late maturing varieties , better technology in processing of cane juice, reduction in total losses, the sucrose recovery is rotating just around 10 per cent during the last 50 years.

In this connection it can be mentioned that the Australian Sugar Industry Which boats of 14.25 per cent sugar recovery is making extensive use of varieties which were originally developed at coimbtoor. Among many sugarcane varieties NCO 310 is the most preferred for higher sugar recovery in some Australian Sugar factories. The Burdkin district of Australia gets sugarcane with as much as 16 per cent sucrose in cane resulting into average recovery of 14.25 per cent on cane. This is Highest in the world. Secondly, it is also observed that the average productivity of cane ia also much lower as compared to number of countries in the world.

This can be easily seen with the help the help of following table. Yield of sugarcane & sucrose Recovery:

Year	*Yield of Sugarcane Tonnes/per ha*	*Averages sucrose Recovery%*
1930-1931	30.9 tonnes/pha	8.96
1960-1961	45.5 tonnes/pha	9.92
1997-1998	66.5 tonnes/pha	10.00
1999-2000	70.8 tonnes/pha	10.20

Where as the Sugarcane yield in Kenya 100.2 MT/P/ha, Egypt 100.3, Colombia 83.5 Australia 74.5 & Hawaii 150 M.T. per ha for the period of 24 months crop & the recovery in these countries is always more than 12 per cent.

Therefore, it is the need of the time the Indian sugar industry should concentrate on to development the high sugar content & higher yielding varieties of sugarcane which play a key role in the sugar industry.

Need to the Promote & Export of Raw Sugar

The cost of producing raw sugar in fairly low as compared to white sugar. It is because of less use of chemicals & utilization of higher crushing capacity. At present 55% of the world sugar trade is in raw sugar. Asia itself imports about

8 million tones of raw sugar perineum. Indian sugar industry can use this opportunity & should promote the production of raw sugar for international market.

Since raw sugar is generally exported in bulk, there can be considerable saving in the handling expenses such as bagging and allied costs etc. If large scale export of raw sugar is undertaken on a regular basis India can switch over to mechanical handing , which will accelerate the rate of loading & thus can earn additional amount of foreign exchange.

Indian raw sugar has an edge over the raw sugar of other countries as its sugarcane has no dextrose content which makes it easy for refining.

The Country can built up a very big clientele in Russia, Japan, South Korea, Malaysia China, Indonesia along with European union. Here, the porting raw sugar to these countries. This will also help to stabilize the domestic market.

Need to Improve the Quality of Sugar

The international sugar trade is based on certain quality norms prescribes by ICUMSA (International Commission for uniform method of sugar Analysis) The sugar importing countries usually insist on colour value less than 100 ICUMSA unit. In India the sugar quality is assessed by crystal size & luster s. The co lour is judged by visual comparison with Indian sugar standards supplied by National Sugar Institute Kanpur.

The colour of sugar is judged in the foreign countries by ICUMSA units. The codex commission judging the quality norm of sugar production now announced that method 10 would be the new testing mechanism for solving any international trade disputes in sugar. Till now the codex was using method 9 which was disadvantageous for Indian sugar because it consistently showed to have more than 150 ICUMA level.

According to experts, method 9, is a flaw because it is designed for testing beet sugar produced by the European union & not cane sugar produced by countries like India . Cuba, Brazil. Colombia , Thailand & Australia . It was nothing but a anomaly in testing norms which shows the poor quality of sugar. The newly adopted Method 10 is designed especially for cane sugar which will help to increase the marketability of Indian sugar . Now the sugar mills in India are required to make necessary changes in the quality norms of their sugar manufacturing which will help them to become more competitive in the international market.

CHALLENGE BEFORE SUGAR INDUSTRY

Challenge are not new to sugar industry tracing a little back, we come to know that the private sugar factory was powerful not only in Maharashtra but Bihar & Uttar Pradesh . But the government passed the shilling act and imposed rest auction on holding land . It adversary affected the private sugar industry which was based on the cultivation sugarcane of a thousands acres of land . This created the first big challenge of supplying sugar to the ever increasing population before the co-operative sector . However the first co-operative sugar industry was lunched at Pravaranagar in Ahamadnagar District of Maharashtra. Statistically speaking there are 465 sugar factories functioning all over the country . But of these , there are 140 factories in Maharashtra done and 180 are functioning with their full capacity.

Co- operative sugar Industry was served to organize thousands of laborers. It has created cheerful and promising future for the Farmers and has contributed immensely to change the face of the rural Maharashtra. It has built the hospitals, opened educational & trailing units, & prepared roads to make the life in the rural area more developed and prosperous. The sugar industry with its beneficial approach to the member terms and customers, has also efficiently attended on cultivating sugar can & producing quality sugar .The following date would convince the efficiency and work of the sugar industry. The investment of the annual turnover is around 4000 crores. Near about 700 to 1000 laborers get wages on permanent on contractual basis. Around 5000 other benefic ions are there which include can-cuting labours cane transferred and sugar exchange business. The government has invested around 220 crores in the state co-operative sugar industry .Around 1590 crores deposits are owned by the sugar industry and the share of Maharashtra is 1/3 of the national sugar production , but presently the sugar industry has been tracing a big challenge today in the spate of new economic reforms the scarcity of water, draught and invariability of resources also add to the complexity of the situation.

Along side the conventional problems like party-politics, inefficient administration, weak management , and malfunctioning factories, the new challenges knock the sugar industry in the new millennium. Following are some of the major challenges:

1. Without of government capital under the pretext of globalisation.
2. The indifference of credit-societies in providing financial assistance to the sugar industry.
3. The sugar Industry has ceased to have share in the stock market.
4. The increase in state government restrictions on the sugar industry.
5. Renewed exposure of the industry to newly imposed tare policies.
6. Least distance between tow sugar factories thereby shooting cut-throat competition.
7. The advent of multi-national companies has created shortage of sugarcane production. This may result into the increase of the production cost.
8. The cane-cutting laborers may lose their wages with the introduction of operative machines in the sugar factories.
9. The skilled and unskilled human power engaged in the sugar industry is the sugar industry is facing the problem of up gradation in technology and advance training.

10. There is need to pay attention to human resource development and financial management.
11. There is rapid increase in the membership of the non-sugar-cane producers
12. The young generation of the cane-cutting laborers is willing to be free from the manual hard work 13. There is a cut- throat competition between sugar factories on allotting good tares to farmers.
14. There is need to give emphasis on research and new technology.
15. Co-operative bank in the state do not seem to be extending their helping hands to the sugar industry.
16. Mechanism of sugar industry can severely affect the employment sector. IT. Enormous increase in electricity and water charges, increase in salary, in the chemicals have added to the problems in sugar industry.

CONCLUSION

Economy liberalization, privatization on one hand have created big challenges before sugar industry and natural calamities on the other hand add to the severity of the situation. The industry needs strict economic discipline, high efficiency, managerial skill, clean leadership and sincere efforts to overcome the problems and to survive the challenges successfully.

In short, the path of development lies in competition and sugar industry has to prove its competence in the newly changing scenario.

REFERENCES

Dr. G. A. Nikam, "WTO and It's Impact on Indian Sugar Industry Research paper Published in the Special Edition of, "International Conference" namely Globalization and India Economy". Apratim Publication Aurangabad.

* Dr. G. S. Nikam, Management of Co-operative Sugar Factories in Maharashtra.

* Dr. P.R. Dubhashi. Perestroika in Co-operation and other Essays.

*> Dr. J. P. Sing (2001), Iodays Sugar Industry's Need more Sugar Content High Yielding Varieties of Sugarcane". Co-operative Sugar, February, Vol. 32

No. 6 P. 465»> Editorial 'Indian Sugar Industry unbound', Co-operative Sugar, June 2001 Vol. 9 P .689 <* Editorial "Bitter Sugar Policy" *The Economic Times,* New Delhi

10/4/2001. *J* Editorial Diabetic Sugar Policy, Co-operative Sugar Press News October 11, 2001 Vol. 32 No. 37, P. 20 & 21.

•J* M. R. Desai (2000), 'Regional Sugar Policies and Its Impact on Sugar Industry in Asian Countries', Co-operative sugar September, Vol. 32 No. 1 pp. 29-33.

»> N.N. Shrinivas, India Scores A Win as WTO set New Sugar Testing Norms. Co-operative Sugar Press News , July 19, 2001, Vol. 32, No. 25, p. 36,37.

t Ranvir Nayar (2001), "India to Take up Sugar Quota with E.U", '*Economic Times*' 6/4.

Chapter-18

A BRIEF ANALYSIS OF SOME CHALLENGES FACED BY AGRIBUSINESS ALONG THE VALUE CHAIN

Vinodh K. Natarajan & J. Cyril Kanmony

INTRODUCTION

The global agribusiness is gradually being dominated by value chain relationships in which lead firms exercise vertical coordination. There is a startling variety of forms of such linkages in agribusiness value chains, including out grower schemes, contract farming, category management by supermarket suppliers, marketing contracts, etc. It is these linkages that small and medium enterprises can enter and add value to agricultural products. A number of strategies are available as a means of adding value to agricultural commodities. Strategies can involve certification or closer link with traders, producers, retailers or small farm producers. The adoption of these strategies by small producers in poor or developing countries is not very easy.

Meeting these challenges means organizing agribusiness value chains so that they are able to deliver what is required by global buyers and food safety regimes. As Van Roekel et al. (2002) state that integrated supply chain is a vital tool for competing in tool in today's globalizing business economy. Also it has been suggested that a defining characteristic of the agro-industrialization phenomenon is the growing number of complex contractual arrangements replacing spot markets (Cook and Chaddad, 2000).

Before we can explore the challenges faced by agribusiness, it is important to understand the various actors and relationship involved in the agribusiness value chain. Given below is a simplified agribusiness value chain diagram.

The above figure shows a simplified agribusiness value chain. Further it also shows the concentration of business activities at various stages in a value chain. Here at the first or input stage, concentration of chemical and seed companies are evident. The second stage or at the production stage there is concentration of agricultural producers. In this stage there are a large number of producers whose nature of concentration is based on the nature of products

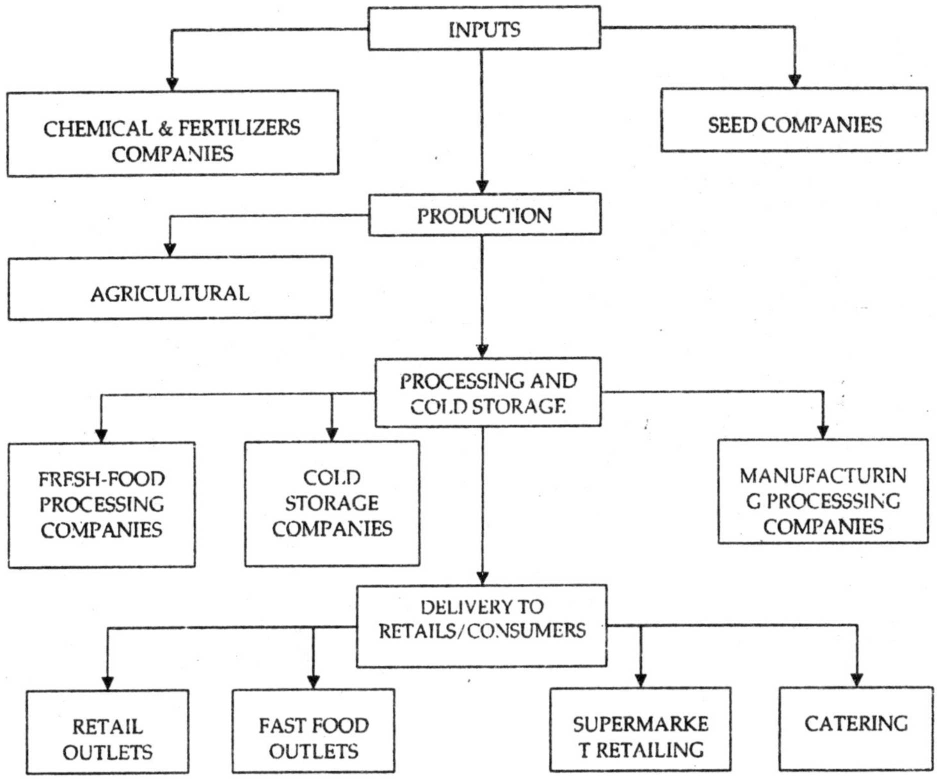

Source: Author

Figure 1: A Simple Agribusiness Value-chain Diagram

being produced. Climatic and soil conditions play a very important role in the nature of agricultural crops that can be cultivated in a particular region. For e.g., cultivation of cotton crop needs a dry climate, where as cultivation of rubber needs a rainy climate. This is an important criterion for emergence of agribusiness clusters among agricultural producers.

The third stage covers the processing industry. The processing industry covers a broad range of activities. At one end there are processors of fresh produce and at the other end, agricultural processing can involve the transformation of agricultural raw materials into a variety of processed products. In the processing stage value is added through packaging, preparation, innovation and keeping products fresh (involvement of cold storage chains) and transferring them quickly (logistics and supply chain management) from farm to delivery points or retail shelf. It must be noted that the benefits of processing in case of fresh vegetables has favoured large exporters who are able to undertake necessary levels of technical expertise and investment.

The last stage in the agribusiness value chain is the delivery to retailers or point of sale to consumers. Concentration in this space is also increasing with the emergence of supermarket retailing in developing countries. The rise of supermarket retailing indirectly has a profound effect on the structure of the production and processing industry. For e.g. in the 1970's Mc Donald reduced the number of its domestic ground-beef suppliers in the United States from 175 to 5. Food and grocery retailing has been consolidating in Europe and North America, where as in developing countries like, India China, and Brazil etc it is still in the evolving stage.

Concentration at the retail level is not only about size. It also changes the value-chain relationships as large buyers or supermarkets have transformed themselves from resellers of products made by others, into firms that find suppliers for the products they can sell under their brand to their customers. Increasingly they play an active role in branding, product development, supplier selection and distribution. The position of retailers within agribusiness is shown with the help of the table below.

Table 1
The Agricultural Supply Chain

Stage in Value Chain	*Number of Actors*
Consumers	160 million
Customers	89 million
Retail outlets	170,000
Supermarket formats	600
Buying desks	110
Manufactures	8,600
Semi-manufacturers	80,000
Suppliers	180,000
Farmers/Producers	3,200,000

Source: Grievink (2002).

The above table shows the different level of actors and the level of concentration prevailing in the food value chain in Europe. The above data clearly shows that the market power of key actors in agribusiness value chain comes from high levels of concentration at certain points in the chain. The consequence of these trends implies that there would be less income following to less concentrated parts of the value chain, mainly small farmers or producers. Therefore the need to look into the challenges faced by small producers and take steps to increase their incomes while adding value to their products must be given at most priority in the developing countries. If not the above value chain model will be replicated even in developing countries and the small producers will be marginalised.

The increasing influence of retail and branded markets as one of the main agents of globalisation was brought out by Gereffi (1994). He termed theses firms as manufactures without factories as they did not engage directly in manufacturing production themselves, but played an important role in product design, supplier selection and value chain coordination. A good example which highlights the role of firms participating through the global value chain can be seen through the way Nike conducts its business. It designs and markets footwear and clothing, but it does not own any footwear or clothing factories. It works with suppliers across various countries to deliver a rapidly changing range of products to shops and retailers spread across the world. Its core competences are design and branding, and not manufacturing. Logistics and supply chain management have been core competences, but these are increasingly outsourced to first-tier suppliers.

This type of business model is gaining prominence among agribusinesses and hence posing challenges as well as opportunities for small producers and farmers in developing and poor countries. The process of adding value along the value cum supply chain requires that the identity and distinctiveness of the product is established at the point of origin and maintained as it moves along the value as well as supply chain. Adding value need not involve physical transformation of the product. Global buyers such as supermarkets and large processors are not solely buying a physical product. They are buying a product that is bundled with a set of value-adding services. In other words, adding value to traditional agricultural export commodities often involves the same types of challenges as seen in the production and trade of non-traditional agricultural exports.

Value-chain analysis suggests a number of strategies for adding value. In particular, it emphasizes the opportunities for adding value through increasing "buyer service" elements of the total product package delivered to buyers. Increasing revenue streams from agribusiness by adding value should be the objective of any government policy. This challenge is one which has confronted policymakers not only in agriculture, but in export manufacturing as well.

THE IMPORTANCE OF AGRIBUSINESS ALONG THE VALUE CHAIN

The growth of agriculture sector is of primary importance for any country. Historical experience suggests that agricultural sector growth and increases in agricultural productivity may be a prerequisite to broader-based sustained economic growth and development (Department for International Development, 2002, UK Govt). Also many studies have documented the fact that agricultural growth is more effective in poverty eradication than growth of mining, manufacturing or services sector, since agriculture forms the backbone of any economic activity in rural areas. Moreover it can be said that agricultural growth provides a direct link to the poor as seen from the fact that forty to sixty per cent of the world's poor live in rural area (World Development Report 2000). Therefore, many economists have backed the agriculture sector as the engine for kick-starting growth among developing and poor countries

One opportunity for achieving higher agricultural growth lies in increasing export of agricultural products of poor countries in the global markets. The above argument is based on a theory which equates high economic growth with higher exports. Therefore for any country to achieve higher economic growth, the country must expand its export sector. Although this theory is debatable, many studies have brought out the fact that a higher export in any one sector accelerates economic growth. A major reason for articulating the idea that promoting agricultural exports will reduce poverty among developing and the poorest countries is based on the fact that the potential for export growth from the mining, manufacturing and service sectors is poor among developing and poor countries.

In short increasing the agricultural exports of poor and developing countries is not only important for economic growth but also a critical factor in reducing poverty. But, increasing exports by taking part in the global agricultural trade or being part of the global value chain, the agricultural sector provides both opportunities and challenges, which will be dealt later in the paper. The section below will bring out a brief outlook of the global agricultural scenario, which will be the basis on which some of the challenges faced by the agribusinesses will be dealt in detail.

The Global Agriculture Sector–An Overview

In the last decade or so there has been a rise in agricultural trade especially among developing countries. Improvements in transportation technology have played a vital role in promoting agricultural trade. Further the last quarter of a century has also seen large scale increase as well as transformation in global trade in agriculture sector. But it should be noted that not all sectors of agriculture provide the same opportunity for export led growth. This can be seen from the table given below.

From the above table it is clear that during the last two and half decades, there has been a substantial shift away from traditional tropical products and towards non traditional agricultural exports, particularly horticulture and fish (which includes seafood more generally). This is substantiated with the fact that in the early eighties, traditional tropical products accounted for 39.2 per cent of all food exports from developing countries, where as twenty years later this had fallen to 18.9 per cent. Conversely, during the same period, of the total food exports, the share of horticultural products rose from 14.7 per cent to 21.5 per cent and fish (seafood) rose from 6.9 to 19.4 per cent.

Overall, over the years the share of bulk commodities in total agricultural trade has gone down. Decreased demand for bulk commodities has been compensated by the growth in intermediate processed products, which are essentially processed bulk commodities. The consequences of this shift are also seen at the level of individual products. The rapid expansion of global demand for and trade in horticultural and seafood products created attractive export opportunities, while the relative decline of traditional tropical products, most notably coffee, created problems.

Table 2
The Changing Structure of Agricultural Trade (Percentage of Export Value)

	Total for Developing Countries	
Products	*1980-81*	*2000-01*
Traditional Tropical Products		
Coffee, Cocoa and Tea	18.3	8.5
Natural Fibres	8.0	3.3
Sugar and Confectionery	10.5	4.3
Nuts and Spices	2.4	2.8
Subtotal	39.2	18.9
Temperate Products		
Meats, Fresh and Processed	7.2	6.0
Dairy Products	0.3	1.1
Grains, Raw and Processed	9.3	7.0
Oilseeds and Edible Oil	4.6	5.5
Animal feed	7.5	8.5
Subtotal	28.8	28.1
Fish and Horticulture		
Fish, Fresh and Processed	6.9	19.4
Fruits, Vegetables and Flowers	14.7	21.5
Subtotal	21.6	40.9
Other Products		
Tobacco and Cigarettes	2.6	3.3
Beverages	1.1	3.6
Other Processed Food	6.7	5.2
Subtotal	10.4	12.1
Total	100	100

Source: Jaffee (2005).

A deeper look at the reasons why this shift from traditional tropical products to fish and horticulture by small farmers in developing countries happened might as well provide us with some interesting facts useful for framing policies for reducing poverty in developing or poor countries.

The advantages which the small producers experienced in shifting to horticulture production were many folds. Firstly, it offered them favourable price and quantity trends. Secondly, the horticulture industry is highly labour-intensive. Often horticultural production requires twice as much, sometimes up to four times as much labour than the production of cereal crops. Therefore it is a sector which generates relatively high levels of employment (Weinberger *et al.* 2005). Thirdly, some types of horticultural production yield the same amount of production using just a fraction of an acre needed to grow other crops. This helped the small farmers experience economies of scale and provided them with relatively high incomes per hectare of land in use.

Therefore, it is not surprising that a lot of effort has been devoted to promoting the production and export of non-traditional agricultural products with particular emphasis given to horticulture and fresh and processed produce. Moreover small farmers benefiting from huge increase in agricultural income do not shift their additional farm income on imported or capital intensive goods as done by large concerns. This is highlighted by the fact that reduction in poverty has been larger in countries where small and medium sized farms have driven agricultural growth.

As it has been said earlier that promoting agricultural exports is fundamental for reducing poverty, it is imperative that small and medium enterprises (SMEs) and poor producers being able to gain access to the value chains involved in the production, processing and distribution of these agricultural products. As poverty reduction depends on the economic growth of small producers it is very apt to look into some of the challenges faced by agribusiness in developing and underdeveloped countries and finding ways to overcome some of these challenges so as to benefit the people who are dependent on the agribusiness for their livelihood.

Global Trends in the Agribusiness

Global agricultural markets have become increasingly complex because of concentration at all points in the value chain. Many initiatives undertaken by many countries have been targeted to benefit the small producers as changes in agricultural trade have imposed new problems and challenges for agribusiness as a whole. Changes like growing disposable income of individuals, urbanization, consumer awareness regarding quality and safety are affecting the global agricultural trade. Therefore realizing the potential benefits of agricultural export growth for poverty reduction requires careful analysis of trends in global markets which are hindering the growth of agricultural exports of poor and developing countries. Some of the major changes that are impacting the global agricultural trade have been discussed below.

The Growth of Food Processing Sector

The faster growing categories in agricultural trade are non-bulk packaged processed food products, which are marketed under different brands. Developed countries have played an important role in promoting trade in processed food products. In developed countries, there is a demand for labour saving and better quality products, due to which the import of high value and processed foods products is more in these countries. On the other hand, in case of developing countries, due to increase in level of incomes and other factors the demand for processed food is slowly but steadily increasing, resulting in higher import as well as local production of these products. But still the share of developed countries in import of processed food products is more than developing countries, whereas in case of bulk commodities share of developing countries exceeds the import of developed countries. However the change in consumption pattern in developing countries caused by numerous factors is accelerating the growth of processed food industry.

Food Safety Initiatives-Standards

Food safety has emerged as an important issue in global agricultural trade. Moreover, increased consumer awareness, especially in developed countries has highlighted the importánt of food safety in agricultural trade. The importing as well as the exporting country are emphasizing hygiene and food safety issues in food production, processing, distribution and preparation. WHO is working closely with the Food and Agriculture Organization of the United Nations (FAO) to address food safety issues along the entire food production chain i.e. from production to consumption. Currently the WTO agreement, the Sanitary and Phytosanitory Measures Agreement (SPS) sets out the basic rules on food safety and animal and plant health standards. The SPS agreement allows countries to set their own standards and adopt different methods of inspecting products. But having different technical regulations and product standards makes life difficult for producers and exporters. Therefore adoption of international standards is a better option for exporters, but it certainly involves significant costs. The high costs involved may discourage manufactures from poor countries from trying to sell their agricultural produce abroad thus preventing access to taking part in the global market.

Growing Ethnic Influence

On the global level food consumption can no longer be confined to food being produced locally. Fast-food burgers, French fries, Chinese noodles and rice, Italian pasta and pizza, Indian curry, Japanese sushi, and many varieties of types of food have spread their reach to all parts of the world. This has lead to the availability of a wider choice of ethnic food. Due to increase in the number of working women, greater disposable household income, increased trade and above all the free movement of people across the boundaries the awareness and demand for and consumption of many ethnic foods is on the rise. The availability of different ethnic food locally has influenced the consumption pattern of people at the global level. This has led to new agricultural products being produced and exported from developed countries to developing countries and vice versa.

Food Retailing

The growth of Modern distribution outlets or retail chains in the wholesale and retail agribusiness are shifting customers from traditional traders to modern retail chains. The rise or modern distribution outlets are a significant gain for the packaged food industry. According to a survey by US Department of Agriculture, packaged food products account for large shares of total food expenditures among consumers in high-income countries where the demand for convenience is growing. The United States, the European Union, and Japan account for over half of total global sales of packaged products. In developing countries, intermediate products such as vegetable oils, dry pasta, and other dried products account for the bulk of retail sales. However, market trends indicate strong growth in sales of packaged food products among developing countries partly due to rapidly growing income levels created by the growth of the manufacturing and service sectors.

In order to safeguard the interests of small farmers it is important for the government, development agencies, as well as private players to undertake several initiatives to include them as part of this organised retailing. Being part of the retail chain business can help the small farmers to gain more income and reduce the poverty level on a larger scale.

Having seen some of the trends that confront the agribusiness, it is worthwhile to look in detail some of challenges affecting the Indian agribusiness taking part in the global value chain in lieu of the changing trends in agricultural trade.

THE GROWTH OF FOOD PROCESSING SECTOR AND FOOD RETAILING

Historically speaking, processing of fruit and vegetables in the simplest form like pickle making, sun drying and or making preserves has been practiced in the country from very ancient times almost in every home. It has generally been the exclusive domain of grandma's who developed their own fine recipes without any formal training except their age-old experience and conventional wisdom.

Worldwide, during the last half a century, the food processing industry has undergone massive changes. It has emerged as a big industry with major sub sectors like, Fruit and Vegetable Processing, Fish-processing, Milk Processing, Meat and Poultry Processing, Packaged/Convenience Foods, Alcoholic beverages and Soft drinks and Grain Processing. Also during the same period, from the age of famines and food importer, the Indian food and food processing sector has evidenced strong growth.

As of 2006 India ranks third in production of food grain (210 million tonnes), is the worlds second largest producer of fruits and vegetables (150 million tonnes) the largest producer of milk (91 million tonnes), the largest producer of tea (820 million tonnes) third largest producer of fish (6.3 million tonnes) has the worlds largest livestock (485 million) and produces 489 million poultry and 4.52 billion eggs annually. Further, during 1998-99 all varieties of spices worth over Rs. 3500 crores (US $ 900million) amounting to 25-30 per cent of world production was produced and processed for value-addition and export. It grows 22 million tonnes of oilseeds covering most of the varieties. In 1999 the total area under fruits and vegetables cultivation was estimated to be at 5.63 and 5.6 million hectares respectively (Annual Report 2006, Ministry of Food Processing Industries (MFPI), India).

India produces large variety of fruits and vegetables - tropical, sub-tropical or temperate. These include mango, banana, apple, orange, chikoo, and pomegranates, and vegetables like potato, tomato, onion, cauliflower, and cabbage. Moreover India is also one of the major producers of plantation products including tea, coffee, cocoa and cashew. Over the last few years, there has been a positive growth in ready to serve beverages, fruit juices and pulps, dehydrated and frozen fruits and vegetable products, tomato products, pickles, convenience veg-spice pastes, processed mushrooms and curried vegetables. The above statistics gives a small but significant picture about the importance of agriculture sector to the Indian sub continent.

Having looked at the agriculture sector as a whole, it is worthwhile to look at some statistics prevalent in the food processing sector. It was in the First World War that some mechanization and commercialisation entered into this industry mainly to meet the demand of the armed forces. The Second World War gave it a much-needed fillip. Since then it has been progressing fairly well and has been meeting the local demand and in a very limited way entered the exports market. It is, however, not a heavy weight industry but has the potential to develop into a Sunshine Industry of the country.

As per a recent study on the Indian food processing sector, during the year 1998-99, the turnover of the total food market is approximately Rs.250,000 crores (US $ 69.4 billion) out of which value-added food products comprise only Rs.80,000 crores (US $ 22.2 billion). During the year 2001 -2002 processed food exports were at around 17,09,813.84 (Million Tonnes) generating revenue of Rs.4381.57 crores. As of 2005-06 processed food exports rose to 19,05,819 (Million Tonnes) generating revenue of Rs.7539.43 crores. Out of these exports, processed fruits & vegetables accounted for 26.34 per cent, animal products accounted for 36.25 per cent and other processed foods accounted for 37.41 per cent. The average growth rate of food processing industry during five years preceding 2003-04 has been 7.15 per cent.

In meat & meat processing sector, poultry meat is the fastest growing animal protein in India India's livestock population is largest in the world with 50 per cent of world's buffaloes and 20 per cent of cattles. As the Indian consumer prefers to buy freshly cut meat from the wet market, rather than processed or frozen meat only 6 per cent of production of poultry meat is sold in processed form. Of this, only about 1per cent undergoes processing into value added products. The total processing capacity in India is over 1 (Million Tonnes) per annum, of which 40-50 per cent is utilized. India is the 5th largest exporter of bovine meat in the world. Indian buffalo meat exports have the potential to grow significantly. The estimated production is 1,500 thousand tones growing at CAGR (compound annual growth rate) of 13 per cent through 1991-2005. Per capita consumption has grown from 870 grams in 2000 to about 1.68 kg in 2005. This is expected to grow to 2 Kg in 2009.

India is the largest milk producer in the world with a production of 91 million tones growing at a CAGR (compound annual growth rate) of 4 per cent. About 35 per cent of milk produced in India is processed. The organized sector (large scale dairy plants) processes about 13 million tonnes annually, while the unorganized sector processes about 22 million tonnes per annum. The quantum of marine products processed and exported during the year 2004-05 was around 4,61,329 (Million Tonnes) generating revenue of Rs. 6647 crores. Size of the semi-processed and ready to eat packaged food industry is over Rs. 4000 crores (US$ 1 billion) and is growing at over 20 per cent.

Primary food processing is a major industry with lakhs of rice-mills/hullers, flour mills, pulse mills and oil-seed mills. There are several thousands of bakeries, traditional food units and fruit/vegetable/spice processing units in unorganised sector. In the organised sector, there are over 820 flour mills, 418 fish processing units, 5198 fruit/vegetable processing units, and 171 meat processing units. India's agricultural production base is quite strong but at the same time wastage of agricultural produce is massive. Processing level is very low i.e. around 2 per cent for fruits & vegetables, 26 per cent for marine, 6 per cent for poultry and 20 per cent for buffalo meat, as against 60-70 per cent in developed countries.

The statistics mentioned above show that Indian food processing sector is in for some tasty times. India can emerge as a leader in the Food Processing Industry in terms of production, consumption, exports and growth prospects due to various factors. Some of the factors which are in favour of India emerging as a leader in the food processing industry are stated below.

- Due to its diverse agro-climatic conditions, it has a wide-ranging and large raw material base suitable for food processing industries.
- It is one of the biggest emerging markets, with over a billion in population.
- Rapid urbanisation, increased literacy and rising per capita income, have all caused a rapid growth of 250 million strong middle class leading to changes in demand patterns, providing tremendous new opportunities for exploiting the large latent market. It is said that an average Indian spends about 50 per cent of his household expenditure on food items.
- Liberalised overall policy regimes, with specific incentives for high priority food processing sector, provide a very conducive environment for investments and exports in the sector.
- Very good investment opportunities exist in many areas of food processing industries like fruit and vegetable processing, meat, fish and poultry processing, packaged, convenience food and drinks, and milk products.

Although the above factors are important for the growth of the food processing industry (FPI), it is imperative that government also frames policies and action plans which facilitate this growth. Having understood the importance of food processing sector, for the economic growth of India, the Indian government has accorded the food processing industry a high priority, with a number of fiscal relief and incentives, to encourage commercialisation and value addition to agricultural produce; for minimising pre/post harvest wastage, generating employment and export growth. Currently the state governments in India have been responsive at the policy level by amending certain sections of the Agricultural Produce Market Committees Act, 1966 to allow effective implementation of contract farming.

As a result of several policy initiatives undertaken since liberalisation in August 1991, the industry has witnessed fast growth in most of the segments. Since liberalisation in Aug 1991 and till Feb 2000 over Rs. 53,800 crores (US$ 13.4 billion) of projects have been proposed in various segments of the food and agro-processing industry by the central government of India. Besides this, the Indian government has also approved proposals for joint ventures, foreign collaboration, industrial licenses and 100 per cent export oriented units envisaging an investment of Rs. 19,100 crores (US$ 4.80 billion) during the same period. The total inflow of FDI in FPI sector up to 2006-07 (upto December 2006) was Rs. 2500.65 crore. In order to give fresh impetus to processing of Fruit and Vegetables, Government in 2004-05 has allowed under I.T. Act, 100 per cent deduction of profit for first five year and 25 per cent deduction for another five years for new upcoming Fruits & Vegetables Processing units. A Vision 2015 on Food Processing Industries has been finalized by the food processing Ministry for giving boost to growth of food processing Sector which envisages increasing the size of the processed food sector by increasing the level of processing of perishables from 6 per cent to 20 per cent, value addition from 20 per cent to 35 per cent and share in global food trade from 1.5 per cent to 3 per cent by 2015. To achieve this the thrust areas identified for strategic intervention are-establishing Mega Food Parks, Modernization of Abattoirs, Cold Chain/Value Addition and Preservation Infrastructure, Upgrading Safety and Quality of Street Food and Establishment / Upgradation of Quality Control Laboratories.

The above statistics and government initiatives speak volumes about the growth rate experienced by the agricultural sector and more importantly the food processing industry. Despite all this bounty, two challenges confront the agricultural sector. One challenge stems from the projected increase in household demand for goods and services in tune with anticipated population growth. The second challenge which is very important from the agribusiness point of view is that despite all world class status achieved among different agri-products less than two per cent of the food produced is processed in any way. This can be attributed to a number of reasons. The reasons for the domestic consumption of value added fruits and vegetable products being low as compared to the primary processed food in general and fresh fruits and vegetables in particular can be attributed to higher incidence of tax and duties including that on packaging material, lower capacity utilisation, non-adoption of cost effective technology, high cost of finance, infrastructural constraints, inadequate farmers-processors linkage leading to dependence upon intermediaries. The smallness of units and their inability for market promotion is also other main reasons for inadequate expansion of the domestic market.

On the whole the food processing industry is facing constraints like non-availability of adequate critical infrastructural facilities like cold chain, packing and grading centres, etc. lack of adequate quality control and testing infrastructure, inefficient supply chain, lack of processable varieties of farm produce, seasonality of raw material, high inventory carrying cost, high taxation, high packaging cost, affordability and cultural preference of fresh food.

The implication is that the Indian agribusiness experiences a huge loss of potential revenue for producers, since processed food generally commands premium rates. Also in India where so much of food is produced, bulk of it gets wasted due to lack of transportation, cold storage and processing facilities (like sorting, cleaning, and freezing and basic preservation methods.). Therefore the food processing is not a luxury but a necessity and this industry provides a huge potential which is waiting to be tapped.

The Indian consumers by and large very much prefer fresh fruit and vegetables. The high cost of packaging pushes up the cost of the processed items and thereby makes them out of reach of the common man. Because of the varied agro climatic conditions some fresh fruit and vegetable are available throughout the year. The fruits like bananas are non seasonal and apples, oranges, and potatoes etc. are put in the cold stores thus prolonging their shelf life and making them available in the off-season. Some fruits like guavas, oranges have two seasons so they are available in fresh form for four to five months in a year. Therefore it can be seen that domestic consumption of processed items is quite meagre because of economic reasons and also as a matter of habit.

In spite of the fact that India, is the second largest producer of fruit and also of vegetables in the world yet the commercial processing of fruit and vegetables is estimated at 2.20 per cent of the total production. The installed capacity of fruits and vegetables processing industry has increased form 11.08 lakh tons on 01.01.1993 to 21.18 lakh tones as on 01.01.2006 and 24.74 lakh tones as on 01.01.2007. Therefore the food processing industry has abundant investment opportunities in the expanding domestic market and export arena. Further increasing acceptance of new products with market development efforts along with changes in export-import policies and exchange rate adjustments have helped improving the export potential of processed foods.

There is a good international demand for certain fresh fruits as well as processed fruits products. Fresh fruits identified as having good export potential are: mango, grapes, banana, lichee and exotic fruits like sapota, ber, pomegranate, custard apple and other tropical fruits. Among vegetables, the items identified as having good export potential are: onion, potato and green traditional vegetables like: okra, bitter gourd, green chillies and other seasonal vegetables. Many non-traditional vegetables mainly processed mushrooms and gherkins, and other like: asparagus, celery, bell pepper, sweet corn, green and lima beans and organically grown vegetables are also increasingly being exported.

Also with its over 8000 km. of coastline, 3 million hectares of reservoirs and 1.4 million hectares of brackish water, India has vast potential for fishes from both inland and marine resources. Units mostly exist in the small scale sector as proprietary/partnership firms or fishermen co-operatives. Over the last decade, the organized corporate sector has become increasingly involved in preservation, processing and export of coastal fish. But the wide variety of fish resources found in Indian inland waters, coastal areas and deep seas comprising India's Exclusive Economic Zone, still remain grossly underutilized.

In developed countries farming cooperatives harvest, grade and preserve their own produce. This not only helps them to limit wastage but also provide them with time to negotiate profitable deals to sell their produce to large food processing companies, whereas in India the farmers have as little as twenty-four hours to strike a deal because of the perishable nature of the produce. In fact the farmer looses out as the day wears on, since fresh produce commands a higher price in the morning. This wastage can be estimated to be as high as 40 per cent. The annual total value loss arising from such wastage can be estimated to be around Rs 50,000 crores. To bring about more value out of the food industry it is imperative that there is a very effective infrastructure and supply chain setup which helps in tapping the value available in the food processing industry.

Although many strategies can be used to improve agricultural infrastructure in the value chain, contract farming is one strategy which can be used in the Indian market especially in the food processing sector. The benefit of contract farming can be seen if contracts are well designed and implemented. On the one hand the farmers and small producers (Small and Medium Enterprises) benefit from guaranteed prices, technical assistance and funding for cold chain infrastructure. On the other hand the big corporates benefit from assured raw materials. Therefore it is a win-win situation for the local farmers as well as big retail corporate or super markets. In India the multinational dairy sector has been one of the largest users of contract farming model which allows many actors to participate in the value chain.

Many big industrial corporates like ITC, Reliance, Birla, and RPG Group, are setting up huge network of retail chains and supermarkets across the country. Retail chains in agricultural products are expected to drive the growth of contract farming, especially in fruits and vegetables. This provides a huge potential for the food processing industry as contract farming helps in solving some of the problems faced by the local farmers through backward integration of business processes. A very good example of a successful contract farming business in India is the Suguna Chicken Company.

Due to massive increase in number of big retail stores, the demand for cold storage chains is increasing. This is another problem faced by agribusiness in India. The current cold chain storage infrastructure in India is fragmented. The major reasons why cold chain storage is not very prevalent in India are high capital and power costs, low utilisation and lack of support structure including human capital, quality benchmarks and food protocols. There are a very few players who operate in the integrated logistics management namely, Snowman, Frick India, Chitanya Cold Storage, Fresh Express and Kausar.

The annual demand for frozen food by organised retail chains is estimated to be around Rs 1500 crore, which presents a huge opportunity for growth. Currently the back end creation investment by all retail players is estimated at Rs 20.5 lakh crore. The government has also initiated action on this front by planning to implement the scheme for infrastructure development comprising the following components to address different aspects of food related infrastructure, like Mega Food Parks, Packaging Centres, Integrated Cold Chain Facility, Value Added Centres, Irradiation Facilities, and Modernized Abattoir across the country. The MFPI has so far approved 54 food parks for assistance out of which 29 are operational as on date. The food parks are based on public-private partnerships with private partners expected to bring in around Rs.400-450 crores for each project.

Because of the liberal government and other developmental measures being taken, to some extent cold chain storage is being provided, which will help in retaining quality, freshness and reduce post-harvest losses. With the new hybrid varieties being added the production season is also being extended. If the above mentioned challenges are looked into and measures are taken to implement them, then it shall result in the greater availability of quality raw materials to the industry. This will result in better capacity utilisation and producing a wider range of products and of international quality and in effect enhancing the success of the Indian agribusiness. With the rise in the per capita income particularly of the middle class accompanied by drastic change in the food habits the processed foodstuff seems to be the winner.

THE NEED FOR QUALITY INFRASTRUCTURE IN AGRIBUSINESS

The presence of quality infrastructure, for conducting agribusiness, is very important for ensuring continued market access and supporting improved competitiveness. The term infrastructure is widely used and if detailed it aims to cover three broad areas that need development for the growth of agribusiness trade. Three broad areas identified within this quality infrastructure requirement are: logistics capability development, inspection and testing infrastructure which are accredited according to international standards and certification agencies.

There is a need for physical and informational infrastructure, visible at airports, seaports, and inland storage centres to support coordination between enterprises and the rapid shipment of products. The speed of product transport and supply-chain coordination depends on effective communication which requires investment in relatively simple, cheap, and reliable Information,

Communication and Technology (ICT) infrastructures. The communication infrastructure helps the suppliers to coordinate their activities with buyers. In short, the above requirements call for a sound logistics capability development within a country.

The importance of quality products with increasing control on the number of substances that can be used in production processes has put a strong demand for the setting up of inspection and physical testing infrastructure. This infrastructure provides a dual function: it provides assurances to producers about the quality of inputs they use and the safety of the products they sell, while at the same time providing assurances to buyers through regular inspections of producers and products. Thirdly, given the increasing importance of standards, governments need to support the development of local certification companies that will provide services at a reasonable cost.

The need for provision of this quality infrastructure by a government is important as there is an increasing importance placed on "buyer service requirements" such as food safety, quality and speed and reliability of delivery in agribusiness trade. Further developing countries like China, Brazil and India are expected to increase their food exports, which face non-tariff barriers such as stringent sanitary and phytosanitory norms.

The area of standards has been dealt elaborately in this paper as it is the area of non-tariff barriers wherein developing countries will be facing the biggest challenge in increasing their agricultural exports in the coming years.

Food Safety Initiatives-Standards

Standards today encompass much more than technical product standards. Hawkins states standards as 'external points of reference', by which a product or service's performance, its technical and physical characteristics, and/or the process and conditions under which it has been produced or delivered can be assessed" (Nadvi and Wältring, 2004).

The standards environment for agribusiness has exhibited some important trends that are important for the structuring of value chains in the agribusiness sector. Increasing awareness of the health risks has led to increasing stringency of public mandatory standards relating to food safety. Tightening of control in areas like pesticide residues, colouring and purity in foods have been seen in the Europe Union.

Satisfying food safety requirements of importing countries have become more complex. This is due to the fact that the range of items as well as the stringency of standards covered by mandatory standards have increased. Not only the agribusiness sector is facing increasing mandatory standards and stringency of standards but also the sector is facing complications in demonstrating compliances with standards because of a shift from product standards towards process standards (i.e. the way products are grown, harvested, processed and transported). Product standards merely define particular outcomes to be achieved; process standards indicate particular procedures that need to be put in place. The shift towards process based standards will require new systems to be established and verified, which imposes additional costs.

With the adoption of Hazard Analysis and Critical Control Point (HACCP) norms in food processing sector many countries have shown a commitment to transit from product standards to process standards controls. Hazard Analysis and Critical Control Point is an important quality assurance system. HACCP is an important requirement for ensuring the quality of products from health and safety aspects and is crucial for exports. This system ensures that the products are safe and of good quality. For e.g. the US has made HACCP mandatory in plants processing meat, poultry, fish and fruit juices. Canada has made HACCP mandatory in the fish processing sector and the EU has made HACCP mandatory for dairy, meat and fish products. The shift towards a process-control approach to food safety is clearly expressed in the law establishing the European Food Safety Authority.

Standards in Agribusiness Value Chain

Standards in agribusiness value chains operate, at multiple points. There are controls by different agents carried out in different ways at different points along the value chain in response to the requirements of private sector companies, coalitions of private-sector standards setters and public agencies. The development of public and private standards involves interventions at multiple points along the value chain. The need and importance of public and private standards can be best explained with an illustration.

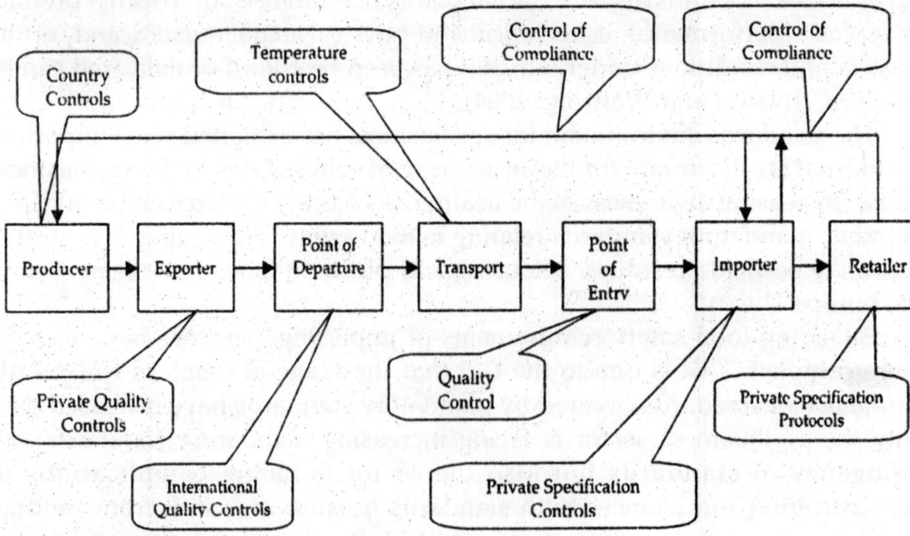

Source: Author

FIGURE 2: **Food Safety and Quality Control in an Agribusiness Supply Chain**

The figure above highlights the various points wherein public and private standards in agribusiness value chain are needed. It illustrates that standards are created, adopted, applied and verified by different actors (enterprises and institutions) at different points in the value chain. Although the above value-chain highlights the range of options available for the enforcement of standards the requirements for public enforcement of standards vary according to the nature of the value chain. On the one hand, when the export sector is fragmented, or when the outputs of the export sector are relatively standardized and sourced through arms-length market relationships, governments can enforce standards through inspection, testing, and certification of producers. In contrast, when products are highly customized and relationships between buyers and sellers are information-intensive, then much of the task of ensuring buyer confidence is achieved through the buyer-seller relationship.

Food safety is viewed as a product of the value chain as a whole, "from primary production to delivery to the consumer", and as a consequence risks have to be managed at all points and traceability guaranteed so that a particular product's chain history can be reconstructed.

Challenges Faced While Adopting Standards

The private sector and civil society organisations have began to play an enhanced role in the regulatory process in the standards environment thus complimenting the public mandatory standards. The term "private standards" has been used to refer to particular labels used by private companies to differentiate their products and to indicate superior quality features. For e.g. the "Nature's Choice" label developed by the UK supermarket, Tesco, is a good example of such a label. Tesco positions the label as guaranteeing superior safety, quality and environmental standards through the monitoring and certification of suppliers. Less visible, but more important, are the collective private standards developed by groups of firms and business associations. In the European food industry, these standards include the EurepGAP standard, developed by EUREP (an association of European fresh produce importers and retailers), the UK British Retail Consortium standard for food processing and the Franco-German International Food Standard.

The consequences of the rapid development of public and private standards have created many challenges and problems for producers in the agribusiness. Firstly producers in developing countries face more standards, more stringent standards and multiple standards developed by different agencies addressing the same issue. The magnitude of this challenge faced by the food industry is evident when we take a look at the list of certification offered by a single company in Switzerland. The table below illustrated the list of certification offered by a Swiss company called ProCert.

Secondly certificates have become indispensable marketing instruments, whether they are visible to the consumer, or required on principle by western retail chains for imported fruit and vegetables. Certification by international

Table 3
Certification Offered by a Swiss Company Called ProCert

Standard	*Title*	*Accreditation*
ISO 9001:2000	Quality management system	SCES 039
ISO 14001:2004	Environmental management system	SCES 039
ISO 22000:2005	Food safety management system	SCES 039
OHSAS 18001:1999	Management System for Occupational Health and Safety	SCES 039
FSIO-DI 2000 (Swiss)	Quality management system for Institutions for the disabled	SCES 039
BRC Global Standard-Food	Food safety management system	SCES 038
IFS (International Food Standard)	Food safety management system	SCES 038
DS 3027	Food safety management system	SCES 039
ELOT 1416	Food safety management system	SCES 039
eduQua	Swiss quality certification for continuous training institutions	SCES 039
EUREPGAP	Euro Retail Produce Working Group for Good Agricultural Practice	SCES 038
Programms AOC (Swiss)	Appelation d'origine contrôlée (AOC) Sbrinz, Rheintaler Ribelmais, Cardon épineux genevois	SCES 038
Programms IGP (Swiss)	Indication géographique protégée (IGP)-Viande desgrisons, Saucisson vaudois, Saucisson aux choux vaudoise	SCES 038
Feed Safety (Swiss)	Feed Safety Management system	SCES 038
Naturane (Spain)	Integrated Production	SCES 038
Fontestad (Spain)	Integrated Production for citrus fruits	SCES 038
Natursense (Spain)	Integrated Production for citrus fruits	SCES 038

Source: http://www.procert.ch/zertifizierungen.

agencies can be costly for developing country producers. For this reason development of local certification agencies is needed in most developing countries. Another question may arise is whether the certification by local certification agencies in developing countries will be acceptable to the authorities in developed countries. Further, developing a different domestic market standard creates the problem of proliferation of standards for companies that wish to produce for both markets. However, it should be noted that governments have a difficult choice to make; particularly when they seek to develop standards for agricultural produce sold domestically as well as exported. If a government decides to apply the same standard prevailing in key export markets to its domestic market, it could place the small producers at a disadvantage. This is due to high costs involved in adapting to international standards as the market for their produce is primarily domestic which is price competitive. A very good example to counter the above stated argument can be seen from the success of AfriCert, the first Nairobi based Certification Company in Eastern Africa. AfriCert has now gained accreditation according to the international ISO 65 standard. AfriCert's seal of approval confirms that producers subscribe to good agricultural practices, namely resource conservation, safe use of pesticides, good post-harvest protection, hygiene, and occupational health and safety. AfriCert now offers growers in Kenya and the region affordable certification in line with internationally recognized standards. "The company has enabled us to close a considerable gap in the value chain of agricultural products. Previously, exclusively European companies offered certification - a costly process that only major growers could afford. Without the EurepGAP certificate, growers are unable to export their goods to European supermarkets as powerful retailers in Europe have begun demanding the EurepGAP certificate from their suppliers. The advantages especially for small and medium-sized fruit and vegetable growers are obvious, rather than spending a lot of time and money on European companies coming here to assess and certify them, the growers are now able to receive the same service at much lower cost from a local company.

Thirdly another challenge posed by standards relates to providing the type of support for achieving certification that is appropriate for small producers. Certification agencies both private as well as public tend to be more focussed on the large enterprises than those of small enterprises or small farmers. This problem arises as small farmers might be unable to bear the costs of obtaining knowledge about standards and certification. Another reason for small farmers in developing or poor countries not willing to obtain certification is that small farmers or producers know that they have limited or no opportunity for exporting their products. So the produces are mainly for local consumption. As the local consumers are not that particular about certified products, due to their poor standard of living conditions, small farmers do not go in for certification. Lastly the challenge facing small farmers relates to the cost of adjusting production systems to the new requirements, so that they comply with the new standards.

Although the necessary quality infrastructure can be built the benefits arising from them might not pass on to small producers living in rural areas. Therefore it is necessary that challenges faced by small producers need to be taken into consideration while building up the quality infrastructure of a country. The analysis of standards pointed out the importance of business associations in collaboration with governments for establishing sector-wide practices and ensuring the overall reputation of the export sector.

CONCLUSION

The issues outlined so far have focused on the trends and changes seen in the global agribusiness which shows the need for governments and development agencies to support agribusiness producers and exporters taking part in the agribusiness value chain. It is important to understand the various actors and relationship involved in the agribusiness value chain so as to have an easy understanding about the problems faced by agricultural businesses.

It was argued that export agribusiness, and in particular non-traditional agricultural exports, had been identified as having an important part to play in poverty-eradication strategies because of their ability to make a difference to the incomes of poor people in rural areas. It is hence suggested that framings of pro-poor policies for agriculture should be equated to pro-poor agricultural growth with improvements in the ability of small farmers to access export markets.

The increasing complexity of the global agricultural trade environment, which creates new risks for buyers, and increasing requirements for traceability do not provide the coordination and control needed by global buyers. Furthermore, there are economies of scale in coordination and control, which work against small farmers. In this context, the top priority for policy is to be realistic, particularly with respect to the opportunities open to small farmers. The poverty reduction goal should not lead to policy interventions that lack sustainable business logic.

Also, more attention needs to be given to the potential of domestic and regional markets in developing countries. This potential has been somewhat overshadowed by the priority given to export markets, and in particular developed-country markets.

Moreover, the assumption of small farms being a more effective route to poverty eradication in rural areas than large-scale farming needs to be re-examined. This type of analysis needs to be extended to see if the conclusions are valid for other sectors and other countries.

There are many difficulties as well as opportunities facing Indian producers and exporters in the food processing and food retailing sector. It is evident that the food processing industry is a sunrise industry having a huge potential in generating revenue. Many suggestions were provided as how to integrate the small farmers into the food processing industry value chain.

Another important aspect discussed is that the provision of quality infrastructure. It is evident that there is an urgent need by the government for speeding up various projects and programs involved in providing quality infrastructure. It is evident that the impact of standards varies from sector to sector. In the food processing sector the impact is felt more strongly in the area of costs. One possible way of increasing the cost-effectiveness of local certification may be through the development of national equivalent standards that are a subset of international standards. This will be beneficial to domestic companies as these standards can act as a stepping-stone for companies wanting to take part in the global trade. This will happen as meeting the domestic standard becomes a partial fulfilment of the export market standard.

Overall, the paper has tried to identify some challenges faced by small producers who wish to take part in the global value chain. The analysis of agribusiness exports along the value chain highlights the increasing challenges facing developing-country farmers' taking part in global markets. Linking farmers to global markets has usually involved the bulking of produce, often through local markets for commodities and state marketing boards. Markets are becoming more complex, more demanding and more differentiated. In this context, policy interventions to support farmers and exporters must be grounded in realistic appraisals of the needs of the market, the capacities of the export sector and competitors in global markets. It will be then only small farmers will be able to take part in the global food trade and the economic benefit arising out of exports will be experienced by small farmers and poverty will decline on strong agricultural growth. Otherwise even though developing countries like India experience huge agricultural growth, poverty reduction will still be a vocal call.

REFERENCE

Bain, Carmen, James Deaton, and Lawrence Busch, (2005), "Reshaping the Agri-food System: the Role of Standards, Standards Makers and Third-party Certifiers", in Vaughan Higgins (ed.), Agricultural Governance: Globalisation and the New Politics of Regulation (London: Routledge), pp. 71-83.

Cook, Michael, and Fabio Chaddad, (2000), "Agroindustrialization of the Global Agrifood Economy: Bridging Development Economics and Agribusiness Research", Agricultural Economics 23 (3), pp. 207-218.

DFID (2002), Better Livelihoods for Poor People: The Role of Agriculture, (London: DFID).

Donaghu, Michael, and Richard Barff (1990), "Nike Just Did It: International Subcontracting and Flexibility in Athletic Footwear Production", Regional Studies 24 (6), pp. 537-552.

Eastwood, Robert, and Michael Lipton (2000), "Pro-poor Growth and Pro-growth Poverty Reduction: Meaning, Evidence, and Policy Implications", Asian Development Review 18 (2), pp. 22-58.

EUREP (2001), "EUREPGAP Protocol for Fresh Fruit and Vegetables", Available online at *http://www.eurep.org/*

FAO (1998), Food Quality and Safety Systems-A Training Manual on Food Hygiene and the Hazard Analysis and Critical Control Point (HACCP) System, (Rome: FAO). Available online at *http://www.fao.org/*

Grievink, J.W. (2002), "The Changing Face of the Global Food Industry", Presentation at OECD Conference, The Hague, February.

Gereffi, Gary (1994), "The Organisation of Buyer-Driven Global Commodity Chains: How U.S. Retailers Shape Overseas Production Networks", in Gary Gereffi and Miguel Korzeniewicz (eds), Commodity Chains and Global Capitalism, (Westport: Praeger) pp. 95-122.

Goldman, Robert, and Stephen Papson (1998), Nike Culture, (London: Sage).

Hendrickson, Mary, and William Heffernan, (2005), "Concentration of Agricultural Markets", Columbia, MO: University of Missouri, Department of Rural Sociology.

Humphrey, John, and Olga Memedovic (2006), "Global Value Chains in the Agrifood Sector", UNIDO.

Jaffee, Steven (2005), "Food Safety and Agricultural Health Standards: Challenge and Opportunities for Developing Country Exports". Report 31207, (Washington D.C.: The World Bank, Poverty Reduction and Economic Management Trade Unit).

Jebaraj, Priscilla (2007), "Supply Chain Infrastructure Needed to Propel Agri-business Boom" *The Hindu*, December 2nd.

Manarungsan, Sompop, Jocelyn O. Naewbanij, and Tanapat Rerngjakrabhet (2004), "Costs of Compliance with SPS Standards: Thailand Case Studies of Shrimp, Fresh Asparagus, and Frozen Green Soybeans", Agriculture and Rural Development Discussion Paper, Washington DC: World Bank, Accessed April 2005.

Nadvi, Khalid, and Frank Wältring (2004), "Making Sense of Global Standards", in Hubert Schmitz (ed.), Local Enterprises in the Global Economy, (Cheltenham: Edward Elgar), pp. 33-94.

Swinnen, Johan (2004), Dynamics of Agri-food Supply Chains in Transition Countries, (Sarajevo).

Unnevehr, Laurian (2000), "Food Safety Issues and Fresh Food Product Exports from LDCs", Agricultural Economics 23 (3), pp. 231-240.

Van Roekel, Jan, Ron Kopicki, Carry Broekmans, and Dave Boselie (2002), "Building Agri Supply Chains: Issues and Guidelines", Available online at *http://www.agrichaincompetence.org/*.

Vorley, Bill (2003), "Food, Inc.: Corporate Concentration from Farm to Consumer". London: International Institute for Environment and Development and UK Food Group.

Weinberger, Katinka, and Thomas Lumpkin (2005), "Horticulture for Poverty Alleviation: The Unfunded Revolution", Working Paper 15, (Shanhua, Taiwan: AVRDC).

Willems, Sabine, Eva Roth, and Jan van Roekel (2005), "Changing European Public and Private Food Safety and Quality Requirements Challenges for Developing Country Fresh Produce and Fish Exporters", Agriculture and Rural Development Discussion Paper, Washington DC: World Bank.

Young, Linda and Jill Hobbs (2002), "Vertical Linkages in Agri-Food Supply Chains: Changing Roles for Producers, Commodity Groups, and Government Policy", Review of Agricultural Economics 24 (2), pp. 428-41.

Websites:

http://www.gtz.de/en/

http://www.eurep.org/

http://www.procert.ch/zertifizierungen

http://www.fao.org/

http://www.wto.org/

Reports

Annual Report 2005-06, Ministry of Food Processing Industry, Government of India.

Chapter-19

IMPACT OF INTELLECTUAL PROPERTY RIGHTS ON DEVELOPING COUNTRIES: AN EVALUATION

Jawahar Lal, Ranjana Sharma & Pramod Kumar Sinha

INTRODUCTION

Traditional concept of factors of production is changing in the era of globalized and liberalized economy. The role of knowledge as "potential contributor" to production is increasingly being recognized. *Marshall*, a great economist remarks, "Capital consists in a great part of knowledge & it is our most powerful engine of production." The economic and producing power of the firm lies in its intangible assets than its hard assets such as plant & machinery. Today, 2/3 of the value of America's large business can be traced to the intangible assets that embody ideas, especially the intellectual property of patents and trademarks. In order to gain the maximum advantages of knowledge economy, we need to create, protect and nurture these knowledge professionals, provide them infrastructure facilities to operate upon and allow them sufficient creative space.

By the end of 20th Century, the things created and invented by human mind were recognized as an "Intellectual Property" (I.P.) of the owner. The distinctive feature of I.P. is that it "relates to information which can be incorporated in tangible objects and reproduced in different locations and can be used by several persons at the same time, unlike immovable or movable tangible property". It is not depleted by use like other forms of tangible assets and it has zero marginal cost to adding more users. True value of IP is upto public demand to decide whether they like or not. IP is also a good investment. Since its value increases gradually over a period of time and exceptionally value may jump significantly in short period.

INTELLECTUAL PROPERTY RIGHTS (IPRs)

Intellectual Property Rights (IPRs) is the right of owner or holder of IP, granted by the state. It enables the owner to prevent or stop others from commercially using their product/work in the market place. IPRs laws define the rights and privileges attached to the ownership of intellectual property. Such rights define ownership and specify the degree to which inventors or creators may get profit from their work, access others and how others may use or improve upon existing works. Rather than monetary benefits, it also urges to scientific works, social recognition and goodwill. The rights conferred by Intellectual Property laws can generally be transferred with or without consideration, licensed or rented or mortgaged to third party as security for loan in same jurisdiction. Basically IPRs was formed to serve the following two purposes:

(i) To control the growth of international trade in "counterfeit" goods and,

(ii) To reduce tariff and non tariff barriers to cross border trade.

The above two factors constitute the entire objectives of TRIPs Agreement as stated in article-7 of the agreement. With the ever growing awareness of the benefits of Intellectual Property Rights (IPRs) have been recognized and accepted all over the world as a foundation of economic development. Thus there is a need to re-engineer modernized management system of IPRs for the purpose of embarking on new benefits areas which is to be perceived.

PROTECTION OF IPRs

The need for a system to protect IP internationally arose when foreign exhibitors refused to attend an international exhibition of inventons in Vienna in 1873, because they were afraid that their ideas would be stolen and exploited commercially in other countries. The Paris convention 1883 was the first measure for the protection of Intellectual Property in the form of Industrial Property Rights.

There is a well established statutory, administrative and judicial frame work to safeguard IPRs in India. Right to privacy, which is not protected even some developed countries has been recognized in India. Protection of IPRs in India continue to be strengthened further by enactment of the Patent (Amendment) Act, Copy Right (Amendment) Act, Industrial Design Bill, Trade Marks Bill (All) in the year 1999. As regards the aspects of enforcement, Indian enforcement Agencies are now working very effectively and there has been notable decline in the levels of piracy in India. Effective protection of IPRs regulates unwanted copying and spreading, which may be reasonable cause for negative growth of free economy.

A natural right which is one of the rational of IPRs, also stresses the inherent authority of innovation to control works they have created. To provide knowledge privately there must be some form of protection, assuming knowledge cannot simply be distributed free of cost. Broader protection of Intellectual Property Rights is required, so that constant creation of new knowledge is not halted. Protection of IPRs is essential to ensure the "inventors" (and their institutions) to get a substantial piece of the cake of commercial success. In offshore business model IPR protection is a significant element.

Bill Gates would not be a richest person in the world, if he had not secured all his Intellectual Property Rights. Sometimes questions arises about protection of IPRs upto which extent? Some authors have advocated for strong Intellectual Property regime, but it is possible that an excessive strong Intellectual Property regime may actually restrict the pace of innovation.

NEW PATENTS REGIME: TRIPs

An ideal regime of Intellectual Property Rights strike a balance between private incentives for innovators and the public interest of maximizing access to the fruits of innovation in an optimum way.

The Intellectual Property Rights can broadly be classified into Copyrights and related rights and Industrial Property Rights. Copyrights & related rights relate to the cultural field and cover all literary and artistic expressions as well as artistic performance and broadcasts. The main purpose of this right is to encourage and reward to creative work. Industrial Property Rights have a great relevance to production and distribution of Industrial goods. The main purpose of this right is to stimulate innovations, design & creation of technology.

During the ***Uruguay Round*** of talks lasted from 1986 to 1994, India along with other developing countries opposed the inclusion of IPRs in Trade Negotiations. However, the agreement on Trade Related Intellectual Property Rights (TRIPs) which is a part of the World Trade Organization (WTO) Agreement ratified and signed by India in 1994 - yokes together all IPRs under one multilateral forum. The TRIPs agreement prescribes minimum standards for protection of wide varieties of Intellectual Property Rights (IPRs). This agreement is applicable to all WTO members as it is a part of total package of WTO agreements. Different member nations have been allowed different time spans for applying its provisions into their legal system keeping in view their economic circumstances. The developed countries were granted transition period of one year, whereas developing countries for five year and least developed countries have an extra transitional period of 11 years. The TRIPs agreement entered into force in most developing countries in Jan. 2005. The battle today is between those that are not equal economically institutions. Its implications will be decided by resolving disputes.

There are variations as to set of rights forming the basket of Intellectual Property Rights. The agreement on Trade Related Aspects of Intellectual Property Rights (TRIPs) includes following within the scope of IPRs.

- Copyrights & related rights.
- Trademarks.
- Geographical Indications
- Industrial Designs
- Patents
- Layout design for integrated circuits.
- Trade secrets (undisclosed information)
- Breeder's rights

The GATT Agreement on Trade Related Aspects of Intellectual Property Rights (TRIPs) covers the first seven categories only and Indian laws are compatible with WTO standards, but it differs sharply from the WTO standards in respect of patents. A brief explanation of all these items are given below:

COPYRIGHTS

Copyrights are rights given by law to the creators of literary, dramatic, musical & artitistic works and producers of cinematographic films and sound recording which come out of imagination. The right consists of rights of reproduction, distribution, communication to the public, translation and adaptation soon. According to Sec. 22 of the Copyright Act 1957, copyrights generally last during the life term and till the end of fifty years after the death of author.

RELATED RIGHTS

Related Rights are rights of performers and broadcasting organizations, who communicate works of authors through performance or broadcasting. In many countries, rights of sound recording producers are treated as part of related rights and not as copyright, unlike the case in India.

TRADEMARKS

Trademarks are distinctive signs which identify a particular product as the product of a particular company/manufacturers. Trademarks can be a visual symbol in the form of words, letters, number, drawing, images, symbols and even sound & smell. Trade marks not only protect the owner's right but also build-up confidence in the product purchased by a customer.

GEOGRAPHICAL INDICATIONS

A geographical indication is a sign used on goods that have a specific geographical origin and possess qualities or a reputation that are due to that place of origin, such as agriculture goods (Basmati rice of Dehradoon) natural goods or manufactured goods in the territory, region or locality. The registration of geographical indications lasts for ten years & can be renewed from time to time.

INDUSTRIAL DESIGNS

Industrial designs are the external features of a product. They are the ornamental or aesthetic aspects of a product which makes the product attractive and appealing and increase their marketability. According to Design Act 2000, industrial designs protection for five years and it can be renewed for fifteen years.

LAYOUT DESIGNS

It is a layout of transistors and other circuitry elements and include lead wires connecting such elements and expressed in any manner in a semi-conductor integrated circuit. The registered proprietor of layout design has exclusive right to the use of the layout designs which last for ten years.

TRADE SECRETS (UNDISCLOSED INFORMATION)

This may be protected as a trade secret as long as reasonable steps have been taken to keep the information secret. The importance of Trade secrets in the ambit of I.P. has gained extensive recognition. TRIPs include provisions for protection of trade secrets.

BREEDER'S RIGHT

A breeder of a new plant variety, which fulfils the requirements of novelty, distinctiveness, uniformity and stability may obtain certain exclusive rights over that variety.

PATENTS

Abraham Lincoln said "the patent system added the fuel of interest to the fire of genius". Any person, who wishes to exploit the invention, must obtain the authorization of the patentee to do so. Thus, inventions are protected by patent rights of the inventors. Patent rights give exclusive right to the inventor to commercially exploit the invention for a specific period of time. The basic purpose of patent is to give incentive to the inventor compensating for his investment and encouraging for further efforts into research and development.

Indian Patent Act was enacted based on the foot print of British system. It was approved by the President of India in 1970 and came into force in 1972. Indian patent laws differ significantly with TRIPs agreement in many respects. The condition for getting patent as per TRIPs agreement is novelty, non-obviousness and practical use. Among developed countries, Japan is having highest number of patent followed by USA & Korea due to technological excellence. Among developing countries, China possesses highest number of patent & it is expected that number of granting patent will be double in next year. The Indian Patent office granted record 15267 patents during 2007-08 which is more than double the patent granted last year 2006-07 was 7359.

Patent has encouraged industrial production & revenue of developed countries, because of effective protection of their IPRs. Developing countries in general & India in particular lag much behind of patents and revenue out of patented from IPRs. India has tremendous potentials and challenges in the area of Bio Technology, IT industries, micro electronics etc. Thus it is required to pay more attention to IPR Protection. India must show commendable results in granting patents to its inventors.

IMPACT OF TRIPs

A weak IPR regime in developing countries leads to losses from "re-engineered products" for original innovators. Thus, the countries of the triad, the U.S.A.,

Europe & Japan have been working towards harmonization of IPR regimes since last two decades. TRIPS is one of the culmination of their efforts.

The countries initiating TRIPS based their actions on the presumption that strong IPR regime is a critical precondition for private investment in research and development, and hence Economic Growth. They contented that an expanded and strengthened protection of IPRs would bring about increased flows of Foreign Direct Investment and technology transfer to developing countries. It would also stimulate local innovation. Finally, it would also enable the multinationals of the developed countries to recuperate markets from local imitators. The developing countries, on the other hand, not so confident about reaping benefits from this global IPR regime, since having access to technological knowledge is perceived as being crucial for economic growth. Many developing countries have had or have to change their IPRs regime quite radically to fulfil the TRIPs Agreements requirement. A UN report suggests that negative short to medium term effects may occur e.g., increased product prices and more difficult access to technologies. Governments in developing countries have to find a balance between the need to protect intellectual property and the requirement to diffuse certain technologies in order to increase welfare. Moreover, domestic output of developing countries and employment of producers of counterfeit goods will decrease. Employment, wages & tax receipts will shrink and governments of these countries will have to invest largely in administrative resources to enforce legislation.

Presently, the developing countries suffer from welfare losses and developed countries could boost their exports. Some developing countries which signed the TRIPs agreement, still are confronted with unilateral relation measures. The burning example of such illegitimate measures is the U.S. threats of imposing sanctions under section 301 of its Trade Act. TRIPs agreement prime objective was not the battle against counterfeiting and piracy cut, but technological protectionism. Developed countries are regarded as innovations and suppliers of products where as, developing countries serve as markets.

The above discussion shows negative impact of TRIPs on developing countries including India. Then the question is why developing countries including India finally afraid to TRIPs? In fact, following two factors have influenced this decision.

(i) The United States threats of bilateral initiatives.

(ii) Developing countries saw some advantages in tariff reductions of agricultural, textile and other products of their concerns through WTO Agreement, but under the single package system they had to agree to all negotiated points under TRIPs.

(iii) In the developing countries, the impact of TRIPs will vary according to each country's economical & technological development. Industrialised country had a major victory by adopting TRIPs Agreement and stronger patent protection, middle income countries like Brazil and Malaysia are likely to benefit from the spur to local innovation. Countries like India and China which are endowed with a large infrastructure, can gain in the long term by stronger IPR protection. However, least developed countries, where formal innovation is minimal, are likely to face higher costs without offsetting benefits.

Impact of IPRs have been analysed under following heads:

Promotion and Protection of Traditional Knowledge

One of the concerns of developing countries is that the process of globalization is threatening the appropriation of elements of collective knowledge of societies into proprietary knowledge for the commercial profit of few. An urgent action is needed to protect these knowledge systems through national policies and international understanding linked to IPR, while providing its development and proper use for the benefit of its holders. We need a particular focus on community knowledge and innovation.

The issue of 'protection' of traditional knowledge should be viewed from two perspectives, the protection may be granted to exclude the unauthorised use by third parties and to preserve traditional knowledge from the uses that may negatively affect the life or culture of the communities that have developed and applied it.

For sharing the benefits of traditional innovation new experiments have started in India to a medicine which is based on active ingredient in plant found in tropical forests of south-western India and collected by Kani tribal people. Scientists at the Tropical Botanic Garden and Research Institute (TBGRI) in Kerala learned of the plant, tested the ingredient and incorporated it into a compound which they called "Jeevani" the giver of life. The tonic is now being manufactured by a major Ayurvedic drug company in Kerala. In 1995, an agreement was struck to share the licence fee and 2% of sales of the product as royalty by TBGRI, which was shared on 50% basic with the Tribe. This makes perhaps for the first time that for IP held by a tribe, a compensation in the form of cash benefits has directly gone to the source of IP holders.

IPR and Traditional Medicine

Traditional Medicine (TM) plays a crucial role in health care and serves the health needs of a vast majority of population in developing countries such as India. Access to 'modern' health care services and medicine in these countries are either limited or out of reach due to various reasons. T. M. becomes the only affordable treatment available to poor people and in remote communities. In India, 60% people are not under reach of modern medicines and depend on traditional medicines.

Traditional Medicines are largely based on medicinal plants, which are accessed directly or through modern tools of breeding and cultivation, including tissue culture, cell culture and transgenic technology. IP issues linked to such endeavours remain unresolved.

The protection of TM under IPRs raises two types of issues. First, to what extent it is feasible to protect, existing IPR system. Certain aspects of TM may be covered by patents or other IPRs. There have also been many proposals to develop *sui generic systems* of protection.

World Intellectual Property Organisation (WIPO) has been sensitive to these concerns. The grant of patents on non-original innovations (particularly those linked to traditional medicines) have been causing a great concern to the developing countries. To solve the problem of traditional medicine, an international support is required by joint efforts of developing and developed countries. To mitigate this problem, the Indian government has taken steps to create a Traditional Knowledge Digital Library (TKDL) on traditional medicinal plants and systems. Eventually the creation of TKDL in the developing countries would serve a bigger purpose in providing and enhancing its innovation capacity. It could act as bridge between traditional and modern knowledge systems and will give a major impetus to modern reach in developing countries on adding further value to this traditional knowledge.

Sustained efforts on the modernization of the traditional knowledge of developing country will create higher awareness at national and international level and will establish a scientific approach, that will ensure higher acceptability of these system by practiceners of modern system and public at large Ideas innovated by ***Swami Ramdev* & *Acharya Bal Krishna*** regarding T.M. in India is the burning example of acceptability by masses at worldwide.

IPR and Essential Medicines

During pre-TRIPs periods, many developing countries including India did not grant product patents but process patents for pharmaceutical industries, enabling domestic research to develop similar products through a process called "reverse engineering".

Thus impact of IPR on essential medicines produced by pharmaceuticals industry can be examined under two heads:-

(a) Pre TRIPs
(b) Post TRIPs

Pre TRIPs

Before TRIPs, essential medicines or drugs were exempted by Indian Patent Act, 1970 and Indian Pharmaceuticals industry have been a glowing example of success. India has emerged as one of the largest producers of entire range of therapeutics in the world, accounting 12% of the world drug requirements and it has achieved global recognition due to low cost/price & high quality medicines with significant international marketing presence in Asia, Middle East, Africa & South America. Due to lower prices, Indian drugs have been affordable to the poor masses and have been in great demand, which increased the market shares of pharmaceuticals firms during 1998-99 to 2003-04.

Post TRIPs

India, like many other developing countries, has been forced to shift from process to product patent regime. Govt. of India forced new patent laws from 1st Jan. 2005 in conformity with Trade Related Intellectual Property Rights (TRIPs) agreement negotiated under WTO.

The adoption of the TRIPs Agreement has entailed significant changes for the protection of pharmaceutical products & processes. The Agreement not only made product patent protection binding to all member countries, but also strengthened *inter alia,* process patents, narrowly defined conditions for establishing exception to patent rights, and limited the possibility of applying especial modalities of compulsory licenses to pharmaceuticals.

Much debate on the impact of product patents on the Pharmaceutical Industry in India has centred on the issues of prices of patented products and their acceptability. A key question is whether the TRIPs regime has led to an increase in the prices of patented medicines. Although many researchers argue that there is no clear relationship between the patents and prices of medicines, there is a strong evidence that average pharmaceutical product prices decline in the face of entry by generic substitutes. Competition is important to keep prices down. It is also true that prices decline with expiry of patents. India has good scope for generic drugs, the patent for which has expired.

According to TRIPs agreement, drugs that were already available in the Indian market by 2005, will not get retrospective patent protection. Thus the TRIPs agreement will only affect the prices of small proportion of drugs available in India. However, the impact will gradually increase over time as virtually al new drugs entering the market in future would be patent protected. It is expected that prices of medicines after 2005 will be more unbearable for the poorer than what it had been in 2001. Such price hike of medicines in India, will produces an immeasurable impact on the vast majority of Indian people who are under BPL lists. Dr. Manmohan Singh the then Finance Minister of India has also remarked that prices of drug will go up after implementation of accord. The granting of product patent will have adverse effect on the Indian Pharmaceutical Industry and the prices of drugs/medicine will rise considerable.

It is evident that patented drug prices have little to do with the cost of production or even innovation. Pharmaceutical companies change the prices of drugs/medicines what the market will bear and monopolist attitude of the firm.

It will also very difficult for MNCs pharmaceuticals firms to offer lower prices for essential medicines in developing countries based on their purchasing power. Because such disparities in prices would be easily revealing the extent of profits involved and may be pressurised to reduce prices in developed countries as well, especially for life saving and mass consumption medicines. By strong patent protection to Indian Pharma, many of essential drugs now being imported at higher prices will start being made hare and prices will fall accordingly. This will also encourage research for production of essential drugs.

The threat perception about rise in pharmaceutical products (medicines) prices is an important consideration in the short run, but effective TRIPs will go a long way to bring FDI and significant R&D activities in this sector. The more impact is manufacture of product patent system and safeguard the public interest. For this purpose enactment of required patent legislation complying with the provision of TRIPs agreement is imperative.

There are a number of options available within TRIPs to ensure affordable access. Compulsory licensing, parallel imports and differential pricing between developed and developing countries have been suggested as instruments to improve access within the broad framework of TRIPs.

Biopiracy

Third world countries heavily rely on domestic agricultural production, which makes IPRs like patents and plant breeders rights an important issue. Plant breeders right are applied in the case of development of new plant verities through conventional methods and they are a kind of sui, generics protection, which does not include re-using of the seed and further research on the basis of developed variety. Although the TRIPs Agreement does not classify protection of new varieties of plant as separate Intellectual Property Right, India provides protection for new plant varieties & rights to farmers through, the protection of Plant Varieties and Farmers Right Act, 2001. The Protection period for new varieties is fifteen years for annual crops and eighteen years for trees and vines.

Biopiracy describes the situation, where some one, either an individual or a corporation, gains a patent on a plant variety already in use by someone else. The Rural Advancement Foundation International (RAFI) points out that in most cases the victims of such action will be farmers in developing countries. The export of agricultural produces and biopiracy is dangerous threats to farmers in these Countries.

India has bitter experience in case of biopiracy. Neem has become a symbol of biopiracy in the new world order. Similarly, one of the must talked cases of biopiracy is that of Basmati rice. An U.S. based company "Rice tech inc.". Patented a modified strain on Basmati Rice, traditionally cultivated in India and Pakistan, and sold it in the international markets as ***Kasmati*** and ***Texmati***.

CONCLUSION

In globalised economic scenario, creativity and innovation are the new drivers of the world economy. An effective intellectual property is the foundation of such strategy. IPR is a dynamic tool for wealth creation providing an income for enterprises and Individuals to create and innovate, encompassing more monopoly element.

To gain with IPRs, Developing countries including India which is integral part of WTO, are introducing harmonized national system of IPRs following an agreed set of minimum Standard of TRIPs Agreement. But there is an urgent need for reform of TRIPs to exclude certain sector from TRIPs & differential treatment depending the state of developing countries. The main objective of GATT/WTO to improve free trade can be achieved by providing competitive opportunities across the nations on non-discriminating basis.

Developing countries in general and India in particular leg much behind of patents and revenue out of patenting from intellectual properties. To meet the requirements of TRIPs, the entire Patent Act, as operative in India will have to be changed and India must show a commendable result in granting patents to its inventions. More attention is required to IP protection for IT sector and biotechnology industries because of its abundant scientific and technical manpower.

The threat perception about escalation in pharmaceutical product prices is important from the short term point of view but effective TRIPs will go a long way to bring in Foreign Direct Investment (FDI) and facilitate R & D activities.

A common man comes across the intellectual property from down to desk. So they must have knowledge of IPRs, since their life is very closely linked with articles protected by law under IPRs. To Streamline IPRs, educational institutions should comprise the band wagon for nurturing the professional thoughts.

REFERENCES

Aggarwal, Pradeep and P. Saibaba (2001), "TRIPS and India's Pharmaceutical Industry," *Economic and Political Weekly*, September 29-October 5, pp. 3787.

Collection of Documents on Intellectual Property, compiled by World Intellectual Property Organisation (WIPO) Worldwide Academy (2002), WIPO Publication No. 456(E), p. 3.

Datt, Ruddar and Sundharam, K.P.M. (2004), *'Indian Economy'* S. Chand and Company Ltd., Ram Nagar, New Delhi, p. 69.

Frank, Richard and Salkever David (1992), 'Pricing, Patent Laws and the Market for Pharmaceuticals,' *Southern Economic Journal*, Vol. 50, No. 2.

Fink, C. (2006), Intellectual Property Rights, Market Structure, and Transnational Corporations in Developing Countries, Berlin: Mensch-und-Buxch-Verlag.

Messner, Sophie (2001), 'Implications of the TRIPS-Agreement under the GATT for Developing Countries'.

The Protection of Plant Varieties and Farmers' Rights Act, 2001.

UN (1996), The TRIPS Agreement and Developing Countries, Geneva: United Nations Publication.

WTO (2001c), Intellectual Property Protection and Enforcement Retrieved 27 October 2001.

Wadhave Charan D. (1994), 'Economic Reforms in India and the Market Economy', Allied Publishers Ltd., New Delhi, p. 57.

CHAPTER-20

SEGMENTATION OF INVESTORS BASED ON SAVING MOTIVES

R. KASILINGAM & G. JAYABAL

INTRODUCTION

FINANCING socio-economic activities in a country requires large amount of resources, which is not possible to secure from taxation alone. It can be carried through only by a rise in the rate of capital formation. In the opinion of L.G.Whyte (1976) the future welfare of any country depends, to a great extent upon a high level of investment on capital goods. This is possible only by the generation of an adequate volume of savings. Developing economies lay great emphasis on the importance of domestic savings as they are the source of investment to break the vicious circle of poverty and under employment. Arthur Lewis (1963) asserts that the obstacle to greater investment in the less developed countries is that their current propensity to save is too low.

It has been estimated that the rate of saving in the initial stages of growth of present day advanced economies remained nearly 20 per cent of their national income. A study on the pattern of savings in Japan during the post war period revealed that the exceptionally high rate of capital formation in Japan resulted from consistent rate of saving of over 20 per cent throughout the period, and with such a high rate of savings, Japan could easily surpass even some of the highly industrialized economies of the west (Sinha, 1964). In a study (Andrea Poltho, 1975) it has been shown that Japan invested 31.8 per cent of its GNP(at constant prices) between 1953 and 1972 and during the same period ,it was 25.1 per cent for West Germany,23 per cent for France, 20.2 per cent for Italy,17.3 per cent for UK and 17.0 per cent for USA.

The volume of aggregate saving is made up of private saving by individuals or business, saving by the companies, and public saving by the government. The composition may vary from country to country and time to time in the same country. In the democratic welfare states like the United Kingdom, Sweden and France, contribution of corporate and government savings to the total savings is more than 60 per cent, whereas in India, Canada and Japan individuals' saving is more, especially in India it is more than 80 per cent. This indicates that the higher percentage of corporate savings is due to high industrialization. The reason for less government savings in welfare states like India is that they have invested a large amount on social services and social well being by borrowing on a large scale. People as individuals need to save not only to meet emergencies and uncertainties in future but also to maintain their status in the society.

Many research works have been carried out to find out the variables which could affect the savings rate of the households. The variables identified by the previous researchers are economic variables, psychological variables, social variables and behavioural variables. To put it in simple term the saving is the product of ability to save and willingness to save. The ability to save is influenced by income and wealth of individual. The willingness to save is determined saving motives. In absence of other factors the individual saving is the function of their saving motives. Hence it can be presumed that the highly motivated people will save more than the least motivated people. As the motivation level of highly motivated people is high, convincing them to make investment will not require much effort. To sell more with limited effort, the institutions who offer investment products can concentrate on highly motivated segment. To device effective marketing strategy, it is necessary for them to understand the characteristics of this motive segment. Therefore it is necessary to segment the investor into highly motivated and least motivated based on the level of motive. The present study aims to serve that purpose.

REVIEW OF LITERATURE

While it is common to associate interest in motives with psychologists, economists have long been interested in motives for saving. For example, Adam smith (1776/1993) speculated that "the principle which prompts us to save is the desire of bettering our condition, a desire which is generally calm and dispassionate, comes with us from the womb, and never leaves us still we go into the grave". John Maynard Keynes (1936) proposed eight saving motives: the precautionary, life cycle, intertemporal substitution, improvement, independence, enterprise, bequest, and avarice i.e., inhibitions against acts of expenditure as such. More recently, neo-classical economists have emphasized four motives for saving, including the desire: 1) to maintain consumption in the face of income fluctuations, particularly during retirement; 2) to prepare for income shocks and other emergencies (precautionary saving); 3) to transfer wealth to future generations (bequest motive); and 4) to purchase big ticket items such as consumer durables, education, or a vacation (target saving). The first three are expected to influence long term saving, and the fourth to affect short to medium term saving and dissaving patterns (Sturm, 1983). At the same time, as Owens (1993) says, "these motives are not mutually exclusive, and saving decisions will generally be influenced by more than one of them". Empirical studies observe that Americans generally cite retirement, emergencies, and education as the primary motives for saving (Avery *et al.*, 1986; Bernheim, 1994; Modigliani, 1988; Sturm, 1983). However, it is quite possible that the silence of particular motives varies by socioeconomic status (Solmon, 1975; Avery *et al*, 1986).

Several of these motives were developed into formal economic models (Browning & Lusardi, 1996). The most influential saving model is the life cycle models (Ando & Modigliani, 1963). This model states that current consumption spending depends on current wealth and lifetime income so that consumers borrow and save to smooth out their consumption throughout their life cycle. This model thus implies a saving motive for retirement. This model was further revised to include intergenerational transfer motive (saving for children) (Barro, 1978; Kurz, 1984) and precautionary motive (Saving for emergencies) (carroll, 1997). Empirical studies using U.S. data were conducted to investigate saving behaviour associated with saving motives for emergencies and retirement (Johnson & Widdows, 1985; Yuh, Montalto & Hanna, 1998). Using U.S. macro data, Feldtein (1974, 1996) found that social security reduces private savings, indicating that social institutions affect private saving motives. Many economists have noted the limitations of the life cycle model. For example, Wolff (1981) divided families into three classes: the capitalist, the primary working class, and the secondary work force. He found that only the primary working class takes the form of life cycle wealth. Katona (1960, 1980) stressed the importance of psychological aspects of people's economic behaviour and empirically studied saving motives and behaviour using survey methods, which were earlier versions of the Survey of Consumer Finances. His study showed that people's new saving motives emerge when the old saving needs is met and the income is positively related to the number of saving motives (Katona, 1960). Kennickell, Starr-McCluer, & Surette, (2000) using the 1998 survey of consumer Finances data shows that the proportion of families reporting education related reasons for saving has risen since 1989.

METHODOLOGY

The primary data have been collected by conducting survey among teachers working in Government colleges and Universities in Tamil Nadu by using well structured questionnaire. The population size was 11867 and the sample size of 614 was calculated by using formula $n = Z^2 * p * q * N / e^2 * (N-1) + Z^2 * p * q$ (Kothari.C.R., 2005) where n is the minimum sample size required. The 614 sample respondents were selected by using multi stage random sampling. The questionnaires were distributed to all 614 selected respondents in person by the researcher. After repeated persuasion only 586 filled in questionnaires were received and the remaining respondents did not respond. For the purpose of final analysis 552 questionnaires were used after rejecting some of the questionnaires which were not completed properly. The non response rate and rejection rate totally amounts to 10 per cent. The margin of error for the present sample size of 552 is 1.454 per cent. The content validity of the questionnaire was verified by group of people comprising experts from the fields of statistics, psychology, management, commerce and investment consultancy. The reliability of the survey instrument was tested using Cronbach Alpha method. The standardized item alpha was 0.6879 and the Hotelling's T-square was 909.2650 and probability was 0.0000. This shows that these statements are reliable and will produce desired result consistently.

SAVING MOTIVES

Saving was treated as residual unspent income (Lunt & Livingstone, 1991). Consistent with this view, Keynes described eight factors which were believed to lead individuals to refrain from spending out of their incomes. Furnham (1985) summarized these findings as follows:

(1) *Precaution:* To build up a reserve against unforeseen contingencies.

(2) *Foresight:* To provide for an anticipated future relation between the income needs of the individual or his or her family different from that which exists in the present (i.e., for old age, education).

(3) *Calculation:* To enjoy interest and appreciation, because larger real consumption in the future is preferable to a present smaller consumption.

(4) *Improvement:* To enjoy a gradually increasing expenditure, since most people look forward to a gradually improving standard of living.

(5) *Independence:* To enjoy a sense of independence and the power to do things, without a clear idea of definite intention of specific action.

(6) *Enterprise:* To secure a capital mass to carry out speculative or business enterprise.

(7) *Pride:* To bequeath a fortune to others.

(8) *Avarice:* To satisfy pure miserliness.

Keynes also offered a corresponding list of motives of consumption which include enjoyment, shortsightedness, generosity, miscalculation, ostentation and extravagance.

PRIORITIES OF MOTIVES

The investors were asked to rate their motives level in five points Likert rating scale. The value 1 is assigned for very strongly disagree and 5 is assigned for strongly Agree. The mean value of importance assigned to every motive by the investors is given in the table.

The investors give more importance to precautionary motive which means that people want to build reserve to meet unforeseen contingencies. The Indian investors have not shown much interest for the speculative motive which is otherwise called enterprise motive. In the order of priority people want to save money mainly for precautionary motive and least priority is given to speculative motive. The mean values of two motives namely Enterprise and Avarice are less than three which indicate that most of the people do not agree

Table 1
Priorities of Motives

Motives	*Mean Value*	*Rank*
Precaution	3.95	I
Foresight	3.80	II
Improvement	3.45	III
Independence	3.35	IV
Pride	3.27	V
Calculation	3.16	VI
Avarice	2.42	VII
Enterprise	2.30	VIII

with the existence of such motives for the purpose of saving. The mean values of all other six motives are more than three which explains the existence of such motives for saving. As the motive has influence on saving and the presence of strong motive for saving among Indians makes them save more though their per capita income is less when compared to developed countries.

FACTORISATION OF MOTIVES

To reduce the number of variables into minimum manageable variables, factor analysis is performed. The suitability for factor analysis is tested using two analysis namely KMO test and Bartlett's test of Sphericity. The Kaiser-Meyer-Olkin Measure oi Sampling Adequacy is a statistic which indicates the proportion of variance in the variables which might be caused by new factors. High values generally indicate that a factor analysis may be useful with the data. If the value is less than 0.50, the results of the factor analysis probably won't be very useful.

Table 2
Kmo and Bartlett's Test

Kaiser-Meyer-Olkin Measure of Sampling Adequacy		0.731
Bartlett's Test of Sphericity	Chi-Square	804.442
	df	28
	Sig.	0.000

The above table shows that the KMO value is 0.731 which indicates that the factor analysis is useful with the data. The chi-square value for Bartlett's test of Sphericity is 804.442 and the significant value is 0.000 which is significant at more than 99 per cent level of confidence. For the purpose of extraction, Principal Component Analysis is used and for the rotation Varimax rotation is used which is the standard rotation method (Kaiser,1958). The factors which have Eigen value greater than unity are taken as reduced factors which are used as new factors for further analysis. From the factor analysis two factors are extracted from original eight variables. Five variables (motives) are grouped under the first factor and another three variables are included in the second factor. The first factor can be named as self support motive and the second factor can be designated as family oriented motive. The motives which are included in the each factor along with their loadings are given below.

SELF SUPPORT MOTIVE

Self support motive is a motive related to needs and wants of an individual. People mainly want to reserve some money for the purpose of meeting their own future contingencies. The variables included under this motive along with their respective loadings are given in the Table 3.

Table 3
Factor Loadings For Self Support Motive

Statements	*Factor Loading*
I save because I desire to provide for anticipated future needs like old age.	0.762
I save because I desire to build reserve for unforeseen contingencies.	0.684
I save because I desire to enjoy an enlarged future income like interest and appreciation	0.654
I save because I desire to meet gradually increasing expenditure in order to improve the standard of living	0.624
I save because I desire to enjoy a sense of independence and power to do things	0.609

The need to save for future anticipated requirements and the need to save for future unexpected contingencies are the primary motives included under self support motive. People also save to live independently and to have higher standard of living.

FAMILY ORIENTED MOTIVE

People not only reserve money for the purpose of meeting their own needs and they also give equal importance to family related needs. They want to leave some assets to their family members after their death. For the purpose of creating more assets to their family members, they may spend less during their life time and may involve into some business to earn more money.

Table 4
Factor Loadings for Family Oriented Motive

Statements	*Factor Loading*
I save because I desire to carry out speculation business.	0.830
I save because I desire to spend less (satisfy a purely miserly instinct)	0.686
I save because I desire to pass the fortune to next generation (bequeath a fortune)	0.636

From the above analysis, the eight motives of saving given by Keynes are reduced into two factors namely self support motive and family oriented motive. For the purpose of future analysis only these two motives are considered.

STRENGTH OF MOTIVES

The following table shows mean value for the self support motive and family oriented motive which signifies the importance of each motive.

Table 5
Strength of Motives

Motive	*Mean*	*Rank*
Self Support	3.54	I
Family Oriented	2.66	II

Of those two motives self support motive is very dominant than family oriented motive and its presence is very strong among individual investors. The average level of self support motive among individuals is 3.54 which indicates that its presence is very predominant among individuals.

Table 6
Self Support Motive

	Frequency	*Per cent*
Disagree	29	5.3
Agree	523	94.7
Total	552	100.0

About 95 per cent of people agree with the need to save to support them in future. The self support need mainly comprises of the need to save for meeting future unforeseen contingencies and future anticipated expenses. The presence of strong motives among Indians indicates that people will definitely save if they have any surplus money after meeting their basic consumption needs.

Table 7
Family Oriented Motive

	Frequency	*Per cent*
Disagree	265	48.0
Agree	287	52.0
Total	552	100.0

Of the total investors only 52 per cent of investors agree with the need to reserve money for family oriented needs. The family oriented need is represented by need to create assets to leave it for their future family use. The presence of family oriented motives among investors is much less than self support motives.

VARIANCE EXPLAINED

The Eigen value and variance explained by each factor (motive) is given in the following table.

Table 8
Variance Explained by Factors

Factors	*Eigen Value*	*% Variance Explained*	*Cumulative %*
Self Support Motive	2.597	29.337	29.337
Family Oriented Motive	1.604	23.173	52.510

The reduced two factors explain 52.5 per cent of total variance which is fairly significant. Among the two motives, self support occupies pivotal position and it alone explains 29.3 per cent of total variance. This indicates that the primary motive of every individual is self support motive and individuals differ from each other mainly on the level of their self support motive.

SEGMENTATION OF INVESTORS BASED ON MOTIVES

The individual investors can be grouped on the basis of similarities between these two factors namely self support motive and family oriented motive. Cluster analysis is performed for the purpose of segmentation of investors based on the level of motives they have on self support motive and family oriented motive.

Table 9
Final Cluster Centers

	Cluster	
	1	*2*
Self Support	3.75 (I)	3.37 (II)
Family Oriented	3.38 (I)	2.09 (II)

If the investors are divided into two groups then the first group can be called highly motivated group because their level of motivation is high in both self support motive and family oriented motive.

Table 10
Final Cluster Centers

		Cluster	
Motives	*1*	*2*	*3*
Self Support	3.72 (II)	2.81 (III)	3.85 (I)
Family Oriented	3.51 (I)	2.12 (III)	2.18 (II)
Average	3.61	2.46	3.01

If the investors are grouped into three segments then the first group can be called as highly motivated group because their average level of motivation is high when compared to the other two groups and they can also be called as family oriented group because they rank first in the family oriented motive. The second group can be called as least motivated group because they are not agreeable to the existence of both self support motive and family oriented motive. The third group can be christened as average level motivated group because their average level of motivation is around three which is in the middle of 1 to 5 point scale. The third group can also be called as self centered group because they have very strong self support motive.

Table 11
ANOVA

	Cluster		Error			
Motives	*Mean Square*	*df*	*Mean Square*	*df*	*F*	*Sig.*
Self Support	50.253	2	0.283	549	177.428	0.000
Family Oriented	118.658	2	0.241	549	492.222	0.000

The Anova table explains that both motives are playing influential role in dividing the investors into three groups. The Anova table also indicates that there exists a significant difference in the mean scores of these three groups on both self support motive and family oriented motive. The significant difference in mean score indicates that these three groups can be explained by using these two motive categories.

CHARACTERISTICS OF MOTIVE SEGMENTS

A brief description of the three motivation groups namely highly motivated, least motivated and self centered segments is given below.

HIGHLY MOTIVATED INVESTORS

The motivation level of this group is high in both the family oriented motive and self support motive as the mean values of both motives are above three in the five point rating scale. They rank among the top in the family oriented motive, second in the self support motive and first in the over all average of mean values of both motives. Though they are second in the self support motive they can be termed as highly motivated group because their motivational level is high in both motives. In the sample of 552 respondents 206 respondents are in this group which means that 37 per cent of investors are highly motivated.

LEAST MOTIVATED INVESTORS

The second segment of people with respect to motives of savings is called Least Motivated Investors because people in this segment have least level of motivation for savings. This group has very less level of motivation on family oriented motives and self support motives and the mean values of both these motives are less than three in the five point scale. They also rank third in both motives. They also have less level of motivation for saving in the over all average of mean values. In the overall investor population, around 25% of investors are in this category.

SELF CENTERED INVESTORS

The average score of mean values of both motives of this segment is 3.01; hence this group can be treated as average motivation groups. This group can also be treated as self support motivated group because they have very high level of self support motive. As these groups have high level of self support motive and very least and insignificant level of family oriented motive, this group of investors can be called as self centered investors. Around 38 per cent of investing population is in this category.

Table 12
Number of Cases in Each Cluster

Cluster	1	206.000	37%
	2	137.000	25%
	3	209.000	38%
Valid		552.000	100%

The above table explains the number of people present in each cluster. The highly motivated group and the self centered group account for 75 per cent of the population.

Table 13
Number of Cases in Each Cluster

Cluster	1	246.000	45%
	2	306.000	55%
Valid		552.000	100%

If the investors are grouped into two clusters then 45% of the investors are highly motivated investors and 55% of the investors are least motivated investors. The self centered people are mainly grouped into least motivated group because they have insignificant level of motivation in family oriented motives.

TESTING SUITABILITY OF SEGMENTATION

The investors are classified into three clusters based on the level of motives they have for savings. The three identified clusters are highly motivated clusters, self centered clusters and least motivated clusters. Around 37 per cent of investors are treated as highly motivated people and 25 per cent of investors are least motivated people and 38 per cent of the investors are self centered people. The next primary question is whether the identified clusters are genuine and each cluster differs from the other significantly and both motives play a role in separating investors into three segments. For this purpose discriminant analysis is used.

Table 14

Tests of Equality of Group Means

	Wilks' Lambda	F	df1	df2	Sig.
Self Support	0.607	177.428	2	549	0.000
Family Oriented	0.358	492.222	2	549	0.000

Wilks' lambda is the ratio of the within-groups sum of squares to the total sum of squares. Wilks' lambda is very small for family orientation which means there is a strong group difference among the three motive segmentation in a family orientated motive. The mean values of family oriented motive are significantly different among the three segments. Wilks' Lambda for self support motive is comparatively high because there is no much difference between the first segment and the third segment in the mean values of self support motive. The F statistic is a ratio of 'between-groups variability' to the 'within-groups variability'. The value of F ratio with respect to degrees of freedom is very significant which is indicated in the significance value. The low value of significance indicates that there exists a significant difference in motivational levels among the three groups. The above two facts explain that the present segmentation is right and there exists a significant group difference.

Table 15

Eigen Values

Function	Eigen value	% of Variance	Cumulative %	Canonical Correlation
1	1.809	75.9	75.9	0.802
2	0.573	24.1	100.0	0.604

The Eigen value is the ratio of 'between-groups sum of squares' and 'within-groups sum of squares'. The largest Eigen value corresponds to the maximum spread of the groups' means. Small Eigen accounts for very little of the total dispersion. The Eigen for first discriminant function is very high when compared to second function. For the three clusters two discriminant functions can be formed and there will be two canonical correlations. The canonical correlation is a tool used to measure the association between discriminant functions and the two motives. The canonical correlation between the first function and the two motives is very high which is 0.8, but canonical correlation for the second function is only 0.6. The Wilks Lambda table indicates that both canonical correlations are significant.

Table 16

Wilks' Lambda

Test of Function(s)	Wilks' Lambda	Chi-square	df	Sig.
1 through 2	.226	814.879	4	0.000
2	.636	248.443	1	0.000

Wilks' lambda for the first function is 0.226 which indicates the group means are different in the first function which is the function of family oriented motive and Wilks lambda for second function is 0.636 which also indicates that group means are different but not to the extent of the first function. The second function is the function of self support motive where the group difference is less. A chi-square transformation of Wilks' lambda is used along with the degrees of freedom to determine the degree of significance. The significance value is small for the first function which is 0.000. It indicates that group means differ very much significantly in the first function which is represented by family oriented motive. The Chi-square value for the second function is 248.443 which is also significant by 0.000.

The structure matrix indicates that two functions can be formed for the three clusters. These two domain functions can be used separately, to describe the characteristics of population. The two domain functions are Z1 = 0.994 * Family oriented motive, Z2 = 0.970 * Self Support motive.

Table 17
Structure Matrix

	Function	
	1	*2*
Family Oriented	0.994*	-0.112
Self Support	0.244	0.970*

The following group centroids diagram shows that all the three clusters are distinctive clusters having different group centroids and different mean values. The cluster members are aligned separately from other group members.

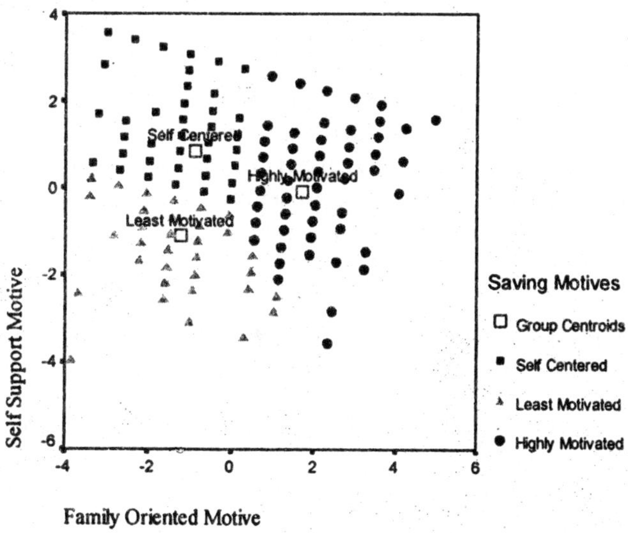

FIGURE 1: Group Centroids for Motive Clusters

The Classification of Results table measures the degree of success of the classification on the basis of motives. The number and percentage of cases correctly classified and misclassified are displayed in the table. Here 203 cases or 98.5 per cent of highly motivated segments are correctly classified and only 3 cases are included in to self centered segment. In the least motivated segment 134 cases accounting for 97.8 per cent are correctly classified. In self centered, it is 100 per cent correctly classified. From this it can be clearly inferred that the segmentation of investors based on motive is correct by more than 98.9 per cent.

Table 18
Classification of Results

			Predicted Group Membership			
		Saving Motives	*Highly Motivated*	*Least Motivated*	*Self centered*	*Total*
Original	Count	Highly Motivated	203	0	3	206
		Least Motivated	3	134	0	137
		Self centered	0	0	209	209
	%	Highly Motivated	98.5	0.0	1.5	100.0
		Least Motivated	2.2	97.8	0.0	100.0
		Self centered	0.0	0.0	100.0	100.0

98.9% of original grouped cases are correctly classified.

CONCLUSION

It can be concluded from the above analysis that around 95 per cent of Indians agree with the existence of motives to save and 75 per cent of the people have high level of motivation to save. Another important finding of the study is that the level of motives has a significant influence on size of saving. India has high saving rate because Indians' have high level of motives to save. The present high level of saving rate will continue as long as Indians have high level of motives. Hence the savings in India depends mainly on the ability to save. Understanding the requirements and characteristics of various segments, the marketers of investment products can tailor different instruments exclusively for different segments to fit their needs. This will help them to tide over the competition effectively and efficiently which might arise out of globalisation.

REFERENCE

Ando, A. and Modigliani, F. (1963), The "Life Cycle" Hypothesis of Saving: Aggregate Implications and Tests. *American Economic Review*, 53, 55-84.

Andrea Poltho (1975), Japan: An Economic Survey, 1953-1972, Oxford University Press, p. 76.

Arthur Lewis, W. (1963), Economic Development with Unlimited Supplied of Labour, in Agarwala and S.P. Singh (Ed.) The Economics of Underdevelopment, Oxford University Press, New York, p. 416.

Avery, Robert, B., Elliehausen, G.E., (1986), Financial Characteristics of high Income Families, Federal Reserve Bulletin, March 1986, pp.163-177.

Barro, R. J.(1978), The Impact of Social Security on Private Savings, Washington, D.C: American Enterprise Institute.

Bernheim, B.D. (1994), Personal Saving, Information, and Economic Literacy: New Directions for Public Policy. In Tax Policy for Economic Growth in the 1990s pp. 53-78. Washinton, DC: American Council for Capital Formation.

Browning, M. and Lusardi, A. (1996), Household Saving: Micro Theories and Macro Facts, *Journal of Economic Literature*, 34, 1797-1855.

Carrol, C. D. (1997), Buffer Stock Saving and the Life Cycle/Permanent Income Hypothesis, *Quarterly Journal of Economics*, 112, 1-55.

Feldstein, M. S. (1974), Social Security, Included Retirement, and Aggregate Capital Accumulation, *Journal of Political Economy*, 82(5), 905-926.

Feldstein, M. S. (1996), Social Security Saving: New Time Series Evidence, National *Tax Journal*, 49(2), 151-154.

Furnham, A. (1985), Why do People Save? Attitudes to, and Habits of Saving Money in Britain, *Journal of Applied Social Psychology*, 15(4), 354-373.

Johnson, D. and Widdows, R. (1985), Emergency Fund Levels of Household, Proceedings of the 31st Annual Conference of the American Council on consumer Interest, 235-241.

Kaiser, H. F. (1958), The Varimax Criterion for Analytic Rotation in Factor Analysis, Pyrometrical, 23, 197-200

Katona, G. (1960), The Powerful Consumer, New York: McGraw-Hill.

Katona, G. (1980), Essays on Behavioural Economics, Institute for Social Research, University of Michigan.

Kennickell, A.B., Starr-McCluer, M. and Surette, B.J. (2000), Recent Changes in U.S. Family Fiancés: Results from the 1998 Survey of Consumer Finances, Federlal Reserve Bulletin, 86, 1-29.

Keynes, J. M. (1958), The General Theory of Employment, Interest and Money, New York, Harcourt, Brace and Company. (Original Work Published 1936).

Kothari, C.R. (2004), Research Methodology-Methods and Techniques, New Age International Publishers, New Delhi.

Kurz, M. (1984), Capital Accumulation and the Characteristics of Private Intergenerational Transfers, Economica, 51. 1-22.

Lunt, P.K. and Livingstone, S.M. (1991), Psychological, Social and Economic Determinants of Saving: Comparing Recurrent and Total Savings, *Journal of Economic Psychology*, 12, 621-641.

Modigliani, F. (1988), The Role of Intergenerational Transfers and Life Cycle Saving in the Accumulation of Wealth, *Journal of Economic Perspectives*, 2, 15-40.

Owens, J. (1993), Taxation and Saving, in A. Heertje (Ed.), World Savings: An International Survey, pp. 100-138, Cambridge, MA: Blackwell.

Sinha M. R. (1964), Savings in the Economic Growth of Post War Japan, Indian Institute of Asian Studies, Asian Studies Press, Bombay, 1984, pp. 2-3.

Smith, A. (1993), An Inquiry into the Nature and Causes of the Wealth of Nations, New York, Oxford University Press. (Original work Published 1776).

Solmon, L.C. (1975), The Relation between Schooling and Savings Behaviour; An Example of the Indirect Effects of Education. In F.T. Juster, Education, Income and Human Behaviour, pp. 253-293. New York: McGraw-Hill.

Sturm, P. H. (1983), Determinants of Saving: Theory and Evidence, OECD Economic Studies, I, 147-196.

Whyte L. G. (1976), Principles of Finance and Investment, Vol. II.

Wolff, E. N. (1981), Accumulation of Household Wealth over Life Cycle: A Micro Data Analysis, Review of Income and Wealth, 27(1), 75-96.

Yuh, Y., Montalto, C.P. and Hanna, S. (1998), Are Americans Prepared for Retirement? Financial Counseling and Planning, 9(1), 1-12.

Chapter-21

IMPACT OF THE WORLD TRADE ORGANIZATION ON INDIAN ECONOMY

N. Radhakrishnan & K. G. Selvaraj

GLOBALIZATION

Globalization is a buzz word that refers to the trend for people, firms and governments around the world to become increasingly dependent on and integrated with each other. This can be a source of tremendous opportunity, as new markets, workers, business partners, goods and services and jobs become available, but also of competitive threat, which may undermine economic activities that were viable before globalization.

Usually, the term is synonymous with international integration, the spread of free markets and policies of liberalization and free trade. The process is not the result simply of economic forces. The decisions of policymakers have also played an important part, although not all governments have embraced the change warmly.

The driving force of globalization has been multinational companies, which since the 1970s have constantly, and often successfully, lobbied governments to make it easier for them to put their skills and capital to work in previously protected national markets.

Firms enjoying some national protection, and their (often unionised) workers, have been some of the main opponents of globalization, along with advocates of fair trade. Despite all the talk of globaliz during the 1990s, in some respects the world economy was more integrated in the late 19th century. The labour market was certainly more global. For example, the flow of people out of Europe, 300,000 people a year in the mid-19th century, reached 1m a year after 1900.

There are numerous advantages in the shift to a global economy including the possibility to increase benefits from economies of scale. The breaking down of global barriers allows companies to benefit from the largest and cheapest workforces, raw materials, and technology. For example, "many North

American publishers actually write and produce much of their software in countries such as India."

Other advantages that companies benefit from include: the opportunity for smaller companies to quickly expand globally, having more choices when recruiting a workforce and the opportunity to target a larger customer base (which translates to greater earning potential).

It is obvious how global economy also helps in promoting international cooperation and peace for the nations involved in the international trade by increasing mutual-dependence. For instance, India and Pakistan are often in dispute over land territory such as Kashmir. It can be argued that it would be less likely that these two countries will enter into combat due to the severe negative effects on their economies. However it can alternatively be argued that countries that are shun out of global trade are more likely to resort to armed combat for the same reasons that are mentioned above, therefore the subject needs a proper study to draw any conclusions on globalization's effect on world peace.

WTO AND GLOBALIZATION

Economic liberalization the world over has paved the way for globalization. The most prominent trend of this process is the emergence of trade agreements as instruments, that are legally binding and enforceable and ones, which are primarily developed by a few developed countries for the developing countries to follow. The World Trade Organization, which is a multilateral trading body, is a polished sword in the scabbard of the industrialized nations for organizing and enforcing global economic governance.

India has been a signatory to the WTO the day it was formed in 1995. Earlier it was a partner country in GATT, WTO's predecessor. Being a member country it is bound by the trade agreement and policies set out in the charter of the World Trade Organization.

India that till now has adopted process patent has been directed by the WTO to do away with it and adopt product patent to comply with the rules charted in the TRIPs agreement. According to the WTO agreement India has been given time up to year 2005 to amend its IPA to allow product patent instead of process patent.

Trade cross-retaliation is one prime problem that India will have to encounter if it does not comply with the specified regulations. In the light of this, an attempt has been made to study the impact of WTO directives post-2005, in the pharmaceutical sector in India. Given the current industry scenario in India, it is in no way a minnow to the global pharmaceutical majors. Yet it is beset with many implications. The policies of the Government apropos of, the pharmaceutical industry show promise and the current budgetary announcements scatter a ray of hope. The pre-WTO scenario (till year 2005, after which WTO regulations would be enforced in India) is characterized by rapid consolidations, acquisitions, mergers, extensive copying of patented drugs, restructuring by TNC's, preparations by them to take the Indian pharmaceutical industry by storm post-WTO and the pre-emptive strengthening of Indian pharma companies to thwart the entry of foreign majors. On the other hand, the post-WTO scenario is likely to be characterized by soaring drug prices, intense competition, new drug discovery and introduction into Indian markets, large expenditures on research and development, large scale downsizing, increase in social costs, etc.

World Trade Organization (WTO) is the only international organization dealing with the global rules of trade between nations. Its main function is to ensure that trade flows as smoothly, predictably and freely as possible. The result is assurance. Consumers and producers know that they can enjoy secure supplies and greater choice of the finished products, components, raw materials and services that they use. Producers and exporters know that foreign markets will remain open to them.

The result is also a more prosperous, peaceful and accountable economic world. Virtually all decisions in the WTO are taken by consensus among all member countries and they are ratified by members' parliaments. Trade friction is Channeled into the WTO's dispute settlement process where the focus is on interpreting agreements and commitments, and how to ensure that countries' trade policies conform with them. That way, the risk of disputes spilling over into political or military conflict is reduced.By lowering trade barriers, the WTO's system also breaks down other barriers between peoples and nations.

At the heart of the system—known as the multilateral trading system—are the WTO's agreements, negotiated and signed by a large majority of the world's trading nations, and ratified in their parliaments. These agreements are the legal ground-rules for international commerce. Essentially, they are contracts, guaranteeing member countries important trade rights. They also bind governments to keep their trade policies within agreed limits to everybody's benefit.

The agreements were negotiated and signed by governments. But their purpose is to help producers of goods and services, exporters, and importers conduct their business. The goal is to improve the welfare of the peoples of the member countries. The World Trade Organization (WTO) is an international organization designed to supervise and liberalize international trade. The WTO came into being on January 1, 1995, and is the successor to the General Agreement on Tariffs and Trade (GATT), which was created in 1947, and continued to operate for almost five decades as a de facto international organization.

The World Trade Organization deals with the rules of trade between nations at a near-global level; it is responsible for negotiating and implementing new trade agreements, and is in charge of policing member countries' adherence to all the WTO agreements, signed by the bulk of the world's trading nations and ratified in their parliaments. Most of the WTO's current work comes from the 1986-94 negotiations called the Uruguay Round, and earlier negotiations under the GATT.

The organization is currently the host to new negotiations, under the Doha Development Agenda (DDA) launched in 2001. The WTO is governed by a Ministerial Conference, which meets every two years; a General Council, which implements the conference's policy decisions and is responsible for day-to-day administration; and a director-general, who is appointed by the Ministerial Conference. The WTO's headquarters are in Geneva, Switzerland.

The WTO's stated goal is to improve the welfare of the peoples of its member countries, specifically by lowering trade barriers and providing a platform for negotiation of trade. Its main mission is "to ensure that trade flows as smoothly, predictably and freely as possible". This main mission is further specified in certain core functions serving and safeguarding five fundamental principles, which are the foundation of the multilateral trading system.

FUNCTIONS OF WTO

Among the various functions of the WTO, these are regarded by analysts as the most important:

It oversees the implementation, administration and operation of the covered agreements. It provides a forum for negotiations and for settling disputes.

Additionally, it is the WTO's duty to review the national trade policies, and to ensure the coherence and transparency of trade policies through surveillance in global economic policy-making.

Another priority of the WTO is the assistance of developing, least-developed and low-income countries in transition to adjust to WTO rules and disciplines through technical cooperation and training.

The WTO is also a center of economic research and analysis: regular assessments of the global trade picture in its annual publications and research reports on specific topics are produced by the organization..

Finally, the WTO cooperates closely with the two other components of the Bretton Woods system, the IMF and the World Bank.

The WTO establishes a framework for trade policies; it does not define or specify outcomes. That is, it is concerned with setting the rules of the trade policy games.. Five principles are of particular importance in understanding both the pre-1994 GATT and the WTO:

Non-Discrimination. It has two major components: the most favoured nation (MFN) rule, and the national treatment policy. Both are embedded in the main WTO rules on goods, services, and intellectual property, but their precise scope and nature differ across these areas.

The MFN rule requires that a WTO member must apply the same conditions on all trade with other WTO members, i. e. a WTO member has to grant the most favorable conditions under which it allows trade in a certain product type to all other WTO members."

Reciprocity. It reflects both a desire to limit the scope of free-riding that may arise because of the MFN rule, and a desire to obtain better access to foreign markets. A related point is that for a nation to negotiate, it is necessary that the gain from doing so be greater than the gain available from unilateral liberalization; reciprocal concessions intend to ensure that such gains will materialize.

Binding and enforceable commitments. The tariff commitments made by WTO members in a multilateral trade negotiation and on accession are enumerated in a schedules (list) of concessions.

These schedules establish "ceiling bindings": a country can change its bindings, but only after negotiating with its trading partners, which could mean compensating them for loss of trade. If satisfaction is not obtained, the complaining country may invoke the WTO dispute settlement procedure

IMPACT OF GLOBALIZATION ON INDIAN ECONOMY

Notwithstanding the low level of globalization of Indian economy, the impact of globalization has been highly positive in all most all spheres of economic and social life and virtually no negative effect. It is only because of opening of the hitherto closed, govt.-oppressed and controlled economy to the process of globalization that has helped Indian economy to grow rapidly in the last 10-12 years, India's economic growth has been high, exports have boomed, incidence of poverty has been reduced, employment has surged, begging by India for economic aid has stopped, long-term inflation rate has gone down, scarcity of goods have disappeared, the quality of products available have improved substantially and overall India has become progressively vibrant and internationally competitive. Indian companies are setting up companies abroad,

India has better technological development for the benefit of the common man (mobiles, road transport, cheap clothes, etc.)- only because of globalization.

REFORMS IN AGRICULTURE

India has done very little reforms in agriculture to enable private and individual economic initiative that would help harness the benefits of globalization. Despite this govt. created hurdles to globalization, Indian agriculture has benefited substantially from whatever little globalization that has been allowed in Indian agriculture. The farmers that got the exposure to global links of markets, technology and investment, benefited in terms of improving their yields, getting better prices and secured off-take.

In many areas of the country, tomato growers, potato farmers and fruit growers, farmers benefited from tie-up and collaborations with ketchup, potato chips, fruit juices, etc. Indian agricultural exports have grown where Indian farmers in selected pockets are competitive: these include spices made from agricultural produce, flowers, mangoes, other fruits rice, vegetables, pickles, tobacco, etc.

The e-choupals network created by an Indian company and the spread of mobile telephones have provided on line market price and climatic information on on-line real-time basis and helped them to get the best prices and sell to the most attractive buyers and brought them freedom from the clutches of the middlemen and traders.

Because of the resistance from the traders and the politicians, more and more farmers are not getting the benefits of globalization: vested interests are stopping the entry of more professional and honest buyers of agricultural produce of high quality for supply to urban areas through network of malls.

Fishermen in Kerala have increased their incomes using mobile phones to find out the best *mandis* where the prices are the highest on each day. There have not been any negative effect of globalization on Indian farming. But faulty and restrictive policies of Indian politicians have made it difficult for farmers to consolidate their holdings for larger scale commercial farming, access to large, high paying buyers with retail chains, support of well-organized transparent *mandis* not ruled by traders.

As a result in many areas farmers have committed suicides because of crop Failures and high indebtedness. Using the old British Indian laws of land acquisition, the state govts. Are forcing farmers to sell their lands for industries at prices they consider justified rather than asking industrialists and companies to bid for agricultural land which will increase the market prices of land.

Once these policy impediments are removed, globalization will proceed in Agriculture and farming in the proper way and benefit Indian agriculture and farming throughout the country. India does not need all the land under agriculture now for agricultural use: much less area would suffice to feed the nation and export if agricultural productivity can be raise substantially through private investment in agriculture by companies that need agricultural produce for their business growth and India's economic growth. Indian economy and take away our national sovereignity in the same manner they have done this in China, Russia, Vietnam etc.

To reiterate, There are absolutely no negative effects of globalization on Indian farming. The politicians are spreading rumours to get votes from farmers promising to save them from the threats of globalization. There is however threat to farmers to some extent: they may have to sell land against compensation to allow industrialization to progress. There would also be displacement of agricultural labor as a result and they have to be compensated, rehabilitated and absorbed in the expanding industrial, construction and other service sector.

But all these have to take place whether India globalizes or not. India's economic growth in future will demand significant rise in agricultural productivity so that some part of agricultural lands can be diverted for industrial growth and residential accommodations. Without releasing agricultural land for industry, development of roads etc,. Agriculture itself will suffer along with the farmers.

The farmers should be careful that they get fairly compensated instead of getting fooled by govts. And industries saying that they are offering more than market price. There is no active market for agricultural land in India. Industries and Govt. should be in competitive bidding process to buy any agricultural land to get real fair price which may be much higher than what they are getting now.

Farming in India urgently needs consolidation of holdings, large sized farms and considerable investments that would raise India's farm output many fold even after giving up a part of agricultural lands for industrial and infrastructure development. The food prices world over are going to shoot up. Indian farming needs to be allowed to make the maximum gains.

Today, politicians are keeping the urban poor happy by keeping most farmers poor that helps keep food prices low. But this policy will soon fail and India may have to import grains if farming sector does not radically improve its productivity.

EFFECT OF GLOBALIZATION ON INDUSTRY

3. Effect of globalization on Indian industry has been very positive, though some industrial firms with the baggage of high cost, inefficient plants and processes inherited from the past because of closed economy's government dictated industrial policies and priorities had to face serious problems in the beginning. But soon most of the industries have become more and more efficient; customer focused and improved their international competitiveness in terms of costs, prices, product quality and variety. Industrial growth has been very high and strong during the past decade because of globalization. Exports have increased tremendously. Indian industries are also expanding abroad. Foreign companies have substantially increased their investments in Indian industries.

Wages of industrial labour has increased substantially as they have become very productive. Lock out and strikes have declined to insignificantly low levels because industrial labor is happy. Those who cannot be efficient and past their prime age tio retrain themselves in modern methods and processes have been retired with very attractive voluntary retirement schemes. The trade unions are finding it difficult to influence industrial workers into agitation because labor has started benefiting from the positive fallout of globalization on the prosperity and growth of the industrial sector.

Talented and merited labor is commanding premium compensation in the labor market. Several new type of industries have also come up. Small scale industries of the past has fast grown into medium scale companies. Incidence of industrial sickness has gone done drastically.

NEGATIVE EFFECTS OF GLOBALIZATION ON INDIAN INDUSTRY

1. Rise in demand for labor and the rise in wage rates leading to some increase in costs.
2. Effect on Indian farming sector:

3. Weakening power of the trade unions over labor in emerging industries and growth sectors like IT, entertainment, internet and mobile services, airlines, banking, insurance, banking services.
4. Too much competition in the market leading to continuous pressure on raising productivity, enhancing consumer service, improving product quality, in order to survive.
5. Voluntary retirement for many public sector units.
6. Too many sales person chasing customers.
7. Too many cars on the road and traffic congestion.
8. Growth of consumerism.
9. Instability in profits due to too much choice among customers.
10. Shortage power and infrastructure affecting industrial expansion.
11. Closure of inefficient units supplying costly and shoddy products and loss of jobs.
12. Two years of large increase in textile industry jobs followed by large loss of jobs due to Rupee appreciation making Indian industry uncompetitive.
13. Problems of dealing with uncertainty in the international market in terms of demand, supply and prices.
14. The fears in the minds of many people that multi-national companies and the USA will exploit.

GLOBALIZATION AND THE FUTURE OF INDIAN ECONOMY

Globalization is an inevitable, irreversible process despite some vested interests trying to thwart it and some other vested interests trying to take better advantage og globalization than others. This is because the increasing prosperity of people at large of each and every country in the World is dependent on global trade, economic cooperation and global integration of economic activities in all spheres- trade, commerce, financial services, technology commercialization, conservation of exhaustible resources, information and knowledge acquisition, protection of environment, ecology, food and health security, enrichment of cultural diversity, tourism, travel, and so on.

This is being increasingly realized by more and more common citizens of almost every country. The vested interests of military/dynastic ideological exploitation and oppression are getting exposed and will not be able to able to keep common people away from globalization and its benefits for long. Indian economy will also benefit and grow at a rapid rate, ensuring radical improvements in standards of living and quality of life for more than 1.1 billion Indians over the years. The increasing trend towards regional trade agreements and bilateral trade agreements will make India realize that India is already on the fast march on the path of globalization. India is becoming more expert in sorting out issues at WTO.

This may create problems for politicians and their parties, they will not be able to live the comfortable luxurious lives and enjoy the privileges of power to control the lives of the masses, keeping them at their mercy for long. In command economies or liberal democracies, the common people will increasingly revolt against any move or extant systems that deny them the better life globalization offers on the basis of "ism'istic/ religious/ racial ideologies or beliefs. The alternative to globalization will be to perish. Globalize and globalize even more or perish.

REFERENCES

Bhasa M.P. WTO and Indian Pharmaceutical Industry: A Study Infosys Technologies Limited-Business Transformation Labs of SET Labs.

Panduranga Rao D. (2001), WTO and Competitiveness-Challenges for India Business and Management, ed., Excel Books.

CLEM TISDELL (2005), Globalization and World Economic Policies (Vol. 2) Serial Publications New Delhi.

CHAPTER-22

IMPACT OF THE WTO ON INDIAN AGRICULTURE–A STUDY

N. RADHAKRISHNAN

INTRODUCTION

AGRICULTURE is the engine of India's national growth and development Accounting for nearly 65 per cent of the country's employment, and being the major supplier of raw materials for several industries, agriculture is not only the backbone of the nation's economy and food security, but also a way of life and anchor of the overall livelihood of Indian people.

But, in recent years several unfavourable trends in Indian agriculture farmers suicides, declining prices of several crops, widening disparities between agricultural and non-agricultural sectors and a marked slowing down in the rate of agricultural growth. Farmers have been committing suicide (or) eating rat meat. This is what we have been hearing from different parts of the country over the last five years. Why does this happen? Why do farmers take this extreme step? Is income from cultivation not enough to meet consumption and other expenditure? Are farmers heavily indebted due to lower income from cultivation and increased cost of cultivation? or are farmers not able to cope with the new competitive environment after economic reforms?

People are driven to the extreme step of suicide not only because of imprudently large borrowing from high cost sources and for non-productive uses but also because the increase in net incomes from loans used for productive purposes falls far below expectations. In the case of Bt cotton, the input costs (especially for seed) are very high, but the expectation is that these are more than made up by higher yields. The performance of these varieties depends crucially on the availability of adequate and reliable irrigation and the quality of input supplies. It is significant that cotton farmers in Gujarat cultivate Bt cotton mostly under irrigated conditions and can access seeds of indigenously developed new varieties at a fraction of the price of varieties developed and propagated by the MNCs. During the last five years their prices have actually declined thereby compounding loss of incomes due to yield declines. The unfavourable prices trends for these crops are, to an important degree, the result of liberalization of imports of agricultural products.

The magnitude of exports and imports of agricultural and livestock products has no doubt increased substantially, the increase in imports being much more than exports. This has had a significant averse impact on domestic prices of some crops and on the farm economy of regions where they play a significant role.

But, overall, the increase in the volume of foreign trade is still too small relative to the country's agricultural production to made a significant impact on domestic production and pattern of resource use at the national level. Available evidence does not corroborate apprehension that liberalization has adversely affected domestic prices of farm products generally (or) shifted the terms of trade against agriculture.

There are strong indications of increasing disparities in income, employment opportunities and living conditions between agricultural and non-agricultural sector and between rural and urban areas. Despite unprecedented growth of output and a considerable expansion of employment growth in non-agricultural activities, the dependence on agriculture as the main source of employment and livelihood remains high. The share of agriculture in total employment has declined only marginally and at a much lower rate than its share in total GDP.

Table 1
Growth Rates in Various Sectors

Year	*Agriculture & Allied sector*	*Industry*	*Services*	*Total*
1993-94to1996-97	4.47	9.71	7.61	7.08
1997-98 to2000-01	0.99	4.2	8.37	5.43
2001-02 to2004-05	2.51	6.18	7.95	6.3

Source: CSO.

The details of the overall growth rate in various sectors are shows in Table 1. The primary sector's long run trend rate of growth since Independence was 3 per cent and the post reform period was the first when it actually fell well below that. It is observed that during the economic reform era, the overall growth rates in India have been declined tremendously. For instance during the period of 1993-94 to 1996-97, the growth rate was 7.08 per cent but it was decreased to 5.43 per cent in the period of 1997-98 to 2000-01, further it was increased to only 6.3 per cent during 2001-02 to 2004-05.

It indicates that there is no significant improvement in the overall GDP growth rates due to implementation of new economic policy in India. It is understood that the sharpest decline in the agriculture sector during the period of economic reforms when compared to the other sectors. For instance during the period of 1993-94 to 1996-97, the agricultural growth rate was 4.47 per cent but it was decreased to 0.99 per cent in the period of 1997-98 to 2000-01. It reveals that there were severe impacts on the agriculture sector during the economic reforms period.

INDIA'S AGRICULTURE TRADE IN POST-REFORMS

Trends in export show that India has not been able to maintain steady flow of export of commodities like non-basmati rice, wheat, cotton, sugar. In the post WTO period export of oil, groundnut, spices, tea, and coffee, has been affected adversely.

Table 2
India's Agriculture Trade in Post Reforms

				*Trade as of GDP Agriculture**		
Year	*Exports $ Million*	*Imports $ Million*	*Net exports $ Million*	*Export*	*Import*	*Total*
1990-91	3352	672	2679	4.13	0.83	4.95
1991-92	3203	604	2599	4.59	0.87	5.46
1992-93	2950	938	2011	4.73	1.50	6.23
1993-94	4013	742	3271	5.67	1.05	6.72
1994-95	4211	1891	2320	5.18	2.33	7,51
1995-96	6098	1761	4337	7.34	2.12	9.46
1996-97	6806	1863	4943	7.23	1.98	9.21
1997-98	6685	2364	4321	7.02	2.48	9.51
1998-99	6064	3462	2601	6.28	3.58	9.86
1999-00	5842	3708	2134	6.01	3.81	9.82
2000-01	6273	2646	3627	6.59	2.78	9.36
2001-02	6183	3408	2775	6.28	3.43	9.71

Source: Agricultural statistics at a Glance ministry of Agriculture, GOI, Various issues.

India's total agricultural exports were at $ 3.35 billion during 1990-91, which corresponds to 4.13 per cent of GDP of agriculture sector. Devaluation of exchange rate by 22.5 per cent in one go in 1991 followed by subsequent depreciation in the exchange rate, coupled with lifting of some restrictions on export, helped the country to double its exports in next six years. Imports also moved on a rising trend in the same period but increase in export was much higher than the increase in agricultural imports. Consequently, the net exports increased from $ 2.67 billion during 1990-91 to $ 4.94 billion by 1996-97.

The increase in export and import raised the proportion of trade in agricultural GDP from less than 5 per cent in the beginning of reforms to close to nine and a half per cent by 1995-96. After 1996-97, value of export started shrinking as international prices started falling. Due to falling international prices imports into the country became more attractive and were facilitated due to liberalization of imports followed due to WTO commitments.

NEGLECT OF AGRICULTURAL SECTOR–THE MAJOR SIN OF ECONOMIC REFORMS

A major criticism of the process of economic reforms is the neglect of agriculture. Data reveal that foodgrains production increased from 129.6 million tones in 1980-81 to 176.4 million tonnes in 1990-91 resulting in annual compound rate of 3.1 per cent. But during the 13-year period of economic reforms, foodgrains production increased from 176.4 million tonnes in 1990-91 to 212.0 million tonnes in 2003-04, indicating an annual average growth rate of 1.4 per cent, which was lower than the growth rate of population. Complacency on the foodgrains front can certainly cost the nation very dearly in the coming decade.

Various reasons have been assigned for this situation. Firstly, the reform process has emphasized the growth of manufacturing and service sectors and thus neglected agriculture. Secondly, as per the data provided in the *Economic Survery (2004-05)* gross capital formation in agriculture indicated that public sector investment (at 1993-94 prices), indicated a decline from Rs. 4,967 crores in 1994-95 to Rs. 4,359 crores in 2002-03, a fall by 12.3 per cent. This big drop in public investment in agriculture, including rural development and irrigation adversely affected foodgrains production. Thirdly, NABARD accumulated Rs. 13,500 crores under its Rural Infrastructure and Development Fund (RIDF), but was able to utilize it to the extent of only 30 per cent-a very dismal performance. This lack of development of irrigation infrastructure by withdrawing public sector investment with the hope that the private sector investment will expand irrigation, did not materialise. This was specially the case in backward states like Bihar, Madhya Pradesh and Orissa, which indicates very poor growth rates in foodgrains production - even lower than the national average. Last but not the least, whereas the green revolution states like Punjab, Haryana, Uttar Pradesh have reached a plateau, the country could not trigger higher yields in backward states. Dr. G. S. Bhalla and G.R. Singh (1997) in their study have pointed out "a sharp pick-up in agricultural growth experienced by the Eastern Region has been facilitated by a remarkable increase in area under irrigation triggered by a substantial private investment in pumpsets and tubewells."

According to Economic Survey (1999-2000) "The decline in public investment in agriculture is mainly due to the diversion of resources into current expenditure in the form of subsidies for food, fertilizers, electricity, irrigation, credit and other agricultural inputs rather than on creation of assets.

If we study the implementation of the Water-Seed Fertilizer technology (popularly known as the Green Revolution) then during the decade 1970-71 to 1980-81, irrigated area indicated an annual average growth rate of 3.6 per cent, which declined to 2.7 per cent during the decade 1980-81 to 1990-91 and further to merely 1.9 per cent during 1990-91 to 1997-98. Since irrigation is the basic input which helps the fuller utilisation other inputs seeds and fertilizers, we also observe declining growth rates in the irrigated area under rice and wheat from seventies to eighties and nineties. In case of pulses, irrigated area growth experienced a negative growth rate of the order of 1.5 per cent per annum. A similar trend was observed in the case of extension of area under HYV in case of paddy and rice. Fertilizer consumption indicated a sharp decline from 8.5 per cent annual average growth rate during the eighties to just 3.7 per cent during the nineties.

Table 3
Growth Rates of Agricultural Production in India

Particulars	*Pre-Reform Period 1990-91 over 1980-81*	*Post-Reform Period 2003-04 over 1990-91*
Foodgrains	3.1	1.40
(a) rice	3.3	1.06
(b) wheat	4.3	2.10
(c) coarse Cereals	1.2	1.20
(d) pulses	3.0	0.36
Oil Seeds	7.1	1.98
Sugarcane	4.6	1.47
Cotton	3.4	2.68
Jute & Mesta	1.2	0.52
Index of Agricultural productions	3.8	1.54

Source: Economic Survey (2005-2006).

In this connection, it is relevant to consider the trend in major and minor irrigation. Major irrigation acts as a supplement to minor irrigation in keeping the water table high, while minor irrigation provides water-security to the peasant in case of failure of rains. The slowing down of the growth rate of irrigated area under minor irrigation from 3.5 per cent during eighties to 2.3 per cent during nineties is another contributing factor to slow down of over–all agricultural growth. Economic reforms did not pay adequate attention to expansion of irrigation and this is a major sin responsible for low growth of agricultural production and productivity during the nineties.

Although the reform process has neglected agriculture and as a result, growth rate of agricultural production which was 3.8 per cent during the eighties, came down to 1.54 per cent during 1990-91 and 2003-04, the population dependent on agriculture has not indicated any decline.

The upshot of the entire analysis is that the major sin of economic reforms is gross neglect of agriculture the mainstay of livelihood of over two-third of the population. Although the Ninth Plan fixed a target of 4.5 per cent for annual growth in agriculture, but actual achievement of GDP growth in agriculture during 1997-2002 was of the order of 2.0 per cent per annum-that is, 44 per cent of the target,. This is more so in view of the fact that though India had seven good monsoon years in succession, agricultural production indicated year- to -year fluctuations. This casts a shadow on sustainability of agricultural growth, unless there is a reorientation of priorities with much greater emphasis on agriculture and rural industrialisation. The state, instead of withdrawing from investment in agriculture, irrigation and rural infrastructure, has to strengthen public sector investment in these areas.

CONCLUSION

Indian economic reforms undertaken since 1991 in the beginning neglected the agricultural sector and measures initiated for agriculture are of recent origin, lacking in cohesiveness. Against this background, an attempt is made in the following aspects to outline a probable agenda for reforms in agriculture.

The National Agricultural policy (NAP) envisages attaining a sustainable growth rate of over 4 per cent per annum in agriculture. The broad thrust of the reforms needs to be on ridding the input and output markets of distortions in agriculture with a view to calibrating them and developing a market -based price discovery mechanism.

Public investment in rural infrastructure and revamping of the supportive institutions in credit and marketing are critical for imparting dynamism in agricultural activity, as also the removal of some legal hurdles, such as ban on leasing on land. However, economic policies have an important role, and if used judiciously an supplement (or) support technological and institutional developments.

While larger investment outlays are necessary, the emphasis and focus must be not on the magnitude of investment expenditure, but on the composition of improvements that increase the product potential of land and water resources already under use. This requires a significant increase in allocations for improvement and modernisation of existing systems to reduce waste and achieve better control over water distribution and increased allocation for integrated watershed development for rain-fed areas. The focus must not be only on the magnitude of investments allocated to these activities but on their efficient implementation.

India has many small and marginal farmers. They depend entirely on agriculture. The rise in input costs of production encourages farmers to use less chemical fertilizers and the pesticides. This encourages environmental conservation but in absence other options, farmers adopt other measures that harm environment. The most crucial impact of globalisation is on small and marginal farmers in some of the states like Andhra Pradesh, Karnataka. In these states, farmers are committing suicide many. The reasons are non-remunerative prices of form products and the failure of monsoon rains. The positive impact of gloablisation is felt only in capital intensive larger farming units that constitute a smallest share of total Indian agriculture.

REFERENCES

Clem Tisdell (2005), Globalisation and World Economic Policies (Volume-2), Serials Publications, New Delhi.

Ruddar Datt and Sundharam K.P.M. (2006), Indian Economy, S. Chand and Company Ltd., New Delhi.

Vaidyanathan A. (2006), "Farmer's Suicides and the Agrarian Crisis", *Economic and Political Weekly*, Vol. XLI, No. 38, September, 23-29.

Narayanamoorthy, A. (2006), "State of India's Farmers", *Economic and Political Weekly*, Vol. XLI, No. 6, February, 11-17.

MUNIAN, A. (2008), "Economic Reforms and Agricultural Growth: A Study", *Southern Economist*, Vol. 47, No. 1, May 1.

Chapter-23

EMERGING TRENDS IN DAIRY PRODUCTS–WITH REFERENCE TO MADURAI DISTRICT, TAMILNADU

N. Namasivayam & C. Raja

The livestock sector best known as a sub-sector of agriculture plays an important role in the national economy and socio-economic developments of the country by providing employment and income to millions of people and also by providing nutritional security to the people. During the last couple of decades significant progress has been made in the dairy sector. The livestock sector produced 90.7 million tonnes of milk, 45.2 billion eggs, 2.12 million tonnes of meat and 44.5 million kgs of wool in 2004-2005. Total export earnings from livestock sector was worth of Rs. 5120/- crores. The share of livestock in the gross value of agricultural output (at 1993-94 prices) has increased from 18.6 per cent in 1971-72 to 35.5 per cent in 2001-2002. The dairy sector contributes the largest share in agriculture GDP.

Due to the changes in international trade following the rising of GATT and the emergence of the World Trade Organization (WTO) in 1995 Indian dairy industry has an opportunity to take its bow as exporter. However, a number of developing countries including India consider the livestock production system to be vulnerable to trade liberalization because of the domination of small scale product system. In contrast commercial production system found to have significant advantages in access capital for investments and new technologies. The export of milk products from India are picking up in a snail pace. Now, Gujarat co-operative federation limited is best known as India's largest exporter of dairy products.

Dairy Development Project during 1998-99 to 2001-2002 with full financial assistance of central government. The brief objectives of the IDD project were;

1. To increase the existing milk production and distribution of hybrid cows/high yielding cows/buffaloes which are on the route of milk collection centre.

2. To revise routes of milk collection centre in order to strengthen the milk co-operative society and to improve milk there of
3. To establish milk processing and distribution centres in the districts
4. To provide technical services such as health/hygiene and artificial insemination of animal to the milk producers from animal husbandry department
5. To provide feeds and fodder with suitable rates to the selected farmers with encouragement to undertake forage development programme
6. To increase the knowledge level of farmers by arranging extension activities.

The importance of dairying lies not only in the production of milk, but in its capacity to bring about significant changes in the socio-economic structure of rural economy. Its role in employment generation is well recognized. It has provided numerous small/marginal farmers and agricultural labourers with supplementary employment and a regular source of jobs equivalent to 25 million a year. The significant role played by co-operatives in stimulating dairying has also proved to be an important source of progress. The India Diary Corporation (IDC) was set up under Company's Act on 13th February 1970. It is a Government of India Dairy Corporation. It is to handle the commercial and financial transaction of India-World Food Programme (IWP) popularly known as 'Operation Flood'. This has become mainly a financing-cum-promotional agency of the central government.

OBJECTIVES

The following are the objectives of study:

1. To analyse the cost and return of milk production and compare them in terms of the milk of cows and buffaloes.
2. To assess the break- even output for milch animals during loctation period and inter calving period.
3. To analyse the price spread of milk in different channel.

DATA AND METHODOLOGY

For this study, the data with regard to milk producers, milk agents and the consumers of milk in madurai district are collected. The data comprise demographic variables, cost components of production, and procurement price. The structured differences of milk yield between cows and buffaloes by using the Cow's test, F-test, Break-Even Analysis and marginal value productivity against unity. The formula for calculating the break-even point is as follows;

$$\text{BEP (in units)} = \frac{\text{TFC}}{\text{ASP-AVC}}$$

$$BEP\,(\text{in sales value}) = \frac{TFC \times Sales}{ASP - AVC}$$

Where,

BEP(in units) = Break-even output of milk in litres

BEP(in sales volume) = Break-even output of milk in sales volume (in Rs.)

TFC = Total fixed cost

ASP = Average selling price of milk per litre

AVC = Average variable cost of milk per litre

The consumers differ in their opinions on milk vendors, co-operatives and corporate bodies. The Garrett's ranking technique is used to assess the important reason/problem in the given information by using the following formula.

$$\text{Present position} = \frac{100(R_{ij} - 0.5)}{N_j}$$

Where,

R_{ij} = Rank given for i^{th} factor by the jth households

N_j = Number of reasons ranked by the jth households.

RESEARCH AND DISCUSSION

Price-spread in Channel of Marketing

The observation of the data given in the Table 1 reveals that in Channel-1 the producer's price is Rs. 9.00 (69.23%) per litre, marketing margin is Rs. 2.65 (20.38%) and marketing cost is Rs. 1.35 which accounts for 10.39 per cent of the selling price (Rs. 13) thus, the price-spread is Rs. 4.00 (30.77%). In Channel-11 the producer's price is Rs. 8.44 (64.92% of selling price) per litre, marketing is Rs. 1.03 (7.92%) and marketing cost is Rs. 3.53 which accounts for 27.16 per cent of the selling price, (Rs. 13) thus the price-spread is Rs. 4.56 (35.08%). In Channel-111 the producer's price is Rs. 8.72 (62.29%) of selling price per litre, marketing margin is Rs. 1.36 (9.71%) and marketing cost is Rs. 3.92 which accounts for 28 per cent of the selling price (Rs. 14), thus, the price-spread is the highest at Rs. 5.28 (37.71%). The producer's price and the marketing margin is the highest in Channel-I and the Channel-I has a price-spread of Rs. 4.00. Therefore, Channel-I is more efficient than Channel-II and channel-III.

Cost and Retúrn-loctation Period

It is observed in Table 2 the cost and returns per milch animal during loctation period . The quantum of milk in litre cows is 2115.03 and 1903.92 litres buffaloes. The value of milk for cows is Rs. 17977.76 and Rs. 19032.92 for buffaloes. The value of dung for cows is Rs. 552.33 and Rs.689.27 for buffaloesds The gross returns of cows at Rs. 18530.09 and Rs.19722.19 for buffaloes. The net returns over variable cost are Rs. 8123.21 for cow and Rs. 8789.29 for buffalo. Whereas, the net return over total cost are Rs.664.44 for cows and Rs.6616.54 for buffaloes. The rate of return by the ratio of gross returns to variable cost is higher in the case of buffaloes (1.80) while it is lower (1.78) in the case of cows. The ratio of grosser turns to total cost is the same for both cows and buffaloes (1.50) during the lactation period.

Table 1
Price-Spread in Different Channels of Marketing of Milk

(in Rs.)

Particulars	Channels *I*	*II*	*III*
Producer's price	9.00 (69.22)	8.44 (64.92)	8.72 (62.29)
Marketing Margin	2.65 (20.38)	1.03 (7.92)	1.36 (9.71)
Marketing Cost	1.35 (10.39)	3.53 (27.16)	3.92 (28.00)
Consumer's Price	13.00 (100)	13.00 (100)	14.00 (100)
Price-Spread	4.00 (30.77)	4.56 (35.08)	5.28 (37.71)

Source: Madurai District Co-Operative Milk Producers Union Madurai.

Table 2
Cost and Returns-Lactation Period

Return	*Cow*	*Buffalo*
Annual Returns		
Quantum of milk yield (in litres)	2115.03	1903.29
Value of milk yield (in Rs.)	17977.76	19032.92
Value of during (in Rs.)	552.33	689.27
Gross Returns	18530.09	19722.19
Net Returns		
Net Return Over Variable Cost	8123.21	8789.29
Net Return Over Total Cost	6164.46	6616.54
Rate of Return per Rupee		
Gross Return/Variable Cost Ratio	1.78	1.80
Gross Return/Total Cost Ratio	1.50	1.50

Source: computed data

Cost and Returns-inter-calving Period

Proper feeding of the milch animal during inter-calving period, gives a good result. The Table 3 reveals that the quantum of milk in litres for cows is 2115.03

litres and for buffaloes it is 1903.29 litres. The value of milk is Rs. 17977.75 for cows and Rs. 19032.92 for buffaloes. The gross returns for cows are observed to be Rs. 18726.00 and Rs. 19919.87 for buffaloes. The net returns over the variable cost of cows are Rs. 4627.68 and Rs. 5851.45 for buffaloes and the net returns over the total cost for cows are Rs. 6360.37 and Rs.6814 for buffaloes during inter-calving period. The rate of returns by the ratio of gross returns to variable cost is higher in the case of buffaloes (1.42) while it is lower (1.33) in the case of cows during the inter-calving period. The ratio of gross returns to the total cost is higher in the case of buffalo (11.53) while it is lower (1.51) in the case of Lows.

Table 3
Cost and Returns-inter-calving Period

Return	*Cow*	*Buffalo*
Annual Returns		
Quantum of milk yield (in litres)	2115.03	190?.29
Value of milk yield (in Rs.)	17977.76	19032.92
Value of during (in Rs.)	784.25	886.95
Gross Returns	18726.00	19919.87
Net Returns		
Net Return Over Variable Cost	4627.69	5851.45
Net Return over Total Cost	6360.37	6814.22
Rate of Return per Rupee		
Gross Return/Variable Cost Ratio	1.33	1.42
Gross Return/total Cost Ratio	1.51	1.52

Source: computed data.

Break–even Output–lactation Period

Table 4 gives a picture of the break–even output during the lactation period. It is 547.21 litres for cows and 509.33 litres for a buffaloes The break–even sales volume is Rs. 4651.26 for cows and Rs. 5093.31 for buffaloes. The profit volume ratio is 42.11 per cent for cows and 42.62 per cent for buffaloes, and the margin of safety is 74.13 per cent for cows and 73.20 per cent for buffaloes. Thus, the percentage of break–even output to total output is 25.87 per cent for cows and 26.80 per cent for buffaloes. The profit per unit is Rs.2.65 for cows and Rs. 3.12 for buffaloes. The contribution per unit is Rs. 3.58 for cows and Rs. 4.26 for buffaloes. The average selling price per unit is Rs. 8.50 for cows and Rs. 10 for buffaloes. The profit volume ratio for cows and buffalo is more or less the same but the break–even sales volume is higher in the case of the buffaloes, when compared to the cows.

Break–even Output–inter-calving Period

Table 5 gives an idea about the break–even output during inter–calving period. It is 1446.69 litres for cows and 1073.65 litres for buffaloes. The break–even sales volume is Rs. 12296.86 for cows and Rs. 1075.59 for buffaloes. The profit volume ratio is 21.58 per cent for cows and 26.11 per cent for buffaloes. The margin of safety is 31.60 per cent for cows and 43.75 per cent for buffaloes. Therefore, the percentage of the break- even output to the total output is 68.40 per cent for cows and 56.25 per cent for buffaloes. The contribution per unit is Rs. 1.14 for buffaloes. The contribution per unit is 1.83 for cows and Rs.2.61 for buffaloes. The average selling price per unit is Rs.8.50 for cows and Rs.10 for buffaloes. The profit volume ratio for buffaloes is higher, but the break even sales volume is higher, in the case of cows.

Table 4
Break-even Output-lactation Period

	Cow		*Buffalo*	
Capacity factor	*Per Unit*	*Total*	*Per Unit*	*Total*
Average yield (in litre)	-	2115.03	-	1903.29
Sales (in Rs.)	8.50	17977.96	10.00	19032.90
Variable Cost	4.92	10406.88	5.74	10924.88
Contribution	3.58	7571.08	4.26	8108.02
Fixed Cost	0.93	1958.76	1.14	2169.75
Profit	2.65	5612.32	3.12	5938.27
Profit Volume Ratio	-	42.11	-	42.60
Break-even Points (in liters)	-	547.21	-	509.33
Break-even Points (in Rs.)	-	4651.26	-	5093.31
Margin of Safety (percentage)		74.13		73.20
Percentage of BEP Output Total Output	-	25.87	-	26.50

Source: computed data.

Table 5
Break-even Output-lactation Period

	Cow		*Buffalo*	
Capacity factor	*Per Unit*	*Total*	*Per Unit*	*Total*
Average yield (in litre)	-	2115.03	-	1903.29
Sales (in Rs.)	8.50	17977.96	10.00	19032.90
Variable Cost	6.69	14098.32	7.39	14065.31
Contribution	1.83	3879.44	2.61	4967.59
Fixed Cost	1.25	2653.55	1.47	2797.84
Profit	0.58	1225.55	1.14	2169.75
Profit Volume Ratio	-	21.58	-	26.11
Break-even Points (in liters)	-	1446.69	-	1071.65
Break-even Points (in Rs.)	-	12296.86	-	10715.59
Marginal Safety	-	31.60	-	43.75
Percentage of BEP Output Total Output	-	68.40	-	56.25

Source: computed data.

Problems of Milk Production

Table 6 reveals the problems faced by the milk producing-respondents. In the production of milk high cost of feed is the first problem for the animal, Insufficiency gets the second rank.

Table 6
Problems

Problem	*Means score*	*Rank*
High Cost of Feed	71	I
High Price of the Animal	66	II
Insufficiency of Veterinary Facilities	57	III
Low Productivity	54	IV
Difficulties Associated with artificial Insemination	47	V
Short Supply of Fodder	41	VI
Insufficiency of Loan Facility	40	VII
Short supply of grazing facility	31	VIII

Source: computed data.

Opinions of the Consumer

There are diffrent opinions of the consumer respondents regarding the quality, density, price, packaging, and advertisement of milk supplied by the co-operatives, milk vendors and corporate bodies. The method of analysis of variance (ANOVA) is applied for calculating the variations. Table 7 shows the results. It confirms that 'price' is significant at 5 per cent level among all the three groups co-operatives, milk vendors and corporate bodies. 'Packaging' and 'advertisement' are significant at 5 per cent level among the co-operatives and the corporate bodies. There is a significant difference in the means obtained from the three groups of sample such as milk vendors, co-operatives and corporate bodies.

Table 7
'F' Test for the Opinions of the Consumer

Variable	*Sum of Squares*	*Df*	*Mean Square*	*F value*
Quality				
Between Groups	2.048	2	1.0240	1.630
Within Groups	91.711	146	0.628	
Density				
Between Groups	6.338	2	3.169	5.059
Within Groups	91.461	146	0.626	
Preservation (price)				
Between Groups	1.235	2	0.618	0.850
Within Groups	106.120	146	0.727	
Packaging				
Between Groups	7.636	1	7.636	11.522
Within Groups	96.786	146	0.663	
Advertisement				
Between Groups	3.661	1	3.661	5.019
Within Groups	106.491	146	0.729	

Source: computed data.

CONCLUSION

From the analysis it is clear the corporate bodies of the private sector have entered into the marketing of milk, subsequent to the introduction of liberalization. Most of the corporate bodies that have entered the market mainly procure process and market the product. They have infused a sense of competition between themselves and the existing co-operative sector. These corporate bodies as part of their strategy try to create a distinct product image by imbibing modern marketing practices such as advertising, sales promotion, packaging and the like. The milk production has indicated that income from farm-bred animals is higher despite higher maintenance cost, than the income from farmer-bred animals. It is found that increase in the maintenance cost, especially the expenditure on feed, would increase the returns from dairying. The dairy farming in general depends upon the natural resources such as grazing land, infrastructural support, supply of feed, and also upon marketing. To improve the production of milk, the dairy form should adopt innovation techniques for higher milk production. The commercial production of milk can be improved if the dairy farmers get a remunerative price.

REFERENCES

Waghmare P. R. and D. N. Hedgier (2007), "Econometric Analysis of Integrated Dairy Development Programme in Prabhani District", *Agricultural Situation in India*, Vol. 3.

Agro-Economic Research (2007), "Evaluation of Integrated Dairy Development Project (IDDP) in Non-operation Flood, Hilly and Backward Area-A Study in Mizoram", *Agricultural Situation in India*, Vol. 3.

Shangita Shah, F.E. (2006), *"India is World Largest Milk Producers"*, *Agriculture and Industry Survey*, Vol. 16.

Manu Saini (2006), "The National Dairy Research Institute (NDRI) Success Story", *Agriculture and Industry Survey*, Vol. 16.

Mallikarjuna Reeddy. R. and S. Subramanyan (2002), "Factors Affecting Productivity Gap in Dairy Farming", *Agricultural Situation in India*, Vol. 1.

Rajendra, K. and R. Prabharan (1993), "A Study on Production, Consumption and Disposal of Milk in Dharmapuri District of Tamilnadu", *Indian Journal of Dairy Science*, Vol. 46.

C.A.R. (1988), *"Feeding of Dairy Cattle and Buffaloes"*, Indian Council for Agricultural Research, Krishi Anusandhan Bhavan Pusa, New Delhi.

Chapter-24

INTELLECTUAL PROPERTY RIGHTS AND ITS IMPACT ON DEVELOPING COUNTRIES

K. A. Rasure

INTRODUCTION

Twenty first century will be the century of knowledge, indeed the century of mind. Innovation is the key for the production as well as processing of knowledge. A nations ability to convert knowledge into wealth and social good through the process of innovation will determine its future. In this context, issues of generation, valuation, protection and exploitation of intellectual property are going to become critically important all around the world. Intellectual property rights will no longer be seen as a distinct or self-contained domain, but rather as an important and effective policy instrument that would be relevant to a wide range of socio-economic, technological and political concerns. The development of skills and competence to manage IPR and leverage its influence will need increasing focus, in particular in the developing countries.

An ideal regime of intellectual property rights strikes a balance between private incentives for innovators and the public interest of maximising access to the fruits of innovation. This balance is reflected in articles 27 of the 1948, Universal Declaration of Human Rights, which recognizes both that "Everyone has the right to the protection of the moral and material interest resulting from any scientific, Literacy or artistic production of which he is the author", and that "Everyone has the right to share in scientific advancement and its benefits". The burning question seems to be balancing the interest of the inventor and that of the society in an optimum way.

The present paper makes a moderate attempt to summarise and discuss the impact of intellectual property rights on developing countries in accordance with the Trade Related Intellectual Property Rights (TRIPS) Agreement. This paper is exclusively depends on published information.

THE IMPACT OF TRIPS ON DEVELOPING COUNTRIES

Trade Related Intellectual Property Rights (TRIPS) agreement in multilateral trade negotiations under World Trade Organisation (WTO) mechanism is viewed as one of the most redundant and controversial aspects. The implication of TRIPS agreement on India has several dimensions including economic, environment, biodiversity, food security, livelihood of indigenous communities and their indigenous knowledge. The integration of local economy with the global economy under the regime of WTO reflecting a greater adoption of western pattern of production and consumerism has resulted in bio-piracy and erosion of indigenous knowledge. Besides, the unauthorised commercial exploitation of bio-diversity, bio-piracy and granting of illegal patenting over indigenous knowledge system relating to utilization of bio-resources, have prevented economic benefits accrue to indigenous communities.

In developing countries 75 per cent of population directly rely on traditional medicines, which are extracted from forests, for primary health care, in developed world perhaps, 25 per cent medical drugs are based on forest ecosystems. The global market value of pharmaceuticals derived from genetic resources is estimated at $ 75-$ 150 billion. Thus it cannot be undermine the relevance and importance of forest based bio-resources in the area of life saving pharmaceutical industry. It is feared that the IPRs regime is largely against the indigenous communities in developing countries. Also this is to protect the interest of the developed world at the cost of developing countries. It is also alleged that IPRs would escalate bio-piracy in the name of scientific and economic development thereby natural resources in developing countries would be affected largely.

The developing countries have been forced to agree the TRIPS. According to the WTO, the developing country status grants those nations certain transitional periods for the implementation of the agreements. The developing countries are granted a transitional period of five years for the integration of TRIPS into their legal systems. If these countries had no protection of product patents in certain technological areas before they signed TRIPS, they are granted an additional five year period. Least developed countries have a transitional period of 11 years, untill 2006. The council for TRIPS may extend these periods.

Many developing countries have had or have to change their IPRS regime quite radically to fulfil the TRIPS Agreements requirements. A UN report suggests that negative short to medium term effects may occur, e.g. increased product prices and more difficult access to technologies. Nevertheless, the authors believe in long term benefits, e.g. the protection of domestic inventions and the augmentation of innovative spirit. Governments in developing countries have had and have to find a balance between the need to protect intellectual property and the requirement to diffuse certain technologies in order to increase welfare.

It is a fact that valuable knowledge is primarily in the hands of enterprises in the developed countries and developing countries have to import this know-how. The UN States that stronger protection of IPRs will inevitably lead to increased royalty payments for licenses of technical knowledge and higher prices due to the monopoly. Like position of the foreign title holder. Developing countries are concerned that a strengthened, worldwide IPRs system may lead to anti-competitive tendencies with negative effects on welfare in these countries. Transnational Corporations may abuse their monopoly-power, gained through their intellectual property, or the transfer of technology may be restricted. TRIPs Agreements Prime objective was not the battle against counterfeiting and piracy but "technological protectionism". Developed countries are regarded as innovators and suppliers of products whereas developing countries serve as markets. Especially in the US strong industrial lobbies such as the pharmaceutical, software, and returns on R and D.

US pharmaceutical industry claims to lose $ 500 million a year in India, due to the country's bad IPRs protection. On the other hand, in 1998, the US received royalty payments of $ 36 billion. In view of this, stronger patent protection is mainly in the interest of the industrialised countries. Correa- said that TRIPs is tailor made for developed countries but disregards essential differences between capabilities of countries in the North and those of the South. In 1990 only 4 per cent of world R&D expenditures came from developing countries, which makes clear who will benefit most from strengthened IPRs regimes.

FOREIGN DISTRICT INVESTMENT (FDI)

This form of investment would be the greatest benefit for developing countries, since they could catch up with their technological development. The developed nations described stronger IPRs regimes in developing countries as the basis for an increase in FDI, but there is no evidence that there is a positive correlation without additional measures. The TRIPs requirement that patent protection has to be ensured even if a product is just imported and not locally produced will hamper more FDI in developing countries. As a consequence, countries can be supplied with finished products, which are protected but produced elsewhere. Developing countries in particular, will not unconditionally benefit from foreign direct investment or transfer of technology.

THE PHARMACEUTICAL INDUSTRY AND TRIPS

The infections diseases which are from a scientific point of view, treatable, account for 14 million deaths each year, most of them in developing countries. A number of factors worsen the situation in these countries, e.g. poverty and lacking access to health services. Efficient and affordable medicines could cut down this death toll if people had access to each drugs. 25 million people out of the 36 million who are infected with HIV worldwide live in sub Saharan Africa and the enormous share of infected people of the whole population has a dramatic impact on life expectancy in this region. Again, affordable medicines could help. In developed countries live saving drugs have raised life expectancy of HIV infected people dramatically but this treatment is unaffordable for people in developing countries, where 95 per cent of people who have AIDS.

The high prices of medicines are the result of patents, which give their holders the right to restrict competition and therefore sell a certain drug in a monopolistic environment. TRIPs requires many developing countries to enforce their patent protection, which will restrain innovation and information flows. Moreover, prices of medicines will continue to rise, making access more difficult and damage local pharmaceutical industries. Production of genetic equivalents to expensive branded drugs will be limited because of the 20 year patent protection for pharmaceutical products and processes. In pre-TRIPs times many developing countries including India, did not grant product patents but process patents for pharmaceuticals, enabling domestic researchers to develop similar products through a process called reverse engineering. The implementation of TRIPs put an end to this practice and fears are growing that through the timely shift of product and process application or minor changes of the ingredients of drugs, protection for medicines may be extended to illegitimately long periods.

BIO-PIRACY

Developing countries heavily rely on domestic agricultural production, which makes IPRs like patents and plant breeders rights an important issue. Plant and plant breeders rights an important issue. Plant breeders rights are applied in the case of the development of new plant varieties through conventional methods and they are a kind of suigeneric protection, which does not include re-using of the seed and further research on the basis of the developed variety. Three criteria have to be fulfilled in order to obtain a 15-20 year protection, the variety has to be distinct, uniform and must keep its characteristics upon reproduction. The export of agricultural products and bio-piracy is a dangerous threat to farmers in these countries. Bio-Piracy describes the situation where someone, either an individual or a corporation, gains a patent on a plant variety already in use by someone else. The Rural Advancement Foundation International (RAFI) points out that in most cases the victims of such action will be farmers in developing countries and the perpetrators mostly are companies in industrialised nations. As a consequence, the title holder may prevent importance of the product in question or demand royalty payments.

TERMINATOR CROPS

Terminator or Traitor seeds are genetically modified to be sterile and not usable for replanting. As a consequence, farmers using these seeds would be forced to purchase new grain every sowing season. This makes quite clear how dangerous Terminator technology is, primarily for the 1.4 billion people worldwide who heavily rely on farm saved seed and who could not afford to buy new seed every year. Moreover, this technology could be used to develop plants which may be dependent on chemical treatment in order to become fertile or healthy giving Gene Giants the power to control agriculture and thus food supply worldwide. The US ignores experts warnings and is actively involved in the further development of a technology aimed at exploiting the poorest of the poor. The patentability of Terminator technology not only legitimates but also even fosters further research in this field, which one day will lead to the commercial application and unimaginable consequences for millions of people on earth.

CONCLUSION

To summarise the situation, developing countries are in a serious situation if they try to comply with the obligations imposed on them by the TRIPs Agreement. I see the urgent need for a reform of TRIPs although in some cases a different interpretation of the regulations would be sufficient in order not to discriminate against developing countries, their economies and their people. Intellectual property rights form the basis for scientific and economic development because they offer an incentive to someone, either individuals or organisations to invest time and knowledge in research activities. Inventors are given the right to derive monopoly profits, which means that only they are allowed to exploit their invention during a certain period of time. As a consequence this exclusive right has to be legally enforceable. The whole society should benefit from these works, as they drive economic growth and technological development. Admittedly, the effects of IPRs depend on various economic variables such as the social value or the existence of substitutes. Consumption of a public goods by someone does not influence someone else's opportunity to consume this goods as well. To maximise welfare within a society it would be better not to price the use of know-how in order to keep the marginal cost at zero but nobody would then be interested in providing knowledge.

REFERENCES

Jayashree Watal (2002), "Intellectual Property Rights-In the WTO and Developing Countries", Oxford University Press, New Delhi.

Roy Ellen (1996), "Indigenous Environmental Knowledge and its Transformation-Critical Anthropological Perspective", Harward Academic Publishers. India.

Shiva Vandana (2002), "WTO and Free Trade-A War Against the Farmers of India". CPI Publication. New Delhi.

World Resource Institute (1998), "World Resources-A Guide to the Global Environment, Environmental Change and Human Health", Oxford University Press, New York.

Correa, C. (2000), "Intellectual Property Rights, the WTO and Developing Countries: The TRIPs Agreement and Policy Options. London: Zed Books.

Fink, C. (2000), "Intellectual Property Rights, Market Structure, and Transnational Corporations in Developing Countries, Berlin: Mensch-and Buch-Verlag.

Messner, Sophie (1997), "Implications of the TRIPs Agreement under the GATT for Developing Countries".

Pass, C. Lowes B. and Davies L (1993), "Collins Dictionary of Economics 2nd Ed. Glassgow: Harper Collins Publishers.

RAFI (2001a), USDA says yes to Terminator, 2 November.

RAFI (2001b), New Terminator patent goes to Syngenta, 2 Nov.

RAFI (2001c), Enola Bean patent challenged 2 November.

UN (1996), The TRIPs Agreement and Developing Countries, Geneva, UN Publications.

Jayashree, Watal (1999), "Intellectual Property Rights and Agriculture: Interests of Developing Countries, Oxford University Press, New Delhi.

WTO (2001a), The WTO in brief. Retrieved: 27 October.

WTO (2001b), The multilateral trading System–Past, Present and Future, Retrieved 27 October.

WTO (2001c), Intellectual Property:Protection and Enforcement. Retrieved 27 October.

WTO (2001d), Who are Developing Countries in the WTO? Retrieved 27 October.

Chapter-25

WTO AND INDIA

M.C. Patel & Ms. S. M. Pillai

INTRODUCTION

The World Trade Organisation (WTO) was established on 1st January 1995. The WTO is the embodiment of the Uruguay Round results and the successor to the General Agreements on Tariffs and Trade (GATT). At the heart of GATT are the WTO agreements, negotiated and signed by the bulk of the world's trading nations and ratified in their parliaments. The WTO is to work towards the liberalisation of international trade and investment to promote economic welfare. The WTO endeavours to ensure that trade is as fair as possible and as free as practicable by negotiating rules and abiding by them. The rule book of trade for WTO is GATT. The Uruguay Round also created new rules for dealing with trade in services, relevant aspects of intellectual property dispute settlement, and trade policy reviews. The complete set runs to some 30,000 pages consisting of about 30 agreements and separate commitments made by individual members in specific areas such as lower custom duty rates and services market-opening. One such commitment made is in the area of Intellectual Property Rights.

Intellectual property may be described as creations of human mind. The legal right of creators to prevent unauthorised use of their intellectual property is referred to as intellectual property rights (IPRs). IPRs give the creators an exclusive right for a certainperiod of time. They are pieces of information with property status and could be exchanged for a value. This commercial aspect makes them the most valuable asset in a knowledge-driven economy. Customarily, IPRs are classified into copyrights and rights related to copyright, and industrial property.

The WTO's intellectual property agreement amounts to rules for trade and investment in ideas and creativity. The rules state how copyrights, patents, trademarks, geographical names used to identify products, industrial designs, integrated circuit layout-designs and undisclosed information such as trade secrets-"intellectual property"—should be protected when trade is involved. One of the most controversial outcomes of the UR is the Agreement on Trade Related Aspects of Intellectual Property Rights including Trade in Counterfeit Goods (TRIPS). TRIPS along with TRIMS and services were called the "new issues" negotiated in the Uruguay Round. Protection of intellectual property rights has become an issue of wide and serious discussions with the formation of the General Agreement on Trade Related Aspects of Intellectual Property Rights (TRIPS) under the Uruguay Round Agreement of the GATT, which is now the WTO.

The UR Agreement on TRIPS covers seven intellectual properties, viz.,

1. Copy and related rights (i.e., the rights of performers, producers of sound recordings and broadcasting organizations),
2. Trademarks including service marks,
3. Geographical indications including appellations of origin,
4. Industrial designs,
5. Patents including the protection of new varieties of plants,
6. The layout-designs of integrated circuits,
7. Undisclosed information, including trade secrets and test data.

On copyrights and related rights, the Agreement requires compliance with the provisions of Bern Convention to which India is signatory and the new Copyright Act of India already meets the requirements of the TRIPS Agreement. Trade and Merchandise Marks Act of !958 was replaced by a new Act, namely, The Trade Marks Act, 1999, so as to provide for the protection of service marks also.

OBJECTIVES OF PROTECTION OF INTELLECTUAL PROPERTY

The objectives of the Protection of Intellectual Property are:

- To encourage and reward creative work.
- To provide protection for the results of investment in the development of new technology, thereby to give incentive and means to finance research and development activities.
- To stimulate and ensure fair competition among producers.
- To protect consumers by enabling them to make informed choices between various goods and services.
- To facilitate the transfer of technology in the form of foreign direct investment, joint ventures and licensing.
- To strike a balance that has been between the legitimate interests of right holders and of users.
- To benefit the society by the proper Patent system.
- To provide an opportunity to re-coup the cost of invention and to make profits out of invention.

- Encourage research and development and thereby contribute to the well being of the society.

COMPARISION BETWEEN INDIAN PATENT ACT, 1970, AND THE UR AGREEMENT

But the UR Agreement on patents is in substantial variance with the Indian Patent Act of 1970 and so has led to lot of controversy in India, some of the main differences between both the laws are highlighted below:

- The Patent laws under the UR Agreement are more rigid and strong than the Indian law.
- Under the Indian Patent Act of 1970, only process patent is applicable in respect of inventions relating to substances intended for use as food, drug or medicines, or substances produced by chemical processes is limited to the methods or processes of manufacture only. This practice has been prevailing in the Indian pharmaceutical industry. The UR Agreement requires both product and process patents.
- Again, under the 1970 Act, patent expiry is of about 5 to 7 years for some products and 14 years for other products, whereas the UR Agreement stimulates 20 years for all products.
- Likewise, plants and animals, including micro-organisms, and biological and microbiological processes for the production of plants or animals are not patentable, under the 1970 Act, while in the UR Agreement, except plants, animals and biological processes, micro-organisms and non-biological and micro-biological processes are patentable.
- Compulsory licensing of any patent is granted for three years if requirements of public interests such as sufficient availability or reasonable prices are not satisfied in the Indian Act, but under the UR Agreement compulsory licensing of any patent allowed only under exceptional and very strict conditions.
- In the Indian Act, a patent is treated as ' working' only when it is used in local manufacturing i.e., used for production in India, while in UR Agreement a patent is treated as 'working ' even when it is not local manufacturing.
- There is ceiling on the royalty or fee that the patent holder can demand from a licensee under the 1970 Act, but in the UR Agreement there no ceiling on the fee or royalty that can be charged from a licensee by the patent-holder.

IMPACT ON INDIAN PHARMACEUTICAL INDUSTRY:-

One of the biggest fear of the UR Agreement is that if the product patents are accepted, it will hinder the growth of the Indian pharmaceutical industry and will also create monopolistic environment in the drug market. But this fear seems to be an illusion because a study shows that the patented drugs constitute only less than 16 per cent of the Indian pharmaceutical market. Again ore than half of the drugs have other therapeutic equivalents. It would not be very easy to increase the prices as the Indian Govt. can make efforts to prevent monopoly abuse by controlled prices. According to a study, Indian pharmaceutical companies faced a challenge as against the favourable climate in 1970. Imports were largely freed and placed on the OGL system and import tariffs were reduced. Inspite of the drawbacks, a favourable factor is the Industrial Licensing Policy that abolishes licensing for almost all bulk drugs. This may encourage the Indian pharmaceutical companies to produce as much as the desire and export freely. Thus the major obstacles to the growth of Indian pharmaceutical companies have been removed.

Moreover with a view to introduction of product patent by 2005 in place of Indian Patent Act, 1970, according to TRIPS agreement, more and more Indian pharmaceutical companies are investing in R&D in order to enter the international product regime. Again a number of MNCs are looking for the Indian partners to develop their R&D in the pharmaceutical industry since India has the advantage of low-cost but highly skilled manpower. As per a study, nearly 29 German companies including Bayer, Deguss Hulls, Adams Armacturen, Beumer KG, Lutzpumpen, Schwarze Alphine, Dechena, Hansturck, Impetus, Krishna Amtroxidant, Arbit Research Associates, Samson Control, Wika Instruments and E-Merck had visited India in late 2002 searching for partners. This will give Indian companies a great thrust to exports.

Major Indian companies are also looking for such enormous production facilities in the US as this country accounts for nearly 50 per cent of the world market. Similarly with a $4 billion pharmaceutical market, Brazil is enticing many Indian companies. As access to medicines is a major problem in Brazil, which has a population of about 17 crores and only about 50% of the population has access to the medicines, out of which only 20 per cent can afford to buy the prescribed drugs. Hence Indian pharmaceutical companies find Brazil as an attractive destination. Indian companies including Ranbaxy, Cadila Pharmaceuticals, Orbindo Pharmaceuticals, Acrolab and Lupin Pharmaceuticals are investing in manufacturing facilities in Brazil.

Thus, Indian Pharmaceutical Industry is one of the largest among the developing countries; in terms of volume, it ranks fourth in global marketing and in terms of value it is the only 13th largest in the world. Therefore, it would be a mistake to state that the TRIPS Agreement would strangle the growth of the Indian pharmaceutical industry.

REFERENCES

Francis Cherunilam (2003), "International Business Environment" September, edition.

Mohd Izhar Ahmad, (2005), "Impact of Intellectual Property Rights on Developing Countries", WTO and The Agriculture, edition.

Dr. P. Palanichamy and Lt. CDR G. Shaumugasundaram, (2004), "Impact of Globalisation on the Pharmaceutical Industry", Facts For You, March, pp. 19 to 22.

John Kishore and Dr. V. K. Somasundaram.

WTO (2001b), The Multilateral Trading System-Past, Present and Future, Retrived: 27 October 2001.

WTO (2001c), Intellectual Property: Protection and Enforcement. Retrived: 27 October 2001.

WTO (2001d), Who are Developing Countries in the WTO? Retrived: 27 Otober 2001.

CHAPTER-26

WORLD TRADE ORGANISATION-AN APPRAISAL

R. SRINIVASAN & B. B. MANSURI

INTRODUCTION

IT is widely felt that, no countryside can remain in isolation. Trade plays an useful role in economic development of a country. There are three international institutions ,namely, IMF, World Bank and World Trade Organization. dominates and control the world. W.T.O. came into existence from 1995, earlier it was known as GATT (General Agreement on Trade and Tariff).

It is acclaimed that, W.T.O. is the supreme sovereignty to control, regulate and regular demeanor of World Trade. Nearly 140 countries are members and China recently joined W.T.O.

In 1944, Western diplomats, in order to reconstruct their war torn economies met at Breton Woods, New Hampshire, USA, to construct the post war International Monetary System. The revival of the gold standard was in the offing. Two New organizations, the International Bank for Reconstruction and Development (IBRD) now called the World Bank, and the International Monetary Fund (IMF) were sought to be created. The reconstruction phase also saw the readiness of nations to cooperate among themselves to promote international trade. The main intention was to create a third institution, the International Trade Organization (ITO), to join the two other Breton Woods institutions[1].

Since the beginning of trade between nations, trade has brought general economic benefits but has simultaneously, also harmed specific domestic interest groups. Even during periods of economic growth, one hears complaints from domestic firms about the damaging effects of foreign competition on their industry.

INSTITUTIONALISATION OF INTERNATIONAL TRADE

In an effort to give an early boost to trade liberalization after the Second World War and to begin to correct the large overhang of protectionist measure which remained in place from the early 1930's–tariff negotiations were opened among the 23 founding GATT "contracting parties" in 1946.[2]

THE FINAL ACT

Ever since the GATT was established after Second World War, it has been striving hard (along with the World Bank and the International Monetary Fund) to achieve international economic cooperation. Towards this objective, GATT has been carry out several trade rounds (Table 1), the latest being the Uruguay Round which is the most expensive. Consensus was finally arrived and the agreement, called the Final Act was signed in April, 1994 at Marrakech, Morocco[3].

Table 1

Year	*Round*	*Area covered*	*No. of Countries*
1947	Geneva	Tariffs	23
1949	Annecy	Tariffs	13
1951	Torquay	Tariffs	38
1956	Geneva	Tariffs	26
1960-61	Dillon	Tariffs	26
1964-67	Kennedy	Tariffs and Anti-dumping	62
1973-79	Tokyo	Tariffs, Non-Tariff measures and Framework Agreements	102
1986-94	Uruguay	Tariffs, Non-Tariff measures, GATS, TRIPS, TRIMS, Dispute Settlement, Textiles, Agriculture, Creation of WTO etc.	123

Source: Compiled from K. Aswathappa, Essentials of Business Environment, 7th Edition, Himalaya Publishing House, P. 85.

WORLD TRADE ORGANISATION

One of the most important developments in the millennium that had far reaching implications in the world economic system is the formation and functioning of the World Trade Organisation (WTO)[4].

The WTO's creation on 1st January 1995 marked the biggest reform of international trade since the Second World War[5].

The World Trade Organisation (WTO) was established in 1st January 1995. Governments had concluded the Uruguay Round negotiations on 15th December 1993 and Ministers had given their political backing to the results by signing the Final Act at a meeting in Marrakech, Morocco in April 1994. The 'Marrakech Declaration' of 15th April 1994, affirmed that the results of the Uruguay Round would 'strengthen the world economy and lead to more trade, investment, employment and income growth throughout the world'. The WTO is the embodiment of the Uruguay Round result and the successor to the General Agreement on Tariffs and Trade(GATT)[6].

The WTO represents the culmination of a long drawn process directed at establishing a formal world trade body after 47 years of de facto trade regulation under GATT. With the completion of the Uruguay Round of Trade Negotiations in December,1993, the Final Act as well the Marrakech Agreement meeting of the GATT held in Marrakech in April,1994, paving the way for beginning of a new era in world trade. The WTO formally commenced its operations on 1st January 1995[7].

GENESIS

The genesis of WTO can be traced to the GATT which was founded in 1948 by 23 countries including India. The 8th round of talk under GATT (1986-1994), known as Uruguay Round led to the birth of WTO on 1st January 1995. Till then, GATT covered issues related to Trade in goods. The Uruguay Round , however, added new Agreements viz, General Agreement on Trade in Services (GATS) and Agreement on Trade Related Aspects of Intellectual Property Rights (TRIPS). All the three major agreements along with their associate agreements, now rest under the umbrella organization–WTO[8].

WTO is the only international body dealing with the rules of trade between nations. At its heart are the WTO agreements, negotiated and signed by the bulk of the worlds trading nations. These documents provide the legal ground-rules for international commerce. They are essentially contracts, binding Governments, to keep their trade policies within agreed limits. Although negotiated and signed by Governments, the goal is to help producers of goods and services, exporters, and importers conduct their business[9].

PRINCIPLES OF WTO

The underlying principle of the WTO is to create an international environment that enables the free flow of goods, services and ideas. The four main WTO guidelines are:

(a) Trade without Discrimination
(b) Predictable and Growing Market Access
(c) Promoting Fair Competition and
(d) Encouraging Development and Economic Reforms[10]

THE MAIN FUNCTIONS OF WTO

The main functions of WTO are:

1. Administering WTO Trade Agreements.
2. Acting as a Forum for Trade Negotiations.
3. Settling Trade Disputes.
4. Reviewing National Trade Policies.
5. Assisting developing countries in trade policies, through technical assistance and training programmes.
6. Co-operating with other international organizations[11].

DIFFERENCE BETWEEN GATT AND WTO

The WTO is not a single extension of GATT. On the contrary, it completely replaces its predecessor and has a very different character. The major differences between the two bodies are the following:

GATT	*WTO*
It is a set of rules and multilateral agreement.	It is a permanent institution.
It was designed with an attempt to establish International Trade Organisation.	The WTO commitments are full and permanent.
It was applied on a provisional basis. Its rules are applicable to trade in merchandise goods.	Its activities are full and permanent. Its rules are applicable to trade in merchandise and trade in services and trade in related aspects of intellectual property.
GATT was originally a multilateral instrument, but plurilateral agreements were added at a later stage.	Its agreements are almost multilateral.
Its dispute settlement system was not faster and automatic	Its dispute settlement system was fast and automatic

Source: Subba Rao P., "International Business-Text & Cases", Himalaya Publishing House, 2nd revised edition, May, 2002, p. 147.

MEMBERSHIP OF WTO

The WTO currently has (*144*) countries as members including India. The entry is subject to fulfilling the commitments enshrined in WTO agreements and principles[12]. *(coddissia book, p. 22).*

WTO: THE ORGANISATION

The WTO, headquartered at Geneva, Switzerland headed by a Director General having a term of four years[13].

DECISION MAKERS AT WTO HIGHEST AUTHORITY

Ministerial Conference

The Ministerial Conference comprising the designated Minister of the member nations, is the supreme decision making forum. The ministers meet atleast once in two years. The Ministerial Conference can take decisions on 'all matter' under any of the multilateral agreements.

Second Level

Day-today work is handled by the General Council, which also acts as 'The Dispute Settlement Body' and the ' The Trade Policy Review Body'. The General Council acts on behalf of Ministerial Conference and meets under the three different terms of reference.

Thrid Level

Three more councils, each handling a different broad area of Trade, report to the General Council: the Council for Trade in Goods (overseeing GATT, the Council for Services (overseeing GATS) and the Council for TRIPS (overseeing TRIPS)[14].

THE WTO STRUCTURE MINISTERIAL CONFERENCE

The structure of the WTO is dominated by its highest authority the Ministerial Conference. This body is composed of representatives of all WTO members. It meets at least every two years and is empowered to make decisions on all matters under any of the multilateral trade agreements. (see chart).

GENERAL COUNCIL

The day-to-day work of the WTO is entrusted to a number of subsidiary bodies; principally, the General Council, also composed of all WTO members, which is required to report to the Ministerial Conference. The General Council also convenes in two particular forms-as the Dispute Settlement Body and the Trade Policy Review Body. The former oversees the dispute settlement procedures and the latter conducts regular reviews of trade policies of individual WTO members.

The General Council delegates responsibility to three other bodies namely the Councils for Trade in Goods, Trade in Services and Trade Related Aspects of Intellectual Property Rights. The Council for Goods oversees the implementation and functioning of all the agreements have their own specific overseeing bodies. The latter two Councils, have responsibility for their respective WTO agreements and my established their own subsidiary bodies as deemed necessary.

Three other bodies are established by the Ministerial Conference who report to the General Council. The Committee on Trade and Development is concerned with issues relating to the developing countries and especially, to the 'least developed' among them. The Committee on Balance of Payments is responsible for consultations among WTO members and countries, which resort to trade restrictive measures in order to cope with their balance of payments difficulties. Finally, issues relating to WTO's financing and budget are dealt with by a Committee on Budget, Finance and Administration.

Each of the plurilateral agreements of the WTO–those on civil aircrafts, Government procurement, dairy products and bovine meat-establish their own management bodies which are required to report to the GeneralCouncil[15].

MINISTERIAL CONFERENCE

As per WTO Agreement, a Ministerial Conference composed of trade and commerce ministers of WTO member-countries shall meet at least once in every two years.

Till now 5 Ministerial Conference held.

1. First Ministerial Conference of WTO at Singapore in 1996.
2. Second Ministerial Conference of WTO at Geneva in 1998.
3. Third Ministerial Conference of WTO at Seattle in 1999.
4. Fourth Ministerial Conference of WTO at Doha in 2001.
5. Fifth Ministerial Conference of WTO at Cancun 2003.
6. Sixth Ministerial Conference of WTO at Hong Kong 2005.

WTO AGREEMENTS

The various agreements of WTO is explained below:

The WTO Agreements cover:

- Goods (main agreement GATT) e.g. all industrial products, consumer durables etc.
- Services (main agreement GATS) e.g. Banking, Insurance, and Consultancy etc.
- Intellectual Property (TRIPS) e.g. Patents, Copyrights, Trademarks etc.

GATT & GATS follow three part structure viz. general principles; associate agreements/annexes on specific sectors/issues and commitments of members countries.

The TRIPS agreement contains general principles only that are to be followed by members.

GUIDING PRINCIPLES OF WTO

The guiding principles of WTO (many inherited from GATT) are:

(a) Most Favoured Nation (MFN) Treatment- No discrimination among Member Countries–Any trade concession offered by one member of WTO to another member, must be offered to all members.

(b) National Treatment–Equal treatment to lawfully imported and domestic products–imported goods should not be discriminated against the domestic goods–same treatment to be accorded to both.

The agreements seek to address, broadly speaking, three concerns:

Same Rule for All

To restrict Governments or organizations from 'distorting ' normally trade by way of subsidizing, dumping, discriminatory licensing policies etc., which can hurt the business within the country or outside the country. To rationalize Govt. policies to eliminate the distorting effects (e.g. WTO allows exports to be relieved of all indirect taxes as Excise, Sales Tax etc. having cascading effect on cost of the product, but prohibits direct tax benefits as Income Tax waiver on export earnings.

Administration of Agreements

To provide detailed guidelines on how the agreements should be administered at national level (as in anti-dumping proceedings) or how the standards be used (as in Sanitary and Phytosanitary Measures) or how the dispute between the nations are to be resolved (through dispute settlement mechanism).

Fair Deal to Business

To create rights for the business community e.g. right to information, right to present evidence etc. (e.g. Agreement on Customs Valuation provides right to importer to justify the value of imported goods or requires customs to give in writing the reasons for rejecting value disclosed).

THE AGREEMENTS

The WTO agreements cover goods, services and intellectual property. The spell out the principles of liberalization with guidelines, permitted exceptions and include member countries commitments to lower tariff and other trade barriers and set procedures for settling disputes. Governments are obliged to make their trade policies transparent by notifying the WTO their laws in force and measures adopted, on a continuing basis.

CONCLUSION

One must remember that good trade policy begins at home. The surest way to liberalize and progress is to reform one's domestic economy. Whether one follows the regional or multilateral track, reforming the domestic economy is imperative in order to maximize the gains from trade liberalization. All are aware, WTO has been introduced in India with an aim of developing the economy of the country. The country's economy can be enhanced only through the support of industrial productivity and marketing. The components of free trade has been identified and grouped into five categories; viz., reducing import bans, removal of Quantitative Restrictions (QR), reduction of customs duty, easy exchange rate policies and change of trade bindings with the consent of trading partners. Even though the situation prevails, The opportunities available to the Indian industry for taking the full benefits of WTO and its agreement, are listed below:

(a) Easy access to foreign markets
(b) Opening of new markets
(c) Trade without fear
(d) Bound rates of duty
(e) Benefits Importers

NOTES

1. Arijay Chaudhry (2002), GATT (A Developing Country Perspective), Asian Books Private Limited, New Delhi-2, 1st Edition, p. 2.

2. Final Course Study Material Paper 7, World Trade Organisation International Trade Joint Ventures and Foreign Collaborations, Published by Directorate of Studies and Publications, The Institute of Company Secretaries of India, p. 6.
3. K. Aswathappa, Essentials of Business Environment, 7 th Edition, Himalaya Publishing House, p. 85.
4. *www.cdos-india.comwtoregime*
5. Final Course Study Material Paper 7, World Trade Organisation International Trade Joint Ventures and Foreign Collaborations, Published by Directorate of Studies and Publications, The Institute of Company Secretaries of India, p. 32
6. K. Aswathappa, Essentials of Business Environment, 7th Edition, Himalaya Publishing House, p. s82
7. *www.cdos-india.comwtoregime*
8. A Guide to Small Business on WTO, Published by Coddissia, p. 12.
9. Final Course Study Material Paper 7, World Trade Organisation International Trade Joint Ventures and Foreign Collaborations, Published by Directorate of Studies and Publications, The Institute of Company Secretaries of India, p. 35
10. (Panduranga Rao book, p. 3).
11. *www.wto.org*
12. A Guide to Small Business on WTO, Published by Coddissia, p. 22.
13. A Guide to Small Business on WTO, Published by Coddissia, p. 12.
14. A Guide to Small Business on WTO, Published by Coddissia, p. 23
15. K. Aswathappa, Essentials of Business Environment, 7th Edition, Himalaya Publishing House, p. 83, 84 & 85.

Chapter-27

WTO AND ITS IMPACT ON PERFORMANCE OF SMALL SCALE INDUSTRIES (SSI) SECTOR IN INDIA

M. K. Radhakrishnan, V. S. Ganesamurthy & A. Sengottaiyan

INTRODUCTION

The Small Scale Industry (SSI) sector has emerged over four decades as highly vibrant and dynamic sector of the Indian economy as it accounts for 35% of gross value of output in the manufacturing sector and over 40% of the total exports from Indian economy. The contribution of this sector to employment is next to agriculture sector. Small scale units not only play crucial role in providing large scale employment opportunities at lower capital cost than large scale sector industries, but also help in industrialization of rural backward areas,. there by reducing regional imbalance, assuring more equitable distribution of national income and wealth.

Small scale industries in India are now facing more threats for their survival than ever before. They have begun to feel hardships in doing their business on two accounts. As the Indian economy has been practicing open market economy from the year 1991, India's market is integrated with world market. It results in severe competition from multinational corporation (MNCs) for local industries including SSIs.

OBJECTIVES OF THE STUDY

1. To evaluate the performance of SSI in India with reference to selected variables such as number of units, production and employment.
2. To find out problems faced by SSI in India.
3. To study the impact on SSI sector in pre WTO regime and post WTO Regime.
4. To study the challenges for the small scale sector in India.
5. To summarise the main findings of study by offering suitable suggestions for improvement of SSI in India.

GENERAL IMPLICATION OF WTO

The world Trade Agreements and negotiations have a direct impact on all economic activities including developing and promotion of the small scale sector. WTO Agreement are likely to affect the SSI sector in the following ways.

1. The impact the WTO and its agreements is being left on every economic activity may it be agriculture, trading service or manufacturing.
2. World markets are opening up due to lowering of tariffs and protections are being dismantled.
3. Developing countries will have greater opportunities in sectors in which they have cost based comparative advantages.
4. Exports markets will become tougher because of competition among developing countries with similar comparative advantages.
5. There is a wave for standardization–hence products from developing countries will face tougher quality standards.
6. Every company will have to cost audit and compare with global markets.
7. International trade is increasingly becoming "knowledge–based".
8. Every aspects of trade has Legal backed hence every unit must be in a position to fight legally.
9. Removal of Quantitative Restrictions (QRS) will allow free and cheap imports and will result in still competition the SSIs.
10. In view of the agreement of Trade Related Intellectual Property Rights (TRIPs) it would be difficult for the SSI sector to continue with the reserve engineering and manufacture many items without royalty with to the patent holders.
11. In terms of sanitary and phytosanitary measures SSIs will have to adopt international standards with regard to quality, health and hygiene.

DEFINITION OF SMALL–SCALE INDUSTRY

The definition of Small-Scale Industry at present is related to investment celling on the original value of the installed plant and machinery. A Small-Scale Industry is defined as "an Industrial undertaking in which the investment in fixed assets in plant and machinery whether held in ownership terms or lease or by hire purchase does not exceed Rs. 100 lakhs". After 2005 the name was changed as small and medium enterprises (SMEs).

IMPACT OF WTO ON SSI

World Trade Organisation is responsible for changing the economy of world. Globalization represents a kind of global reality considerably influencing competition trade and investment 148 members of WTO contribute to over 98% of the world exports. Agreement gives 5624 bilateral agreement. It shows that WTO can shape the economy. Here an attempt has been made to evaluate the impact of WTO on SSI sector. The following table shows that the Number of units, production, Employment and Export of Pre-WTO period and Post-WTO period.

Table 1
Impact on the Small Scale Industrial Sector (Growth Pattern of Small Scale Industrial Sector) (Pre WTO Regime) 1985 To 1994

Year	*No. of unit (Lakhs Nos)*	*Production (Rs. Crores)*	*Employment (Lakhs Nos)*	*Export (Rs. Crores)*
1985-86	13.53	61228	96.00	2769
1986-87	14.62 (8.05)	82250 (18.00)	101.00 (5.20)	3643 (31.56)
1987-88	15.83 (8.28)	87300 (20.83)	107.00 (5.94)	4372 (20.00)
1988-89	17.12 (8.14)	106400 (21.88)	113.00 (5.60)	5489 (25.55)
1989-90	18.23 (6.48)	182320 (24.36)	119.60 (5.84)	7625 (38.91)
1990-91	19.48 (6.87)	155340 (17.40)	125.30 (4.77)	9664 (26.74)
1991-92	20.82 (6.88)	178699 (15.04)	129.80 (3.59)	13883 (43.66)
1992-93	22.86 (9.79)	209300 (17.12)	134.06 (3.28)	17785 (28.11)
1993-94	23.81 (4.16)	241678 (15.47)	139.38 (3.97)	25307 (42.29)
1994-95	25.71 (7.98)	293990 (21.65)	146.56 (5.15)	29068 (14.86)
Avg. Growth Rate	6.66	17.18	4.33	27.19

Source: Annual Report-Small Industry Development Bank of India.

Table 2
Impact on WTO on Small Scale Industrial Sector of [Post WTO Regime] 1995-96 to 2004-05

Year	*No. of unit (Lakhs Nos)*	*Production (Rs. Crores)*	*Employment (Lakhs Nos)*	*Export (Rs. Crores)*
1995-96	27.24	356213	152.61	36470
1996-97	28.57 (4.88)	412636 (15.84)	160.00 (4.84)	39249 (7.62)
1997-98	30.14 (5.50)	465171 (12.73)	167.20 (4.50)	44437 (13.22)
1998-99	31.21 (3.55)	527515 (13.40)	171.20 (2.62)	49481 (11.35)
1999-00	32.25 (3.33)	578470 (9.66)	177.30 (3.33)	54200 (9.54)
2000-01	33.7 (4.50)	639024 (10.47)	185.64 (4.70)	69797 (28.78)
2001-02	34.64 (2.79)	690552 (8.06)	192.23 (3.55)	71244 (2.07)
2002-03	35.1 (1.33)	824363 (19.38)	200.79 (4.45)	86013 (20.73)
2003-04	36.41 (3.73)	886526 (7.54)	273.97 (36.45)	97844 (13.75)
2004-05	58.05 (5.28)	931168 (5.04)	282.91 (3.26)	109634 (12.05)
Avg. Growth Rate	3.49	10.21	6.77	11.91

Source: Annual Report-Small Industry Development Bank of India.

Table 3
Comparative Performance of SSI in Terms of Average Growth Rates

	Average Growth Rates (Amt. in Percentage)	
Area of Performance	*1985-94*	*1995-05*
No. of units	6.66	3.49
Production	17.18	10.21
Employment	4.33	6.77
Exports	27.17	11.91

Source: 1st and 2nd Table.

COMPARATIVE PERFORMANCE OF SSI IN TERMS OF AVERAGE GROWTH RATES

The number of SSI unit went up from 13.53 (lakhs) in 1985-86 to 38.05 (lakhs) in 2004-05 and their production increased from Rs. 61228 (crores) in 1985-86 to Rs. 931168 (crores) in 2004-05. So far as the value of export are concerned, they increased from Rs. 2769 crores in 1985-86 to Rs. 109634 (crores) in 2004-05. Employment increased from Rs. 96 (lakhs) in 1985-86 to Rs. 282.91 (lakhs) in 2004-05. This is a creditable achievement. But the data in the table indicates that, the Average Growth Rate of the number of units declined from 6.66 per cent during Pre-WTO period to 3.49 per cent during the Post-WTO period, Production from 17.8 per cent to 10.21 per cent and Exports from 27.17 per cent to 11.91 per cent, but employment increased from 4.33 per cent to 6.77. The policies of globalisation and liberalisation have affected the growth pattern of Indian Small Scale Industries to a great extent.

CORRELATION ANALYSIS

The Correlation Analysis between number of units and employment, production and export is presented in Table 4. The result of number of units and employment was more during pre WTO regime. The correlation value was 0.994 but it declined to 0.835 during post WTO period. This may be due to stiff composition , de-reservation free import of goods, etc.

Table 4
Correlation Analysis

Dependent variable	*Independent Variable*	*Pre WTO*	*Post WTO*	*Remarks*
No. of Units	Employment	0.994 (25.57)*	0.835 (4.23)*	Significant 1 per cent level
Production	Export	0.95 (8.72)*	0.989 (18.90)*	Significant 1 per cent level

* Figures in brackets t values and significant at 5 per cent level.

Source: Computed.

Similarly the production and export correlation value during Pre-WTO period the correlation value was 0.989. This shows that production and Export value increased during Post WTO period. It may be due to expansion of market, technology up gradation and favourable govt. policies.

PROBLEMS OF SSIs

Small Scale Industries are facing many problems as specified below.

Impact of WTO Agreement

The agreements of world Trade organisation are likely to create some far reaching implications for the small enterprises specifically with regard to their competitive ability and integration with the global market. WTO will affect all types of small enterprises whether producing for the domestic market or for the international market.

Labour Problem

Lack of availability of skilled labour. There are mainly unskilled and untrained Labours. Due to this reason the productivity is low.

Outdated Technology

The technologies used by these industries are outdated technology. Old expellers (Kohllu) and handlooms are still in use. The result is fall in the quantity of output and the goods produced are of inferior quality. Such goods have very little demand.

Competition with Large Scale Industries

One of the main problem of these industries is that they have to face competition of large industries. Finished products of large industries are relatively cheap and of good quality. So, they can not compete with large scale industries.

High Cost of Production

Cost of production are very high in these industries. It is due to high cost of Raw material, old methods of production and high fixed costs because of small quantity of production.

Lack of Advertisement

Owners of SSIs don't have resources for advertisement. Due to lack of advertisement demand for goods is low.

Problems of Raw Material and Power

These industries do not get raw material in adequate quantity. Whatever raw material they get is poor in quality and high in price. It increases the cost of production are of inferior quality. These industries also suffer from shortage of power and coal.

Marketing Constraint

These industries have to face lot of difficulties in selling their goods at fair price and in sufficient quantity. For example, because of high cost of production, price of finished product increases very high and secondly, outward appearance of the finished product is not so appealing the goods also lack in uniformity.

Financial Problem

Non-availability/inadequate financing for working capital, non-availability of collateral free loans, high cost of loans and delayed disbursements of the sanctioned loans are the main obstacles in the development of small scale industries.

Lack of Able Entrepreneurs

These industries face shortage of competent entrepreneurs to run them, workers are mostly illiterate and conservative. Due to lack of education, they are ignorant of new equipment and modern technique of production. Therefore, they are unable to organise their industries. According to a report by State Bank of India, one of the reasons of the failure of these industries is the Lack of able and efficient entrepreneurs.

CHALLENGES

In the context of Globalisation and WTO regime, the challenges for the Small Scale sector in India are:

1. India is not a party of the agreement on Government procurements, but still the right to purchase from domestic manufacturers has come under severe attack in the WTO. If it materlize, domestic manufactures supplying goods to PSUS/Government will have a tough time, in the years to come.
2. Increased competition in the consumer goods sector, particularly in the electronic goods, computer hardware, aerated soft drinks is being experienced by the SSIs in India.
3. Inability of SSI in upgrading their technologies, improving product quality standard in accordance with the international standards and securing foreign collaboration, both financial as well as technical, has led them to a disadvantageous position while competing in the domestic market.
4. All the items under reserved category have been placed on OGL List. This step will have a serious set back to the future growth of SSIs in these product lines when technology is more for SSIs.
5. Permitting non-SSI Units to expand or create new capacities in the reserved sector with the export obligation of 50 per cent has made SSIs lose their sales share in the domestic market.

6. With the reduction in tariff a celling bindings of 40 per cent advalorem on finished goods and 25 per cent on intermediate goods in the non-Agriculture segment, competition has increased. The implication of removal of all quantitative restrictions on SSIs are expected to be as under.
   - Stiff competition from imports.
   - Large Scale dumping of cheap priced goods.
   - Some industrial units may tie-up with MNCs and become vendors and some may vanish.
   - Imported products of quality, high tech standard and competitive price will prevail in the domestic market. This will change tastes and preference of consumers. Consequently, it will lead to shrinking demand for local products.
   - Reserved item manufacture may feel it very difficult at once to switch over to standards, economies of scale, new production processes etc.

FINDINGS

- Compared to pre WTO export increased during Post WTO regime. It shows that the post WTO provided opportunities for higher export. The correlation co-efficient value is found to be significant at 1% Level.
- Compared with Pre-WTO to Post-WTO the correlation co-efficient between Production and export increased in Post-WTO period. It shows that the Post-WTO period provided opportunity for higher export.
- The Average Growth Rate of the number of units declined from 6.80 per cent during Pre-WTO period to 3.49 per cent during the Post-WTO period.
- The Average Growth Rate of Production declined from 17.18 per cent during Pre-WTO period to 10.21 per cent during the Post-WTO period.
- The Average Growth Rate of employment increased from 4.33 per cent during Pre-WTO period to 6.77 per cent during the Post-WTO period.
- The Average Growth Rate of Exports declined from 27.17 per cent during Pre-WTO period to 11.91 per cent during the Post-WTO period.

SUGGESTIONS

- Infrastructure should be strengthened to attract small scale industries.
- Export procedures have to be simplified and they must be made transparent to SSIs.
- Quality of telecommunication infrastructure will have to be improved to enable fast and inexpensive information.
- People must develop a positive and favourable attitude towards small scale industries which would facilitate the fast growth of small sector. People

have to accept privatisation and globalisation by realizaing the benefits without opposing it.

- WTO implication and its benefit to SSIs must be given wide publicity in an organized way in order to remove their apprehensions and make them strong enough to face the challenges in international market.
- Supportive environment must be provided to ensure quality inputs to the manufacturers in the small sector to meet global bench marks.
- Organization structure has to be made free from bureaucratic procedures to help them take fast decisions in the light of an existing opportunity.
- Immediate protection must be provided to industries such as chemical and pharmaceuticals against adverse implications of TRIPs on patents by suitably amending patent act to have automatic licensing provision and making patent information freely available to SSIs.
- Differential rate of interest should be given to SSI Units.

CONCLUSION

The small scale sector has played a very important role in the development of socio-economic condition during the 50 years and it contributed to the over all growth in terms of the Gross Domestic Product (GDP) employment generation and export. The performance of the small scale sector has a direct impact on the growth of the overall Indian economy.

Small-scale sector registered higher growth rate than overall industrial sector after effect of GATT/WTO in terms of numbers of units, production, employment and export. Globalization and Liberalization have affected Indian Small Industries to a great extent. But, it has created beneficial opportunities as well. The removal of quantitative restrictions and the reduction of import duties. Particulary after the setting up of WTO 1995, have opened up foreign market to Indian Market to Indian Small Industry as much as the Indian market has opened up to the foreign goods. Many efficient and export oriented small firms would have gained out of the development. The Indian SSI sector after WTO has performed well.

REFERENCES

Annual Report-Small Industry Development of India from 1985-1986 to 2004-2005.

Naik S. D. (2002), "Small Industries: Prepare for the WTO Challenges", *The Hindu Business line*, Chennai, July 12, p.6

Raghurama A. (2005), "Globalisation and Challenges for Small Sector in India", *Southern Economist*, Vol. 43, No. 19, Feb. 1, pp.13-18.

Raghavalu M. V. (2005), "Performace of Small Scale Industrial Units in the Indian Economy", *Economic Affairs*, Vol. 50, qr. 3, Sept., pp.171.

Rama Prasad (2003), "WTO and its implication on Indian SSI", *Indian Economic Panorama*, Vol. 13, No. 2, July, pp. 12-14.

Sharma S. K. (2000), "WTO and some Vital Issues for SSIs", *Laghu Samachar*, Jan-March, pp.40-45.

Sukanta Kumar Sahoo (2004), "Small Scale Manufacturing Industries in India", *Indian Economic Journal*, Vol. 51, No. 1, April, June, pp. 52-58.

Vellaichamy D. R. (2006), "Globalisation and Challenges for Small-Scale Industries", *Southern Economist*, Vol. 49, No. 10, Feb., pp. 7-9.

CHAPTER-28

TRADE LIBERALISATION AND POLICIES IN INDIA FOR EDIBLE OIL SECTOR: AN OVERVIEW

RAMA SHANKAR SINGH & AMALENDU KUMAR

INTRODUCTION

AGRICULTURAL sector in India again is witnessing major policy changes under the environment of liberalization and globalization after green revolution. Where the major objectives of the former was achieving food security the latter is expected to make the sector globally competitive by improving the utilization efficiency of inputs, and processing units by way of providing a more free environment for their operation. The implication of policy measures and their impact on various sections of the society has remained a debatable issue. The process of liberalization that was initiated in the early 1990's has been seen to start affecting various sub-sectors within the Indian Economy. The phenomenon is expected to affect the agricultural sector through import of inputs and of the possibilities of exports. The increasing dependence on market in an open economy frame work through the channel of liberalisations the essential feature of the process would have impact at the macro and micro levels. At the macro level, the net benefits to the agricultural sector through the import and export needs to be studied. At the micro level, response of the farmers to the changing situation, their adaptability and response in terms of area, cropping pattern and the accompanying changes in cost of cultivation, incomes and profitability assume importance. The decision of the farmers in this regard would affect the allocation of resources and pricing in output and input markets.

The trade liberalization assumes importance for the edible oil sector in India due to the complete reversal of the policy governing trade of the same. Till, 1994, imports of oilseeds and edible oil were canalized through State Trading Corporation (STC) and were distributed through the Public Distribution System (PDS). Imports restrictions and various programmes for increasing area and production under traditional and non-traditional oilseeds during late 1980's made India nearly self sufficient though at the cost of high oil prices for the consumers of edible oils.

However, with the initiation of India's own programme of economic liberalization and the Uruguay Round Agreement, major policy decision relating to edible oils was taken. These were put under open general license and the duty was lowered from 65 per cent to 15 per cent fro a period of fro 1994 to 1998. Consequently, imports increased to the benefit of consumers. In the mid 1990's imports reached to their lowest level and thereafter started increasing again. Overall, with opening up of trade, the import of edible oil has started increasing. The share of imports which was around 4 per cent in early 1990's has gone up to around 30 per cent of the total available oil up to 2001. In the above background, the present paper has been prepared to evaluate the effect of trade liberalization on edible oil in present trade policy regime under the broad objective. Under the study, it has been tried to present the scenario of area and production of oilseeds at national level, impact of imports of edible oils in domestic market under trade liberalization, etc. For the purpose of study, only secondary level data was utilized. The study is based on data from 1980-81 to 2000-01 on national level. This period can be subdivided into two phases-i.e., pre-reform period and the post reform period. The major focus is to analyse the changes taken place during liberalization period for domestic and imported edible oils.

REVIEW OF LITERATURE

Anderson and Tyres (1993) found that the gains from trade would be accompanied by higher prices for the consumers and an skewed distribution. Gulati *et al.* (1996) in their study expressed about higher profitability of oilseeds cultivation and area shifts from food grains to oilseeds and inefficiencies in the resource use in the process of shift. It was felt that productivity augmentation was more important than providing price incentives to the cultivators for edible oils. Gulati again in 1999, found that a positive gain with a similar cost of living with trade liberalization, took a macro view and argued that the comparative advantage for certain commodities such as food grain lies in domestic production whereas for some other commodities such as edible oils it lies in their import given the existing technology, the small country assumption, exchange rate and the cropping pattern etc.

Singh and Asokan (1999) observed that in the oilseed sector, the major concern expressed through the literature was declining area under oilseed dueto import of oilseeds. The argument is that the substitutability between different edible oils and availability of cheap imported oilseeds would reduce desired demand for the oilseeds and would lead to a decline in area under the crop. On the background of great potential for increase in the demand for edible oils, increasing imports would again put strain on the country's balance of payment (BOP). They also found in their research that except soybean, oilseeds were protected till 1990's. The oilseed price except that of soybean were kept above the world price during 1980's and early 1990's.

RESULTS AND DISCUSSION

The edible oil sector in India is comprised of two broad segments i.e., the oilseed crops & the cultivators first and secondary edible oil and the processors. In the former case, oilseeds occupy an important position in terms of area and production among the agricultural commodities.

1. At National level, the area under oilseeds is growing at the rate of about 3 per cent and the production at the rate of double of area since 2001. This particular phenomenon was termed as "Yellow Revolution" in Indian agriculture. As per a report (Gulati, 1999) it was said that India had 17 per cent of total world acreage while it was 9 per cent in world production under major oilseeds. It was also stated that cropping pattern brought changes in area under coarse cereals which was replaced by oilseeds and pulses. The major problem of oilseed sector is lower yield of oilseed crops. during 2002, the average yield of oilseeds in the world was 1662 kg/ha while it was only 885 kg/ha in India.
2. If the area and production increases, it will increase the final product i.e., oil-the second segment of the sector in the consumption basket of population. The NCAER elasticity estimate shows that the per capita demand for edible oils was 9.81 kg per annum during the year 1999-2000 which would rise to 11.55 kg, 13,95 kg and 16 kg by 2004-05, 2009-10 and 20014-15, respectively (Damodaran and Hegde, 2000). At present, per capita consumption of edible oil is 7.5 kg as against the world average of 15 kg.

As far as the oilseed industry in India is concerned, it is the largest and most heterogenous in the world. It is widely recognized that the level of inefficiency is very high in the oilseed processing industry due to excess capacity in large units and inefficiencies in the smaller ones. The impact of trade liberalization is likely to be felt by these in terms of lower margins due to cheaper imports. With cheaper imports, the high cost of processing industry is expected to get adversely affected possibly with the consequences on the oilseeds cultivation.

The above table indicates that there is a vast gap between the capacity and Utilization (Table 1). In fact, after liberalization and the era of delicensing, deregulation and decontrol since 1991, the number of units and the capacity increased tremendously.

It can be seen from the Table 2 that the both domestic availability and imports of edible oils showed the increasing trend since, 1991. However, though the total availability is increasing steadily, the share has been changing, too. The domestic production has been increasing with much stable rate. In 1999, India stood first in the total edible oil import replacing china. Thus it seems that edible oil sector have a potential to grow further with the increasing demand for the product.

Table 1
Profile of Oilseed Processing Industry in India

Units	*Number*	*Annual capacity (lakh tonnes)*	*Capacity Utilisation (%)*
Oil crushing units	1,50,000	425 (seeds)	10-30
Solvent extraction units	818	345 (oil bearing materials)	34
Refineries	300	50 (oil)	32
Vanaspati units	201	31.5 (vanaspati)	33

Source: GOI, 2002.

Table 2
Availability of Edible Oil in India

Year	*Domestic production*	*Imports*	*Total (in million tones)*
1990-91	6.49	0.34	6.83
1991-92	6.81	0.20	7.01
1992-93	6.93	.33	7.26
1993-94	7.19	1	8.19
1994-95	7.22	1.4	8.62
1995-96	7.42	1.75	9.17
1996-97	6.79	2.08	8.87
1997-98	7.37	3	10.37
1998-99	7.48	3.21	10.69
1999-2000	7.39	3.27	10.66
2000-01	7.62	3.43	11.05

Source: *The Economic Times*, June, 2001.

TRADE POLICY CHANGES AND THE EDIBLE OIL SECTOR

The trade liberalization assumes importance for the edible oil sector in India due to the complete reversal of the policy governing trade of the same. Till, 1994, imports of oilseeds and edible oil were canalized through State Trading Corporation (STC) and were distributed through the Public Distribution System (PDS). Imports of oilcakes were also restricted. Exports of oils, oilseeds were banned, however, for those of oilcakes were kept free. Rising demand of edible oils during 1970's put strain on the balance of payment due to the heavy imports of edible oils led the government to take steps towards self sufficiency in edible oils. Imports restrictions and various programmes for increasing area and production under traditional and non-traditional oilseeds during late 1980's made India nearly self sufficient though at the cost of high oil prices for the consumers of edible oils. The subsequent policy changes were directed towards increasing the protection to the edible oil through increasing the tariffs. Throughout 1980's domestic prices were maintained at more than double the international prices except soybean. Thus the oilseed growers derived protection that were given to the edible oils. The area under oilseeds expanded indiscriminately and the cultivators received high prices ,often 20-30 per cent higher than the minimum support price (MSP). However, with the initiation of India's own programme of economic liberalization and the Uruguay Round Agreement, major policy decisions related to edible oils were taken. These were put under open general license (OGL) and the duty was lowered from 65 per cent to 15 per cent. The details of the trade policy changes for edible oils are given below:

Tariff Related Measures: The date and year wise tariff related measures are being described in Table 3.

Table 3
Under Trade Policy Tariff Related Measures Taken in India (May, 1994 to 2000-01 Budget)

Date	*Policy Decision*	*Import (%)*
May 14, 1994	Edible oils placed under restricted list	65
May 15, 1994	Palmoline placed under OGL	65
March 31, 1995	Edible oils except coconut oil,red Palmoline Stearine placed under OGL	65
April 1, 1995	Import duty reduced	30
1996-97 budget	Import duty reduced	25
July 9, 1998	Import duty reduced on edible oils except coconut oil, 3 varieties of palmoline	15
November 21, 1999	Import duty hiked on refined oils as-Soybean Palmoline & Palm oilGround nut/Sunflower Vanaspati	45654555
December 30, 1999	Import duty hiked on refined edible oils	27.5
20000-01 budget	Import duty hiked on refined oils except soybean Import duty hiked on crude edible oils	8575

Source: Damodaran and Hegde (2000).

Table 4
Production of Edible Oil (in lakh MT) in India

Oils	*1981-82*	*1991-92*	*1994-95*	*2000-01*
Ground nut	11.29	16.33	18.56	18.34
Mustard	7.08	17.93	15.78	17.29
Sesame	1.38	2.20	1.82	2.96
Safflower	0.66	0.40	0.83	1.84
Sunflower	0.24	4.38	4.18	5.23
Niger seed	0.29	0.38	0.40	0.64
Soybean	0.24	4.30	4.38	8.29
Cotton seed	2.49	3.46	4.24	3.94
Coconut	1.76	2.98	3.93	5.21
Total	25.60	50.22	53.48	63.74

Source: Indian Agriculture, as quoted in Solvent Extraction Association of India, 2001.

The Table 4 shows that during the past two decades (1981-2001), production of edible oil was on increasing mainly increase in ground nut, mustard, coconut and cotton seed. It may also be observed from the table that in between 1981-

82 to 2000-01,the production of edible oil increased from 25.60 lakh MT to 63.74 lakh MT, more than two folds increase.

MAIN FINDINGS

The study finds that the impact of trade liberalization was visible on increasing imports of edible oils and falling of prices of domestic edible oils. The trade liberalization is characterized by increasing tariff on edible oils with the duty on edible oil reaching its limit (45%) as per WTO regulation. The secondary data shows that at national level, area and production have been rising even after imports of cheaper edible oils but at a slow rate. The study finds that there is a possibility for increasing area and production and increasing demand for edible oils if the prices of oilseeds are not affected due to cheaper imports. As it has already been mentioned that the second phase of trade liberalization is characterized by increased tariffs with the duty on edible oils reaching its limit. Hence, given the comparatively higher rate of tariffs, any change in the price of imported edible oils would depend upon the domestic as well as external factors.

POLICY IMPLICATION

The cultivation of oilseeds depends on the market signals of demand and supply. The study reveals that there is no support for edible oils provided by the government to the producers as well as consumers. It may also be noted that in various states, minimum support price for oilseeds is not properly implemented which results in the slow and steady growth in area and production of oilseeds. Therefore, it is suggested that the concerned department in various states must take proper initiative in this direction so that the productivity, area and ultimately total production could be increased.

REFERENCES

Singh, Gurudev and S.R., Asokan (1999), Impact of WTO on Indian (Edible) Oil Sector in Datta, Samar, K. and Satish Deodhar's Report on Impact of WTO Agreement on Indian Agriculture, Submitted to the Ministry of Agriculture,Vol. II, IIM, Ahmedabad.

Gulati, Ashok *et. al* (1996), Self Sufficiency and Allocative Efficiency: Case of Edible Oils, *Economic and Political Weekly*,Vol. 31 (13), Review of Agriculture, p. A-15 to A-24.

Gulati, Ashok (1999), Trade Liberalisation and Indian Agriculture, Oxford University Press, New Delhi.

Annual Report, Ministry of Consumer affairs and Public Distribution and Department of Sugar and Edible Oils, GOI, 1999-2000, New Delhi.

Handbook on Oilseeds and Oil Statistics (1990), Department of Agricultural Resaerch and Education, Ministry of Agriculture.

6. Solvent Extraction Association of India (2000),SEA Millenium Handbook on Indian Vegetable Oil Industry and trade, Mumbai.

CHAPTER-29

IP ENFORCEMENT MECHANISMS IN SINGAPORE AND BANGLADESH WITH SPECIAL REFERENCE TO SOFTWARE PIRACY**

MOHAMMAD MONIRUL AZAM & ABDUL HAMID CHOWDHURY

INTRODUCTION

SOFTWARE piracy, the unauthorized duplication and distribution of software, is a worldwide problem that is growing at an epidemic pace. Software piracy occurs within businesses, among colleagues and friends, and in large global counterfeiting rings. Furthermore, ease of distribution, and lack of consistent intellectual property laws beyond country borders make software piracy a global problem. Application software and networks such as peer to peer, IRC, BBS provide the means and ease for any computer user to engage in the illegal act of making software copies. Software piracy can be as easy as surfing the World Wide Web or as complex as running a world wide counterfeit ring.

The cost and impact of software piracy is enormous. Whenever a piece of pirated software is used, a company is deprived of its earnings. Piracy undermines the software market, making it less lucrative for software companies to continue to offer innovative and high quality software. It also hurts the consumer. Frequently, pirated software does not include documentation or provide access to customer support, and, or, future software upgrades. Most importantly, pirated software is illegal and a crime in most countries. International, regional and national legal measures are increasingly empowering software creators to protect their assets. An increase in penalties for pirating software and a larger push for wider enforcement are attempts to curb the rising piracy rates worldwide. Furthermore, new anti-piracy technologies are being incorporated to prevent and deter the software piracy.

In this paper we first attempt to define software piracy and its global scenario. In the second section, we outlined the causes of piracy, the debate between the free software and software protection. It also includes the socio-economic impact of software piracy, impacts on the users and its alleged involvement with the organized crime. In the third section, we discussed the legal mechanisms to curb software piracy at the international and national levels. The next section deals with the alternative measures to tackle the software piracy. Section five analyzed the effectiveness of the international and national legal measures to combat software piracy. We attempt to examine the national measures in the light of the TRIPS agreement because it is the most comprehensive IP agreement adopted at the international level, which imposed upon all the member countries of the WTO to ensure effective enforcement mechanisms. This agreement not only pressed for the national enforcement measures but also provides dispute settlement mechanisms for IP related issues between the member states. Finally we examined the effectiveness of the enforcement mechanisms in Singapore and Bangladesh to combat software piracy and concluded with a few recommendations to deter software piracy and thereby to exploit the benefits of IP.

WHAT IS SOFTWARE PIRACY?

"Software" is the set of instructions, which tell a computer what to do[1]. Without software, a computer is just a useless lump of silicon, metal and plastic. As the cost of computer hardware has declined, the importance of software has increased; software is where the action and the money are these days.

"Software piracy" to a large extent has become a generic term for the illicit duplication of copyrighted computer software. However some organization working to prevent infringement of software copyright prefer to use the term software theft rather than software piracy because sometimes the term piracy create a shadow that it is not illegal rather simply prohibited practices and thereby relegating the seriousness of the theft.

Software piracy, or theft, occurs when users illegally duplicate software for profit, produce counterfeit copies of a software package and sell it as a legitimate product, or make multiple copies of software and distribute it to others. Parties that participate in software piracy include commercial users, software resellers, consumers and computer hackers. Even it is now possible to find literally hundreds of websites devoted to software piracy. While all types of software piracy are illegal, software piracy can be categorized based on scale, severity, monetary motivation, and the ability for enforcement. Considering the nature and scope of the piracy, it can be divided into (1) commercial piracy[2]; (2) corporate piracy[3]; and (3) softlifting[4].

The law of most of the countries does not expressly address contributory infringement for software piracy[5]. In fact, specific or particularized knowledge of infringing activity is not essential to liable anyone for contributory infringement. Therefore, the term software piracy is expanding day by day. Keeping in mind this broad perspective, it can be considered that a person who has a role in copying, or who provides facilities, directions, knowledge or encouragement, will be liable for software piracy.

SOFTWARE PIRACY-THE GLOBAL SCENARIO

Although there is no universally well-recognized report on software piracy, it is undisputable fact that software piracy is a global problem increasing day by day. For every two-dollar's worth of PC software purchased legitimately, one dollar's worth was obtained illegally. In the Third Annual Business Software Alliance's (BSA) and IDC Global Software Piracy Study[6], May, 2006 on 97 countries, the median piracy rate was 64 per cent—meaning half of the countries studied in the report have a piracy rate of 64 per cent or higher[7]. Therefore, whether developed or developing countries, software piracy is a problem around the world. Even the seizures of pirated Microsoft products alone exceeded $1.7 billion[8].

In a comparative analysis of the software piracy of last two years, BSA study of 2006 reported that the worldwide personal computer (PC) software piracy rate stayed the same at 35 per cent while losses increased by over $1.6 billion and the PC software piracy rate increased in four of the regions, including Western Europe, Asia Pacific, Latin America and the European Union. However, in Middle East/Africa and Central/Eastern Europe the rate is decreased slightly and in North America stayed the same.

CAUSES OF PIRACY

Quantitative and Qualitative Approach of the Phenomenon

Software is an integral part of the global economy. The large growth in software application makes developing software a big business with potentially large profits. Software enables users and business to do more with their systems, and the need for software is growing. But software is not free, and depending on the type of software, it can cost large amounts of money. Wherever there is potential for large profits and there exists a high demand, illegal methods for satisfying the demand at a lower cost also exist. But money is not the only motivation. Power, satisfaction, and lack of education are also factors for fueling the software piracy industry.

The BSA Study of May 2006 identified the following factors[9] that contribute to differences in piracy rate across the regions or country to country—

- the strength of intellectual property protection,
- the availability of pirated software and
- Cultural differences.

It is worth noting to mention the study of *Donald Merron and David G Steel*[10], where they identified the following factors for the causes and increase of software piracy–

(a) Income level and development of the country concerned,

(b) Cultural notion of rights (Private Vs Collective),

(c) Social and Economic Institutions and

(d) Well-educated population and state expenditure for research and development (R&D).

On the other hand, some scholars would like to say that the ultimate reason of the causes of software piracy is two folds[11]-

(i) Failure of the public authorities and commercial organizations to communicate to the consuming public of the dangers from the use of unauthorized products and of the harmful social welfare effects from this trade and

(ii) The inadequacy of deterrent penalties by the judicial authorities.

Furthermore, Internet facilitating the easy reproduction and distribution of pirated software.However, enormous scale of software piracy is successful owing to the unique nature of computer programs[12].

Free Software and Protection

Free software development, also known as 'open source[13],' is a phenomenon in which volunteer programmers collaboratively develop software on the Internet, and then make it available, along with its source code. Interestingly, free software has recently become a competitive alternative to unauthorized copying. Many free software solutions have finally sufficient functionality to replace proprietary systems and they are available 'Free as in speech, not as in beer.'

Free software makers or developers although not gaining direct economic benefits for disclosing the whole source code, it offers a possibility to market their skills globally and thus might help in finding jobs from rich countries or-more realistically-from a local subsidiary of a multinational software company.

However at the international legal regime as developed by WIPO and WTO has not given that much concern for free software because most of the member countries especially developed countries has feared that opening the door for a discussion about the limits of intellectual property rights under the free software agenda could have unwanted long-term implications to their national interests. This is why, Lois Boland, director of international relations for the U.S. Patent and Trademark Office said that *"...open source software runs counter to the mission of WIPO, which is to promote intellectual property rights[14]"*

Interestingly countries like India, Chile and Brazil, which have been pushing otherwise aggressively for more flexible intellectual property rights regime, have not yet forced the issue on the table. Even in the WIPO Development Agenda, which is mostly sponsored by the developing countries, refers to free software ("open source") only once.

Although there is fundamental political debate between the free software and strict IP law to protect software, it is possible to find some common ground for the proponents of strong intellectual property and the free software movement. In the developed countries strict IP law could protect software. But in the developing and least developed countries situation may be different. In the developing countries the promotion of free software could be used as a non-controversial way to teach about the fundamental concepts of copyright. Consequently, if free software could help creating a social norm "one should obey copyright", which would be beneficial in the long run for every copyright industry equally and obviously software industry as well[15]. Thus, instead of fighting against free software, it could be used as a tool because to create a field for future protection is better than not getting any benefit forever.

Impact of Software Piracy

Economic and Social Impact

Software piracy has many depressing economic consequences: local software industries crippled by competition with pirated software from abroad and Government do not get tax revenues and non creation of new jobs from lack of a legitimate market. In December 2005, IDC and the BSA released their second study on the economic benefits of lowering piracy[16]. In a software market that is projected to grow to over $70 billion from $40 billion within the next five years, the industry is poised for tremendous losses due to piracy. According to the Organization for Economic Co-Operation and Development, counterfeit and pirated items including software piracy that are traded internationally are thought to account for about 176 billion US dollars even by conservative estimates[17].

In the study, IDC concluded that decreasing piracy by 10 percentage points over four years would add more than 2.4 million new jobs and almost $70 billion in tax revenues to local governments worldwide. Most of that new employment and most of an additional $400 billion in GDP would be added to local economies.

The European Union, United States and Canada experienced significant dollar losses, yet had relatively low piracy rates. This is because their markets are so large, and in such enormous markets even small piracy rates can add up to large losses. Only in 2005, the United States lost $6.9 billion as a result of software piracy[18]. The software piracy rate in EU is 37%. The cost of software publisher in the region is over 8 million Euros[19].

As counterfeiting activities have become rampant, counterfeiters create distribution channels and establish an economic and even political presence in society. Some economies are supported by these activities, which create local job opportunities[20].

Such attitude of the government may have long-term harmful effects on the foreign direct investment (FDI) in the software and ICT sector in a country and local software industries. The lack of IP protection will discourages manufacturers of legitimate goods from establishing their facilities in those countries. Such decisions result in a loss of FDI, as well as the concomitant technology transfer and foreign know-how, which normally accompany FDI. Loss of FDI also manifests itself in a loss of foreign income, which ultimately affects a country's balance of payments[21]. Local creators, inventors, and SMEs, in the field of ICT and software industry may also be discouraged that their products will be illegally copied and sold, thus precluding a return on investment and future growth.

In social terms, the damage suffered by businesses because of counterfeiting and piracy is reflected ultimately in its impact upon employment. Initially, employment may improve in those countries where pirate and counterfeit goods are produced. However, where local industries are developed which are dependent upon intellectual property rights, the local capacity to produce infringing products may have an ultimately harmful effect upon employment. Only considering EU, with a 10 point drop in software piracy rates, Western Europe's IT sector could grow to over 330 million euros by 2006, adding over 200, 000 new jobs[22].

Effects on Consumers/Users

To the extent that consumers participate in a contraband market, this undermines respect among ordinary citizens for the law. Studies have shown that the initial act of law breaking can influence subsequent behavior. Once people develop a taste for cheating, they keep on cheating. Thus, a key societal consequence of participating in a contraband market is that it serves to sanction tax evasion and other forms of law breaking[23].

Again, using pirated software is also risky for users. Apart from the possible legal threat of using pirated software, those who use pirated software may also face the following problems:

- Increase the chances that the software will not function correctly or will fail completely;
- Forfeit access to customer support, upgrades, technical documentation, training, and bug fixes;
- Have no warranty to protect themselves;
- Increase their risk of exposure to a debilitating virus that can destroy valuable data;
- May find that the software is actually an outdated version, a beta (test) version, or a nonfunctioning copy;
- Are subject to significant fines for copyright infringement; and
- Risk potential negative publicity and public and private embarrassment and in the case of an organization, negative publicity that could cause irreparable harm to the business etc[24].

Piracy and Organized Crime

Organized criminal elements are deeply involved in counterfeiting and piracy of software due to opportunities of easy reproduction technologies, need less investment of time, physical space and money, high-profit potential and relatively low risk. There are a number of reasons for the dramatic increase in IP crime in recent years.

- First, many forms of IP can be produced with minimal start up costs making IP crimes accessible to larger numbers of people;
- Second, international enforcement of IP laws is virtually nonexistent; and
- finally, domestic enforcement of IP laws has been inadequate and consequently the level of deterrence has been inadequate.

Profits from counterfeiting and piracy of software and other goods are often used to fund other criminal activities; and unfortunately, the criminal enforcement infrastructure as well as the public, does not always view counterfeiting and piracy of software as the serious crimes that they are. The active involvement of organized crime in counterfeiting and piracy is a proven, irrefutable fact[25]. Counterfeiting and piracy is becoming more attractive than drug trafficking, since high potential profits can be obtained without the risk of major legal penalties. Organized criminals often combine counterfeiting and piracy with terrorism and smuggling[26].

The World Economic Forum in Davos in January 2003 was informed by the World Customs Organization (WCO) that the trade in counterfeit and pirate products was as high as US$450 billion per annum and was controlled by organized crime and was being used to fund terrorist activity[27].

At the Third Global Congress on Combating Counterfeiting and Piracy held in Geneva from 30 to 31 January 2007, government officials, business leaders, and international law enforcement bodies like Intellectual Property Crime Unit of Interpol and WCO officials also hinted towards the link between the organized crime, terrorism and piracy and that is why called for an even greater marshalling of efforts and resources to counter the escalation in counterfeiting and piracy[28].

HOW TO TACKLE SOFTWARE PIRACY?

Cooperation and Coordination at the International, Regional National Level

Software piracy has serious repercussions on the entire ICT industry and on the broader knowledge economy. As mentioned earlier, software piracy not only carry mere infringement of intellectual property rights but also constrain growth within the software industry and weaken economies in the form of lost jobs and tax revenues. Against this backdrop intellectual property right is meaningless unless they can be enforced into practice. Therefore, cooperation and coordination at the international, regional and national levels is a must for technical, financial and legal initiatives to deter piracy.

Enhancing the Legal Framework

International Legal Measures

At first it is the Berne and Paris Convention incorporated certain provisions relating to enforcement against counterfeit and pirated goods[29]. These conventions provided that disputes between countries could be brought before the International Court of Justice. But no Member State has ever resorted to this remedy[30]. Perhaps due to voluntary or non-binding nature of these enforcement provisions discouraged the member countries to take recourse to this mechanism.

However, compulsory or mandatory enforcement mechanism was first taken up in the Uruguay Round and resulted in the TRIPS Agreement. Part III of the TRIPS Agreement specifies certain minimum standards for the enforcement of IPRs. All Members are under obligation to implement these standards, which include General Obligations, Civil and Administrative Procedures and Remedies, Provisional Measures, Special Measures Related to Border Measures, and Criminal Procedures.

These provisions obliges signatories to provide a enforcement mechanism so that IPR holders can effectively assert their rights, seize infringing goods, seek remedies against criminal enterprises and infringing goods, and seek the assistance of those agencies of government which have responsibilities in these matters, such as the courts, police, customs, and other administrative agencies.

On another level, when Members of WTO have disputes with other Members concerning, *inter alia*, the effective enforcement of IPRs, they are able to proceed in certain stages to bring their complaints through the Dispute Settlement Mechanism. These procedures are based upon mandatory jurisdiction in the WTO where there are sufficiently weighty remedies to ensure compliance, and in the event of proven noncompliance, to effect remedial compensation to the aggrieved Member. This is a noteworthy experiment to ensure the enforcement of intellectual property under the multilateral trading system.

Furthermore, in 1996 to address the growing trends of online piracy, the World Intellectual Property Organization (WIPO) adopted new copyright treaties to enable better and more effective enforcement against digital and online piracy. In order to ensure protection of copyrighted works in the digital age, countries need to update national copyright laws to implement the obligations of the WIPO copyright treaties.

These treaties address provisions on new tools to fight software piracy by technological protection measures and Internet piracy. Some countries have already implemented them in their national legislation, new legal actions are being taken and a new body of case law is growing up, which can successfully take the enforcement fight into cyberspace as well[31].

National Legal Measures

Although with the launching of the TRIPS agreement now there is effective international framework to deal with software piracy, without effective national legal measures in line with TRIPS agreement software piracy will continue to increase. Ultimately it is the national authority or court that has to deter software piracy within their national borders. To impose a fear of consequences, there must be some form of liability for the act of software piracy and this liability must be able to be proven in a court of law. The liability may rest with the pirate and the provider of the distribution. In this paper we will deal with national law of Singapore and Bangladesh to deter software piracy. At first, it will deal with the laws of the Singapore, a country having very deterrent law to curb software piracy and has considerable success to reduce piracy when it is increasing globally. Finally it will deal with the laws of Bangladesh to combat software piracy, which is a least developed country (LDC) and yet to implement the TRIPS agreement (enjoying the transitional period until July 11, 2013), but trying to fight huge amount of software piracy in the local market.

ALTERNATIVE MEASURES

Technological Measures, Ethical Measures, Social Measures

Apart from the absolute legal protection measures, there are some alternative methods like technological (protective) measure and ethical and social (preventive) measures to prevent software piracy. Technological devices with adequate legal support would be a most effective measure for curbing software piracy by the offline users and online pirates as well.

A large number of ways to prevent software piracy at the technical level have been researched and implemented. A distinction can be drawn between those controls that act to prevent the duplication of software, and those that increase the likelihood of offenders being caught and prosecuted.

Technical measures that increase the difficulty of duplicating software can be categorized as obfuscation, encryption and simple checks. Code obfuscation is the deliberate altering of program code, whether at the source, object or machine code level[32].

Encryption can also be used to encipher program input and output streams, whether they are streamed to disk files or to other devices. A key is then required to be able to make use of the encrypted matter.

Another simple check is registration systems, which involve the user of the software acquiring a special unique string of characters and digits that the program demands are entered before it is first run, or at the time of installation[33].

"Guards" are hardware or software modules that monitor the running program and ensure that it has not been tampered with in any way[34].

The WIPO Internet Treaties, the WCT and WPPT, bind the Contracting Parties to provide legal protection and effective remedies against the circumvention of effective technological measures that are used by the right holders.

Article 11 of the WCT, entitled "Obligations Concerning Technological Measures," provides:

> *"Contracting Parties shall provide adequate legal protection and effective legal remedies against the circumvention of effective technological measures that are used by authors in connection with the exercise of their rights under this Treaty or*

***the Berne Convention and that restrict acts, in respect of their works, which are not authorized by the authors concerned or permitted by law."*[35]**

The social and ethical issues of software piracy are another way to counter piracy. In fact it considers that the "right to fair compensation" is a basic principle of "universai" ethics. If we consider that purchasing software is the only fair compensation for the authors and distributors of that software, then software piracy is in breach of this set of ethics and social norms.

Greater Awareness among the Stakeholders

Role of the Educational Institutions

The Educational institutions can play a prime role for the promotion and protection of the intellectual property rights and at the same time it will aware the people about IP rights and will encourage the students to come up with their new innovation and to seek protection for their IP rights as well. Ultimately when consumers will not be interested to buy pirated software due to educational campaign, piracy will diminish automatically. As the saying goes, when the buying stops the selling stops[36]. The Ministry of Education in the developing and least developed countries may take steps to heighten public awareness for IPR protection by including a standard IP education part in the textbooks at the school and college levels. In Bangladesh under the street law program students of schools and colleges are provided basic education on IP, Environment and Democracy[37].

Role of the Software Users and Corporate Bodies

Software user especially corporate bodies have a great role to play to fight against the software piracy. Every corporate body should use genuine software and should encourage their employee to do the same. Ultimately, the fight against counterfeiting and piracy has to involve the public, since it is its purchasing power, which causes these practices to flourish. National anti-counterfeiting and anti-piracy campaigns could be used to indicate the link between intellectual property, crime and job losses, the debilitating effects of organized crime, and the dangers to health and safety of infringing goods.

Role of the Software Developers

As intellectual property rights are ultimately private rights, right holders have the largest immediate financial stake in ensuring the protection of those rights. For this reason, rights holders have been particularly willing to assist in enforcement efforts by providing information to assist in the identification of infringing products and in co-operating in awareness and training programmes.

The border control provisions of the TRIPS Agreement envisages that in the first place it will be the rights holders who will apply to the Customs authorities to intercept shipments of counterfeit and pirated products. Inevitability the rights holders will be in the best position to identify infringing products[38]. Therefore, software developers should also act as united force against the software piracy[39].

Pro-active Role of the Intellectual Property Offices

The role of the IP offices is crucial for the development of IP culture in a particular country. Intellectual Porperty offices may take initiatives to aware the peoples about IPR's and at the same time it should conduct frequent raid/ visit as the case may be, in the hot-spots (places where software piracy is rampant), super markets and bringing criminal cases against the pirates. Furthermore, IP offices should also review its action and effectiveness of the relevant laws and regulations time to time and will submit reports to the Government to reshape the IP laws and enforcement mechanisms in the country. In some countries special units within the government apparatus have been set up to deal with IP matters[40]. Their functions includes from receiving complaints to investigate, bring matters before the jurisdiction of competent courts and cooperation with other relevant bodies and rights holders.

EFFECTIVENESS OF THE LEGAL ENFORCEMENT MEASURES: A SURVEY OF ISSUES

Effectiveness of the International Legal Measures (WIPO Treaties and TRIPS Agreement)

As mentioned earlier, although Berne and Paris convention provides for the enforcement of IP rights at the international level, theses provisions are not effective. The main reason of the no-effectiveness of these provisions is mainly due to the inherent jurisdictional problems of the International Court of Justice (ICJ), which is primarily responsible for the judicial enforcement of IP rights under the Berne and Paris Convention. International court of justice as opposed to the national courts follows the voluntary nature of jurisdiction. Therefore it has no mandatory enforcement mechanisms like the national courts. The jurisdiction of the ICJ is still depends on the consent of the states to initiate any proceedings before it[41]. Therefore unless or until both the states consented to any measures or voluntarily refer any case before ICJ, it lacks jurisdiction to entertain the same, which is the major drawback to enforce the IP rights through ICJ[42].

Whereas the obligation under the TRIPS agreement although has incorporated mandatory and effective enforcement mechanism, it is yet to be implemented by all the WTO member states. The agreement will be implemented by different member stated under the different time frame on the basis of the stage of development of that particular country. Suppose in this study, the author is concentrating on the enforcement efforts of USA, Singapore and Bangladesh, which has three separate time frames for TRIPS-compliance system[43]. Therefore, despite mandatory provisions, the enforcement mechanism is yet to be fully effective across the member states.

As mentioned earlier, major feature of TRIPS is its requirement in Part III that WTO members include a specific minimum set of effective enforcement procedures for all categories of IP, including copyright (but not including moral rights)[44]. Even developed states which have long been accustomed to enforcing IP rights may need to change their laws and practices to comply with TRIPS obligations; so it is not surprising that developing states also may have to make changes.

The general obligations that TRIPS imposes include, in broad detail, the following:

- Remedies to prevent and cure infringement must be expeditious and must be effective to deter further infringement (art. 41.1).
- Abuses of procedure and barriers to legitimate trade should be avoided (art. 41.1).
- Due process must be guaranteed (arts. 41.2 - 41.4, & 42). In particular, there must be:
- Fair procedures that are "not unnecessarily complicated or costly" and that do not impose "unreasonable time-limits or unwarranted delays[45]".

Thus TRIPS provided a framework of minimum obligation for enforcement to the extent that it is possible under the infrastructure and socio-economic circumstances prevailing in the concerned member countries. But it failed to adopt an approach of complete harmonization in the field of enforcement of intellectual property rights. During the negotiation process, the approach of universal recognition and execution of trans-boundary court judgments (Judgments of one country in another country) was also rejected from the outset because this would probably work only in a relatively 'homogenous environment'. In fact, the formulation of 'minimum basic stock of procedural regulations guided by the intention to achieve the 'best possible effectiveness' and tie this stock of regulations to result oriented criteria instead of setting out all the details reflects a certain Anglo-American pragmatism which need not necessarily always conform with Continental-European concepts of formal procedural fairness. This result oriented approach triggered in the adoption of vague phrases such as 'effective', 'expeditious', 'reasonable, 'undue', 'unwarranted', 'fair and equitable', and 'not unnecessarily complicated', or costly etc[46].

But what kind of remedies will be effective and what not and when it would be expeditious and adequate yet to be explored. There have been no WTO panel reports or Appellate Body decisions to date regarding inadequate enforcement of IPRs. There has been only one complaint filed in the WTO against inadequate IPR enforcement—a complaint filed by the United States in June 1998 against Greece and the European Union because of the Greek Government's failure to enforce its intellectual property laws effectively against television stations that broadcasted U.S. copyrighted works without authorization. On March 22, 2001, after extensive consultations, Greece, the European Union and the United States formally resolved this WTO dispute without a decision by a dispute settlement panel.

Again, given the financial requirements and legal and factual sophistication in identifying inconsistencies and effectiveness in intellectual property laws and trade practices and thereafter in bringing complaints to the WTO-Dispute Settlement Body (DSB), the developed countries like the USA, EU countries, Canada or Japan are structurally best positioned. On the other hand, the developing and least developed countries have to face formidable challenges while taking of the benefits under the DSB due to lack of specialized human resources and financial resources. The size and amount of trade or economic power of a particular developing or least developed country is so marginal, which made it unlikely that such retaliation would harm the opposite developed country[47]. At the same time, the voluntary nature of determine compensation is also a major drawback of the dispute settlement system. The right of filling official cases and obtaining ruling from the Panel has to expand to include additional actors beyond the sovereign member states. Individuals and certain groups that bear the effect of the WTO rulings have to be able to hold their governments. The initiative of including reports of civil society in the panel hearings is already a step in the right direction, but is not sufficient. Leveling the playing fields for all participants of the process by providing more assistance to developing and least developed countries is necessary to preserve the integrity of the system.

Effectiveness of the National Legal Measures (Compliance with TRIPS)

Singapore

Singapore recognizes the importance of intellectual property as a national resource and in attracting foreign investment in its development as a knowledge-based economy. To develop intellectual property as a strategic and competitive resource and to make the country as the hub of IP, Singapore has already adopted an essentially pro-active IPR policy for the development of high value added and creative-content industries. Intellectual Property of Singapore (IPOS) is very active in policy making and in the drafting of legislation relating to enforcement of intellectual property rights.

In Singapore generally the rights holders themselves via civil actions can enforce IP rights whereas the Intellectual Property Rights Branch of the Criminal Investigations Department of the Singapore Police Force responsible for the criminal enforcement activities (e.g. raids on software pirates). Border enforcement measures are carried out by Singapore Customs.

The Intellectual Property Rights Warrant Enforcement Unit (IPRWEU) was set up on 15 Feb 1995 as a dedicated law enforcement unit for the execution of Intellectual Property Rights (IPR) related search warrants. In the year 2000, the unit expanded into the present Intellectual Property Rights Branch (IPRB). The formation of the Branch demonstrated the Singapore Government's strong stance against intellectual property rights offences.

In Singapore, enforcement procedures and remedies (including border measures) are available under the various intellectual property legislations or under the common law to enable effective action against acts of infringement[48]. Both civil and criminal remedies may be resorted to. In a civil action injunction, damages or account of profits maybe ordered. The court may also order the delivery up and/or destruction or other disposal of infringing goods and materials and implements for their production. In criminal prosecutions imprisonment, monetary fines, seizure, forfeiture and destruction of infringing goods and materials and implements for their production may be ordered.

In relation to software piracy on a commercial scale, if a person who, at a time when copyright subsists in a work, makes for sale or hire, sells or lets for hire, or by way of trade offers or exposes for sale or hire or by way of trade exhibits in public or imports for the purposes of trade or distributes either for the purpose of trade or for other purpose but to such an extent as to affect prejudicially the copyright owner any article which he knows, or ought reasonably to know, to be an infringing copy of the work shall be guilty of an offence carrying a fine of $10,000 per infringing article up to a maximum of $100,000 and/or an imprisonment sentence of up to 5 years[49].

In addition, it is also an offence carrying a fine up to a maximum of $20,000 and an imprisonment term of 2 years to make or to have in one's possession an article specifically designed or adapted for making infringing copies when the person knows or ought reasonably to know that the article is to be used for making infringing copies. Singapore law provides that where a person is found to have more than 5 copies of any one's work, it is presumed that the infringing copies were not for personal use[50].

Under Section 139 of the Copyright Act, any person who, by any means, publishes, or causes to be published, in Singapore an advertisement for the supply in Singapore (whether from within or outside Singapore) of a copy of a computer program which is an infringing copy shall, unless he proves that he acted in good faith and had no reasonable grounds for supposing that copyright would or might thereby be infringed, be guilty of an offence and shall be liable on conviction to a fine of up to $20,000 or to imprisonment for a term not exceeding 2 years or to both.

Since the enactment of the Manufacture of Optical Discs Act (MODA)[51] in 2004, Singapore police regularly visit various plants to prevent the manufacturing of unauthorized optical discs, which are mostly used for software piracy. Again under the Regulation 3 of Imports and Exports Regulations, any party who wishes to import replication and mastering equipment for manufacture of optical discs must obtain permit from the Director General of Customs to do so.Any party who imports without permit shall be guilty of an offence[52]. The initiatives of Singapore Police and Custom to destroy the counterfeiting rings and to tackle piracy were very significant over the years.

Statistics on Number of Raids and Total Value Seized by Singapore Authorities.

Year	*Copyright Raids*	*Trademark Raids*	*Total Raids*	*Total Value Seized*
2000	308	146	454	S$ 16,310,436.28
2001	308	183	491	S$ 15,553,324.95
2002	284	207	491	S$ 9,415,266.00
2003	266	160	426	S$ 33,185,092.00
2004	126	190	316	S$ 12,665,969.00
2005	61	168	229	S$ 19,774,083.00

Source: Singapore Police Force, Films and Publications Department and Customs and Excise Department.

It is worth noting that the Judiciary of Singapore considers the cases of piracy and counterfeiting very seriously. In this regard, the observation of Yong Pung How CJ in the case of *Ong Ah Tiong v Public Prosecutor [2004] SGHC 11*[53], *is remarkable:*

> *"Singapore is a prominent business hub with a reputation for upholding intellectual property rights. It is manifestly in the public interest to deter potential criminals who are inclined to use Singapore as a distribution centre or a base for transshipment of counterfeit products to neighboring countries. I therefore agreed with the sentiments of the trial judge that the appellant's intention of re-exporting the counterfeit items rather than of selling them in Singapore was not of any mitigating value whatsoever".*

The CJ further held that the trial judge rightly recognized the *government's strong efforts to promote Singapore as a regional intellectual property centre and the concomitant need to clamp down on piracy of intellectual property.*

In is also fascinating to know that in the original suit the trial judge, while determining a sentence for piracy and counterfeiting considered *"all the circumstances in which the offences were committed, including the nature and extent of the infringements, and the manner in which the infringements were carried out*[54]*" (Emphasis added).*

It is also worth noting that Singapore adopts the 3 'Es' (Education, Engineer and Enforcement) approach in combating piracy[55].

Education: IPRB consider that education is the one of the most effective ways to fight piracy. As the saying goes, when the buying stops the selling stops. In Singapore, the Intellectual Property Office of Singapore (IPOS) is responsible for educating the public to heighten its awareness on piracy issues. The IPOS conducts regular anti-piracy campaigns like mobilising artists for walkabouts, concerts and school talks to propagate the message to members of public that the intellectual property of artists and rights owners should be respected. IPOS also works with the IPRB to spread the message across to the schools.

Engineer: Singapore Government promotes an environment where public can gain easy access to genuine products with reasonable pricing. In this, the intellectual property owners are strongly encouraged to price their products reasonably. In government agencies and schools, only genuine products are used. The Singapore government is actively promoting innovation and creativity among Singaporeans to be inventors and creators ourselves. With more and more genuine ideas generated, people will respect the intellectual property of others.

Enforcement: When the two above 'Es' do not produce the desired results, the 3rd 'E'-Enforcement is the last resort. The IPRB adopts a 2-prong approach-police initiated and collaborative, towards enforcement. The police initiated approach is targeted at syndicates, icons and hot spots and the collaborative approach is targeted at retail piracy.

Under the collaborative approach, the IPRB act in the interest of justice by executing the Search Warrant, ensuring law and order during the raids and to take custody of the seized exhibits. No arrest is made in this instance. The benefit of this approach is that the IPR owners determine the pace and scope of the enforcement action. In addition, the punishment meted out can be similar to that of the criminal proceeding, depending on the merits of the case.

On the basis of analysis of law, relevant case law, working procedure and communication with relevant bodies, it is reflected that the reasons behind the success of the Singapore in reducing software piracy are as follows:

1. Education and Campaign programs by IPOS along with relevant national bodies and non-governmental organization having expertise in the relevant field[56].
2. Effective Cooperation and coordination among the Singapore Custom, Police and other relevant bodies to ensure different remedies where appropriate.
3. Tough law to prevent software piracy (as amended in 2005, which has very positive impact to reduce piracy).
4. Very active role of the Singapore Police and its special unit to raid hot spots, markets and to initiate tough proceedings against the pirates.
5. Active role of Singapore Custom to prevent software piracy and manufacture and export and import of related equipments under Manufacture of Optical Discs Act and Export and Import Regulation.
6. prevent internet piracy by prohibiting any kinds of technological means for software piracy.
7. Cooperation between the law enforcing agency and the rights holders.
8. Last but not the least, the successful application of the 3 'Es' (Education, Engineer and Enforcement) approach in combating piracy.

Bangladesh

Piracy of intellectual property rights including software piracy is a common phenomenon in Bangladesh[57]. Although Bangladeshi nationals feel piracy keenly, the harm from piracy in Bangladesh is significant for the U.S. and other foreign right holders. Piracy is so rampant, Bangladeshi record/music producers compelled to take it so seriously to enforce their own rights, calling it "a matter of life and death" for their local Bangladeshi companies[58]. But responses of the government of Bangladesh are not adequate, both in terms of the results from enforcement actions taken, as well as from the standpoint of publicizing results of actions in order to create necessary deterrence[59].

However, as least developed country, *Bangladesh* required to implement the TRIPS agreement by July 11, 2013. Bangladesh has already started the process and recently promulgated new legislations in the field of intellectual property rights and is in the process of strengthening its IPR regime. The Copyright law as enacted in 2000 is almost TRIPS compliance and the law commission of Bangladesh drafted new patent and design law and trademarks law in compliance with the TRIPS agreement, which will replace the existing laws in the concerned fields. With the help of WIPO and EU, intellectual property offices of Bangladesh especially the Trade Marks Registry and the Patents Office are being in the process of modernization both in terms of facilities and working procedures. Enforcement mechanisms to deter software piracy in Bangladesh is depends not only on intellectual property related laws but also some other general laws like the civil enforcement mechanism is regulated by Copyright Act along with Code of Civil Procedure, 1908 and criminal enforcement mechanism is regulated by the Copyright Act and Code of Criminal Procedure, 1898.

Under the Code of Civil Procedure, 1908 (Order 39, rule 2) a court has powers to order temporary injunctions. A temporary injunction may be passed to restrain an infringement of an intellectual property right[60]. Under the Code of Civil Procedure (Order 39, rule 7), the court has the authority to pass an order for the preservation, detention or inspection of any subject matter of the suit[61]. The law authorizes judges to order the payment to the right holder of adequate damages to compensate the injury he suffered. Section 76 of the Copyright Act, 2000, empower the court to order the infringer to pay adequate damages to the right holder to compensate for the injury that he has suffered because of the infringement. Section 93 of the same Act authorizes the police to raid and seize the pirated software. But unfortunately this provision is hardly applied due to lack of knowledge among the law-enforcing agency regarding the software piracy and gravity of it.

Customs has a more visible and important role with respect to enforcing IPRs at the borders, as the TRIPS Agreement provides detailed provisions on customs procedures. But due to the low policy priority given to IPR enforcement, customs offices in Bangladesh have scarce resources to combat piracy at the border. Custom authority has the power to order that infringing goods are to be placed outside channels of commerce or destroyed[62].

Although section 15 of the Customs Act, 1969 empowered the custom authority of Bangladesh to take border measures against the pirated goods[63], similar provisions yet to be included in copyright law (which is mainly applied in Bangladesh for software protection) and that is why, Custom authority is either reluctant to take action or ignorant about the pirated software.

Criminal Offences in Bangladesh can either be cognizable or noncognizable[64]. All offences under the Copyright Act are cognizable. Under the Copyright law[65] and Penal Code[66] of Bangladesh, criminal penalties are available against copyright piracy and trademark counterfeiting. The Court before which any offence under the Copyright Act is tried may, whether the alleged offender is convicted or not, order that all copies of the work or plates or recording equipment in the possession of the alleged offender, which appear to it to be infringing copies, or plates, or recording equipment used or intended to be used for the purpose of making infringing copies, be destroyed or delivered to the owner of the copyright or otherwise dealt with as the Court may think fit[67].

It is quite interesting to note that although copyright law in Bangladesh protects software, law-enforcing agency in most of the occasions and even software developers proceed to take action against the software piracy under the penal code. Till date as per study of this author on the law reports of Bangladesh as decided by the Supreme Court of Bangladesh, there is no case law on the software piracy. However, District Judges Court in Dhaka[68] for the first time decided a case on Software piracy in 2002. In that case more popularly known as the *Bijoy Keyboard Case*, the Court applied the Copyright Act and showed very tough view against the software piracy and illegal use of trademark of Plaintiff's software (*Bijoy*) by the defendant. Again in another case, the Supreme Court of Bangladesh showed a very liberal approach towards the application of international IP related conventions/treaties/agreements, as case may be within the domestic jurisdiction of Bangladesh[69]. This is a very remarkable development in Bangladesh for the effective enforcement of intellectual property laws in line with international standard like the TRIPS agreement and WCT[70] etc.

On the basis of field reports, interview with experts and officials, relevant laws and case laws, it is reflected that the enforcement mechanisms of Bangladesh to prevent software piracy is not satisfactory due to following reasons:

1. Lack of effective and deterrent criminal enforcement system
2. Most of the procedural laws in Bangladesh like Code of Civil Procedure and Code of Criminal Procedure is yet to be updated, which are mostly enacted during the British colonial time and not suitable to address the modern phenomenon of software piracy and other computer crime (hacking, cracking, virus distribution etc)[71].

3. Lack of competent police and custom officials having expertise on intellectual property laws.
4. Lack of awareness among the general user regarding the gravity of software piracy.
5. Poor infrastructure and resources for the intellectual property teaching in general and awareness program on piracy in particular[72].
6. Delay in civil and criminal adjudications and cost of litigations[73].
7. Despite the enactment of information technology law in 2006 to provide protection for technological protection measures to prevent software piracy, due to lack of technological knowledge among the police and custom officials to monitor internet piracy, it is not effective till date.
8. Extremely poor border procedure to deter software piracy from the outside of borders[74].
9. Low priority and ignorance about the gravity of software piracy.
10. Lack of coordination and cooperation among the official of different bodies.
11. Last but not the least, the debate or dilemma in Bangladesh among the scholars despite its WTO membership that TRIPS may not be beneficial for Bangladesh let alone it's enforcement mechanisms. For the proper implementation of the TRIPS agreement (being a member of the WTO) and for introducing the effective enforcement mechanisms Government should settle this dilemma immediately on the basis of proper study[75].

RECOMMENDATIONS AND CONCLUDING REMARKS

All member countries of the WTO are under obligation to comply with the enforcement provisions of the TRIPS Agreement. In developed countries, there is good evidence that intellectual property is, and has been, important for the promotion of invention in some industrial sectors, particularly the pharmaceutical, chemical and petroleum industries as well as biotechnology and software and ICT industries. For developing countries, the nurturing of indigenous technological capacity through the intellectual property system has also proved to be a key determinant of economic growth and poverty reduction. The enforcement of intellectual property rights thus protects local commercial and industrial innovation, as well as encouraging technology transfer and foreign investment. Enforcement is therefore is to be considered as a developing country's economic development strategy as well.

Thus, for true economic, social, and cultural development to occur, intellectual property must play a crucial role and to ensure that crucial role of IP, they must be enforced throughout society. However, enforcement is a multilayered concept. It cannot be achieved only through the police, customs, and courts. Without political will, the appropriate legislative framework, and a sustainable IP practices, there can be no enforcement, and ultimately, the country and its economy will suffer.

To fight against piracy in general and software piracy in particular (as that is the most used IP rights in this digital age) and to declare a country as the 'Home of IP' (IP protector country) to attract foreign direct investments in the ICT sector and to harness the 'Beauty of IP' (benefits of IP) to ensure economic growth and sustainable progress of the software industries and IP intensive enterprises, a country at least should take following steps:

Implement the TRIPS and WIPO Copyright Treaty

A country should make its laws in compliance with the TRIPS agreement and at the same time it should adopt the provisions of the WCT to prevent online software piracy[76]. Among other things, these measures make sure that software cannot be pirated by ensuring that protected works are not made available online without the author's permission, and that copy protection tools are not hacked or circumvented.

Not Mere Paper Tiger and Awareness is the Key

Strong copyright laws are vital, but worthless and would be mere paper tiger without effectual mechanisms to inflict them. Governments must accomplish their obligations by adopting and enforcing IP laws unswerving with the TRIPS agreement. However mere hard-hitting law without alertness among the peoples may not be effective. Reducing software piracy requires a fundamental budge in the public's stance. In this regard, the successful application of the 3 'Es' (Education, Engineer and Enforcement) approach in combating piracy in Singapore may be a effective model to be replicated in other countries.

Trained and Knowledgeable Enforcement Staffs

Too often, software piracy is treated harmless or not considered as a serious offence and the punishment is too insignificant to be an effective deterrent. In this regard, Countries should elevate their enforcement of intellectual property by:

(a) creating specialized intellectual property enforcement units at the national and local levels, and providing dedicated resources to investigate and prosecute intellectual property theft,

(b) increasing cross-border mutual cooperation among police, custom and other enforcement agencies to improve coordination among law enforcement in various countries[77], and

(c) supporting training of law enforcement and judiciary officials and providing better technical assistance to ensure that the people on the front lines of piracy enforcement are equipped with the tools they need to deal with the changing nature of intellectual property theft.

Set Example

One of the most effective mechanisms for public persuasion may stem from governments themselves by sending a strong and clear signal that the government will not tolerate software piracy, and is vigorously managing its own software assets[78].

Let us contribute in our respective countries for the effective enforcement of IP rights and thereby making our respective country *'Home of IP'* to exploit the *'Beauty of IP'*. IP protection to deter software piracy cannot be viewed in isolation. It is a global effort, which requires all stakeholders to work closely with one another. Again, solving software piracy requires a combination of education, technology, legislature, and enforcement. Anti-piracy methods must be effective in deterring piracy and not hinder the legal use of the software by the user. A successive and viable solution for piracy prevention is a solution that incorporates both hardware and software protection in conjunction with education about intellectual property rights. It is also important to provide choices for quality software at fair prices[79].

NOTES

** While writing this article the author used substantially another paper of them published by the World Intellectual Property Organisation, Collection of Research Paper series 2006, Geneva, Switzerland.

1. In the United States of America, under the copyright Act of 1976, A Computer Program is defined as "a set of statements or instructions to be used directly or indirectly in a computer in order to bring about a certain result." 17 U.S.C. § 101. Computer programs fall within the definition of literary works. *Lexmark Int'l, Inc. v. Static Control Components, Inc.*, 387 F.3d 522, 533 (6th Cir. 2004). The EU Directive 91/250 does not define the term computer program as such, however it has made several provisions regarding the protection of computer programs. Article 10.1 of the TRIPS agreement requires member states to recognize computer programs as literary works. But there is no definition of the software or computer program in the TRIPS agreement. As it is not defined in the TRIPS agreement, members may keep the definitions they adopted under their domestic laws prior to entry into force of TRIPS. See for details, Resource Book on TRIPS and Development, UNCTAD-ICTSD in IPRs and Sustainable Development, Cambridge Univ. Press, USA, p. 152.

2. Commercial piracy refers to the illegal duplication of software for the purpose of distribution and sale. In *Microsoft v. CMOS Technologies, Inc., et. al., 872 F. Supp. 1329 (D. N.J., 1994)* USA, the defendants purchased and sold nearly 30,000 units of stand alone counterfeit software after receiving notice of its counterfeit status. Microsoft filed suit and obtained seizure and temporary restraining orders. The Court found that defendants engaged in the unauthorized distribution of counterfeit software. In Microsoft v. Grey Computer, *et. al.*, 910 F. Supp. 1077 (D. Md. 1995), co-defendants purchased and copied Microsoft software without the accompanying personal computers and sold the software

to others. Here, the defendants asserted their alleged lack of knowledge as a defense. The Court found that the defendants had in fact received notice of the counterfeit products and were computer software professionals and therefore held liable for copyright infringement.

3. Corporate piracy entails copying of software for direct financial gain. Corporate pirates often find that the size and scope of their company's software usage makes tracking and enforcement of software copyrights exceedingly difficult. Corporate piracy encompasses the activities of not only corporations and businesses, but also educational institutions, government entities, etc.

4. Softlifting is the software equivalent of shoplifting. Softlifting occurs when a person purchases a single licensed copy of a software program and loads it on several machines, in violation of the terms of the license agreement. When one copies a friend's software package, or brings a backup copy home from work for personal use, or borrows a program from the library and makes a copy of it, each of these acts amounts to softlifting. Softlifting is that piracy which goes on in our homes and behind closed doors, where no one can see it happening. It is not intended for direct financial gain, and is believed by many to be perfectly legal.For details see, D. Hornik, *Recent Development Combatting Software Piracy: The Softlifting Problem,* 7 J.L. & Tech 377, 378 (1994).

5. Nevertheless, US federal courts have held that a person who knowingly causes, induces, or materially contributes to the infringing conduct of another may be held liable as a contributory infringer. See for details, *Playboy Enterprises, Inc. v. Russ Hardenburgh, Inc.,* 982 F. Supp. 503, 508 (1997).

6. Despite the report of BSA is higly controversial, the author used the data due to lack of any other source on global software piracy from any universally recognised authority. The main criticism against the BSA is that it is simply serving the interest of a corporate lobby, self appointed global police and legislature and even examining the situation of other countries without considering the knowledge of the law of that particular country, ignoring the sovereign right of law making of a country BSA simply consider US law and sometimes campaign using disgraceful notice to even genuine customers. It is quite interesting to note that in a Belgian case, the Court declared the campaign of BSA to some extent illegal and to be removed immediately and it has also forbidden BSA to operate as a Non-Profit Organisation as the Court consider the activities of BSA entirely commercial. See for deials, J. Douglas, BSA (A) Belligerence Stepping on Sovereignty, available at *www.zdnet.com/au/mews/business/soa/BSA_A_belligerencesteppingonsovereignty/0,139023166,120265924,00.htm and IT Week December 1, 1997, available at www.itweek.co.uk/vnunet/mews/2095430/bsa-campaign-illegal-rules-belgian-judge/*

7. The Third Annual Business Software Alliance's (BSA) and IDC Global Software Piracy Study, May, 2006, p. 1.

8. Statement of R. Lamagna (Microsoft Corporation) before the House Subcommittee on Courts, the Internet, and Intellectual Property, *Oversight Hearing on International Copyright Piracy: Links to Organized Crime and Terrorism,* (March 13, 2003).

9. *Supra note* 11, p. 5.

10. D. Merron and D. Steel, *Which Countries Protect Intellectual Property? The Case of Software Piracy*, Eco.. Inquiry, April 2000, pp. 159-174.

11. M. Blakeney, *Overview of IPR Enforcement Developments*, EC-ASEAN Intellectual Property Rights Co-operation Programme (ECAP II), May, 2003, Bangkok.

12. This unique nature of software, which is facilitating piracy may be illustrated as follows:In most countries those who seek to ride on the backs of others must first take time to understand and recreate the work of their competitors. Thus the original work enjoys 'lead time' over the imitations it has inspired, in which time it can begin to eatablish a footing on the market. However, in the computing insdutry, the digitisation of information allows programs to be copied, manipulated and disected at such a great speeds and at such a little expense that 'lead time' is virtually non-existent. Consequetly consumers cannot distingush between the original and the second generation work. The only obvious difference is likely to be their relative price. See for details, D.J.M. Attridge, *'Copyright protection for computer programs'* in EIPR Issue 12 2000 p. 563.

13. The term 'free software' is often misunderstood. The father of free software Stallman clarifies its meaning by explaining that it refers to software that is 'Free as in speech, not as in beer.' Thus, the term describes software that one is able to use freely, without limiting restrictions. There are many software programs that are available at no cost, such as freeware or shareware, yet they do not provide the same freedoms that 'free software' provides. Stallman states that a piece of software can be called 'free software' if a user has the freedom to use it for any purpose, to modify it, and to redistribute either copies of modified versions, either without cost or for a fee. For details see, R. Stallman, "The GNU Operating System and the Free Software Movement," available at *http://www.opensource.org/advocacy/faq.php*, accessed on November 12, 2006.

14. The biggest beneficiaries of free software are currently big information technology service firms such as IBM and HP–most of them based in the U.S. Also, the most important Linux-distribution companies RedHat and SuSE (i.e. Novell) are from the U.S. This makes the U.S position quite complex.

15. One of the possible mechanism to use free software for IP enforcement is to encourage the software companies to distribute software freely or with a minimum price to the educational institutions in the developing and least developed countries with a precondition that there must be a mandatory course curriculum on the IP and negative impacts on the piracy. It may be somehow a bit different from the idea of free software as prevalent now. Whereas as the cocept of Stallman when he states that a piece of software can be called 'free software' if a user has the freedom to use it for any purpose, to modify it, and to redistribute either copies of modified versions, either without cost or for a fee may be used for the Government Campaign to promote the respect of IP law from the view point that people will have the option to use this kind of software and to exploit the benefits of it and in other kinds of software user

have to pay and can be used under some restrictions. Therefore, in this way customer would be educated not to use pirated software or to use with restrictions or without restrictions , as the case may be.

16. Available at *www.bsa.org/idcstudy*, accessed on October 30, 2006.
17. To view the preliminary findings of the OECD study 'Counting the Cost: The Economic Impacts of Counterfeiting and Piracy' presented at the WIPO conference, availavle at *http://www.oecd.org/dataoecd/12/7/38015608.pdf*, accessed on February 15, 2007.
18. Software Piracy in the United States-Fact Sheet, available at *www.bsa.org*, accessed on September 25, 2006.
19. BSA and IDC Global Software Piracy Study, 2004.
20. *Supra note* 1, p. 309.
21. *Ibid*, pp. 312-13.
22. BSA and IDC Study on the Benefit of Reducing Software Piracy, 2003.
23. M. Blakeney, *Guidebook on Enforcement of Intellectual Property Right*, Queen Mary Intellectual Property Research Institute Queen Mary, University of London, UK, 2003, p. 10.
24. for details see; *http://www.siia.net/piracy/faq.asp*; accessed on September 25, 2006.
25. *Suprq note* 1, p. 309.
26. *Supra note* p. 13; According to media reports, the FBI had compiled strong evidence that the terrorists who bombed the World Trade Center in 1993 financed their activities with counterfeit textile sales from a store located on Broadway in New York City.
27. *Supra note* 23, p. 11.
28. See for details proceedings of the Third Global Congress on Combating Counterfeiting and Piracy held in Geneva from 30 to 31 January 2007, details available at *http://www.wipo.int/edocs/prdocs/en/2007/wipo_pr_2007_475.html*
29. Article 28 of the Paris Convention, 1883 and Article 33 of the Berne Convention, 1886 respectively.
30. *Supra note* 1, p. 313.
31. *Supra note* 193, p. 309.
32. The idea is to hide the very purpose of the code, thereby making it more difficult to understand and alter . This is a protection against reverse engineering, which may allow a pirate to duplicate more easily by analysing the code for protections against duplication and circumvent these. Obfuscation may be carried out statically, or it may be introduced as part of the executing code.
33. This occurs in most popular business and development software, for example Microsoft Office (Office 2002) and Macromedia Dream weaver (Dream weaver 2002).
34. It works as a system to guard against illegitimate modification of code by implementing a network of mutually reinforcing software agents within an

executable program. The guards use checksums on key areas of code and on each other to ensure no modifications have taken place and take some action such as crashing the program if a modification is detected.

35. WIPO Copyright Treaty, Article 11 (Adopted December 20 1996).

36. For details See,Intellectual Property Crime Prevention initiatives in Singapore (on file with author, collected by email communication with Singapore Custom, Police and IPOS)

37. In fact the University law students under the supervision of Faculty members conduct all these street law classes. The author of this paper has the experience to conduct street law programs both as a student and faculty member as well.

38. An example of rights holder co-operation with the enforcement authorities is the establishment in the People's Republic of China of the Quality Brands Protection Committee (QBPC), which was founded in 2000. The QBPC consists of 76 foreign companies, such as Compaq, Siemens and Kodak, with investments in China totalling some $US 14 billion. The QBPC cooperates in the fight against counterfeiting with local administrations.

39. In Bangladesh, a number of copyright owners (especially software and audio-video) formed an organisation named after 'Movement Against Piracy(MAP)' which campaign against piracy around the country and with the aid of law enforcing agency visit different hot spots and super markest time to time to seize pirated software and CD-VCD; See for details, A report on the activities of MAP published in Daily Shamokal, January 15, 2007, Dhaka, Bangladesh.

40. See for details, A. Hirst, *The role of the Government authorities in the enforcement of Intellectual Property rights*, WIPO Workshop for Judges, Beirut, December 7, 1999.

41. Article 36(2) of the Statute of the International Court of Justice.

42. For details on the jurisdictional problems of the ICJ see, R. Anand, *ICJ and Contemporary conflicts*, New Delhi, 1974, N. Singh, *The role and Record of the ICJ*, Nijhoff Publishers, The Netherlands, 1989, R. Hoque, *Jurisdictional Problems of the ICJ: Towards an Alternative Framework of the ICJ, BJL*, Vol. 3, No.1, 1999.

43. For USA, January 1, 1995, For Singapore, January 1,2000 and for Bangladesh July 11, 2013 (for Pharmamceutical patents untill January 1, 2016)

44. Articles 41.1 and 9.1 of the TRIPs Agreement.

45. The establishment of a special IP court is not mandatory or not required by the TRIPS (art. 41.5).

46. See for details, F.K.Beier-G.Schricker (Eds.), *From GATT TO TRIPS-The Agreement on Trade Related Aspects of Intellectual Property Rights, IIC Studies*, Max Planck Institute, Munich, Germany, 1996.

47. For example, in Bannana III case before the WTO-DSB, Ecuador received WTO authorisation to cross retaliate the EC (now EU) by targetting European Intellectual property rights and trade in services as well as product based tariffs.

But the size and power of the Ecuadorian economy is not so strong to harm the EU countries. See for details, Dispute Settlement System under the WTO: An Appraisal, *CU Journal of Law*, Vol. VII, 2002, pp. 107-120.

48. Review of Singapore Legislation on Enforcement at the TRIPS Council, IP/Q/SGP/1, September 20, 2000, p.1.
49. Section 136 of the Copyright Act of Singapore.
50. From Official Communication with Singapore Police (on file with author).
51. Under section 4 of the Manufacture of Optical Discs Act, no party shall engage in the manufacture for sale or other commercial purpose of any CDs,VCDs, CD-ROMs, DVD-ROMs in any place except under the authority, and in accordance with the terms and conditions of a licence.
52. This regulation is very important to control piracy from the source/root or point of origin. The penalties for a first conviction are a fine not exceeding S$ 100,000/-or upto 3 times value of goods, whichever is greater and/or imprisonment for up to 2 years. For a second conviction the fine payable shall not exceed S$200,000/-or upto 4 times value of goods, whichever is greater and/or imprisonment for upto 3 years.
53. In this case, the appellant appealed that the sentence inflicted on him was excessive. He was the managing director of a company selling electronic goods, was the sole partner actively involved in running the business. He was convicted on three charges of having in his possession for the purposes of trade articles with falsely applied trade marks unders 49(c) of the Trade Marks Act (the "TMA"). Three charges were taken into consideration for sentencing purposes. The appellant was sentenced to a total of 32 months' imprisonment.
54. The trial judge referred *OhCheng Hai v Ong Yong Yew* [1993] 3 SLR 930 at 937 case to consider what kind of punishment may be awarded.
55. The author collected information about this approach using email communication with IPOS, Singapore Custom and Police Authority.
56. The necessity of education programs side by side the role of police is reiterated by the A.Jong, Head of Singapore police forces IP Rights Branch: 'Our actions against pirates addressing the supply side of the piracy problem whereas education is also important to discourage the public and consumers from looking for and using pirated software'. (Communication with Singapore Police and collection of an interview of A. Jong, Head of Singapore police forces IP Rights Branch-on file with author).
57. As reported in International Intellectual Property Alliance 2007 Special 301 Report on Bangladesh: The local music companies are regularly complaining about growing piracy problems, especially the fact that music albums of the leading Bangladeshi music labels are being pirated in the outskirts of key urban areas. The music industry of Bangladesh is at the same time undergoing steady growth in terms of new music production companies in the sector. These companies aspire to create quality music and have no intention to engage in

piracy, so protecting their interests should be paramount to the Bangladeshi government. As to broadcast piracy, the local television industry has also expanded with four new channels coming into operation, Channel One, Bangla Vision, Baisakhi, and STV.

58. See *Bangladesh Music Producers Take Law Into Own Hands To Fight Piracy*, August 17, 2006, at *http://www.channelnewsasia.com/stories/entertainment/view/225343/1/html* (describing a record producer-launched "Movement Against Piracy" campaign, raiding shops in the capital Dhaka and the southeastern port city of Chittagong to catch traders selling pirated CDs and cassettes, and quoting senior campaign member, and CEO of G-Series, Nazmul Haq, as saying, "we had no choice but to take the law into our own hands as piracy has almost sent our business to the graveyard. It's (a) matter of life and death for us"). Raids run by local industry revealed 99% piracy. Haq was further quoted as saying, "in the last four years alone, as many as 10 big and respected companies have had to close because of piracy."

59. In Bangladesh's Trade Policy Review at the World Trade Organization in September 2006 (minutes released in November 2006), the government of Bangladesh essentially indicated that it does not keep regular copyright enforcement statistics, but that "efforts are being made for collecting such data," that the records/data in relation to seizure or confiscation are maintained by Bangladeshi Customs manually in a register, but that there are other enforcement agencies like BDR (Bangladesh Rifles), Coast Guard and Police who are also responsible for enforcement of copyright regulations within their respective jurisdictions, and can supply such information "when available and [when] a request is received." In addition, the government noted that "since several agencies are involved in enforcement of copyright, no consolidated information [on raids, prosecutions, convictions, etc.] is available right now." With respect to optical disc plants and piracy, the government indicated that it took note of the concerns expressed in the report regarding optical disc manufacture in Bangladesh and would place the matter "under investigation." See World Trade Organization, Trade Policy Review Body, 13 and 15 September 2006, WT/TPR/M/168/Add.1 (published November 10, 2006).

60. In granting a temporary injunction, there has to be firstly, a prima facie case, secondly, the accrual of irreparable loss or injury and lastly, the balance of inconvenience in the favour of the petitioner.

61. Such an order may be passed on application by any party to the suit. An application by the plaintiff for such an order may be made after notice to the defendant at any time after the institution of the suit.

62. Section 16 of the Customs Act, 1969 provides that the Govt. by notification in the official Gazzette may prohibit or restrict importation of goods of specified description by air, land or sea. Section 17 of the same Act empowered the authority for the confiscation of the prohibited and pirated goods.

63. Goods specified under section 15 shall not be brought, whether by air or land or sea, into Bangladesh.

64. In respect of cognizable offences the police are authorized to initiate criminal proceedings on its own on information of the offence being committed. In the case of noncognizable offences, the police initiate criminal proceedings at the order of a magistrate to whom a complaint has been made under Section 190 of the Code of Criminal Procedure, 1898.

65. Section 84 of the Copyright Act, 2000 as amended by section 38 of the Copyright (Amendment) Act, 2005 provides that person liable for software piracy shall be punishable with imprisonment which may extend to three years, or with fine which may extend to TK. three lac, or with both

66. Section 482-488 of the Penal Code, 1860. Section 486 provides that ...Whoever sells, or exposes, or has in possession for sale or any purpose of trade or manufacture, any goods or thing with a counterfeit trade mark or property mark be punished with imprisonment of either description for a term which may extend to one year, or with fine or with both.

67. Section 84-89 of the Copyright Act, 2000.

68. Which is the court of first instance to deter piracy and software piracy as well. But judgment of this court is not reported in any law reports.

69. *Sunil Kumar Das Vs. Canon Kabushiki Kaisha*, 57 DLR, 2005 pp. 93-100, in this case the court held that new dimension has been added to traditional concept of local market. The world has become a small one for all practical purposes and one should not strictly adhere to the traditional concept of national/local market. There are free movement of the commodities and capitals. Keeping in mind all these factors, the law must be given a new interpretation to suit the needs of the day. Finally the court applied the well-known provision of the Paris Convention not to allow a national company from using a popular mark and thereby preventing imitation of marks.

70. WCT is yet to be ratified by Bangladesh.

71. Code of Civil Procedure and Code of Criminal Procedure enacted in 1908 and 1898 respectively.

72. Although Chittagong, Dhaka and Rajshahi University respectively offering intellectual property program and some awareness programs, all these are not adequate.

73. On and average to settle a dispute under the regular procedure of the court, it takes around 10 years due to huge backlog of cases and workload of the judges. Judges who supposed to decide IP infringement cases are already burdened with huge cases, therefore IP cases are given mostly low priority.

74. Bangladesh having a very long land and coastal border with India and Myanmar, it is very difficult by the Bangladesh Custom to prevent software piracy from the outside of borders without the active support of Custom of Indian and Myanmar. One of the Custom officials from Bangladesh (unwilling to disclose his identity) said in fact at least 50% of software piracy in Bangladesh can be eliminated with the active support of Indian Custom to prevent entry of cheap blank optical discs and pirated software. (Field Visit on January

20-25, 2007). Unfortunately till date there is no cooperation regarding this and even it is not in the agenda of two countries while discussion among the Custom and border forces of two countries.

75. However in a recent case for piracy (by the successful invocation of the TRIPS agreement and WPPT) against the one Indian film director for piracy of the song of one Bangladeshi music group, Indian Court ruled in favour of Bangladeshi music group. This case gained a momentum to show that to some extent TRIPS would be beneficial for the Bangladesh to protect the creative works like software, songs, books of Bangladeshi authors in abroad; The Hon. Justice S. K. Mukherjee of Calcutta High Court took *prima facie* cognizance of the matter and passed an interim order on 19 May 2004. In his learned judgment, the justice ordered the respondents to remove the pirated song from the soundtrack of the movie *Murder*. The court order further barred the respondents from manufacturing, selling, distributing or marketing any music cassette or disc containing the song and the order as to award for damages was pending for final adjudication. See for details, (WTO Case Study 3 available in *www.wto.org*), A.K.Azad, Managing *The Challenges of WTO Participation: Rock 'N Roll in Bangladesh: Protecting Intellectual Property Rights in Music.*

76. However, Microsoft urges to include the provisions of the WCT in the TRIPS agreement to give them more weight for enforcement.

77. Cooperation with Interpol and WCO for IP crime should be strengthened.

78. This can be achieved by implementing software management policies to set an example that the private sector should follow. For a government to demonstrate its commitment to enforcing intellectual property protections in the private sector, it must demonstrate that it is willing to do so in the public sector as well.

79. For details on the importance of fair and reduced price of software as an alternative method to curb software piracy and ensure greater software protection, see, the study of A Story, *Intellectual Property and Computer Software-A Battle of Competing Use and Access Visions for Countries of the South,* UNCTAD-ICTSD Project on Intellectual Property Rights and Sustainable Development, May 2004, Geneva, Switzerland.

Chapter-30

PROBLEMS AND CHALLENGES OF MULTINATIONAL CORPORATIONS: ROLE OF INTERNATIONAL BUSINESS NEGOTIATIONS

Kameshwar Pandit

INTRODUCTION

The basis of International Economic Relations is the international trade. International trade or foreign trade refers persons and firms of different countries for exports and imports of goods and services, multinationals and external assistance also provides basis to international economic relations. The Uruguay Round of GATT negotiations concluded on 15th April, 1994 at Marrakech, Morocco. The final Act incorporating the eight round of multinational trade negotiations consists of,

(i) the WTO Agreement which covers the formation of the organization and the rules governing its working, and
(ii) the Ministerial decisions and declarations which contain the important agreements covering trade in goods, services, intellectual property and plurilateral trade. They also contain the dispute settlement rules and trade policy review system.

The WTO Agreement is in fact, the Uruguay Round Agreement whereby the original GATT is now part of the WTO which came into force from 1st January, 1995. India is a founder member of both GATT and its successor organization WTO where India automatically avails of most Favoured Nations and National Treatment from all WTO members for its exports and its participation in this increasingly rule-based system is aimed towards insuring more stability and predictability in the governance of international trade. (Reeta Mathur, 2003).

Globalisation of business refers to the process of integration of world into one huge market. Such unification calls for removal of all trade barriers among countries. At the company level, globalization means two things'

(i) The company commits itself heavily with several manufacturing locations around the world and offer products in several diversified industries,

(ii) It also means ability to compete in domestic markets with foreign competitors.

A company which has gone global is called Multinational (MNC) and Transnational (TNC). The global company has several benefits to the host countries as well as to their home countries. The benefits from MNCs to the host countries are transfer of technology , capital and entrepreneurship, creation of local job and career opportunities, improvement in balance of payments, greater availability of products for local consumers, improved competition in local economy and better utilization of resources, and greater access to high quality managerial talents etc.. The benefits to their home countries are acquisition of raw materials from abroad at lower prices and steadier supply, technology and management enterprise acquired from competing in global markets, export of components and finished goods for distribution in foreign markets, inflow of income from overseas profits, royalties, licensing fee and management contract and job opportunities abroad in connection with overseas operations.

Besides the several benefits of the MNCs, it has brought several problems and challenges before the host countries. The main focus of this paper is to highlight the problems and challenges before the multinational corporations and the role of the International Business Negotiations to handle the problems. The entire paper is based on theoretical perspectives of the subject and divided into four major parts excluding introduction. The researcher has taken in to consideration the following aspects to study the subject,

(i) What are the problems and challenges brought by MNCS to Host Countries?

(ii) What are the problems and challenges before MNCS in the Host countries?

(iii) What are the roles of International Business Negotiations to handle the challenges and problems?

(iv) What are the important guidelines for improving International Business Negotiations?

PROBLEMS AND CHALLENGES BROUGHT BY MNCS TO HOST COUNTRIES

The role of MNCs in society, as well as its relationship to governments has to be objectively considered as each business has a responsibility to its host communities. Consideration for native population must take priority when a large company moves into underdeveloped community. Social responsibility is the keys to success of business and an important objective for a company should be to become a respected addition to the community. A community often welcome big business, but a company sometimes affects a community and people negatively. A few problems and challenges brought by MNCs to the host countries may be highlighted as under,

(i) Host country is likely to lose its economic sovereignty. Multinational company negotiate with government more like another sovereign state. For example, Enron for Dhabole Power Project in Maharastra.

(ii) MNCs use host country as an export base. This may not happen if we ask MNCs to develop infrastructure and core sector. In India foreign investment initially had gone into consumer items like colas, corn flakes and fried chicken etc. Now MNCs have invested in manufacturing and infrastructural development items. MNCs were invited in India to setup new plants but foreign capital used for requiring local companies and not for creating additional manufacturing capacities.

(iii) Social and cultural differences among nations are big challenges for the MNCs and its managers. Differences in language, values of population can create business and human conflicts. Most serious threat faced by the host country citizens is the loss of their *cultural moorings* in the name of globalization. MNCs usher in their own dress and food habits which is grabbled by youth in the host countries. Youth today are more familiar with Piza, Burger, Fried Chicken, Colas, etc.

(iv) The MNCs have now realized that they must fit into the culture of host nations and help in accomplishment of social improvements better by staying in nation, than by leaving it. MNCs benefits far outweigh the problems they create. MNCs are change agents and are welcome in developing countries, where improving standard of living of mass in a top priority.

However , MNCs have to operate in host countries in such a way that their economic sovereignty is not eroded and they work for long-term development plans.

PROBLEMS AND CHALLENGES BEFORE MNCS IN THE HOST COUNTRY

There has been tremendous changes in international business. The world is getting smaller day-by-day. As rise barriers among nations get reduced , communication, travel and transport have made the world a smaller place, customer needs across the world are getting homogenized. Global marketing is the only way to satisfy these needs . Global marketing differs from export and international market inc. in terms of locus, goals and content. In global marketing the firm's focus is the world as a market place, thus, diffusing the difference between .the home, domestic or foreign markets.. The goal is to maximize efficiency and returns on investments in the world market and strategy is dictated by local country market conditions like customer preferences, laws and competition. In evolving a global marketing strategy the firms has to consider alternatives like standardization , differentiation , localization and nichemanship. Lead market model and insiderization are also important tools for developing a global product. Headquarters should involve local management teams for an effective marketing strategy and gaining higher market penetration in different country markets.

Indian Corporations particularly in software and pharmacy are operating in various locations abroad. Many more sectors are joining to take advantage of new business avenues. This globalization of business is forcing managers to handle with complex issues so that they can gain or sustain a competitive advantage. Recently, cases of discrimination against Indian IT professionals in Malaysia and USA came to light.

There may be various factors, but one factor important is lack of cultural awareness of host country. Professional have to develop global attitude, cross-cultural and international politics. Some vital issues and challenges related to host country may be highlighted as under;

(i) Diverse workforce and MNCs strategies to manage diversity,

(ii) Awareness of certain key aspects of host country's environment , i.e. political-legal, socio-cultural , economic and technological '

(iii) Ethics and corporate social responsibility,

(iv) International Business negotiations,

(v) Focus on some human resource management and industrial relations practices.

Diverse Workforce and MNCs Strategies to Manage Diversity

The basic challenges and problems before MNCs to manage diverse workforce. The Diverse work force is a multi-racial , multi-ethic, multi-lingual and highly educated workforce which have life styles, values ,beliefs, ideals and practices different even in language and religion , code of social behaviour. The workforce will include more women and older persons as women require flexible work schedules and child care programmes and will also include a larger proportion of minority workers and disabled individuals. These diversity should be managed to bring out the best with them. The MNCs to mange the diversity should adopt the strategies and multifaceted approach and to learn details of different cultural norms which will help managers to operate more effectively may be as under,

(i) The organization should develop open culture in which all kinds of workers will be welcome–without discrimination based on age, creed, religion, ethnic background or gender.

(ii) Mangers will need to understand the culture of their employees and develop tolerance.

(iii) Employees in host country will require more skill training and technical expertise and need to trained .

(iv) Education and business will have to unite to create practical opportunities to learn that will better equip employees for "real world".

(v) Management to improve labour-management relationships in which employees are treated with respect, dignity and granted autonomy.

(vi) Management to conduct and support the company's multi-cultural events and strongly encourage the employees to attend and participate.

(vii) MNCs should require all managers of high potentials to become facilitators and trainers of pluralism workshops.

(viii) The Company should send high potential people at all levels to other countries on assignments to become familiar with foreign culture and learn from it.

(ix) MNCs to make a conscious effort to locate plant/unit in a wide variety of communities to build diverse workforce.

(x) To survive in a globally competitive economy, the organization must make all employees , regardless of race, ethnicity , gender, religion, age, lifestyle, full participatory members in their corporate objectives. They must recognize that a heterogeneous group will produce better ideas and strategies than a homogenous group.

Awareness of Host Country Environment

MNCs must be aware and alert to environmental conditions i.e. politicals-legal, socio-cultural, economic and technological aspects in international dimensions of their environment. (James, A. F. Stoner). A manager must have knowledge in both the domestic and international environments. It is important to understand the current state of the environment and to monitor and predict global changes. When a company is setting up in a new location, it puts great emphasis on learning local customs, laws, values and so on. Otherwise ,it runs such risks as unwittingly breaking the law, alienating its new workers, or offending local officials. Thus, managers have to pay particular attention to the environmental factors of economic, socio-cultural, political-legal, technological and market constraints etc. when they are assessing the attractiveness of entering or remaining in a particular country and are considering how to reduce the risk of doing so in day-to-day operations to perform efficiently and effectively in the country.

Ethics and Corporate Social Responsibility

Corporate social responsibility issues are very complex and controversial. It is wrong notion that company's only responsibility is to maximize profits for shareholders within the law. But broader views requires company should adopt the role of a 'good citizen' and balance the interests of shareholders with the best interest of the society.(Bhatia S.K.) The global world presents a critical challenges for MNCs to identify common ethical values that underlie cultural, religious and philosophical differences. Some common fundamental *core human values* followed throughout the world are, *good citizenship, respect of human dignity, respect of basic rights and equity.* (Bhatia. S.K.). Application of core human values is the basic duty of MNCs include the following of adequate workplace and environmental health and safety standard , the payment of living wages , equal employment opportunities, refraining form use of child labour, allowing workers to organize and forms unions, providing basic employee training and education,. Good citizens support good works and charities and bear fair share taxes and take up protection of environment and natural resources. The Caux Round Table developed *principles for business conduct* in 1994 by Japanese, European and North American business leaders in Caux , Switzerland , is the first international ethics code for business and that aims to set a global bench mark against which individual firms can write their own codes and measure the behaviour of their executives. The Caux principles aim to further the twin values of living and working together and human dignity by promoting free trade, environmental and cultural integrity, and prevention of bribery and corruption. (Peter J. Dowling).

International Business Negotiations

One of the important features of international business negotiations is involvement of multiple parties, i.e. host country's government and foreign collaborator and many other interests, i.e competitors , industrialists, politicians, bureaucrats, etc. particularly when joint venture is under considerations. The government of host nation plays a very important role by way of controls and regulations they enforce due to overall concern of industry. Host collaborator is interested in profit, while host governments wants to promote local ownership, modern technology transfers, savings of foreign exchange.

A corporation can be successful in international business negotiation only, if it is able to achieve congruence at various levels , i.e. between the corporation and host government, between corporation and the foreign company, between foreign company and foreign government, etc. While other elements such as-place. Time, language and process of negotiation etc. are important for international business negotiations.

Focus on some Human Resources Management and Industrial Relations Practices

In today's global business world human resources management and industrial relations are also big challenges before the MNCS. Multinationals have to take the some important aspects of focus on human resource practices of shift to host country nationals, cross-cultural training, criteria for appraisal of performance and reward and compensation. MNCs emphasis has to shift from expatriates to host country nationals as it is open to more external influences such as interest groups put more pressure on foreign companies. There has to right mix of managers and employees from host country. Cross- cultural training of managers are needed to be equip the managers with knowledge, skills and attitudes which enables them to achieve the adjustments and effectiveness i.e. personally adjusted, professionally effective, inter- personally adjusted which are indicators of international success. Global or Cross- cultural training will imparts an understanding of other cultures . values and ways of life, with a view to adapting one's own ways to the imperatives of other culture which are needed in global business.

The difference in criteria for appraisal of performance between national and international managers working in similar positions in many case is qualitative in nature. Some criteria for top management personnel evaluation of performance are strategic thinking, capacity to grasp changing environment and market possibilities, competitive threats so as to formulate strategic response, Initiating change- capacity to convey strategic vision and make people involve and motivate employees, Relationship management-capacity to influence and seek cooperation success such as customers, trade unions, government institutions and lobby activities.

The globalization process is trying to reduce the gap in pay across the countries. It is a paradoxical situation for most of companies as they are trying to adopt softer issues of people management through empowerment and team building strategies, but they have not been able to pass the benefit of the performance and contribution across the organization which is hurting the team feeling and morale of the workforce. There is need for a creative compensation design. The success of a reward and compensation strategy depends to a great extent on the attitudes of the managers in creating high degree of commitments, involvement and cooperation among employees. It has to ensure that employees' contribution and performance are rewarded through competency-based pay, team productivity and innovation awards and profit sharing tied to performance criteria and non-financial awards.(Beatty and Schneier, 1997, Henderson, 1997). In today's organization which are becoming more flexible, flat, networked, diverse and global, these kinds of reward inputs will surely play a fecilitating role in helping them in achieving competitive advantage for excellence. (Sami A. Khan, 2000).

ROLE AND TACTICS OF INTERNATIONAL BUSINESS NEGOTIATIONS TO HANDLE THE ISSUES

International Business Negotiations are intended for the resolution of business deals, particularly at international level, to the satisfaction of all the parties involved. It is a process of negotiation involves interaction between two or more people (or group of people) in organizations who communicate with each other in order to reach mutually satisfactory agreement, will depend on communication, human behaviour, and cross-cultural aspects of the parties. Negotiating strategy involves a way of thinking that considers the negotiating party's power and objectives, and how one or both of these can effectively be used to secure the other. Effective negotiation must lead to situation where there is a "win-win" solution rather than "win-lose" solutions. Each party must come out of a negotiation with feeling that they had the best possible deal. There is a constant tension between the self-interest of each party to get the most on the one hand and their mutual dependence on the other, this is called

"Negotiator's dilemma." The effective business negotiation is that where integrative agreements (i.e. in which the cake is enlarged and all parties emerge satisfied with outcome) can be achieved. Negotiators must estimate what they call "BATNA" or the *"Best Alternative to Negotiated Agreement"*. Often, the negotiator fixes his "BATNA" at too high level and after losing a great deal of time reduces the "BATNA" . It might have been better to begin with the lower "BATNA" , so that agreement could have been reached with a larger area of *common grounds* between the parties. Negotiators must try to understand what they really need as an outcome. They must also understand what would satisfy the other parties. Having identified the needs and various positions that can satisfy them, a good negotiator thinks of various offers that can 'discard' during negotiations, which he can offer a concessions for which he can demand concessions in return. These 'discards' are similar to a bridge player discarding unwanted cards. Discard are concessions and negotiator can design a package of such concessions in advance. They may not cost him but give the other party some benefit. He can thus appear reasonable. He can then demand some concessions in return. The concept of a "bargaining zone" in which both parties find "common ground" within which they can satisfy their mutual needs. Both parties to identify "BATNA" for each side. Negotiator then back his minimum requirements with strong arguments with persuasive and convincing way. He also give arguments to show the consequences of no agreement could be for worse.

The role of power and communication is very important factor for influencing the outcomes of negotiations. The negotiator must understand that it is not so much the reality of power, but the perception of it is important. Communication must not merely to put words together. But to constantly test whether the communications has actually reached the other party in the way he meant it to. So, communicator must first of all very clear as to what he wants to convey. Negotiator must know of non verbal communications, i.e. body language signs, for example, legs, eye contact, tone of voice, body tension and distance from the communicator. Signals such as hands clinched across the chest, body squeezed into a corner of chairs, legs, and feet tightly crossed, lips firmly pressed, eyes frequently looking elsewhere, one hand on the mouth holding the words back-these together indicate rejection and hostility. Communication style which pushes arguments on the other party through logic, facts, debates, emphasis on goals by negotiating. Thus negotiator must know which style is appropriate at what stage.

The governments of the both nations, especially of host nation , play very important roles by way of controls and regulations they enforce due to overall concern of industry. Host collaborator is interested in profit, while host government wants to promote local ownership, modern technology transfer, saving of foreign exchange. The firm can be successful in international negotiations only, if it is able to achieve congruence at various levels, i.e. between the firm and host governments, between firm and foreign company.

The role of *four 'C's i.e. Common interest, Conflicting interest, Criteria interest, and Compromise level* must be analysed during course of business negotiations.

Influence of cultural differences also play vital role in international business negotiations. Negotiating style vary between national cultures. (N.J. Adler) Jean M. Hiltrop and Sheila Udall have suggested to adopting *culture-specific strategies on cultural differences in multinational organizations.* Most people are aware of cultural differences between nations. Managers involved in international negotiations often view them at the best as handicap to effective problem solving. As a result , they continue to adhere to the theory of uniformity and universality- some singles best way of doing things- when it comes to managing their *inter-cultural negotiations.*

CONCLUSION

With the globalization of the economiy and the increasing need to carry out business world over, under diverse cultural environments, the need for transnational managers or global leaders, who can think and act across national and subsidiary boundaries are required. They have to acquire effective cross-cultural awareness for which cross-cultural training is needed. Managerial transfers play a critical role in integration and coordination. He must understand world markets business environments from a global perspective, rather than a single-country perspective. He must be skilful at working with people from many different cultures and be able to not only loving in other cultures but also using cross-cultural skills on regular multi-cultural business trips and in daily interaction with foreign colleagues and clients world-wide. Cultural diversity is one of the major challenges facing global business organizations, as it is important success and vitality of the organization. Multinationals have to take some positive steps such as,

- Prepare transnational managers for foreign assignments.
- Develop biasfree HR policies and practices.
- Avoid discrimination and provide equal opportunities.
- Educate employees with proper training to change mind set and prejudice.
- Develop organization culture for valuing differences. Open culture develops tolerance for cultures of their employees.
- To foster mutual adaptation is the only approach works in managing diversity. To make harmonious workplace people and employees try to keep *"their identity"* while on the other hand they are being *"homogenized"*.
- Top Management to support the company's multi-cultural events and encourage employees to attend.
- Managements must recognize that a heterogeneous group will produce better ideas and strategies than homogenous group.

- A *"world culture is a dream"*. We have to be more realist in taking above steps.

India is emerging as the most attractive country for foreigners to invest foreign capital . Merger and acquisition of companies are taking place and global competitions are source of both a threat and an opportunity. For success of the companies and to mitigate the effects of globalization the mangers have *to think global but to act local.*

The business manager while improving negotiation strategies, they have to follow some important guidelines such as:

- Begin with positive overture means begin with a small concession which tend to be reciprocate and lead to agreements.
- To give emphasis on win- win solutions that can allow others party's interest as well as yourself.
- Address problems, not personalities. One should concentrate on the issues in bargaining and not on opposite party's characteristics.
- To create an open and trusting climate by being better listeners and ask more questions which do no irritate an opponent.
- Use congenial accommodation when harmony is important.

Thus, the concept of integrative bargaining must be promoted to provide better outcomes that will satisfy all parties and will build lasting relationship.

REFERENCES

Reeta Mathur (2003), "Recent Trends in Indian Economics", Sublime Publications , Jaipur.

James, A. F. Stoner, "Management" Third edition, Ptintice-Hall of India Pvt.Ltd.

Bhatia, S. K. (2003), "International Human Resource Management: A Global Perspective", Deep & Deep Publications Pvt. Ltd, New Delhi.

Bhatia, S.K. , *Ibid.*

Peter J. Dowling, "International Human Resource Management", Third Edition , South- Western Publications.

Beatty and Schneier (1997), " Human Resource Management".

Henderson, Richard, "Compensation Management", Reston Publishing Company, Reston. (Quoted by S.K. Bhatia.)

Sami, A. Khan (2000), " Reward and Compensation Strategy-Management and Change" Vol. 4, No. 1, (Jan.-June)

N. J. Adler (1991), " International Dimensions of Organisation Behaviour", Bostan.

Jean. M. Hiltop and Sheila Udall, "The Essence of Negotiation" Prentice Hall of India Pvt. Ltd. New Delhi.

CHAPTER-31

PERFORMANCE EVALUATION OF TEA INDUSTRY IN INDIA

R. EZHIL JASMINE

INTRODUCTION

TEA is a significant beverage crop of India. It is part and parcel of Indian social, economic and cultural life. It is the only industry where India has retained its leadership over the last 160 years. The global tea industry is dominated by India–the largest producer and consumer of black Tea. Around 32000 million kgs of tea is produced annually in the world and India accounts for 27.5% of it. Besides, it is also one of the major exporters of tea in the world. However India is facing stiff competition in the International tea market.

OBJECTIVES OF THE STUDY

(1) To study the production performance of Tea industry in India.

(2) To study the export performance of Tea industry in India.

(3) To study the prices of Indian Tea at different auction centres.

(4) To study the problems of Tea industry in India.

PRODUCTION OF TEA IN INDIA

India has 39,700 tea estates (32000 in the south and 6700 in north) and a tea-producing workforce of over 1.1 million people. India produces varieties of tea grown in different regions of the country. The range of tea offered by India–from the original Orthodox to CTC (Crushed, Tear and Curl) and Green Tea, from the aroma and flavour of Darjeeling Tea to the strong Assam and Nilgiri Tea–remains unparalleled in the world.

Since independence, tea production has grown over 250% while land area has just grown by 40%. Tea is grown in 16 Indian states, of which Assam, West Bengal, Tamil Nadu and Kerala are the largest producers accounting for about 96% of the total tea production. The north Indian states have a larger share of land (77%) under tea cultivation and production. The principal tea-growing districts of northern India are in the Assam Valley and Cachar, in the districts of Darjeeling and Jalpaigure (more commonly known as the Duars) and in Terai in West Bengal. In southern India, tea is grown in the elevated region overlooking the Malabar Coast in Kerala and in the Nilgiris Hills.

Tea production in India has registered a slow growth rate over the last few years because of the closure of about 70 tea gardens in Assam due to the widespread recession in the industry.

Table 1
Production of Tea in India (Year-wise)

Year	*Production (Qty. in M kgs)*	*Index 2000 = 100*	*Increase / Decrease*
2000	846.92	100.0	-
2001	853.92	100.8	+ 0.8
2002	838.47	99.0	- 1.0
2003	878.13	103.7	+ 3.7
2004	892.96	105.4	+ 5.4
2005	927.90	109.6	+ 9.6

Source: Tea Board of India.

$\chi^2 = \Sigma \left\{ \frac{(O\text{-}E^2}{E} \right\} = 0.08$

Table value at 5% for 5 degrees of freedom is 11.0. Hence the production of Tea is proved to be significant during the given years.

It is clear from the analysis that the production of tea in all the given years (except 2002) has recorded an increase as compared to the base year 2000. There is a Compound Annual Growth Rate (CAGR) of only 1.9 per cent in the Tea production during the period.

North India is the leading producer of Tea when compared to South India. Especially, Assam (North India) is the largest producer of Tea in India. Tamilnadu is the leading producer of Tea in South India.

Table 2
Production of Tea in India–Area wise

(in Million kgs)

Area	*2003*	*% share*	*2004*	*% share*	*2005*	*% share*	*Increase/decrease 2005/2004*
Assam	435	49.5	436	48.8	474	51.0	+ 38 (8.7)
West Bengal	201	22.9	215	24.1	215	23.2	Nil
Others	12	1.4	12	1.2	12	1.3	Nil
North India	648	73.8	662	74.1	701	75.5	+ 39 (5.8)
Tamil Nadu	167	19.0	163	18.3	155	16.8	- 8 (4.9)
Kerala	58	6.6	62	6.9	67	7.2	+ 5 (8.1)
Karnataka	5	0.6	6	0.7	5	0.5	- 1 (16.7)
South India	230	26.2	231	25.9	227	24.5	- 4 (1.73)
Total	878	100	893	100	928	100	+ 35 (3.9)

Source: Tea Board of India.
Note: Figures furnished in parentheses denotes percentage of increase or decrease of production.

The production of Tea in North India has recorded an increase of 39 m.kgs in 2005 (701 m.kgs of production in 2005 as against 662 m.kgs in 2004). But the production of Tea in South India has recorded a decline of 4 m.kgs in 2005 (227 m.kgs of production in 2005 as against 231 m.kgs in 2004). Tamilnadu and Karnataka are the areas where the production has declined.

Table 3
India's share of World Tea Production

	Production (Qty in M. kgs)		
Year	*World*	*India*	*India's share %*
2000	2908.96	846.92	29.11
2001	3035.27	853.92	28.13
2002	3055.04	838.47	27.45
2003	3174.06	878.13	27.67
2004	3,305.97	892.90	27.01
2005	3,344.72*	927.90	27.74

* Subject to revision.

Source: ITC Annual Bulletin & Tea Board of India Monthly Reports.

Coefficient of Correlation between Indian Tea production and World Tea production is + 0.63. Hence there is positive relationship between them.

India is the leading producer of Tea in the world followed by China, Srilanka, Kenya and Indonesia. But the share per cent of India in the world Tea production has reduced during the recent years. Though India is the topper in production, the growth rate of production is not as high as countries like China and Kenya.

India exports 15 to 20 per cent of its total tea production and the remaining 80 to 85 per cent is domestically consumed. Out of the 928 million kgs of Tea produced in India in 2005, the domestic consumption is around 750 million kgs.

Table 4
India among Top Tea Producing Countries of the World

(Quantity in Mkgs.)

Country	*2002*	*Rank*	*2003*	*Rank*	*2004*	*Rank*	*2005*	*Rank*	*Compound Annual Growth Rate*
India	838.47	I	878.13	I	892.90	I	927.98	I	3.4%
China	745.37	II	768.14	II	835.23	II	870.00	II	5.3%
Srilanka	310.60	III	303.25	III	308.09	III	317.20	III	0.7%
Kenya	287.10	IV	293.67	IV	324.61	IV	328.58	IV	4.6%
Indonesia	172.79	V	167.65	V	164.82	V	164.19	V	-1.69%

Source: ITC Annual Bulletin & Tea Board of India monthly Reports.

It is apparent from the table that the Compound Annual Growth Rate (CAGR) of Indian Tea production (2002-2005) is 3.4 per cent as against 5.3 per cent in China and 4.6 per cent in Kenya. While India and china have a large domestic market, other countries mainly produce for export purpose. Therefore the international tea prices are closely linked with the prices in Srilanka and Kenya.

MARKETING OF TEA

Marketing of Tea in India consists of both Leaf and Dust Teas in the CTC and Orthodox grades. The consumption of tea is above 600 million kgs per year. Tea trading in domestic market is done in two ways - Auction selling and private selling. The primary marketing of tea is conducted through public tea auction centres licensed by Tea Board of India which are located at Kolkata, Guwahati, Siliguri, Amritsar, Coonoor, Coimbatore and Cochin. Bulk trading is done through the auctions held in these centres. The Tea Board has partially introduced electronic auction system in Guwahati, Siliguri, Coonoor, Coimbatore and Cochin. The Board has also launched an IT portal (*www.indiateaportal.com*) for effective dissemination of information relating to tea industry.

Due to globalization, the consumption pattern of tea has remarkably changed in India, resulting in the growth of branded tea sector. New brands are therefore introduced in the market depending upon the tastes and preferences of the consumers. The best quality tea would now fetch Rs. 58 to Rs.65 per kg, medium quality Rs. 48 to Rs. 55 per kg and low quality Rs. 42 to Rs. 48 respectively. The branded Tea sector in India has two major players who take a lion's share in the industry. Hindustan Lever Limited (HLL) leads this segment with a market share of 31 per cent flowed by Tata Tea with a market share of 21.1 per cent.

Hindustan Lever Limited produces tea brands namely Red Label, Taj Mahal, Taaza, 3 Roses and Lipton Tea. Tata Tea Limited produces Tata Tea, Agni, Kannan Devan, Chakra Gold, Tata Tetley and Gemini.

The Indian tea industry has been adversely affected by fall in prices during the last few years mainly due to supply and demand imbalances. Even though there was an improvement in average auction prices of tea during 2004, auction prices have been lower during 2005. The lower prices are dooming many plantations, especially in Assam, which accounts for more than half of India's tea production.

It is clearly known from the Table that prices of tea in all Indian auction centres have declined in 2005. Some of the estates are facing closure, while others have managed to survive by reducing wages with the co-operation of the workers' unions. The main components of cost of production in Indian tea industry comprises labour cost at 50 per cent, manufacturing cost 14 per cent and administration cost 12 per cent. Labour cost is generally fixed and if production suffers, the cost of production per unit goes up significantly. Cost of production in the competing countries like Kenya and Srilanka is lower due to labour cost advantages, better productivity from younger tea bushes and state support. Indian tea is not price competitive except for some niche segments. The tea industry veterans have predicted that prices could rise by 30 to 35 per cent and cross Rupees 100 per kg mark over the next 2 to 3 years, if the global tea production remains tight.

Table 5
Prices of Tea at Indian Auction centers

Quantity in M. kgs.
Price in Rs/Kg.

Auction	*January to December*						*Increase / Decrease*
	2003		*2004*		*2005*		*2005 over 2004*
centres	*Quantity*	*Price*	*Quantity*	*Price*	*Quantity*	*Price*	*Price*
Kolkata	133.87	68.13	119.32	80.34	140.27	70.02	-10.32
Guwahati	138.67	59.01	127.09	68.78	121.63	60.03	-8.75
Siliguri	87.09	54.58	91.99	64.13	90.42	58.38	-5.75
Amritsar	0.19	28.62	0.15	26.04	NA	-	-
North India	359.82	61.31	338.55	71.57	352.32	63.58	-8.01
Cochin	50.63	45.78	54.60	52.30	55.74	50.23	-2.07
Coonoor	40.59	34.55	44.28	43.30	40.86	36.16	-7.14
Coimbatore	22.33	38.30	18.40	46.50	18.14	40.90	-5.60
TEA SERVE	4.40	30.58	18.53	40.79	13.67	35.73	-5.06
South India	117.95	39.93	135.81	47.01	128.41	42.89	- 4.12
All India	477.77	56.03	473.36	64.54	480.73	58.06	- 6.50

Source: Monthly report 2005 & 2006, Tea Board of India.

Table 6
Price of Tea at Different International Auction Centers

Quantity: (in thousand kg)
Price: (in US dollar/kg)

Auction	*January to December*						*Increase / Decrease*
	2003		*2004*		*2005*		*2005 over 2004*
centres	*Quantity*	*Price*	*Quantity*	*Price*	*Quantity*	*Price*	*Price*
North India	359.82	1.32	338.55	1.58	352.32	1.44	-0.14
South India	117.95	0.86	135.81	1.04	128.41	0.97	-0.07
All India	477.77	1.20	474.36	1.43	480.73	1.32	-0.11
Colombo	273.23	1.54	269.87	1.73	273.06	1.84	+0.11
Mombassa	285.84	1.54	298.09	1.55	306.76	1.47	-0.08
Chittagong	47.78	1.16	52.93	1.06	52.08	1.21	+0.15
Jakarta	33.77	0.95	32.21	1.02	36.14	1.04	+0.02
Limbe	15.90	0.95	17.22	1.00	11.93	0.92	-0.08

Source: Tea Board of India.

There is no single world price for Tea, but rather different prices at different auction centres. Tea prices across on all major international tea auction centres have remained soft in 2005 as against 2004. But price rises have been recorded in Colombo, Chittagong and Jakarta.

IMPORT OF TEA IN INDIA

In 2005, India imported 16.47 million kg of tea with the country's domestic consumption pegged at 805 million kg. The low import price is indeed a matter of concern particularly in the context that significant quantum of tea imported into the country is meant for re-exports.

Table 7
Import of Tea in India

Source Country	*2004 (in M.kg)*	*Rs/kg*	*2005 (in M.kg)*	*Rs/kg*
Indonesia	2.65	57.73	2.26	62.52
Nepal	3.14	59.66	3.64	60.60
Srilanka	0.46	80.90	0.30	121.81
Vietnam	17.28	32.56	3.23	36.90
Kenya	3.29	82.25	3.17	77.73
Others	3.98	97.91	3.87	109.18
Total	30.80	45.88	16.47	58.65

Source: www.blonnet.com

Import of Tea has remarkably decreased in India in 2005 (16.47 m.kgs.) when compared to 2004 (30.80 m.kgs.). The Tea (Distribution and Export) Control Order, 2005 provides that no distributor shall carry on the business of distributing imported tea and no exporter shall export tea or export imported tea except under a business license obtained in accordance with the provisions of the order.

Imports for re-exports have two implications. First, re-exporting sub-standard teas in the guise of Indian tea would tarnish the image of Indian teas in the international market; and second import for re-export would result in additional pressure on supply position in the domestic market, as otherwise this tea could have been exported.

EXPORT OF TEA IN INDIA

Almost every major tea-drinking nation in the world imports some or other variety of Indian Tea. Despite India's historical success in the Tea industry, it is facing stiff competition in the international market. India has registered a decline in exports in recent years. Hence focus on the export front is necessary to promote Indian tea in domestic market through advertisement campaigns. The total net foreign exchange earned from Tea industry per annum is around Rs. 1847 crores. Besides, it also contributes revenue to the national exchequer by way of cess, sales tax, agricultural and corporate income tax.

It is clear from the Table that the export of Tea has decreased in all the given years as compared to the base year 2000. The Compound Annual Growth Rate (CAGR) of Tea Export in India is –1.94 per cent, which shows that there is negative effect in the growth of Tea Exports in India.

Table 8
Export of Tea in India–Year wise

Year	*Export*	*Index 2000=100*	*Increase / Decrease*
2000	206.82	100	–
2001	182.59	88.3	-11.7
2002	201.00	97.2	-2.8
2003	173.68	84.0	-16.0
2004	197.60	95.5	-4.5
2005	187.60	90.7	-9.3

Source: Tea Board of India.

$\chi^2 = \Sigma\left\{\frac{(O\text{-}E^2}{E}\right\} = 0.08$ Table value at 5% for 5 degrees of freedom is 11.0. Hence the production of Tea is proved to be significant during the given years.

India ranks fourth in terms of tea exports in the world. However India's export share to three biggest international tea markets – Russia, UK and Pakistan has been on a decline. Srilanka and Kenya have been eating into India's market share. India's tea exports during January to December 2005 stood at 187.6 million kg. compared to 197.6 million kg. during the corresponding period in 2004. Quality is the major factor and that is why India's Exports are suffering.

Table 9
Export of Tea in India–Area wise

	2004			2005			
Region (M.kg)	*Volume*	*Rs. Crore*	*Rs/kg (M.kg)*	*Volume*	*Rs. Crore*	*Rs/kg*	*% Increase/ Decrease 2005/2004*
North India	100.8	1203.85	119.43	92.7	1079.12	116.41	-8.1 (8.0)
South India	96.8	637.28	65.17	94.9	618.55	65.18	-1.9 (2.0)
All India.	197.6	1841.13	93.17	187.6	1697.67	90.49	- 10.0 (5.1)

Source: *www.blonnet.com & Tea Board of India.*
Note: Figures given in parentheses indicate percentage of increase or decrease in export.

The export of Tea from India has dropped by 10 million kgs in 2005 (8.1 m.kgs reduction in North India and 1.9 m. kgs reduction in South India). However, net exports from the country (export minus import) registered a growth which indicates a positive sign for the industry.

North Indian teas fetch twice as much as South Indian teas because of their quality and the markets they cater to. North Indian teas cater to the American and British markets while South Indian teas go to the Common Wealth of Independent States (CIS market), which offer lower realizations.

Table 10
India's share of world Tea exports

	Export (Qty. in M.kgs.)		
Year	*World*	*India*	*India's share %*
2000	1330.87	206.82	15.54
2001	1391.35	182.59	13.12
2002	1438.76	201.00	13.97
2003	1390.35	173.68	12.49
2004	1536.14	197.60	12.86
2005	1557.63	187.60	12.04

India's export–Tea Board of India.
Source: World–ITC Bulletin.

Coefficient of Correlation between Tea Export in the World and in India is 0. Hence there is no relation ship between them.

The share per cent of India in the world Tea Exports has reduced during the past few years. According to the Tea Board of India, India's earlier dependence on Russia's imports is of the main reasons for the drop in its exports. Besides big buyers like Iran and Iraq have also become inactive due to political reasons. Rising competition from Kenya is yet another factor affecting Indian Tea exports.

Decline is quality of Indian tea has been caused by mushrooming bought leaf factories which produce cheap quality tea by buying and processing green leaf from small growers. Further, blending of Indian teas with cheaper varieties and export of the same as Indian tea has also impaired the quality perception.

Table 11
India among Top Tea Exporting Countries of the World

(Qty. in Th. Kgs.)

Name of the Country	*2002*	*Rank*	*2003*	*Rank*	*2004*	*Rank*	*2005*	*Rank*	*Compound Annual Growth Rate*
India	201.00	I	173.68	I	183.64	I	187.60	I	2.3%
Srilanka	285.99	II	291.89	II	290.65	II	298.77	II	1.4%
Kenya	272.46	III	269.27	III	326.34	III	349.74	III	8.6%
China	252.27	IV	259.98	IV	279.50	IV	295.00	IV	5.3%
Indonesia	100.18	V	88.18	V	96.00	V	104.00	V	1.3%

Source: Tea Board of India & ITC Annual Bulletin.

India is fourth in the row after Srilanka, Kenya and China with a world export share of 12.04 per cent in 2005. But all the major tea-exporting countries have reported explicit improvement in their export performance except India which has recorded a negative growth (Compound Annual Growth Rate of Indian Tea exports is -2.3 per cent).

At present due to drought conditions in Kenya, its tea production is expected to drop by 16 per cent. As such, the export of tea in India could do well in the days to come. India could export tea to United Kingdom due to lower projected output in Kenya. India could also tap the potential in Egypt as the latter has reduced the Import duty for Indian tea to five per cent. For the current financial year 2006-2007, Tea Board of India has set an export target of 100 million kg.

PROBLEMS OF TEA INDUSTRY IN INDIA

The tea industry in India, which has an annual turnover of Rs. 10000 crores has been witnessing sea changes in the past few years. Despite some of the unique advantages, namely, largest production, huge domestic consumer base, diverse and unique climatic conditions, rich cultivation tradition, majestic art of tea making, the tea industry in India is ailing. The various problems are:

(i) Malt-based beverages such as Horlicks and Bournvita are the favourite type of hot drinks in the South, and are also growing at a faster rate. Besides, Soft drinks such as carbonates also represent a significant threat to the ongoing dominance of tea in India. Besides, the aggressive marketing campaigns of leading multinationals successfully persuade many young consumers to migrate from tea to soft drinks.

(ii) Stiff competition from the producing-exporting countries like Srilanka, China, Indonesia and Kenya pose great threat to the Indian tea industry.

(iii) Various tariff and non-tariff measures imposed by importing countries such as Russia, Egypt and Iran pose threat to Indian tea industry.

(iv) Land and labour productivity are two of the most serious banes of the Indian tea industry. The production, productivity and quality of tea are highly affected by the old age of tea bushes in India, with more than 30% of tea area being above the economic threshold age limit. The estimated life of a tea bush ranges from 80-100 years with the most productive age between 30-35 years. About 50% of the Indian tea bushes have crossed 50 years of age.

(v) Mechanization is one of the effective alternatives that can reduce costs. But in countries like India and Kenya where a large number of people are employed in the plantations, they feel that it is a major threat to their livelihood.

(vi) Lack of plucking standards among small growers is another problem in India.

Fresh investments and technology adoption are the primary vehicles to rejuvenate the Indian plantation sector and make it more competitive and viable in the current global scenario. For increasing labour productivity the industry is in discussion with the government and the Unions to go for piece-rate system instead of the traditional time-rate systems. There is also an urgent need to help the small growers in India to improve their plucking standards and to handle the plucked leaf in a proper manner so that the leaves could be transported it to the factories in a fresh condition.

With the slowing down in the rate of domestic consumption of tea, increasing competition from other beverages, particularly soft drinks and developments in the global arena, the tea Board has planned to go in for a massive advertising campaign to change the image of tea and increase its consumption. The TV commercials are a part of the first phase of the Rs. 10 crore internal promotional drive by the Tea Board of India that will be carried out throughout the 2006-07 fiscal year. Further, the Government of India has also planned for a series of initiatives to boost the plantation sector, which has been under rough weather due to growing global competition. A special insurance scheme for plantations, restrictions on import, new marketing initiatives and better compensation during price crash are some of the steps under consideration to boost the industry. Further, the Indian Government would continue to focus on the traditional Indian Tea markets such as Russia, the UK and UAE. "The future of plantation industry depends on research and development" said Mr. Jairam Ramesh, Union Minister of Commerce for state.

FINDINGS

1. India ranks first in the world in Tea production followed by China, Srilanka, Kenya, and Indonesia etc. The compound Annual Growth Rate of Indian Tea production is 1.9 per cent.
2. North India is the leading producer of Tea when compared to South India. Assam is the largest producer in North India and Tamilnadu is the leading producer in South India.
3. India secures the fourth position in the world in Tea exports. But the Compound Annual Growth Rate of exports in India shows a negative effect of -2.3 per cent.
4. High cost of production is a fundamental problem of Tea industry in India.
5. The Indian Tea industry is widely affected by fall in prices during the past years.
6. Blending of Indian teas with cheaper varieties and exporting the same, has impaired the quality perception in the market.

CONCLUSION

In the era of globalization, the buzzword is competition and the bottom line is competitiveness. The road ahead for Indian Tea industry is not rosy, unless the industry drastically reduces the cost and improves its competitiveness. In order to revive the Indian Tea industry, the Central budget 2006-2007 has proposed contribution of Rs. 1 billion towards Special Purpose Tea Fund (SPTF) a 15 year programme, aimed at re-plantation and rejuvenation of Tea. The need for the hour is to increase the productivity of both land and labour. The

Indian Tea Association (ITA) forecasts a high growth in 2006 for the recession-hit tea industry with more exports, production and domestic consumption. The Indian tea industry should gear up to meet the global challenges.

REFERENCE

Monthly Report of Tea, April 2005, Tea Board of India.

Monthly Report of Tea, February 2006, Tea Board of India.

Performance Budget, Ministry of Commerce & Industry 2005-2006, Government of India.

www.agritrade.cta.int/tea

www.blonnet.com

www.commerce.nic.in/annual 2005-2006

www.dailypioneer.com

www.epwrf.res.in

www.hindu.com/2005

www.icra.in

www.indiabudget.nic.in

www.indiatea.org/ccpa

www.indiateaportal.com

www.Indiainfoline.com

www.newkerala.com

www.seattlecentral.org/faculty.

www.swannteas.com/abouttea

www.thehindubusinessline.com

www.teauction.com/industry/indiantea.asp

www.teaauction.com/statistics

www.teacouncil.co.uk

www.tribuneindia.com

www.voanews.com

Chapter-32

RURAL MARKET IN INDIA AND THE ROLE OF INFORMATION TECHNOLOGY

M. V. S. Srinivasa Rao

INTRODUCTION

'Change is the only constant' in all our lives. But the change being witnessed in the Indian economy is particularly interesting. There is a bi-faceted change from National to Global & from Urban to Rural. National to global is a worldwide phenomenon. In India it gained in momentum with the opening up and libèralization of the economy in the 1990s. Arrival of many well known MNCs and international brands up till now were available only in the grey market but now its changing as the MNCs are moving towards rural areas. There is transformation in lifestyle, values and aspirations of rural populace with increasing penetration of media forms. The villager is no longer the person as typified in Hindi movies. Today, there is an exponential increase in demand for goods, services, entertainment forms in rural India.

A powerhouse in global Information Technology (IT) and process outsourcing, and with a vibrant and growing industrial sector, India is well and truly on the path to economic prosperity. Close to 72 per cent of Indian population lives in rural areas, India lives in villages. With India truly on the path of global IT leadership, it first needs to look into itself and consider that does this progress include rural population or not. With the advent of E-Commerce, one area where progress of India is consistently slows in its backbone which is rural India. One reason for the same is that urban markets have all the advantages of technology, while rural markets fail in the same. Rural markets in India have not been able to take advantage of ICT (Information and Communication Technology). Hence this paper will discuss the benefits rural population can derive from the information technologies like E-Commerce, etc. It will also take up cases in India where information technologies have made considerable difference in the rural market.

With this introductory note, this paper is organized as follows. In Section II, characteristics of Indian Rural Economy are discussed. Section III deals marketing activities in Rural India. In Section IV, usage of information technology in Indian Rural Markets is analyzed and Section V has the Conclusion.

INDIAN RURAL ECONOMY

Agriculture is the life-blood of the rural economy. About two-thirds of the Indians are engaged in the agricultural operations. But they account for only a fourth of the country's GDP. The tele-density of the rural population in India is 0.5 per thousand. This is due to the unavailability of information and communication technologies. The type of products they offer is mostly a commodity. The commodities largely grown in the rural areas are rice and other crops. Since these goods are staple goods, the scope for differentiating one's product from another is generally difficult. Achieving differentiation through production process is also not possible. Though it has almost all the characteristics of the perfect market, it is lacking in one of the main features of the perfect market, i.e., availability of information across the markets. Here comes the role of information and communication technologies. It is making available a spectrum of right information across the world at the right time just by a click at the mouse. Internet has the potential to make farm market as close to perfect competition as possible.

A SWOT Analysis

Strengths	*Opportunities*
1. Labor Cost-Cheap	1. Untapped Resources
2. Human Resources are plenty	2. Technology advancement
3. Not tapped by the corporate	3. Enabling rural people to participate in the global market
4. Agriculture-main occupation	4. Can generate more employment opportunities
5. Large Number of consumers	5. Near absence of rural industries
6. Large number of producers	6. Low cost of production
7. Diverse agro climate conditions	7. Existence of reference groups.
Weakness	***Threats***
1. Information asymmetry	1. Rural people's perception towards technology
2. Low literacy rate	2. Integration of the scattered population
3. Low Purchasing power	3. Closer to the mother nature
4. Inadequate infrastructure	4. Conservative society
5. Lack of internet connectivity	5. Migration to urban areas
6. High cost and non availability of credit	6. Different languages
7. Fragmented land holdings	7. Politicization of the rural society.

Source: Ganguly, A. S. (1985), Growing Rural Market in India, *Marketing in India,* New Delhi, p. 37.

According to the census of India, village with clear surveyed boundaries not having a municipality, corporation or board, with density of population not more than 400sq.km and with at least 75 per cent of the male working population engaged in agriculture and allied activities would quality as rural. According to this definition, there are 6, 36,365 villages in the country. Table 1 below gives us the population and village size details in the country.

Table 1
Rural Population Statistics in India.

Population	*Number of Villages*	*Percentage of total villages*
Less than 200	114267	17.9
200-499	155123	24.3
500-999	159400	25
1000-1999	125758	19.7
2000-4999	69135	10.8
5000 9999	11618	1.8
10000 & above	3064	0.5
Total	636365	100

Source: Census of India, 2001.
Understanding: In the country we have 6.36lakh villages out of which only 13 per cent have population above 2000.

Interestingly, for FMCG (Fast Moving Consumer Goods) and consumer durable companies, any territory that has more than 20,000 and 50,000 population, respectively, is rural market. So, for them, it is not rural India which is rural (Refer Table 2).

Table 2
Classification of Town in India–According to FMCG Companies.

Class	*No. of towns*	*Population*
I	400 (Includes 35 metros)	More than 1lakh
II	498	More than 50,000 and less than 1lakh
III	1368	More than 20,000 and less than 50,000
IV	1560	More than 10,000 and less than 20,000

Source: Kashyap Pradeep & Raut (2005), *Rural Marketing Book, New Delhi,* Biztantra Publication, p. 19.

According to National Council for Applied Economic Research (NCAER) study, there are as many 'middle income and above' household in the rural areas as there are in the urban areas. There are almost twice as many 'lower middle income' households in rural areas as in the urban areas. At the highest income level there are 2.3 million urban households as against 1.6 million households in rural areas. According to Personal Products Division of Hindustan Lever Limited (HLL), in 2007, the money available to spend on FMCG products by urban India is Rs. 49, 500crores as against is Rs. 63, 500crores in rural India. Of course, investment in formal savings instruments by 6.6 million rural households compared to 6.7 million in urban India.

As per NCAER projections, the number of middle and high income households in rural India is expected to grow from 80 million to 111 million by 2007. In urban India, the same is expected to grow from 46 million to 59 million. Thus, the absolute size of rural India is expected to be double that of urban India. Table 3 provides the details of demographic classification of rich people in India.

Table 3
Classification of Urban and Raul Rich in India

	No. of Households (million)		
Demographic Classification	*Urban*	*Rural*	*Total*
Very Rich (Greater than 10 Lakh Per Annum)	4.84	1.32	6.16
Well off (Greater than 5 Lakh Per Annum)	29.45	27.36	56.81
Total	34.29	28.68	62.97
% of Total	54%	46%	100%

Source: NCAER, *Rural Infrastructure Report (2007)*, New Delhi.

However, the rural economy contributes nearly half of the country's GDP which is mainly agriculture driven and monsoon dependent. Remember, more than 50 per cent of the sales of FMCG and Durable companies come from the rural areas. The estimated annual size of the rural market for FMCG is Rs.85, 000crore, for Durables it is Rs. 12, 000crore, in Agro-inputs (incl. tractors) it is Rs. 5, 000crore and for 2/4 wheeler vehicles it is estimated as Rs. 12, 000crore.

Similarly, the McKinsey report (2007) on the rise of consumer market in India predicts that in twenty years the rural Indian market will be larger than the total consumer markets in countries such as South Korea or Canada today, and almost four times the size of today's urban Indian market and estimated the size of the rural market at $577 Billion. Let us discuss how the rural marketing activity has gained its momentum.

RURAL MARKETING IN INDIA

In India, leaving out a few metropolitan cities, all the districts and industrial townships are connected with rural markets. The rural market in India brings in bigger revenues in the country, as the rural regions comprise of the maximum consumers in this country. About 285 million people live in urban India whereas 742 million reside in rural areas.

The rural market in Indian Economy generates almost more than half of the country's income. Rural marketing in Indian economy can be classified under two broad categories. These are:

- The market for consumer goods that comprise of both durable and non-durable goods
- The market for agricultural inputs that include fertilizers, pesticides, seeds, and so on

The concept of rural marketing in India is often been found to form ambiguity in the minds of people who think rural marketing is all about agricultural marketing. However, rural marketing determines the carrying out of business activities bringing in the flow of goods from urban sectors to the rural regions of the country as well as the marketing of various products manufactured by the non-agricultural workers from rural to urban areas. To be precise, Rural Marketing in India Economy covers two broad sections, namely:

- Selling of agricultural items in the urban areas
- Selling of manufactured products in the rural regions.

Where as, Rural Marketing is set to clock 20 per cent growth this fiscal with Rs.570crore of promotional budget being spend by major companies on rural marketing and below-the-line activities. Driving the growth are categories like Telecom, IT and Insurance. Players including Air Tel, Hutch, Nokia, HP, Intel, and HDFC Standard Life amongst others are spending considerable amount in taking their product and services to smaller towns and villages.

HLL, according to industry estimates, spent Rs. 517 crore on advertising in 2006. About 10-12% of this budget was spent on rural marketing and promotions. P&G, on the other hand spent Rs.200crore on mass-media advertising, its share on rural marketing hovered around Rs. 5-10crore. But its share is set to increase in next two years. LG and Samsung, too have taken a fancy to rural marketing, though this year (2007) they are expected to spend between Rs. 5-8 crore between them.

The growth areas today, according to industry figures, are in 13,000 villages, with population of more than 5000. of these, 80% of the villages are in seven states–Uttar Pradesh, Maharashtra, Bihar, Andhra Pradesh, West Bengal, Tamil Nadu and Kerala.

IT companies including Intel and HP and mobile companies like AirTel, Hutch and Reliance will be conducting rural marketing fair to showcase PC, Internet, and technology usage and benefits to the villages in UP, Maharashtra and Andhra Pradesh soon.

Auto companies like TVS motors and General Motors (GM) try out rural marketing through mobile road shows. Last year (2006), GM spent between Rs. 1.5-2crore in each of the state of Gujarat, Maharashtra and Punjab to showcase Chevrolet brand.

RURAL TELECOM, CURRENT STATUS IN INDIA

Core sectors like telecom are said to have a direct bearing on transforming consumers into producer and promote economic development. According to the NCAER Rural Infrastructure Report (2007), the demand for telecommunication services are surging across rural India, as middle class and upper classes are growing in most villages but the tele-density levels are very low 1.67 per 100 residents compared with average of 8.59 overall and 25.90 in Indian cities.

Table 4
Details of the Urban-Rural Divide of Telecom Usage in India

	Rural	*Urban*
Mobile Phones	0.01 million	75.685 million
Fixed Lines	13.9 million	36.988 million
Private Operator Share	0.01%	53.54%
PCO's	Approx 20Lakh	Approx 35Lakh
VPTs	5,33,000 villages (as of Sept, 2005)	
VPTs Target	Another 53,800 villages (by 2008)	
Total Number of Phones	Approx. 14 million	Approx 112 million
Teledensity	Approx 2%	Approx 31%
Teledensity Targets	15% (by 2007)	43%

Source: NCAER, Rural Infrastructure Report, 2007.

Till recently it was the government which made an attempt at providing the services in rural India. The Government of India, Bharat Nirman Initiative, 2005-09, plans every village in the country to be connected by November, 2007. The aim is to provide every village in the country with a Village Panchayat Phone (VPTs) by the year end 2008.

Village NET-Basic Framework

E-commerce is business conducted via internet as a world wide distribution channel for goods and services. E-commerce represents a qualitative jump in the ability to bring buyers and sellers closer together. Following frame work is a government regulated Village Net for rural e-commerce. It explains how e-commerce can foster a balanced rural development.

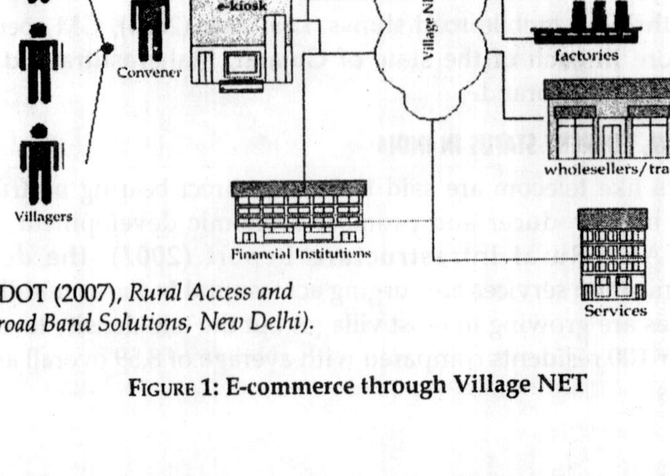

(Source: CDOT (2007), *Rural Access and Broad Band Solutions, New Delhi).*

FIGURE 1: E-commerce through Village NET

Village NET would comprise of several players. They are:

Villagers: They include craftsmen, farmers, laborers, women, milkmen, fishermen and others.

Convener: A convener per village who would serve as a contact point. He would be responsible for management of Village NET in the village.

Financial Institutions: Banks and government agencies. They are the principle enablers of microfinance and e-payment systems.

Services: Insurance companies, health, education and other services.

Government: It would act as a key regulator. There could be a private company also in place of Government that would be responsible for infrastructure and provisioning of e-commerce. It will get a service tax/charge for providing the service in enabling transactions.

Mandi/Commodities Market: It will provide information about current prices of commodities.

Factories: Factories that use raw material that is rual produce like khadi, tea, tobacco, cotton, jute etc.,

Traders/Wholesalers: Traders perform collective e-procurement and sell to retailers and direct customers.

E-kiosks: They will be the interface between the villagers and Village NET. A basic e-kiosk will have a computer terminal connected to Village NET, a web-cam, a speaker and microphone, web-browser.

ITC's E-Choupal and HLL's Project Shakti

For an E-commerce model to be appropriate and successful in any area, be it rural or urban, it should be a two-way model. Also, E-commerce, as one of the information and communication technology tool, should facilitate a two-way communication. Reciprocity of communication should be the optimum one. The E-commerce model should include the participants as both buyers and sellers.

It is in this regard, ITC's E-Choupal scores over HLL's Project Shakti. ITC employs both pull and push strategy. The psuch strategy that ITC adopts is the plan to introduce healthcare products to the rural market. The pull strategy is that the farmers can get the required information about the global market at any time (This has been facilitated by the introduction of E-Choupal). ITC procures crops from the rural farmers besides providing market information to the rural people so that, both the parties have a win-win situation. Whereas, HLL's Project Shakti adopted the push strategy by reinventing their distribution channels in rural areas. It does not see to have any proposal to improve the purchasing power of the rural people.

One of the specialties of ITC's E-Choupal is that the middlemen's role has been redefined as the consumer friendly middlemen. It is this person, who explains the information provided by the kiosks to the rural illiterate tech averse farmers. Thus, ITC has taken the advantage of trust, which the middleman has in their traditional trading. Thus, ITC's E-Choupal has raised the rural people's purchasing power to an extent possible with re-intermediation of jobs.

CONCLUSION

Rural markets are an important and growing market for most products and services. The journey of markets to the rural markets has indeed been fueling growth in the advent of Information Technology. One of the major benefits of Information Technology in marketing of goods and services is that it can provide a cost-effective way to expand into the global arena. It can lower transaction cost by interacting directly with overseas supplier and customers and streamlines one business. Not only that, it can help in removing the intermediaries and traders in the supply chain of global giants. This, along with higher responsiveness and speed at which business takes place has helped in reducing transaction cost, and increase profit margins. This is especially true in case of agricultural commodities. A very good example of this would be ITC's e-Choupal.

With a huge untapped market, rural India is very attractive to marketers. There is immense potential in terms of the services that can be provided to rural India by developing the information technology infrastructure but it needs to be seen as to how far this potential is realized. A road map is now laid for us to progress and it is in our hands whether to follow or not.

REFERENCES

Anderson, James and N. Biliou (2007), "Serving the World's Poor: Innovation at the Base of the Economic Pyramid", *Journal of Business Strategy,* 28(2).

Balakrishnan Mandira (1997), "Rural Market: End of a Long road for Consumer Markets", *Decision,* July, pp.177-184.

Beshouri (2006), "Grassroots Approach to Emerging - Market Consumer", *McKinsey Quarterly,* No. 4.

Bharat Nirman Initiative-2005-09 (2005), *"Report of Government of India"*, New Delhi.

Bhatnagar, S. (2000), *"Enhancing Telecom Options in Rural India: Some Options"*, Indian Telecom Conference. Stanford.

C.K.Prahalad and Stuart L. Hart (2002), *"The Fortune at the Bottom of the Pyramid"*, Strategy and Business, Issue 26.

CDOT (2007), *"Rural Access and Broad Band Solutions"*, New Delhi.

Ganguly, A. S. (1985), *"The Growing Rural Market in India"*, Marketing in India. New Delhi.

Grameen Foundation (2005), *"Village Phone a Tool for Empowerment", USA.*

Gunasekaran V. and F Harmantzis (2007), *Emerging Wireless Technologies for Developing Countries"*, Technology in Society, 29, 23-42.

Gupta Rahul (2006), "Rural India Calling", Voice and Data, June.

Kashyap Pradeep and Raut (2005), *"Rural Marketing Book: Text and Cases"*, New Delhi, Biztantra Publications.

McKinsey Report (2007), *"The 'Bird of Gold: The Rise of Indian Consumer Market"*, McKinsey Global Institute.

NCAER (2007), "*Rural Infrastructure Report - 2007*", New Delhi.

Prahlad, C. K. and Allen Hammond (2002), "*Serving the World's Poor, Profitability*", Harvard Business Review, September, pp. 48-57.

Wellenius, B. (2002), "Closing the Gap in Access to Rural Communication: Chile, 1995-2002, *Info* 4, 3.

INDEX

O

P